An Illustrated Ziyārah Guide to

ʿIRĀQ

Kisa Publications

Table of Contents

Preface

بسم لله الرحمان الرحيم

In the name of Allāh, the Entirely Merciful, the Especially Merciful
All praise is for Allāh, the Lord of the worlds

Dear Zāʾir,

Every person has a goal and purpose for embarking upon a trip, whether it be to conduct business, visit family, or for leisure. Likewise, there is also a purpose upon embarking to perform ziyārah of the Maʿṣūmīn (A), who are our connection to Allāh and the guides to His path. Thus, the goal of a zāʾir (visitor) is to express gratitude, passion, and love towards the Ahl al-Bayt and attain maʿrifah (deep understanding) in order to receive the blessings of Allāh. Upon returning from ziyārah, a zāʾir should have attained a level of maʿrifah much higher than before.

A zāʾir who embarks on a journey to ʿIrāq will have the privilege of visiting the graves of six Imāms (A). To have such an opportunity is truly a privilege and blessing from Allāh, and one should thank Allāh for endowing him/her with this opportunity. The benefits of ziyārah can be seen in this world, as well as the hereafter. The least of these benefits is that the a ʾimmah will visit the zāʾir and accompany him or her during the dark, difficult nights in the grave, especially on the first night.

As I mentioned earlier, the goal of a zāʾir is to increase the ma'rifah and love of the Ahl al-Bayt (A). An increased understanding of the Ahl al-Bayt (A) naturally results in increased love for them. This eventually leads to obedience and following the Ahl al-Bayt (A) in every matter of life. This natural effect is the sole purpose for ziyārah. Ziyārah helps us connect to our aʾimmah such that we attain the highest level of maʿrifah of Allāh, and in turn, our actions become a reflection of the actions of the Ahl al-Bayt (A).

In order to achieve these lofty goals, one must be physically, mentally, and spiritually prepared for this magnificent journey. It is important for one to be aware and knowledgeable about the various locations of ziyārah, including the ādāb (etiquette), duʿāʾs, and relevant historical facts. This book has been written to help a zāʾir achieve exactly this purpose. Although not all historical facts have been mentioned, the primary objective is for the zāʾir to understand the significance of the places he or she will be visiting, as well as the duʿāʾs and ziyārat that are highly recommended to recite in the holy places.

The content of this book was primarily produced by translating text from *Irāq: An Illustrated Ziyārah Guide* (*Irāq: Rahnamayeh Muṣawwareh Safareh Ziyāratī*), with supplemental content produced by us. We hope that you provide us with feedback and share your thoughts on this book as you use it throughout your journey. We kindly request that you report to us any errors that you may encounter. Your feedback will be greatly appreciated and can be sent to info@kisakids.org.

We are thankful for the wonderful team of people who put tremendous effort in writing this book. In particular, we would like to thank Al-Kisa Foundation, Sayyid Ahmad Alawi, and the Kisa Publications team. We ask Allāh to grant this project success and barakah, inshāʾAllāh.

Wassalam,
Nabi R. Mir (Abidi)

Transliteration

Arabic has been transliterated according to the following key:

ء	a, u, i (initial form)	ز	z	ك	k	ـَ	a
ء	ʾ	س	s	ل	l	ـُ	u
ب	b	ش	sh	م	m	ـِ	i
ت	t	ص	ṣ	ن	n	ـَا	ā
ث	th	ض	ḍ	ه	h	ـُو	ū
ج	j	ط	ṭ	و	w (as a consonant)	ـِي	ī
ح	ḥ	ظ	ẓ	ي	y (as a consonant)		
خ	kh	ع	ʿ	ة	ah (without iḍāfah)		
د	d	غ	gh	ة	at (with idāfah)		
ذ	dh	ف	f	ال	al-		
ر	r	ق	q				

Prelude

Etiquette of Travelling

Before Travelling

It is mustaḥab to perform the following actions before embarking on your journey:

- Ask Allāh for khayr (goodness).
- Inform your relatives and friends about your departure and ask for their forgiveness.
- Prepare a will, especially for those things that are wājib. Settle your loans, debts, and khums.
- Read and learn about the holy personalities you are about to visit.
- Pick good people to travel with, who are similar to you in akhlāq and manners
- Pick a good time to travel; it is good to commence travel on Sunday, Tuesday, Thursday, or Saturday. It is makrūh to travel before Jumʿah prayers. If you must leave on any of the other days, it is good to give ṣadaqah first.
- Fast for three days prior to your departure
- Perform a ghusl on the third day with the intention of ziyārah
- Next, recite a two rakaʿāt ṣalāh (like Fajr) and ask Allāh for goodness
- Gather your family and recite the following duʿāʾ:

O Allāh, today I am certainly entrusting you with my life, my family, my wealth, my children, and all those on the same path as me, whether they are present or absent.	اَللّٰهُمَّ اِنِّيْ اَسْتَوْدِعُكَ الْيَوْمَ نَفْسِيْ وَ اَهْلِيْ وَ مَالِيْ وَ وُلْدِيْ وَ مَنْ كَانَ مِنِّيْ بِسَبِيْلٍ الشَّاهِدَ مِنْهُمْ وَالْغَآئِبَ
O Allāh, surely, we seek refuge with You from the dangers of travelling, a negative ending, and misfortunes for our families, wealth, and offspring, in this world and the hereafter.	اَللّٰهُمَّ اِنَّا نَعُوْذُ بِكَ مِنْ وَعْثَآءِ السَّفَرِ وَ كَآبَةِ الْمُنْقَلَبِ وَسُوْءِ الْمَنْظَرِ فِيْ الْاَهْلِ وَالْمَالِ وَالْوَلَدِ فِيْ الدُّنْيَا وَالْاٰخِرَةِ

اَللّٰهُمَّ اِنِّيْ اَتَوَجَّهُ اِلَيْكَ هٰذَا التَّوَجُّهَ طَلَباً
لِمَرْضَاتِكَ وَتَقَرُّباً اِلَيْكَ

O Allah, certainly I turn to You, asking for Your pleasure and closeness to You.

اَللّٰهُمَّ فَبَلِّغْنِيْ مَا اُؤَمِّلُهُ وَاَرْجُوْهُ فِيْكَ وَفِيْ
اَوْلِيَآئِكَ يَا اَرْحَمَ الرَّاحِمِيْنَ

O Allah, so deliver to me that which I hope and wish from you and your close ones, O the Most Merficul!

- Next, recite Āyat ul-Kursī, praise Allāh, recite ṣalawāt, and then this duʿā':

اَللّٰهُمَّ اِلَيْكَ وَجَّهْتُ وَجْهِيْ وَ عَلَيْكَ
خَلَّفْتُ اَهْلِيْ وَ مَالِيْ وَ مَا خَوَّلْتَنِيْ وَ قَدْ
وَثِقْتُ بِكَ فَلَا تُخَيِّبْنِيْ يَا مَنْ لَا يُخَيِّبُ
مَنْ اَرَادَهُ وَلَا يُضَيِّعُ مَنْ حَفِظَهُ

O Allah I turn my face towards You, and I have left with you my family, wealth, and all my possessions. I have faith in You, so do not disappoint me, O He who does not disappoint the one who asks Him and does not lose the trusts given to Him.

اَللّٰهُمَّ صَلِّ عَلٰى مُحَمَّدٍ وَآلِهِ
وَاحْفَظْنِيْ فِيْمَا غِبْتُ عَنْهُ وَلَا تَكِلْنِيْ
اِلٰى نَفْسِيْ يَا اَرْحَمَ الرَّاحِمِيْنَ

O Allah, bless Muhammad and his family, and protect everything I have left behind, and do not leave me to myself, O the Most Merciful.

- After this duʿā', recite the tasbīḥ of Sayyidah Fāṭimah (A) and Sūrat al-Fātiḥah

- Recite Āyat al-Kursī facing the three sides of your home.
- The traveler should recitea Sūrat al-Ikhlāṣ 11 times, Sūrat al-Qadr once, Āyat al-Kursī once, Sūrat an-Nās one time, Sūrat al-Falaq one time, and then begin travel.
- If you have a turbah or tasbīh made from the sand of Imām Ḥusayn (A), then recite the following:

اَللَّهُمَّ هٰذِهِ طِيْنَةُ قَبْرِ الْحُسَيْنِ عَلَيْهِ

السَّلَامُ وَلِيِّكَ وَابْنِ وَلِيِّكَ اِتَّخَذْتُهَا حِرْزاً لِمَا اَخَافُ وَمَا لَا أَخَافُ

O Allāh, this is the dirt from the grave of Imām Ḥusayn (A), who is your walī (guardian), and his son, who is also your walī. I have taken this dust as my refuge from that which I fear and even from that which I do not fear.

- Recite Sūrat al-Fātiḥah (once towards the right side and once towards the left)
- Give ṣadaqah

Imām as-Ṣādiq (A):

أَلْمُرُوَّةُ فِيْ السَّفَرِ كَثْرَةُ الزَّادِ وَطِيْبُهُ وَبَذْلُهُ لِمَنْ كَانَ مَعَكَ وَكِتْمَانُكَ عَلَى الْقَومِ أَمْرَهُمْ بَعْدَ مُفَارِقَتِكَ إِيَّاهُمْ

وَ كَثْرَةُ الْمِزَاحِ فِيْ غَيْرِ مَا يُسْخِطُ اللهَ عَزَّوَجَلَ

Traveling graciously consists of the following: being generous, sharing what you have brought with others, and keeping their secrets after you finish your travels. Be jolly with those whom you travel with in a manner that does not make Allāh angry.

While Travelling

- Take all the items you will need on your trip (See packing list on p. 22)
- Have the best akhlāq with those whom you are traveling with
- Help those who are weak and sick throughout your journey
- Give ṣadaqah to the poor within the places you travel to

Special Duʿāʾ for Ziyārah of Imām Ḥusayn (A)

When you intend to perform ziyārah of Imām Ḥusayn (A), recite the following before leaving your home:

O Allāh, today I am certainly entrusting You with my life, my family, my wealth, my children,	اَللَّهُمَّ إِنِّيْ أَسْتَوْدِعُكَ الْيَوْمَ نَفْسِيْ وَ أَهْلِيْ وَ مَالِيْ وَ وَلَدِيْ
and all those on the same path as me, whether they are present or absent.	وَ كُلَّ مَنْ كَانَ مِنِّيْ بِسَبِيْلٍ الشَّاهِدَ مِنْهُمْ وَ الْغَائِبَ
O Allāh, protect us with Your protection, protect our faith, and be a protector over us.	اَللَّهُمَّ احْفَظْنَـــا بِحِفْظِكَ بِحِفْظِ الْإِيْمَانِ وَ احْفَظْ عَلَيْنَا
O Allāh, place us under Your protection, do not remove from us Your blessings, do not alter the blessings and health You have given us,	اَللَّهُمَّ اجْعَلْنَا فِيْ حِرْزِكَ وَ لَا تَسْلُبْنَا نِعْمَتَكَ وَ لَا تُغَيِّرْ مَا بِنَا مِنْ نِعْمَةٍ وَ عَافِيَةٍ
and increase Your favors upon us. Surely, we are longing for You.	وَ زِدْنَا مِنْ فَضْلِكَ إِنَّا إِلَيْكَ رَاغِبُوْنَ

As you leave your home, keep reciting the following dhikr with humility:

There is no god except Allāh! Allāh is the Greatest! All praise is for Allāh!	لَا إِلٰهَ إِلَّا اللهُ وَاللهُ أَكْبَرُ وَالْحَمْدُ لِلّٰهِ

Special Duʿāʾ for Ziyārah of Imām ʿAlī (A)

When you decide to perform the ziyārah of Imām ʿAlī (A), perform ghusl, wear clean clothes, and apply perfume. When leaving your house, recite the following:

O Allāh, I have left my house seeking Your grace	اَللّٰهُمَّ إِنِّيْ خَرَجْتُ مِنْ مَنْزِلِيْ أَبْغِيْ فَضْلَكَ
to visit the successor of Your Prophet, may Your blessings be upon both of them.	وَ أَزُوْرُ وَصِيَّ نَبِيِّكَ صَلَوَاتُكَ عَلَيْهِمَا
O Allāh, please make this easy for me.	اللّٰهُمَّ فِيْسِّرْ ذَلِكَ لِيْ
Help me internalize [what I attain] and treasure from this visit to him,	وَ سَبِّبِ الْمَزَارَ لَهُ
and take care of my affairs and possessions while I am away in the best manner.	وَ اخْلُفْنِيْ فِيْ عَاقِبَتِيْ وَ حُزَانَتِيْ بِأَحْسَنِ الْخِلَافَةِ
O The Most Merciful!	يَا أَرْحَمَ الرَّاحِمِيْنَ

Recite this dhikr throughout your journey:

All praise is for Allāh! All glory be to Allāh! There is no god except Allāh!	اَلْحَمْدُ لِلّٰهِ وَ سُبْحَانَ اللهِ وَ لَا اِلٰهَ اِلاَّ اللّٰهُ

Practical Laws (Aḥkām) for Ziyārah

- Offering ṣalāh in the ḥarams of the Imāms (A) is mustaḥab; in fact, it is better than praying in a masjid because all of the ḥarams are, in fact, masājid (e.g., Masjid un-Nabī).
- It is good for a person to have ādāb (respect) and be careful not to pray "ahead" of the grave of the Prophet (S) and Imāms (A) in a manner that would be considered disrespectful to the owner of that grave. (If you pray Ṣalāh in a manner that is disrespectful to the owner of the grave, it becomes ḥarām.)
- The ḥaram of Imām Ḥusayn (A), Masjid al-Kūfah, Masjid al-Ḥarām, and Masjid an-Nabī are the four places where a traveler can choose to pray a full prayer or shortened prayer (please see individual chapters for a more detailed explanation).
- When entering the ḥarams of the Imāms, or even their descendants, it is mustaḥab to enter with wuḍūʾ.
- It iḥtiyāt-e-wājib (obligatory precaution) that a person who is in the state of janābah, ḥayḍ, or nifās should not enter the ḥaram of a Maʿṣūm and remain there (passing through is okay). However,it is okay to enter the ḥarams of the other children of the Imāms (e.g., Ḥaḍrat ʿAbbās).
- The ḥaram, in this context, is that room that falls underneath the dome, where the ḍarīh is built.

The Special Days of the Maʿṣūmīn

According to our aḥādīth, each day of the week has been dedicated to some of the Maʿsūmīn. It is recommended to visit the Maʿsūm on that specific day and has more thawāb (rewards). The days are as follows:

- Saturday: Prophet Muḥammad (S)
- Sunday: Imām ʿAlī (A) and Sayyidah Fāṭimah (A)
- Monday: Imām Ḥasan (A) and Imām Ḥusayn (A)
- Tuesday: Imām as-Ṣajjād (A), Imām al-Bāqir (A), and Imām as-Ṣādiq (A)
- Wednesday: Imām Mūsa al-Kāḍim (A), Imām ar-Ridhā (A), Imām al-Jawād (A), and Imām al-Hadī (A)
- Thursday: Imām Ḥasan al-Askari (A)
- Friday: Imām al-Mahdī (AJ)

Etiquette (Ādāb) of Ziyārah

When visiting the Maʿsūmīn, whether in their lifetime or after their shahādah, there are certain etiquette to follow. Some of these are mentioned below:

- Perform a ghusl and enter the ḥaram in a state of ṭahārah
- Wear clean, preferably white, clothes and perfume (within the parameters of fiqh)
- Avoid engaging in vain discussion about worldly matters
- Walk towards the ḥaram with slow, small steps, with humility
- Reciting dhikr as you're walking towards the ḥaram, especially Allāhu Akbar and Alḥamdulillāh
- Ask for permission to enter (idhn ad-dukhūl) along with humility and humbleness
- (khuḍūl - external humbleness and khushūʿ- internal humbleness)
- Enter the ḥaram with your right foot.
- Reciting takbīr 100 times before reciting the Ziyārah
- Face the Ḍarīh with your back towards the Qiblah while reciting the Ziyārah
- Afterwards, offer a two-rakaʿat prayer with the intention of Ziyārah of the Maʿsūm
- Make duʿāʾ and ask for your ḥājāt (lawful wishes) after completing the Ṣalāh of Ziyārah
- Recite Qurān and gift that thawāb (reward) to the Maʿsūm
- Have Hudhūr al-Qalb (presence of heart)
- Seek istighfār (forgiveness) for your sins
- Be nice and respectful towards the khuddām (caretakers) of the ḥaram
- Every time you return to your place of stay, your focus should be to rest and eat and then return to Ziyārah
- When bidding farewell, recite Duʿāʾ al-Widā (farewell duʿāʾ) as your last Ziyārah
- After reciting Duʿāʾ al-Widā, one should leave the ḥaram immediately; as you are exiting, try not to have your back towards the ḍarīh
- When you finish your visitation, you should leave the ḥaram quickly, maintaining the excitement of Ziyārah (When one tends to stay long periods of time and socialize excessively, the excitement of Ziyārah may decrease.)
- Every Ziyārah should be more spiritually uplifting than the previous one
- Give Ṣadaqah and be kind to the poor, as well as the Sayyid families, in the city

Ṣalāh of Ziyārah and the Gifted Ṣalāh

- Reciting the Ṣalātul Ziyārah has only been recommended for the Maʿṣūmīn and a few others, such as Prophet Ādam (A), Prophet Nūḥ (A), and the martyrs of Karbalā.
- For everyone else, it is good to read a Ṣalāh after Ziyārah with the intention of gifting the thawāb to their souls (e.g., the other descendents of the Imāms (A), the scholars, parents, friends, relatives, etc.)

Ziyārat an-Niyābah (Ziyārah on Behalf of Somebody)

- Is it good to perform ziyārah on behalf of someone else (whether they are alive or passed away)
- Both the nā'ib (the one performing the ziyārah) and manūb anhu (the one on whose behalf the ziyārah is being performed) will gain the reward of the ziyārah
- In aḥādith, it is mentioned that Dāwūd Surmī said to Imām Ḥasan al-ʿAskarī (A), "I have performed the ziyārah of your father and have made a nīyyah (intention) for the thawāb to be given to you." The Imām (A) replied, "There is a supreme reward for you from Allāh, and from us, there is praise towards you."
- In another narration, some of the Imāms were asked, "Is there a reward for someone who offers a two-rakaʿat prayer, fasts for a day, performs Hajj or ʿUmrah, or performs the ziyārah of the Prophet (S) or one of the Imāms (A), and gifts that thawāb to their mother, father, or brother/sister in faith?" In response, it was said, "The thawāb of that action goes to the one on whose behalf it was done without taking away any thawāb from the one performing the action."
- In the book Tahdhīb, Shaykh Ṭūsī mentions that the performer (nā'ib) should recite the following salām at the end of their ziyārah:

اَلسَّلَامُ عَلَيْكَ يَا مَوْلَايَ عَنْ "فُلَانِ بْنِ فُلَانٍ" [1]

Peace be upon you, O my master, on behalf of so-and-so.

[1] Instead of saying "fulan ibn fulan," say the name of the person on whose behalf you are reciting the Ziyārah and their father (for example, ʿAlī bin Ḥusayn or Fāṭimah binte Ḥusayn)

اَتَيْتُكَ زَائِراً عَنْهُ فَاشْفَعْ لَهُ عِنْدَ رَبِّكَ

I have come to visit you on behalf of him/her, so intercede for him/her to your Lord.

- Someone who would like to recite Ziyārah on behalf of all of the believers or a specific group of believers can make the nīyyah verbally or in his/her heart before reciting the Ziyārah.
- After the Ziyārah is recited, offer a two-rakaʿat prayer for the Ziyārah and recite the following:

O Allāh, surely I have made this visitation and prayed these two rakaʿāt.	أَللّٰهُمَّ إِنِّي زُرْتُ هٰذِهِ الزِّيَارَةَ وَ صَلَّيْتُ هَاتَيْنِ الرَّكْعَتَيْنِ
And I give the reward of these acts as a gift from me to my master on behalf of my brothers, all the believing men and women,	وَ جَعَلْتُ ثَوَابَهُمَا (هَدِيَةً مِنِّيْ إِلَى مَوْلَايَ) عَنْ جَمِيعِ إِخْوَانِيْ الْمُؤْمِنِيْنَ وَالْمُؤْمِنَاتِ
and on behalf of all those who have asked me to perform ziyārah and supplicate on their behalf.	وَ عَنْ جَمِيْعِ مَنْ أَوْصَانِيْ بِالزِّيَارَةِ وَالدُّعَاءِ لَهُ
O Allāh, accept this from me and them, by Your mercy, O the Most Merciful!	أَللّٰهُمَّ تَقَبَّلْ ذٰلِكَ مِنِّيْ وَ مِنْهُمْ بِرَحْمَتِكَ يَا اَرْحَمَ الرَّاحِمِيْنَ

- After the duʿāʾ, when you return and see one of these brothers and sisters in faith, say, “I performed the Ziyārah of the Maʿsūm on your behalf,” and this statement will be true

Ṣalāh for Marḥūmīn

- According to aḥādīth, Imām aṣ-Ṣādiq (A) would offer a two-rakaʿat Ṣalāh every night for his children and everyday for his parents. In the first rakʿah, he would recite Sūrat al-Qadr after Sūrat al-Fātiḥah. In the second rakʿah, he would recite Sūrat al-Kawthar after Sūrat al-Fātiḥah, and gift the reward of this prayer to their souls.
- In another ḥadīth from Imām aṣ-Ṣādiq (A), it is said that the reward of an action done for those who have passed away has rewards for the deceased, as well as the one performing it.

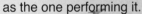

Suggested Packing List

BASICS

- ☐ Passport & color copies
- ☐ Flight itinerary & hotel details
- ☐ Ziyārah group details
- ☐ Cellphone & charger
- ☐ Cash & international credit card
- ☐ Small bag to take to the ḥaram
- ☐ Earphones
- ☐ Emergency contact information
- ☐ Notebook/pen
- ☐ Travel adaptor
- ☐ Prescribed medicines
- ☐ Additional medicine (e.g., tylenol, imodium, cough drops, bandaids etc.)

CLOTHING

- ☐ Shirts
- ☐ Comfortable pants
- ☐ 2-4 Abays (for women)
- ☐ Chador (for women)
- ☐ Hijabs & caps (for women)
- ☐ Comfortable walking shoes
- ☐ Flip flops (for the restroom)
- ☐ Socks (1 pair per day)
- ☐ Sweater/jacket
- ☐ Gloves, hat, scarf (if going in winter)

TOILETRIES

- ☐ Toothbrush & toothpaste
- ☐ Deodorant
- ☐ Attar/cologne
- ☐ Spray bottle (for wuḍūʾ)
- ☐ Shampoo & conditioner
- ☐ Soap
- ☐ Lotion & sunscreen
- ☐ Hairbrush, comb, hairties, etc.
- ☐ Feminine products (for women)
- ☐ Lipbalm/chapstick
- ☐ Hand sanitizer

PRAYER

- ☐ Qurʾān
- ☐ Ziyārah guide
- ☐ Duʿāʾ books
- ☐ Travel prayer rug & turbah

MISCELLANEOUS

- ☐ Tissue packs
- ☐ Snacks (e.g., granola bars, chips, etc.)
- ☐ Reading glasses
- ☐ Empty ziploc bags
- ☐ Travel alarm clock
- ☐ Towel

Notes:

1. For women, a chador and socks are required for entry into the ḥaram. Additionally, refrain from excessive make-up, as you may be prohibited from passing through the checkpoint.
2. While travelling between cities (e.g., from Karbalāʾ to Kaẓimayn), it is recommended to carry tissues, as restroom conditions are not the best.

النجف الأشرف

Najaf al-Ashraf

Najaf al-Ashraf (The Dignified City)

Rasūl Allāh (S) said to Imām ʿAlī (A):

إِنَّ اللهَ قَدْ جَعَلَ قَبْرَكَ وَ قَبْرَ وُلْدِكَ بِقَاعاً مِنْ بِقَاعِ الْجَنَّةِ وَ عَرْصَةً مِنْ عَرَصَاتِهَا وَ إِنَّ اللهَ جَعَلَ قُلُوْبَ نُجَبَاءَ مِنْ خَلْقِهِ وَ صَفْوَةِ عِبَادِهِ تَحِنُّ إِلَيْكُم وَتَحْتَمِلُ الْمَذَلَّةَ وَ الْأَذَىٰ فِيْكُمْ وَ يُعَمِّرُوْنَ وَ يَكْثُرُوْنَ زِيَارَتَهَا تَقَرُّباً مِنْهُمْ إِلَى اللهِ وَمَوَدَّةً مِنْهُمْ لِرَسُوْلِهِ، أُوْلٰئِكَ يَا عَلِيُّ الْمَخْصُوْصُوْنَ بِشَفَاعَتِيْ وَ الْوَارِدُوْنَ حَوضِيْ وَ هُمْ زُوَّارِيْ غَداً فِي الْجَنَّةِ

Certainly, Allāh has placed your grave and the graves of your children in visible, honorable, and heavenly places. He has made the hearts of his chosen and pure servants love you so deeply that they will bear torture, pain, and belittlement in order to come visit your graves. In order to seek nearness to Allāh and strengthen their friendship with the Prophet (S), they will come visit you frequently. O ʿAlī, these servants will receive my intercession and enter the Fountain of Kawthar, and they will be my visitors in Heaven.

Wasāʾil ash-Shīʿah, Vol. 10, P. 298, Ḥadīth 1#

Najaf al-Ashraf (The Dignified City)

Dear Zāʿir,

Welcome to Najaf al-Ashraf, the Dignified City, the city of Amir ul-Muʾminīn (A). This city was once the capital of Islāmic scholarship and knowledge. As you walk these streets, ponder on how these are the same streets where many of our Imāms (A) walked. According to aḥadīth, Imām ʿAlī (A), Prophet Ādam (A), and Prophet Nūḥ (A) are like your spiritual fathers, and you have come to your fathers' house. Therefore, use every single moment wisely by trying to connect with your fathers. Recite as much Qurʿān, duʿāʾs, and ṣalāt as you can.

In this city, you will find three primary landmarks:

1. The holy shrine of Imām ʿAlī (A)
2. The graveyard of Wādī as-Salām
3. The hawzah (Islāmic seminary) and ʿulamā (scholars)

Within the holy shrine, you will find the following:

- The grave of Imām ʿAlī (A)
- The grave of Prophet Nūḥ (A)
- The grave of Prophet Ādam (A)
- The location where Imām Ḥusayn's (A) head was buried previously
- The graves of various companions and scholars

According to our narrations, when one spots the dome of the holy shrine, he/she should ask for seven ḥājāt (wishes/needs), and inshāʾAllāh they will be fulfilled.

Additionally, since the ḥaram (shrine) is also a masjid, it is recommended to offer a two rakāʿah prayer of Taḥiyat-e-Masjid (Greeting and Respecting the Masjid) upon entering.

The Merits of Visiting Imām ʿAlī (A)

Mufaḍḍal narrates the following dialogue[1] between him and Imām aṣ-Ṣādiq (A):

Mufaḍḍal: I went to Imām aṣ-Ṣādiq (A) and said, "I am eager to go to Najaf!"

Imām as-Ṣādiq (A): For what reason?

Mufaḍḍal: I want to perform the ziyārah of Amīr al-Mu'minīn.

Imām as-Ṣādiq (A): Do you know the merits of performing his ziyārah?

Mufaḍḍal: No, O son of Rasūl Allāh, please tell me!

Imām as-Ṣādiq (A): Know that when you visit Amīr al-Mu'minīn, in reality, you have visited the bones of Ādam (A) [the source of mankind], the body of Nūḥ (A) [the root of Prophethood - the first Ulul 'Aẓm Prophet), and the spirit of ʿAlī ibn Abū Ṭālib (A) [the origin of imāmah].

Mufaḍḍal: Ādam (A) came down from Heaven and landed on the mountain of Serendib[2], which is in the east, and it is said that his bones are buried near the Kaʿbah. How are his bones in Kūfah?'

Imām as-Ṣādiq (A): When Prophet Nūḥ (A) was in the ark, Allāh sent him revelation to perform tawāf around the Kaʿbah 7 times in his ark, so he did. Then, he came down from the ark into the water, and the water reached his knees. A coffin, which contained the bones of Prophet Ādam (A), floated up to the surface. Prophet Nūḥ (A) placed the coffin in the ark and performed ṭawāf again, as Allāh had ordered. The ark then came to Masjid al-Kūfah. Here, Allāh sent waḥī (revelation) to the earth to drain the water, and the water drained near Masjid al-Kūfah. Everyone disembarked the ark and went their separate ways. Prophet Nūḥ (A) took the coffin and put it in a cave close to Najaf al-Ashraf. This cave is in the same mountain that Prophet Mūsā (A) went to speak to Allāh. Allāh raised Prophet ʿĪsā (A) to the heavens from this mountain, too.

On this mountain, Prophet Ibrāhīm (A) was named the Khalīl (special friend) of Allāh. And on this mountain, He named Prophet Muḥammad (S) Ḥabīb (beloved one). This mountain was home of many Prophets.

I swear by Allāh that no one in this place is more valuable than these three. So, everytime you go to Najaf, perform ziyārah of the bones of Ādam (A), the body of Nūḥ (A), and the spirit of ʿAlī (A), and in reality, you will have performed the ziyārah of your forefathers.

When the visitors to the shrine of Imām ʿAlī (A) recite du'a, the doors of the heavens open, so do not be unaware of the goodness that exists in this place.

1. Kāmil az-Ziyārāt, Ch. 10, P. 38, Ḥadīth # 2
2. ʿIlalu ash-Sharāʾiʿ, Vol. 2, P. 595

Imām aṣ-Ṣādiq (A):

مَن زارَ جَدّى عارِفاً بِحَقِّهِ
كَتَبَ اللهُ لَهُ بِكُلِّ خُطْوَةٍ
حَجَّةً مَقبُولَةً وَعُمْرَةً مَبرُورَةً ؛

When one performs the ziyārah of my grandfather [Imām ʿAlī (A)] with maʿrifah (deep understanding), Allāh will record for him/her the reward of an accepted Ḥajj and ʿUmrah for each step he/she takes.

Wasāil ash Shīʿa, Vol. 10, P. 294, Ḥadīth # 1

Imām ʿAlī (A): The First Imām

Name:	ʿAlī
Kunya:	Abūl-Ḥasan, Abūl-Ḥasanayn, Abū Turāb
Title:	Amīr al-Muʾminīn
Parents:	Abū Ṭālib & Fāṭimah bint Asad
Birthday:	13th Rajab, 23 years before Hijrah
Birth Place:	Holy Kaʿbah, Makkah
Ring Inscription:	اَلْمُلْكُ لِلّٰهِ الْوَاحِدِ الْقَهَّارْ The Kingdom belongs exclusively to Allāh, the Almighty
Number of Children:	27
Duration of Khilāfah:	4 years and 9 months (36 AH - 40 AH)
Duration of Imāmah:	30 years
Date of Martyrdom:	21st Ramaḍān 40 AH
Place of Martyrdom:	Masjid al-Kūfah
Cause of Martyrdom:	Struck by Ibn Muljim while praying
Lifespan:	63 years
Holy Shrine:	Najaf al-Ashraf
Eras of his life:	■ Childhood: 10 years ■ Alongside the Prophet (S): 23 years ■ Under the Khilāfah of Others: 25 years ■ As Khalīfah: 4 years

The Ṣalāh (Prayer) of Imām ʿAlī (A)

Offer 4 rakaʿāt in 2 sets of 2 rakaʿāt each. In each rakʿah, recite Sūrat al-Fātiḥa once and Sūrat al-Ikhlāṣ 50 times.

The History of Najaf & Imām ʿAlī's (A) Ḥaram

- **19th Ramaḍān 40 AH:** Imām ʿAlī (A) was struck with a poisonous sword in Masjid al-Kūfah while leading Fajr prayers.
- **21st Ramaḍān 40 AH:** Imām ʿAlī (A) attained shahādah. In accordance with his will, Imām Ḥasan (A) and Imām Ḥusayn (A) secretly buried the Imām in Najaf. His grave remained hidden for many years.
- **135 AH:** During the khilāfah of Mansūr al-ʿAbbāsi, Imām as-Ṣādiq (A) revealed the location of Imām ʿAlī's (A) grave for the first time.
- **165 AH:** During the imāmah of Imām al-Kāẓim (A), the first ḍarīh was constructed out of white stone.
- **236 AH:** Mutawakkil al-ʿAbbāsi destroyed the gravesite of Imām ʿAlī (A).
- **283 AH:** Abūl-Hayjā, the shīʿah ruler of Mūṣil, built a grand dome and carpeted the ḥaram.
- **287 AH:** Muḥammad bin Zayd, one of the shīʿah kings of Ṭabaristān, created a grand structure around the grave of Imām ʿAlī (A), including a courtyard with 70 rooms.
- **363 AH:** The shīʿah king ʿAḍud ad-Dawlah expanded the ḥaram and added to its grandeur.
- **436 AH:** Shaykh Ṭūsī migrated from Baghḍād to Najaf and established the ḥawza al-ʿIlmiyyah of Najaf.
- **676 AH:** ʿAṭā Malik Jūwaynī built the first plumbing infrastructure for water to reach Najaf.
- **755 AH:** Due to a fire, the ḥaram and ḍarīḥ were burnt, along with two Qurʾāns handwritten by Imām ʿAlī (A).
- **760 AH**: The Mogul Īl-Khanīd Dynasty and their workers rebuilt the ḥaram.
- **1033 AH:** Shāh ʿAbbas aṣ-Ṣafawī performed ziyārah and ordered that the ḥaram, including the dome and the courtyard, be reconstructed and repaired.
- **1047 AH:** Shāh aṣ-Ṣafawī ordered his wazīr, Mīrzā Taqī Māzandarānī, to expand the courtyards of the ḥaram.
- **1156 AH:** Nādir Shāh Afshār ordered the bricks on the dome to be replaced with gold.
- **1211 AH:** Āghā Muḥammad Khān Qājār gifted a silver ḍarīh
- **1236 AH:** Fātiḥʿali Shāh performed some repairs and construction for the ḥaram
- **1424 AH:** After the fall of Ṣaddām, a great expansion plan was put into place.

N
W
E
S
وادی السلام
Wādī as-Salām
Al-ʿImārah
7
6
شارع الطوسی
Mishrāq
شارع المحیط
شارع الامام زین العابدین
شارع الامام زین العابدین
محل احداث صحن حضرت فاطمه (س)
سوق الکبیر (بازار بزرگ)
شارع الامام الصادق
شارع الصفا
Burāq
Ḥuwaysh
شارع الرسول
شارع بنات الحسن
Judaydah

1 Holy Shrine of Imām ʿAlī (A)

2 Shrine of Ṣāfī Ṣafā Yamānī

3 Maqām of Imām Zayn al-ʿĀbidīn (A)

4 Maqām of Imām Mahdī (AJ) in Wādī as-Salām

5 Shrine of Prophets Hūd and Ṣāliḥ (A)

6 Masjid Ḥannānah

7 Shrine of Kumayl ibn Ziyād

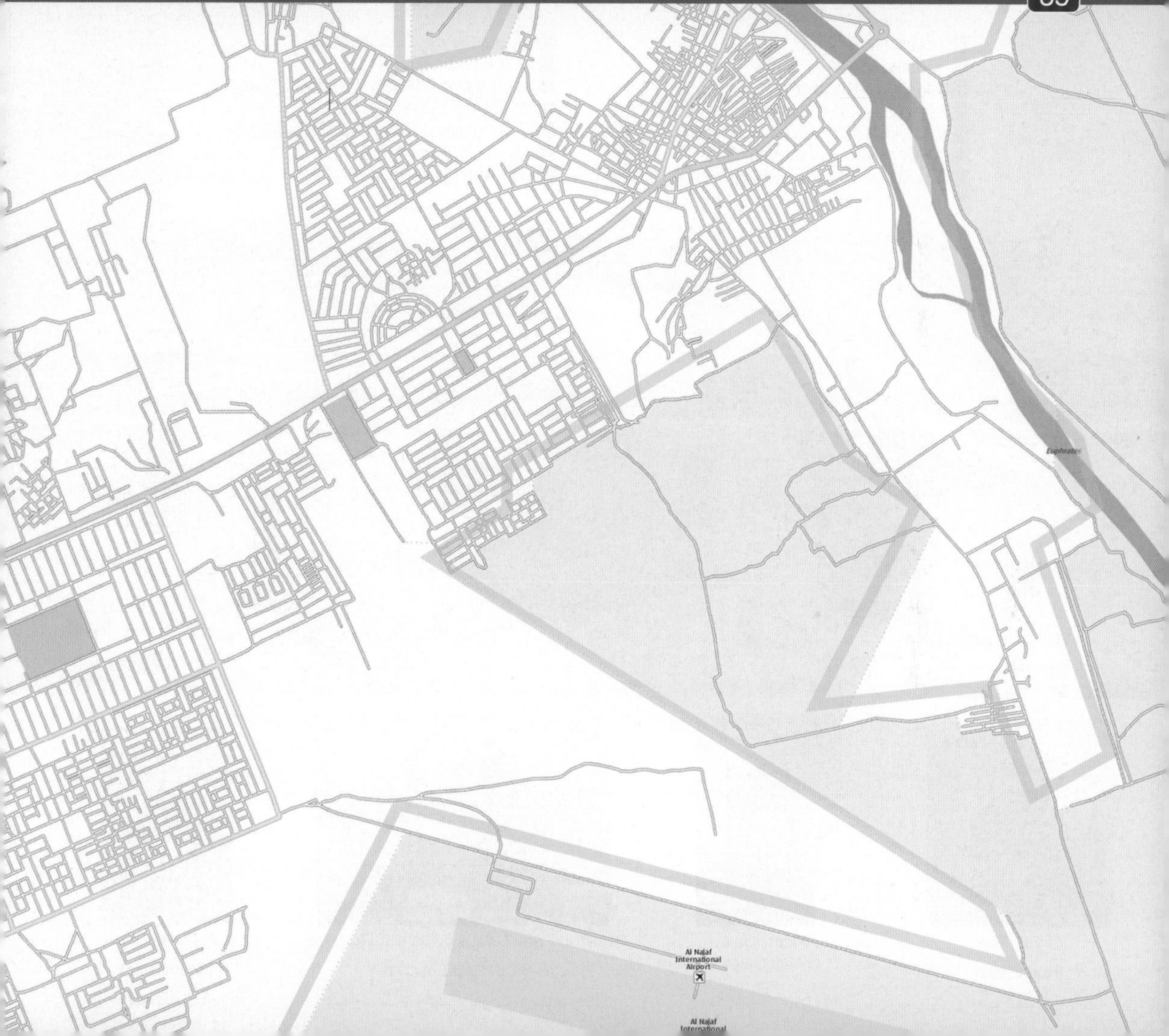
Euphrates
Al Najaf
International
Airport
Al Najaf

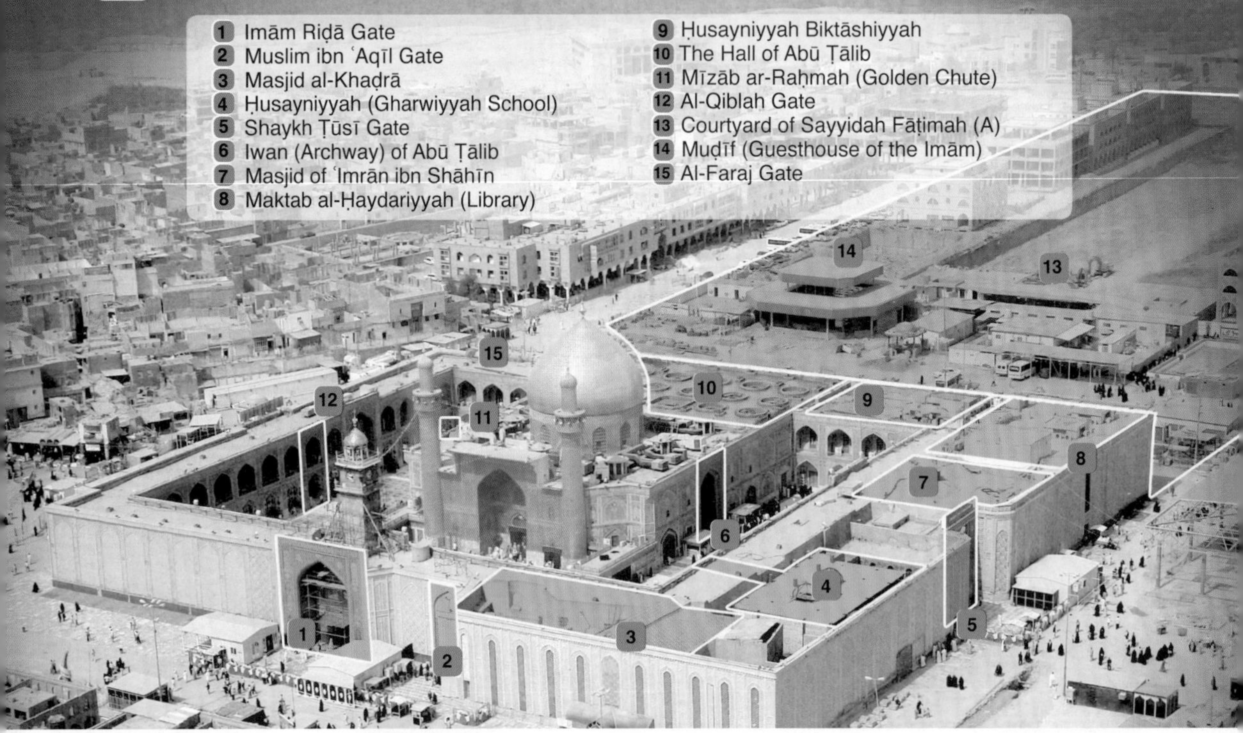

At-Ṭūsī Gate
(North Gate)
باب الطوسي

Al-Faraj Gate
(West Gate)
باب الفــرج

Muslim ibn ʿAqīl Gate and Imām ar-Riḍā Gate
(as-Sāʿah Gate/East Gate)
باب مسلم بن عقيل وباب الامـام الرضا

Al-Qiblah Gate
(South Gate)
باب القبــلة

Scholars Buried in the Ḥaram

- 1. Āghā Ḍiyāʾ ʿIrāqī
- 2. Ismāʿīl Muḥlātī
- 3. Muḥammad Ḥusayn Iṣfahānī Masjid Shāhi; Fatḥʿalī Sulṭān Ābādī
- 4. Sayyid Mūsā Māzandarānī
- 6. Sayyid Muhammad Jawād Tabrīzī Muḥammad Riḍā Nāʾīnī
- 11. Shaykh Aʿẓam Murtaḍā Ansārī; Ṭāha Najaf
- 15. Mīrzā Ḥusayn Nūrī; Shaykh ʿAbbās Qummī
- 21. Mīrzā Ḥusayn Nāʾīnī
- 22. Shaykh al-Sharīʿah Iṣfahānī Sayyid ʿAlī Akbar Khuʾī
- 26. Sayyid Abū al-Ḥasan Isfahānī Sayyid Ḥasan Bajnawardi; Shaykh Ḥabīb Allāh Rushtī Ākhūnd Khūrāsānī;
- 31. Sayyid Abū al-Qāsim Khūʾī;
- 47. Sayyid Muḥammad Kāẓim Yazdī;
- 48. Sayyid ʿAbd al-Ḥusayn Sharaf ud-Dīn.

- Next to the Minarets of Tūs Gate
  ʿAllāmah Ḥillī;
  Muḥammad Ḥusayn Gharawī Isfahanī;
  Sayyid Muṣṭafā Khumaynī;

- Next to the Minarets of al-Qiblah Gate
  Muqaddas Ardabīlī;

- Iwan (Golden Archway) al-ʿIlmā
  Mullā Muḥammad Mahdī Narāqī;
  Mullā Aḥmad Narāqī;

- The Western Entrance of Iwan (Golden Archway) al-ʿIlmā
  Shaykh Muḥammad Fāḍil Sharbiyānī;

- Tomb of Mīrzā Shīrāzī

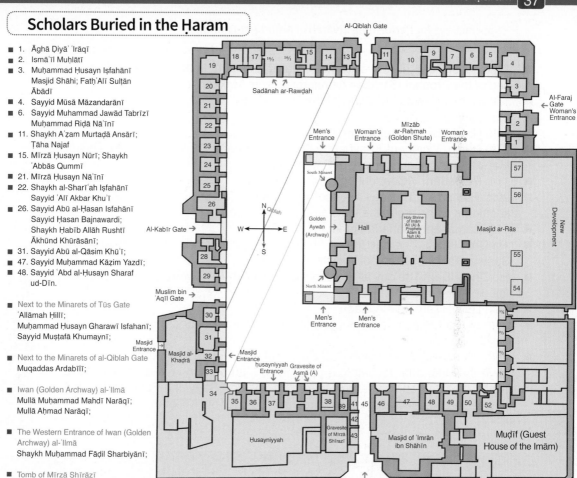

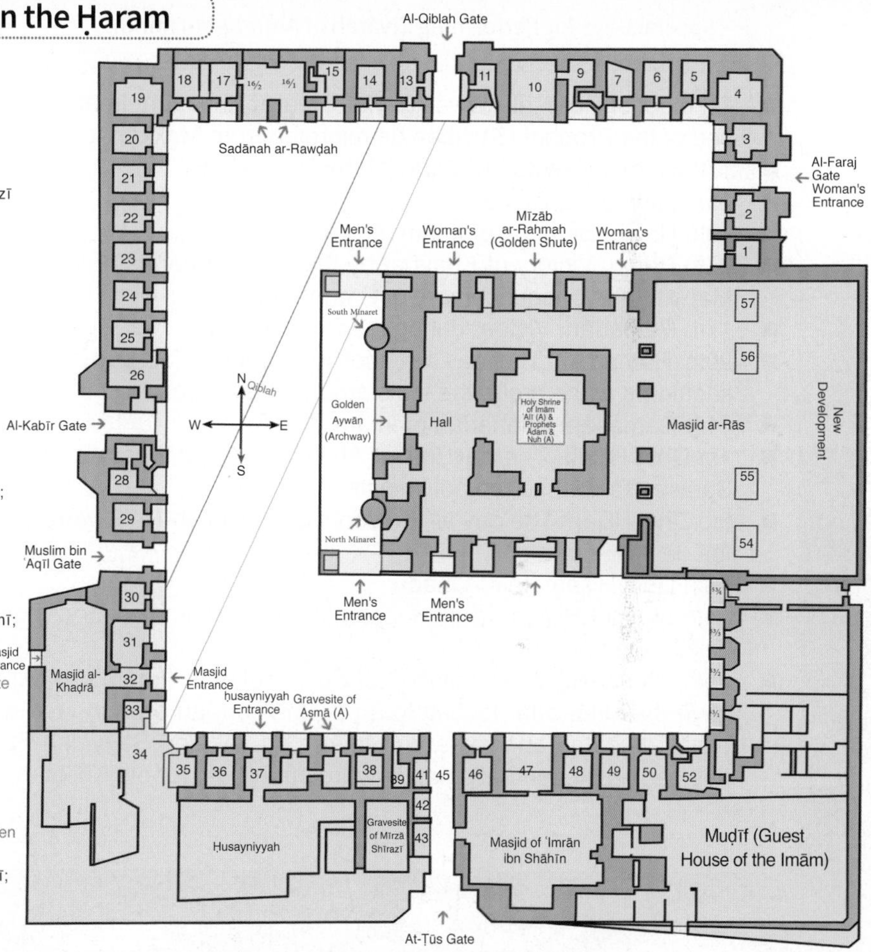

Special Days for Performing Ziyārah of Amīr al-Muʿminīn

- 1st night of Rabīʿ al-Awwal: Laylatul Mabīt (the night Imām ʿAlī (A) slept in the bed of the Prophet (S) when he migrated from Makkah to Madīnah)
- 17th Rabīʿ al-Awwal: Birthday of the Prophet (S)
- 15th Jamāda al-Awwal
- 13th Rajab: Birthday of Imām ʿAlī (A))
- 27th Rajab: Victory of Khaybar by the blessed hands of Imām ʿAlī (A); Day of Mabʿath (the announcement of Prophethood)
- 17th Ramaḍān: Victory during the Battle of Badr
- 20th Ramaḍān: The day Prophet Muḥammad (S) put Imām ʿAlī (A) on his shoulders as he broke the idols around the Kaʿbah
- 21st Ramaḍān: Shahādah of Imām ʿAlī (A)
- 1st Dhul Hijjah: The day Imām ʿAlī (A) was appointed to recite the verses of Sūrat al-Tawbah to the polytheists
- 9th Dhul Hijjah: The day all the doors of Masjid an-Nabī were closed except for the door of Imām ʿAlī
- 18th Dhul Hijjah: ʿĪd al-Ghadīr
- 24th of Dhul Hijjah: ʿĪd al-Mubāhalah; the day Imām ʿAlī (A) gave his ring as zakāh in rukūʿ
- 25th Dhu al-Hijjah: Revelation of Sūrat al-Insān (Imām ʿAlī (A) and his family gave their ifṭār after fasting to a poor person, an orphan, and a prisoner for 3 days); wedding anniversary of Imām ʿAlī (A) and Sayyidah Fāṭimah (A); the day people pledged allegiance to Imām ʿAlī (A) for his Khilāfah.

Biḥār al-Anwār, Vol. 97, P. 383

Ziyārah of Amīr al-Muʾminīn

When you decide to perform the ziyārah, perform ghusl, wear clean clothes, and apply perfume. When leaving your house, recite the following:

O Allāh, I have left my house seeking Your grace	اَللّٰهُمَّ إِنِّيْ خَرَجْتُ مِنْ مَنْزِلِيْ أَبْغِيْ فَضْلَكَ
to visit the successor of Your Prophet, may Your blessings be upon both of them.	وَ أَزُوْرُ وَصِيَّ نَبِيِّكَ صَلَوَاتُكَ عَلَيْهِمَا
O Allāh, please make this easy for me.	اللّٰهُمَّ فَيَسِّرْ ذٰلِكَ لِيْ
Help me internalize [what I attain] and treasure from this visit to him,	وَ سَبِّبِ الْمَزَارَ لَهُ
and take care of my affairs and possessions while I am away in the best manner.	وَ اخْلُفْنِيْ فِيْ عَاقِبَتِيْ وَ حُزَانَتِيْ بِأَحْسَنِ الْخِلَافَةِ
O The Most Merciful!	يَا أَرْحَمَ الرَّاحِمِيْنَ

Recite this dhikr throughout your journey:

All praise is for Allāh! All glory be to Allāh! There is no god except Allāh!	اَلْحَمْدُ لِلّٰهِ وَ سُبْحَانَ اللهِ وَ لَا اِلٰـهَ اِلاَّ اللهُ

Ziyārah of Amīr al-Muʾminīn

Before you enter Najaf, recite:

Allāh is the Greatest! Allāh is the Greatest!	اَللهُ أَكْبَرُ اللهُ أَكْبَرُ
He is the worthiest of exaltation, glorification, and grandeur!	أَهْلُ الْكِبْرِيَاءِ وَ الْمَجْدِ وَ الْعَظَمَةِ
Allāh is the Greatest! He is the worthiest of exaltation, sanctification, glorification, and granting bounties.	اَللهُ أَكْبَرُ أَهْلُ التَّكْبِيْرِ وَ التَّقْدِيْسِ وَ التَّسْبِيْحِ وَ الْآلَاءِ
Allāh is Greater than my fears and worries!	اَللهُ أَكْبَرُ مِمَّا أَخَافُ وَأَحْذَرُ
Allāh is the Greatest! He is my support, and upon Him I rely.	اَللهُ أَكْبَرُ عِمَادِيْ وَ عَلَيْهِ أَتَوَكَّلُ
Allāh is the Greatest! He is my hope, and to Him I turn.	اَللهُ أَكْبَرُ رَجَآئِيْ وَ إِلَيْهِ أُنِيْبُ
O Allāh, You are the guardian of my blessings and the granter of my requests.	اَللّٰهُمَّ أَنْتَ وَلِيُّ نِعْمَتِيْ وَ الْقَادِرُ عَلٰى طَلِبَتِيْ
You know my wishes and those desires that are hidden in my heart and my inner thoughts.	تَعْلَمُ حَاجَتِيْ وَ مَا تُضْمِرُهُ هَوَاجِسُ الصُّدُوْرِ وَخَوَاطِرُ النُّفُوْسِ
I, therefore, ask You in the name of Muḥammad, the chosen one	فَأَسْأَلُكَ بِمُحَمَّدٍ الْمُصْطَفٰى

through whom You have dispelled all doubts and excuses through proof and who You have sent as a mercy to the worlds.	اَلَّذِيْ قَطَعْتَ بِهِ حُجَجَ الْمُحْتَجِّيْنَ وَ عُذْرَ الْمُعْتَذِرِيْنَ وَجَعَلْتَهُ رَحْمَةً لِلْعَالَمِيْنَ
(I ask You) not to deprive me of the rewards for visiting Your successor,	أَنْ لَا تَحْرِمَنِيْ ثَوَابَ زِيَارَةِ وَلِيِّكَ
the brother of Your Prophet, the Commander of the Faithful.	وَأَخِيْ نَبِيِّكَ أَمِيْرِ الْمُؤْمِنِيْنَ
Turn my attention towards him, and place me amongst the righteous ones and his God-conscious followers.	وَقَصْدَهُ وَ تَجْعَلَنِيْ مِنْ وَفْدِهِ الصَّالِحِيْنَ وَ شِيْعَتِهِ الْمُتَّقِيْنَ
By Your mercy, O the Most Merciful!	بِرَحْمَتِكَ يَا أَرْحَمَ الرَّاحِمِيْنَ

Recite the following when the holy dome is sighted:

All praise is for Allāh, for He has bestowed upon me exclusively a pure lineage,	الْحَمْدُ لِلّٰهِ عَلَىٰ مَا اخْتَصَّنِيْ بِهِ مِنْ طِيْبِ الْمَوْلِدِ
and through His honor, He has granted me	وَ اسْتَخْلَصَنِيْ إِكْرَامًا بِهِ
loyalty towards His pious, immaculate, best, and most knowledegable representatives	مِنْ مُوَالَاةِ الْأَبْرَارِ السَّفَرَةِ الْأَطْهَارِ وَ الْخِيَرَةِ الْأَعْلَامِ

O Allāh, accept my efforts towards You and my earnest imploration in Your presence,	اَللّٰهُمَّ فَتَقَبَّلْ سَعْيِيْ إِلَيْكَ وَ تَضَرُّعِيْ بَيْنَ يَدَيْكَ
and forgive my sins, which cannot be hidden from You.	وَ اغْفِرْ لِيَ الذُّنوبَ الَّتِيْ لَا تَخْفَىٰ عَلَيْكَ
Surely, You are Allāh, the Master, the All-Forgiving!	إِنَّكَ أَنْتَ اللّٰهُ الْمَلِكُ الْغَفَّارُ

Before entering the gate to the ḥaram, recite:

All praise is for Allāh, who has guided us to this, and we would not have been guided if Allāh had not guided us.	اَلْحَمْدُ لِلّٰهِ الَّذِيْ هَدَانَا لِهٰذَا وَمَا كُنَّا لِنَهْتَدِيَ لَوْ لَا اَنْ هَدَانَا اللّٰهُ
All praise is for Allāh who has made me travel to His countries, made me ride His animals, and made the distant space seemingly near.	اَلْحَمْدُ لِلّٰهِ الَّذِيْ سَيَّرَنِيْ فِيْ بِلَادِهِ ، وَحَمَلَنِيْ عَلىٰ دَوَآبِّهِ، وَطَوىٰ لِيَ الْبَعِيْدَ
He has kept danger away from me and held off from me what is unwanted	وَصَرَفَ عَنِّي الْمَحْذُوْرَ، وَدَفَعَ عَنِّي الْمَكْرُوْهَ
to the extent that He made me come to the shrine of the brother of His Messenger, peace be upon him and his household.	حَتّىٰ اَقْدَمَنِيْ حَرَمَ اَخِيْ رَسُوْلِهِ صَلَّى اللّٰهُ عَلَيْهِ وَآلِهِ

اَلْحَمْدُ لِلّٰهِ الَّذِيْ اَدْخَلَنِيْ هٰذِهِ الْبُقْعَةَ الْمُبَارَكَةَ الَّتِيْ بَارَكَ اللهُ فِيْهَا، وَاخْتَارَهَا لِوَصِيِّ نَبِيِّهِ

All praise is for Allāh, who has allowed me to enter this gravesite, which Allāh has blessed and has chosen for His Prophet's Successor.

اَللّٰهُمَّ فَاجْعَلْهَا شَاهِدَةً لِيْ

O Allāh, please make this place a witness for me

Stand at the entrance of the courtyard and recite:

اَللّٰهُمَّ بِبَابِكَ وَقَفْتُ ، وَبِفِنَائِكَ نَزَلْتُ، وَبِحَبْلِكَ اعْتَصَمْتُ، وَلِرَحْمَتِكَ تَعَرَّضْتُ

O Allāh, I have stopped at Your gate and reached my ultimate desire. I am clinging to Your rope [of wilāyah] and seeking Your mercy.

وَبِوَلِيِّكَ صَلَوَاتُكَ عَلَيْهِ تَوَسَّلْتُ فَاجْعَلْهَا زِيَارَةً مَقْبُوْلَةً، وَدُعَاءً مُسْتَجَاباً

I beg you by the right of Your guardian, may Your blessings be upon him. So, please accept my visit and respond to my supplication.

When you enter the courtyard, recite the following:

O Allāh, surely, this shrine and holy place belong to You,	اَللّٰهُمَّ اِنَّ هٰذَا الْحَرَمَ حَرَمُكَ وَالْمَقَامَ مَقَامُكَ
and I am entering here to confide in You about those things that You know better than I — my secrets and confidential whispers.	وَاَنَا اَدْخُلُ اِلَيْهِ اُنَاجِيْكَ بِمَآ اَنْتَ اَعْلَمُ بِهِ مِنِّيْ وَ مِنْ سِرِّيْ وَنَجْوَايَ
All praise is for Allāh, the All-Benevolent and All-Munificent, who has made it easy for me to visit my master, out of His munificence.	اَلْحَمْدُ لِلّٰهِ الْحَنَّانِ الْمَنَّانِ الْمُتَطَوِّلِ الَّذِيْ مِنْ تَطَوُّلِهِ سَهَّلَ لِيْ زِيَارَةَمَوْلَايَ بِاِحْسَانِهِ
He has not prevented me from visiting him, nor has He made me disloyal to His divinely appointed guardianship.	وَلَمْ يَجْعَلْنِيْ عَنْ زِيَارَتِهِ مَمْنُوْعاً، وَلا عَنْ وِلَايَتِهِ مَدْفُوْعاً
Rather, He has bestowed upon and granted me (this favor).	بَلْ تَطَوَّلَ وَمَنَحَ
O Allāh, just as You have blessed me with the favor of recognizing him, please also include me amongst his followers,	اَللّٰهُمَّ كَمَا مَنَنْتَ عَلَيَّ بِمَعْرِفَتِهِ فَاجْعَلْنِيْ مِنْ شِيْعَتِهِ
and allow me to enter paradise through his intercession.	وَاَدْخِلْنِي الْجَنَّةَ بِشَفَاعَتِهِ
O the Most Merciful!	يَا اَرْحَمَ الرَّاحِمِيْنَ

After entering the courtyard gate, recite:

All praise is for Allāh who has honored me to recognize Him and His Messenger.	اَلْحَمْدُ لِلّٰهِ الَّذِيْ اَكْرَمَنِيْ بِمَعْرِفَتِهِ وَمَعْرِفَةِ رَسُوْلِهِ
And through His mercy, He has made it incumbent upon me to obey Him.	وَمَنْ فَرَضَ عَلَيَّ طَاعَتَهُ رَحْمَةً مِنْهُ لِيْ
He has bestowed His favor upon me and gifted me with faith.	وَتَطَوُّلاً مِنْهُ عَلَيَّ، وَمَنَّ عَلَيَّ بِالْاِيْمَانِ
All praise is for Allāh, who has allowed me to enter the shrine of His Messenger's brother	اَلْحَمْدُ لِلّٰهِ الَّذِيْ اَدْخَلَنِيْ حَرَمَ اَخِيْ رَسُوْلِهِ
and allowed me to see it in a state of good health.	وَاَرَانِيْهِ فِيْ عَافِيَةٍ
All praise is for Allāh who has placed me amongst the visitors to the grave of His Messenger's successor.	اَلْحَمْدُ لِلّٰهِ الَّذِيْ جَعَلَنِيْ مِنْ زُوَّارِ قَبْرِ وَصِيِّ رَسُوْلِهِ
I bear witness that there is no god except Allāh, alone, without partners.	اَشْهَدُ اَنْ لَّا اِلٰهَ اِلَّا اللّٰهُ وَحْدَهُ لَا شَرِيْكَ لَهُ
and I bear witness that Muḥammad is His servant and Messenger.	وَاَشْهَدُ اَنَّ مُحَمَّداً عَبْدُهُ وَرَسُوْلُهُ
He brought the truth from Allāh.	جَآءَ بِالْحَقِّ مِنْ عِنْدِ اللّٰهِ

And I bear witness that ʿAlī is the servant of Allāh and the brother of Allāh's Messenger.	وَاَشْهَدُ اَنَّ عَلِيًّا عَبْدُاللهِ وَاَخُوْ رَسُوْلِ اللهِ
Allāh is the Greatest! Allāh is the Greatest! Allāh is the Greatest! There is no god except Allāh, and Allāh is the Greatest!	اَللهُ اَكْبَرُ اَللهُ اَكْبَرُ اَللهُ اَكْبَرُ لَا اِلٰهَ اِلَّا اللهُ، وَاللهُ اَكْبَرُ
All praise is for Allāh, for He has guided me and led me successfully to His path.	وَالْحَمْدُ لِلّٰهِ عَلٰى هِدَايَتِهِ وَتَوْفِيْقِهِ لِمَا دَعا اِلَيْهِ مِنْ سَبِيْلِهِ
O Allāh, You are surely the greatest One who is besought and the most honorable One to come to.	اَللّٰهُمَّ اِنَّكَ اَفْضَلُ مَقْصُوْدٍ وَاَكْرَمُ مَأْتِيٍّ
I have come to You, seeking nearness to You through Your Prophet, the Prophet of Mercy,	وَقَدْ اَتَيْتُكَ مُتَقَرِّباً اِلَيْكَ بِنَبِيِّكَ نَبِيِّ الرَّحْمَةِ،
and in the name of his brother, the Commander of the Faithful, ʿAlī the son of Abī Ṭālib, peace be upon them both.	وَبِاَخِيْهِ اَمِيْرِ الْمُؤْمِنِيْنَ عَلِيِّ بْنِ اَبِيْ طَالِبٍ عَلَيْهِمَا اَلسَّلَامُ
So, send You blessings upon Muḥammad and the family of Muḥammad.	فَصَلِّ عَلٰى مُحَمَّدٍ وَآلِ مُحَمَّدٍ
Do not disappoint my efforts, and grant me a merciful look from You through which I am reborn and energized.	وَلَا تُخَيِّبْ سَعْيِيْ وَانْظُرْ اِلَيَّ نَظْرَةً رَّحِيْمَةً تَنْعَشُنِيْ بِهَا

وَاجْعَلْنِيْ عِنْدَكَ وَجِيْهاً فِي الدُّنْيَا وَالْآخِرَةِ وَمِنَ الْمُقَرَّبِيْنَ

And make me illustrious in Your view in this world and the hereafter, and include me amongst those who are brought near to You.

When you reach the entrance to the hall, recite the following:

اَلسَّلَامُ عَلٰى رَسُوْلِ اللهِ اَمِيْنِ اللهِ عَلٰى وَحْيِهِ وَعَزَائِمِ اَمْرِهِ،

Peace be upon Allāh's Messenger, whom Allāh has entrusted with His revelations and ultimate command.

الْخَاتِمِ لِمَا سَبَقَ، وَالْفَاتِحِ لِمَا اسْتُقْبِلَ، وَالْمُهَيْمِنِ عَلٰى ذٰلِكَ كُلِّهِ وَرَحْمَةُ اللهِ وَ بَرَكَاتُهُ

He completed the previous messages, paved the way for the coming blessings (imāmah), and prevails over all things. May the mercy and blessings of Allāh be upon him.

اَلسَّلَامُ عَلٰى صَاحِبِ السَّكِيْنَةِ

Peace be upon the master of tranquility.

اَلسَّلَامُ عَلَى الْمَدْفُوْنِ بِالْمَدِيْنَةِ

Peace be upon the one buried in Madīnah.

اَلسَّلَامُ عَلَى الْمَنْصُوْرِ الْمُؤَيَّدِ

Peace be upon the one who is granted victory and support (by Allāh).

اَلسَّلَامُ عَلٰى اَبِي الْقَاسِمِ مُحَمَّدِ بْنِ عَبْدِاللهِ وَرَحْمَةُ اللهِ وَبَرَكَاتُهُ

Peace be upon the father of Qāsim, Muḥammad, the son of ʿAbdullāh. May the mercy and blessings of Allāh be upon him.

Now, enter the hall with your right foot. Stand at the door of the ḍarīḥ and recite the following:

I bear witness that there is no god except Allāh, alone, without any partners.	اَشْهَدُ اَنْ لَّا اِلٰهَ اِلَّا اللّٰهُ وَحْدَهُ لَا شَرِيْكَ لَهُ
And I bear witness that Muḥammad is His servant and Messenger.	وَاَشْهَدُ اَنَّ مُحَمَّداً عَبْدُهُ وَرَسُوْلُهُ
He has conveyed the truth from Him and verified the (past) Messengers.	جَآءَ بِالْحَقِّ مِنْ عِنْدِهِ وَصَدَّقَ الْمُرْسَلِيْنَ
Peace be upon you, O Messenger of Allāh!	اَلسَّلَامُ عَلَيْكَ يَارَسُوْلَ اللّٰهِ
Peace be upon you, O most beloved of Allāh and the best of His creations!	اَلسَّلَامُ عَلَيْكَ يَاحَبِيْبَ اللّٰهِ وَخِيَرَتَهُ مِنْ خَلْقِهِ
Peace be upon the Commander of the Faithful, the servant of Allāh and the brother of Allāh's Messenger.	اَلسَّلَامُ عَلٰى اَمِيْرِالْمُؤْمِنِيْنَ عَبْدِاللّٰهِ وَاَخِيْ رَسُوْلِ اللّٰهِ
O my master, O Commander of the Faithful!	يَا مَوْلَايَ يَا اَمِيْرَالْمُؤْمِنِيْنَ
My father, my mother, and I are all your slaves.	عَبْدُكَ وَابْنُ عَبْدِكَ وَابْنُ اَمَتِكَ
I have come to you seeking the refuge of your protection,	جَآءَكَ مُسْتَجِيْراً بِذِمَّتِكَ

قَاصِداً اِلىٰ حَرَمِكَ، مُتَوَجِّهاً اِلىٰ مَقَامِكَ

turning to your shrine, aware of your status,

مُتَوَسِّلاً اِلَى اللهِ تَعالىٰ بِكَ

and begging Allāh, the Exalted, in your name.

أَأَدْخُلُ يامَوْلَايَ، أَأَدْخُلُ يَا اَمِيْرَالْمُؤْمِنِيْنَ، أَأَدْخُلُ ياحُجَّةَ اللهِ

May I enter, O my master?
May I enter, O Commander of the Faithful?
May I enter, O proof of Allāh?

أَأَدْخُلُ يَا اَمِيْنَ اللهِ، أَأَدْخُلُ يَامَلَائِكَةَ اللهِ الْمُقِيْمِيْنَ فِيْ هٰذَا الْمَشْهَدِ

May I enter, O trustee of Allāh?
May I enter, O angels of Allāh who reside in this shrine?

يَا مَوْلَايَ اَتَأْذَنُ لِيْ بِالدُّخُوْلِ اَفْضَلَ مَا اَذِنْتَ لِاَحَدٍ مِنْ اَوْلِيَائِكَ،

O master, do you allow me to enter in the best way you have ever permitted any of your close friends?

فَاِنْ لَمْ اَكُنْ لَهُ اَهْلاً فَاَنْتَ اَهْلٌ لِذٰلِكَ

If I am too unworthy to deserve your permission, then You are too exalted to deprive me of it.

Kiss the door of the ḍarīḥ. Then, put your right foot forward and recite:

بِسْمِ اللهِ وَبِاللهِ وَفِيْ سَبِيْلِ اللهِ وَعَلىٰ مِلَّةِ رَسُوْلِ اللهِ صَلَّى اللهُ عَلَيْهِ وَآلِهِ

With the name of Allāh (I begin), in Allāh (I trust), in the path of Allāh, and upon the creed of Rasūl Allāh (I proceed), may Allāh bless him and his household.

اَللّٰهُمَّ اغْفِرْ لِيْ وَارْحَمْنِيْ وَتُبْ عَلَيَّ، إِنَّكَ اَنْتَ التَّوَّابُ الرَّحِيْمُ

O Allāh, forgive me, have mercy upon me, and accept my repentance. Surely, You are the granter of repentance, the Most Merciful.

Then, enter and stand facing the holy ḍarīḥ. Recite the following:

اَلسَّلَامُ مِنَ اللهِ عَلٰى مُحَمَّدٍ رَسُوْلِ اللهِ اَمِيْنِ اللهِ عَلٰى وَحْيِهِ وَ رِسَالَاتِهِ وَعَزَآئِمِ اَمْرِهِ

Peace of Allāh be upon the Messenger of Allāh, whom He has entrusted with His revelations and ultimate command,

وَمَعْدِنِ الْوَحْيِ وَالتَّنْزِيْلِ،

and the source of divine inspiration and revelation.

الْخَاتِمِ لِمَا سَبَقَ، وَالْفَاتِحِ لِمَا اسْتُقْبِلَ، وَالْمُهَيْمِنِ عَلٰى ذٰلِكَ كُلِّهِ، الشَّاهِدِ عَلَى الْخَلْقِ، السِّرَاجِ الْمُنِيرِ

He completed the previous messages, paved the way for the coming blessings (imāmah), prevails over all things. He is a witness over all creations and a luminous lantern.

وَالسَّلَامُ عَلَيْهِ وَرَحْمَةُ اللهِ وَبَرَكَاتُهُ،

May Allāh's peace, mercy, and blessings be upon him.

اَللّٰهُمَّ صَلِّ عَلٰى مُحَمَّدٍ وَاَهْلِ بَيْتِهِ الْمَظْلُوْمِيْنَ

O Allāh, send blessings upon Muḥammad and his household, the oppressed ones,

اَفْضَلَ وَاَكْمَلَ وَاَرْفَعَ وَاَشْرَفَ مَاصَلَّيْتَ عَلٰى اَحَدٍ مِنْ اَنْبِيَائِكَ وَرُسُلِكَ وَاَصْفِيَائِكَ

with the best, most perfect, most exalted, and most honorable blessings that You have ever bestowed upon any of Your Prophets, Messengers, and chosen servants.

اَللّٰهُمَّ صَلِّ عَلٰى اَمِيْرِالْمُؤْمِنِيْنَ عَبْدِكَ وَخَيْرِ خَلْقِكَ بَعْدَ نَبِيِّكَ

O Allāh, send blessings upon the Commander of the Faithful, Your servant, the best of Your creations after Your Prophet,

وَاَخِيْ رَسُوْلِكَ، وَ وَصِيِّ حَبِيْبِكَ

the brother of Your Messenger, and the successor of Your beloved one,

الَّذِي انْتَجَبْتَهُ مِنْ خَلْقِكَ، وَالدَّلِيْلِ عَلٰى مَنْ بَعَثْتَهُ بِرِسَالَاتِكَ

whom You have selected from among Your creations, and a guide to those whom You sent with Your messages,

وَدَيَّانِ الدِّيْنِ بِعَدْلِكَ، وَفَصْلِ قَضَائِكَ بَيْنَ خَلْقِكَ

the one who established the true religion through Your justice, and was the decisive judge amongst Your creations.

وَالسَّلَامُ عَلَيْهِ وَرَحْمَةُ اللهِ وَبَرَكَاتُهُ

May Allāh's peace, mercy, and blessings be upon him.

اَللّٰهُمَّ صَلِّ عَلَى الْاَئِمَّةِ مِنْ وُلْدِهِ الْقَوَّامِيْنَ بِاَمْرِكَ مِنْ بَعْدِهِ،

O Allāh, send blessings upon the Imāms from his offspring, the ones who upheld Your commands after him,

and the immaculate ones whom You have accepted as supporters of Your religion,	الْمُطَهَّرِيْنَ الَّذِيْنَ ارْتَضَيْتَهُمْ اَنْصَاراً لِدِيْنِكَ
keepers of Your secret, witnesses over Your creations, and signs for Your servants.	وَحفَظَةً لِسِرِّكَ، وَشُهَدَآءَ عَلٰى خَلْقِكَ، وَاَعْلاَماً لِعِبادِكَ
May Your blessings be upon them all.	صَلَوَاتُكَ عَلَيْهِمْ اَجْمَعِيْنَ
Peace be upon the Commander of the Faithful, ʿAlī the son of Abī Ṭālib, the successor of Allāh's Messenger, his representative, the one who upheld his commands after him,	اَلسَّلاَمُ عَلٰى اَمِيْرِ الْمُؤْمِنِيْنَ عَلِيِّ بْنِ اَبِيْ طَالِبٍ وَصِيِّ رَسُوْلِ اللهِ وَخَلِيْفَتِهِ وَالْقَآئِمِ بِاَمْرِهِ مِنْ بَعْدِهِ
and the leader of all the Prophet's successors. May Allāh's mercy and blessings be upon him.	سَيِّدِ الْوَصِيِّيْنَ وَرَحْمَةُ اللهِ وَبَرَكَاتُهُ
Peace be upon Fāṭimah, the daughter of Rasūl Allāh, may Allāh's blessings be upon him, the leader of the women of the worlds.	اَلسَّلاَمُ عَلٰى فَاطِمَةَ بِنْتِ رَسُوْلِ اللهِ صَلَّى اللهُ عَلَيْهِ وَآلِهِ سَيِّدَةِ نِسَاءِ الْعَالَمِيْنَ
Peace be upon al-Ḥasan and al-Ḥusayn, the leaders of all the youth of paradise.	اَلسَّلاَمُ عَلَى الْحَسَنِ وَالْحُسَيْنِ سَيِّدَيْ شَبَابِ اَهْلِ الْجَنَّةِ مِنَ الْخَلْقِ اَجْمَعِيْنَ

اَلسَّلَامُ عَلَى الْأَئِمَّةِ الرَّاشِدِيْنَ،
اَلسَّلَامُ عَلَى الْأَنْبِيَاءِ وَالْمُرْسَلِيْنَ

Peace be upon the guiding and nurturing Imāms.
Peace be upon the Prophets and Messengers.

اَلسَّلَامُ عَلَى الْأَئِمَّةَ الْمُسْتَوْدَعِيْنَ ،
اَلسَّلَامُ عَلٰى خَاصَّةِ اللهِ مِنْ خَلْقِهِ

Peace be upon the Imāms who are entrusted (with the religion of Allāh). Peace be upon the elite creations of Allāh.

اَلسَّلَامُ عَلَى الْمُتَوَسِّمِيْنَ

Peace be upon those with honorable character.

اَلسَّلَامُ عَلَى الْمُؤْمِنِيْنَ الَّذِيْنَ قَامُوا بِأَمْرِهِ
وَ وَازَرُوْا أَوْلِيَاءَ اللهِ، وَخَافُوْا بِخَوْفِهِمْ

Peace be upon the faithful believers who have upheld His commands, supported the close friends of Allāh, and have feared for their fear.

اَلسَّلَامُ عَلَى الْمَلَائِكَةِ الْمُقَرَّبِيْنَ،

Peace be upon the closest angels.

اَلسَّلَامُ عَلَيْنَا وَعَلٰى عِبَادِ اللهِ الصَّالِحِيْنَ

Peace be upon us and upon the righteous servants of Allāh.

Ziyārah Near the Ḍarīḥ

Go near the holy ḍarīḥ. Face the ḍarīḥ with your back to the qiblah and recite:

اَلسَّلَامُ عَلَيْكَ يَا اَمِيْرَالْمُؤْمِنِيْنَ
اَلسَّلَامُ عَلَيْكَ يَا حَبِيْبَ اللهِ

Peace be upon you, O Commander of the Faithful. Peace be upon you, O beloved of Allāh.

اَلسَّلَامُ عَلَيْكَ يَا صَفْوَةَ اللهِ، اَلسَّلَامُ عَلَيْكَ يَا وَلِيَّ اللهِ

Peace be upon you, O chosen one of Allāh. Peace be upon you, O close guardian of Allāh.

اَلسَّلَامُ عَلَيْكَ يَا حُجَّةَ اللهِ، اَلسَّلَامُ عَلَيْكَ يَا اِمَامَ الْهُدَىٰ

Peace be upon you, O proof of Allāh. Peace be upon you, O leader of true guidance.

اَلسَّلَامُ عَلَيْكَ يَا عَلَمَ التُّقَىٰ، اَلسَّلَامُ عَلَيْكَ اَيُّهَا الْوَصِيُّ الْبَرُّ التَّقِيُّ النَّقِيُّ الْوَفِيُّ

Peace be upon you, O sign of piety. Peace be upon you, O pious, God-conscious, pure, and loyal successor.

اَلسَّلَامُ عَلَيْكَ يَا اَبَاالْحَسَنِ وَالْحُسَيْنِ، اَلسَّلَامُ عَلَيْكَ يَا عَمُوْدَ الدِّيْنِ

Peace be upon you, O father of al-Ḥasan and al-Ḥusayn. Peace be upon you, O pillar of the religion.

اَلسَّلَامُ عَلَيْكَ يَا سَيِّدَ الْوَصِيِّيْنَ، وَاَمِيْنَ رَبِّ الْعَالَمِيْنَ

Peace be upon you, O leader of the successors (of the Prophet), trustee of the Lord of the worlds,

وَدَيَّانَ يَوْمِ الدِّيْنِ، وَخَيْرَ الْمُؤْمِنِيْنَ، وَسَيِّدَ الصِّدِّيْقِيْنَ

judge on Judgment Day, best of the believers, leader of the truthful,

وَالصَّفْوَةَ مِنْ سُلَالَةِ النَّبِيِّيْنَ، وَبَابَ حِكْمَةِ رَبِّ الْعَالَمِيْنَ

elite of the Prophet's lineage, door to the wisdom of the Lord of the worlds,

وَخَازِنَ وَحِيْهِ، وَعَيْبَةَ عِلْمِهِ، وَالنَّاصِحَ لِأُمَّةِ نَبِيِّهِ، وَالتَّالِيْ لِرَسُوْلِهِ

keeper of His Revelation, container of His knowledge, advisor to His Prophet's people, next to His Messenger,

وَالْمُوَاسِيَ لَهُ بِنَفْسِهِ، وَالنَّاطِقَ بِحُجَّتِهِ، وَالدَّاعِيَ اِلٰى شَرِيْعَتِهِ، وَالْمَاضِيَ عَلٰى سُنَّتِهِ

who sacrificed himself for him (the Messenger), spoke his proofs, invited to his principles, and held fast to his traditions

اَللّٰهُمَّ اِنِّيْ اَشْهَدُ اَنَّهُ قَدْ بَلَّغَ عَنْ رَسُوْلِكَ مَا حُمِّلَ

O Allāh, I bear witness that he carried out the mission conveyed to him by Your Messenger,

وَرَعٰى مَا اسْتُحْفِظَ، وَحَفِظَ مَا اسْتُودِعَ، وَحَلَّلَ حَلَالَكَ، وَحَرَّمَ حَرَامَكَ

delivered and protected what was entrusted to him, deemed lawful that which You made lawful, deemed unlawful that which You made unlawful,

وَاَقَامَ اَحْكَامَكَ، وَجَاهَدَ النَّاكِثِيْنَ فِيْ سَبِيْلِكَ، وَالْقَاسِطِيْنَ فِيْ حُكْمِكَ، وَالْمَارِقِيْنَ عَنْ اَمْرِكَ

upheld Your laws, strove in your path against the oathbreakers, the opposers to Your laws, and the apostates from Your command.

صَابِراً مُحْتَسِباً لَا تَأْخُذُهُ فِيْكَ لَوْمَةُ لَآئِمٍ

He patiently endured, expecting Your reward, and no one can accuse him of having any shortcomings.

اَللّٰهُمَّ صَلِّ عَلَيْهِ اَفْضَلَ مَا صَلَّيْتَ عَلٰى اَحَدٍ مِنْ اَوْلِيَآئِكَ وَاَصْفِيَآئِكَ وَاَوْصِيَاءِ اَنْبِيَآئِكَ

O Allāh, send blessings upon him in the best way You have ever blessed any of Your intimate servants, Your chosen ones, and Your Prophet’s successors.

اَللّٰهُمَّ هٰذَا قَبْرُ وَلِيِّكَ الَّذِيْ فَرَضْتَ طَاعَتَهُ، وَجَعَلْتَ فِيْ اَعْنَاقِ عِبَادِكَ مُبَايَعَتَهُ

O Allāh, this is the grave of Your guardian, whose obedience You have made incumbent (upon us) and whose allegiance has been put on the shoulders of your servants.

وَخَلِيْفَتِكَ الَّذِيْ بِهِ تَأْخُذُ وَتُعْطِيْ، وَبِهِ تُثِيْبُ وَتُعَاقِبُ

And (it is the grave of) Your representative through whom You will give and take, and through whom You will reward and punish.

وَقَدْ قَصَدْتُهُ طَمَعاً لِمَا اَعْدَدْتَهُ لِاَوْلِيَآئِكَ، فَبِعَظِيمِ قَدْرِهِ عِنْدَكَ،

I have turned towards him, seeking what You have prepared for Your intimate servants. So, I beseech You by his supreme standing with You,

وَجَلِيْلِ خَطَرِهِ لَدَيْكَ، وَقُرْبِ مَنْزِلَتِهِ مِنْكَ، صَلِّ عَلٰى مُحَمَّدٍ وَّآلِ مُحَمَّدٍ

his great status in Your view, and his close position to You, to bless Muḥammad and the household of Muḥammad,

وَافْعَلْ بِيْ مَا اَنْتَ اَهْلُهُ فَاِنَّكَ اَهْلُ الْكَرَمِ وَالْجُودِ

and to do to me that which is expected from You, for surely, You are worthy of honoring and granting generously.

وَالسَّلَامُ عَلَيْكَ يَا مَوْلَاىَ وَعَلٰى ضَجِيْعَيْكَ آدَمَ وَنُوْحٍ وَرَحْمَةُ اللهِ وَبَرَكَاتُهُ	Peace be upon you, O my master, and upon your companions Ādam and Nūh. May Allāh's mercy and blessings be upon you.

Now, kiss the holy ḍarīḥ, stand by the holy head, and recite:

يَا مَوْلَايَ اِلَيْكَ وُفُوْدِيْ، وَبِكَ اَتَوَسَّلُ اِلٰى رَبِّيْ فِيْ بُلُوْغِ مَقْصُوْدِيْ	O my master, I have come to you and ask Allah in your name, so that I may reach my goal.
وَاَشْهَدُ اَنَ الْمُتَوَسِّلَ بِكَ غَيْرُخَائِبٍ	I bear witness that one who asks Allāh through you will never be disappointed,
وَالطَّالِبَ بِكَ عَنْ مَعْرِفَةٍ غَيْرُمَرْدُوْدٍ إلَّابِقَضَاءِ حَوَائِجِهِ،	and one who implores Allāh through you, with full cognizance, will never be rejected. Rather, all his needs will be granted.
فَكُنْ لِيْ شَفِيْعاً اِلَى اللهِ رَبِّكَ وَرَبِّيْ فِيْ قَضَاءِ حَوَآئِجِيْ، وَتَيْسِيْرِ اُمُوْرِيْ	So, be my interceder to Allāh, your Lord and my Lord, to settle my needs, make my affairs easy,
وَكَشْفِ شِدَّتِيْ، وَغُفْرَانِ ذَنْبِيْ، وَسَعَةِ رِزْقِيْ، وَتَطْوِيْلِ عُمْرِيْ	relieve my sorrows, forgive my sins, increase my sustenance, extend my lifespan,

and grant me all my requests in this world and the hereafter. O Allāh, curse the killers of the Commander of the Faithful.	وَاعْطَاءِ سُؤْلِيْ فِيْ آخِرَتِيْ وَدُنْيَايَ، اَللَّهُمَّ الْعَنْ قَتَلَةَ اَمِيْرِالْمُؤْمِنِيْنَ
O Allāh, curse the killers of al-Ḥasan and al-Ḥusayn.	اَللَّهُمَّ الْعَنْ قَتَلَةَ الْحَسَنِ وَالْحُسَيْنِ
O Allāh, curse the killers of the Imāms, and subject them to such a painful punishment that You have never subjected anyone in the universe to,	اَللّهُمَ الْعَنْ قَتَلَةَ الْاَئِمَّةِ وَعَذِّبْهُمْ عَذَاباً اَلِيْماً لَاتُعَذِّبُهُ اَحَداً مِنَ الْعَالَمِيْنَ
such a great punishment that never ceases, nor comes to an end, nor reaches a deadline, for what they contended against Your commands.	عَذَاباً كَثِيْراً لَاانْقِطَاعَ لَهُ وَلَا اَجَلَ وَلَا اَمَدَ بِمَا شَاقُّوْا وُلَاةَ اَمْرِكَ
And prepare for them such an intense torture that You have not decided for any of Your creatures. O Allāh, impose upon the killers of Your Messenger's supporters,	وَاَعِدَّ لَهُمْ عَذَاباً لَمْ تُحِلَّهُ بِاَحَدٍ مِّنْ خَلْقِكَ، اَللَّهُمَّ وَاَدْخِلْ عَلٰى قَتَلَةِ اَنْصَارِ رَسُوْلِكَ
the killers of the Commander of the Faithful, the killers of al-Ḥasan and al-Ḥusayn,	وَعَلٰى قَتَلَةِ اَمِيْرَالْمُؤْمِنِيْنَ، وَعَلٰى قَتَلَةِ الْحَسَنِ وَالْحُسَيْنِ
the killers of the supporters of al-Ḥasan and al-Ḥusayn,	وَعَلٰى قَتَلَةِ اَنْصَارِالْحَسَنِ وَالْحُسَيْنِ
and the killers of all those whom were killed because of their loyalty to the Household of Muḥammad,	وَقَتَلَةِ مَنْ قُتِلَ فِيْ وِلَايَةِ آلِ مُحَمَّدٍ اَجْمَعِيْنَ

[and grant them] a painful, increasing punishment in the lowest level of the hellfire.	عَذَاباً اَلِيْماً مُضَاعَفاً فِيْ اَسْفَلِ دَرْكٍ مِّنَ الْجَحِيْمِ
Do not decrease their punishment, and make it so they shall remain in utter despair and endless curse;	لاَ يُخَفَّفُ عَنْهُمُ الْعَذَابُ وَهُمْ فِيْهِ مُبْلِسُوْنَ مَلْعُوْنُوْنَ
they shall be hanging down their heads before their Lord	نَاكِسُوْا رُؤُوْسِهِمْ عِنْدَ رَبِّهِمْ
after they shall find out with certainty regret and long-lasting disgrace, for they killed the members of the household of Your Prophets and Messengers and the righteous servants from their followers.	قَدْ عَايَنُوا النَّدَامَةَ وَالْخِزْيَ الطَّوِيْلَ لِقَتْلِهِمْ عِتْرَةَ اَنْبِيَآئِكَ وَرُسُلِكَ وَاَتْبَاعَهُمْ مِنْ عِبَادِكَ الصَّالِحِيْنَ
O Allāh, curse them both in secrecy	اَللّٰهُمَّ الْعَنْهُمْ فِيْ مُسْتَسِرِّ السِّرِّ
and openly, in Your lands and in Your heavens.	وَظَاهِرِ الْعَلاَنِيَةِ فِيْ اَرْضِكَ وَسَمَآئِكَ
O Allāh, (please do) decide for me a truthful step with Your intimate servants	اَللّٰهُمَّ اجْعَلْ لِيْ قَدَمَ صِدْقٍ فِيْ اَوْلِيَآئِكَ
and make me long for their shrines and their residing-places until You include me with them	وَحَبِّبْ اِلَيَّ مَشَاهِدَهُمْ وَمُسْتَقَرَّهُمْ حَتّٰى تُلْحِقَنِيْ بِهِمْ
and place me among their followers in this world as well as the world to come. O most Merciful of all those who show mercy!	وَتَجْعَلَنِيْ لَهُمْ تَبَعاً فِي الدُّنْيَا وَالْآخِرَةِ، يَا اَرْحَمَ الرَّاحِمِيْنَ

Kiss the ḍariḥ. Then, with your back to the Qiblah, face the grave of Imām Ḥusayn (A) in Karbalā and recite the following:

Peace be upon you, O Abā ʿAbdullāh. Peace be upon you, O son of Allāh's Messenger.	اَلسَّلَامُ عَلَيْكَ يَا اَبَا عَبْدِ اللّٰهِ ، اَلسَّلَامُ عَلَيْكَ يَا بْنَ رَسُولِ اللّٰهِ،
Peace be upon you, O son of the Commander of the Faithful.	اَلسَّلَامُ عَلَيْكَ يَابْنَ اَمِيْرِالْمُؤْمِنِيْنَ
Peace be upon you, O son of Fāṭimah az-Zahrā', the leader of the women of the worlds.	اَلسَّلَامُ عَلَيْكَ يَا بْنَ فَاطِمَةَ الزَّهْرَآءِ سَيِّدَةِ نِسَآءِ الْعَالَمِيْنَ
Peace be upon you, O father of the guiding and well-guided Imāms.	اَلسَّلَامُ عَلَيْكَ يَا اَبَا الْاَئِمَّةِ الْهَادِيْنَ الْمَهْدِيِّيْنَ
Peace be upon you, O the subject of pouring tears.	اَلسَّلَامُ عَلَيْكَ يَا صَرِيْعَ الدَّمْعَةِ السَّاكِبَةِ
Peace be upon you, O master of the disastrous tragedy.	اَلسَّلَامُ عَلَيْكَ يَاصَاحِبَ الْمُصِيْبَةِ الرَّاتِبَةِ
Peace be upon you and upon your grandfather and father. Peace be upon you and upon your mother and brother.	اَلسَّلَامُ عَلَيْكَ وَعَلٰى جَدِّكَ وَاَبِيْكَ، اَلسَّلَامُ عَلَيْكَ وَعَلٰى اُمِّكَ وَاَخِيْكَ

اَلسَّلاَمُ عَلَيْكَ وَعَلَى الْاَئِمَّةِ مِنْ ذُرِّيَّتِكَ وَبَنِيْكَ

Peace be upon you and upon the Imāms from your offspring and descendants.

اَشْهَدُ لَقَدْ طَيَّبَ اللهُ بِكَ التُّرَابَ، وَاَوْضَحَ بِكَ الْكِتَابَ

I bear witness that Allāh has certainly purified the soil (on which you were slain) through you and made His book clear through you.

وَجَعَلَكَ وَاَبَاكَ وَجَدَّكَ وَاَخَاكَ وَبَنِيْكَ عِبْرَةً لِاُوْلِي الْاَلْبَابِ

And He has made you, your father, your grandfather, your brother, and your descendants examples for those who manifest intellect.

يَابْنَ الْمَيَامِيْنِ الْاَطْيَابِ، التَّالِيْنَ الْكِتَابَ،

O son of the blessed, purified ones who recite (and apply) the Book utterly,

وَجَّهْتُ سَلاَمِيْ اِلَيْكَ، صَلَوَاتُ اللهِ وَسَلاَمُهُ عَلَيْكَ

I direct my greetings to you. May the peace and blessings of Allāh be upon you.

وَجَعَلَ اَفْئِدَةً مِّنَ النَّاسِ تَهْوِيْ اِلَيْكَ

And may He make the hearts of mankind yearn for you.

مَاخَابَ مَنْ تَمَسَّكَ بِكَ وَلَجَاَ اِلَيْكَ

Disappointment shall never reach one who adheres to you and resorts to you.

Then, walk towards the holy grave, stand by the footside, and recite the following:

Peace be upon the father of the Imāms, the intimate friend of Prophethood, and the one exclusively chosen for brotherhood (with the Noble Prophet).	اَلسَّلَامُ عَلٰى اَبِي الْاَئِمَّةِ، وَخَلِيْلِ النُّبُوَّةِ، وَالْمَخْصُوْصِ بِالْاُخُوَّةِ،
Peace be upon the upholder of the religion and faith, and the word of the Most Beneficent.	اَلسَّلَامُ عَلٰى يَعْسُوْبِ الدِّيْنِ وَالْاِيْمَانِ، وَكَلِمَةِ الرَّحْمٰنِ
Peace be upon the scale of deeds (by which I weigh my actions), the changer of my conditions (to be better), the sword of the Lord of Majesty (who helps stop me from bad deeds),	اَلسَّلَامُ عَلٰى مِيْزَانِ الْاَعْمَالِ، وَمُقَلِّبِ الْاَحْوَالِ، وَسَيْفِ ذِي الْجَلَالِ
and the one who quenches (the thirst of my soul) with the fresh water of Salsabīl.	وَسَاقِي السَّلْسَبِيْلِ الزُّلَالِ
Peace be upon the most righteous of the believers,	اَلسَّلَامُ عَلٰى صَالِحِ الْمُؤْمِنِيْنَ
the inheritor of the Prophets' knowledge, and the judge on the Judgment Day.	وَوَارِثِ عِلْمِ النَّبِيِّيْنَ، وَالْحَاكِمِ يَوْمِ الدِّيْنِ،
Peace be upon the tree of piety and the hearer of secrets and whispers.	اَلسَّلَامُ عَلٰى شَجَرَةِ التَّقْوٰى، وَسَامِعِ السِّرِّ وَالنَّجْوٰى

اَلسَّلاَمُ عَلىٰ حُجَّةِ اللهِ الْبَالِغَةِ،
وَنِعْمَتِهِ السَّابِغَةِ، وَنِقْمَتِهِ الدَّامِغَةِ

Peace be upon Allāh's conclusive proof, His blessings who help guide to perfection, and His forceful punishment.

اَلسَّلاَمُ عَلَى الصِّرَاطِ الْوَاضِحِ،
وَالنَّجْمِ اللاَّئِحِ، وَالْاِمَامِ النَّاصِحِ،
وَالزِّنَادِ الْقَادِحِ وَرَحْمَةُ اللهِ وَبَرَكَاتُهُ

Peace be upon the clear-cut path, the guiding star, the advising leader, and the guiding light in darkness. May Allāh's mercy and blessings be upon him.

اَللّٰهُمَّ صَلِّ عَلىٰ اَمِيْرِ الْمُؤْمِنِيْنَ عَلِيِّ
بْنِ اَبِيْ طَالِبٍ

O Allāh, send blessings upon the Commander of the Faithful, ʿAlī the son of Abī Ṭālib,

اَخِيْ نَبِيِّكَ وَوَلِيِّهِ وَنَاصِرِهِ وَوَصِيِّهِ
وَوَزِيْرِهِ ، وَمُسْتَوْدَعِ عِلْمِهِ،
وَمَوْضِعِ سِرِّهِ

the brother, guardian, supporter, successor, and advisor of Your Prophet; the storer of his knowledge, the depot of his secrets,

وَبَابِ حِكْمَتِهِ، وَالنَّاطِقِ بِحُجَّتِهِ،
وَالدَّاعِيْ اِلىٰ شَرِيْعَتِهِ، وَخَلِيْفَتِهِ فِيْ
اُمَّتِهِ

the door to his wisdom, the spokesman of his proofs, the caller to his code of law, his represenative in his nation,

the reliever of agony from his face, the terminator of the infidels, the conqueror on the wicked ones,	وَمُفَرِّجِ الْكَرْبِ عَنْ وَجْهِهِ وَ قَاصِمِ الْكَفَرَةِ، مُرْغِمِ الْفَجَرَةِ
the one whose position You have made, in regard to Your Prophet, the same as the position of Hārūn in regard to Mūsā.	الَّذِيْ جَعَلْتَهُ مِنْ نَبِيِّكَ بِمَنْزِلَةِ هَارُوْنَ مِنْ مُوْسىٰ،
O Allāh, befriend anyone who befriends him, be the enemy of anyone who is His enemy, support anyone who supports him, disappoint every one who disappoints him,	اَللّٰهُمَّ وَالِ مَنْ وَالَاهُ وَ عَادِ مَنْ عَادَاهُ، وَانْصُرْ مَنْ نَصَرَهُ، وَاخْذُلْ مَنْ خَذَلَهُ،
and remove Your mercy from anyone who usurped his rights from among the past and future generations.	وَالْعَنْ مَنْ نَصَبَ لَهُ مِنَ الْاَوَّلِيْنَ وَالْآخِرِيْنَ،
And (please do) bless him with the best blessings that You have ever poured on any of Your Prophet's successors. O Lord of the worlds!	وَصَلِّ عَلَيْهِ اَفْضَلَ مَا صَلَّيْتَ عَلىٰ اَحَدٍ مِّنْ اَوْصِيَاۤءِ اَنْبِيَاۤئِكَ، يَا رَبَّ الْعَالَمِيْنَ

Mawḍiʿu al-Iṣbaʿayn
The Place of the Two Fingers

This holy place is located inside the ḍarīḥ, near the head of the Imām (A), and holds great significance.

History narrates that Murrat ibn Qays was an oppressive governor. One day, he was engaging in a discussion about the history of his tribe and ancestors. He came to know that many of them were killed in war. When asked who killed them, he was told that most of them were killed by ʿAlī ibn Abū Ṭālib. When he asked where Imām ʿAlī (A) was buried, they told him, "Najaf."

Murrat prepared an army of 2,000 people and headed to Najaf. The people of Najaf bravely defended their city, but after six days of resistance, they were defeated.

Murrat entered the ḥaram of Imām ʿAlī (A) and began destroying everything. He wanted to exhume the Imām's (A) body from his grave, but just then, two fingers shaped like swords miraculously came out of the ḍarīḥ and cut him in half. The two halves of his body miraculously turned into two stones. These two stones were used as a place for animals to relieve themselves. Later, the enemies took these two stones and hid them.

Jaʿfar Āl Maḥbūbah, Māḍī al-Najaf wa Ḥāḍirihā, P. 232
Jaʿfar Naqdī, al-Anwār al-Alawiyyah, P. 423

Ziyārah of Prophets Ādam and Nūḥ (A)

For the ziyārah of Prophet Ādam (A), turn toward the head and recite:

اَلسَّلَامُ عَلَيْكَ يَا صَفِيَّ اللهِ
اَلسَّلَامُ عَلَيْكَ يَا حَبِيْبَ اللهِ،

Peace be upon you, O chosen one of Allāh! Peace be upon you, O beloved of Allāh!

اَلسَّلَامُ عَلَيْكَ يَا نَبِيَّ اللهِ
اَلسَّلَامُ عَلَيْكَ يَا اَمِيْنَ اللهِ،

Peace be upon you, O Prophet of Allāh.
Peace be upon you, O trustee of Allāh.

اَلسَّلَامُ عَلَيْكَ يَا خَلِيْفَةَ اللهِ
فِيْ اَرْضِهِ، اَلسَّلَامُ عَلَيْكَ يَا اَبَا الْبَشَرِ

Peace be upon you, O representative of Allāh in His lands.
Peace be upon you, O father of all mankind.

اَلسَّلَامُ عَلَيْكَ وَعَلىٰ رُوْحِكَ
وَبَدَنِكَ، وَعَلَى الطَّاهِرِيْنَ مِنْ وُلْدِكَ
وَذُرِّيَّتِكَ،

Peace be upon you and upon your soul and body, and upon the pure ones from your offspring and lineage.

وَصَلَّى اللهُ عَلَيْكَ صَلَاةً لَا يُحْصِيْهَا
إِلَّا هُوَ وَرَحْمَةُ اللهِ وَبَرَكَاتُهُ

May Allāh bless you with innumerable blessings that none can count except Him. May Allāh's mercy and blessings be upon you.

For the ziyārah of Prophet Nūḥ (A), recite:

اَلسَّلَامُ عَلَيْكَ يَا نَبِيَّ اللهِ، اَلسَّلَامُ عَلَيْكَ يَا صَفِيَّ اللهِ،	Peace be upon you, O Prophet of Allāh. Peace be upon you, O chosen one of Allāh.
اَلسَّلَامُ عَلَيْكَ يَا وَلِيَّ اللهِ، اَلسَّلَامُ عَلَيْكَ يَا حَبِيْبَ اللهِ،	Peace be upon you, O intimate servant of Allāh. Peace be upon you, O beloved by Allāh.
اَلسَّلَامُ عَلَيْكَ يَا شَيْخَ الْمُرْسَلِيْنَ، اَلسَّلَامُ عَلَيْكَ يَا اَمِيْنَ اللهِ فِيْ اَرْضِهِ،	Peace be upon you, O chief of the Messengers. Peace be upon you, O trustee of Allāh in His lands.
صَلَوَاتُ اللهِ وَسَلَامُهُ عَلَيْكَ وَعَلٰى رُوْحِكَ وَبَدَنِكَ، وَعَلَى الطَّاهِرِيْنَ مِنْ وُلْدِكَ	May Allāh's peace and blessings be upon you, upon your soul and body, and upon the pure ones from among your offspring.
وَرَحْمَةُ اللهِ وَبَرَكَاتُهُ	May Allāh's mercy and blessings be upon you.

Ziyārah Prayer for Imām ʿAlī (A)

Offer a two rakaʿāt prayer with the intention of ziyārah of Amīr al-Muʾminīn. This can be performed as a regular Fajr prayer, but the following method is better. In the first rakaʿah, recite Sūrats al-Fātiḥah and ar-Raḥmān, and in the second rakaʿah, recite Sūrats al-Fātiḥa and Yāsīn. After salām, recite the tasbīḥ of Fāṭimah az-Zahrāʾ (A). Then, seek forgiveness from Allāh, pray for yourself, and recite the following:

O Allāh, I have offered these two units (rakaʿāt) of prayer, as a gift from me to my leader and master, Your close guardian,	اَللَّهُمَّ اِنِّيْ صَلَّيْتُ هَاتَيْنِ الرَّكْعَتَيْنِ هَدِيَّةً مِنِّيْ اِلٰى سَيِّدِيْ وَمَوْلَايَ وَلِيِّكَ
the brother of Your Messenger, the Commander of the Faithful, and the leader of the Prophets' successors:	وَاَخِيْ رَسُولِكَ اَمِيْرِالْمُؤْمِنِيْنَ وَسَيِّدِ الْوَصِيِّيْنَ
ʿAlī the son of Abī Ṭālib, may Allāh's blessings be upon him and his household.	عَلِيِّ بْنِ اَبِيْ طَالِبٍ صَلَوَاتُ اللهِ عَلَيْهِ وَعَلٰى آلِهِ
So, O Allāh, send blessings upon Muḥammad and the household of Muḥammad, and accept it (the prayer) from me,	اَللَّهُمَّ فَصَلِّ عَلٰى مُحَمَّدٍ وَآلِ مُحَمَّدٍ، وَتَقَبَّلْهَا مِنِّيْ
and grant me that reward that You give to the good-doers.	وَاجْزِنِيْ عَلٰى ذٰلِكَ جَزَاءَ الْمُحْسِنِيْنَ
O Allāh, I have prayed, bowed, and prostrated to You;	اَللَّهُمَّ لَكَ صَلَّيْتُ وَلَكَ رَكَعْتُ وَلَكَ سَجَدْتُ

to You, alone, without associating any partners with You, because prayers, bowing, and prostration are for none but You	وَحْدَكَ لَا شَرِيْكَ لَكَ، لِاَنَّهُ لَاتَكُوْنُ الصَّلَاةُ وَالرُّكُوْعُ وَالسُّجُوْدُ اِلَّا لَكَ،
because You are Allāh; there is no god except You.	لِاَنَّكَ اَنْتَ اللهُ لَااِلٰهَ اِلَّا اَنْتَ
O Allāh, bless Muḥammad and the household of Muḥammad, and accept my ziyārah (visit) and grant me my requests by the right of Muḥammad and his pure household.	اَللّٰهُمَّ صَلِّ عَلٰى مُحَمَّدٍ وَآلِ مُحَمَّدٍ وَتَقَبَّلْ مِنِّيْ زِيَارَتِيْ، وَاَعْطِنِيْ سُؤْلِيْ بِمُحَمَّدٍ وَآلِهِ الطَّاهِرِيْنَ

Ziyārah Prayer for Prophets Ādam and Nūḥ (A)

Next, recite two sets of two rakaʿāt and gift them to Prophet Ādam (A) and Prophet Nūḥ (A). Then, perform sajdah of shukr (thanks) and recite the following:

O Allāh, I direct my attention to You, resort to You, rely upon You.	اَللّٰهُمَّ اِلَيْكَ تَوَجَّهْتُ، وَبِكَ اعْتَصَمْتُ، وَعَلَيْكَ تَوَكَّلْتُ
O Allāh, You are my trust and my hope; so, save me from those things that I am concerned about and those that I am not concerned about (but am unaware of their danger), and that which You know more than I do.	اَللّٰهُمَّ اَنْتَ ثِقَتِيْ وَرَجَائِيْ فَاكْفِنِيْ مَا اَهَمَّنِيْ وَمَا لَا يُهِمُّنِيْ ، وَمَا اَنْتَ اَعْلَمُ بِهِ مِنِّيْ
One who is under Your protection is honored, Your praise is exalted, and there is no god except You.	عَزَّ جَارُكَ، وَجَلَّ ثَنَاؤُكَ وَلَا اِلٰهَ غَيْرُكَ

Send blessings upon Muḥammad and the household of Muḥammad and hasten their relief (the appearance of Imām Mahdī (AJ)).	صَلِّ عَلىٰ مُحَمَّدٍ وَآلِ مُحَمَّدٍ، وَقَرِّبْ فَرَجَهُمْ

Then, place your right cheek on the ground and recite:

Have mercy on my lowliness before You, my earnest imploring to You, my loneliness among people, and my attachment to You.	اِرْحَمْ ذُلِّيْ بَيْنَ يَدَيْكَ، وَتَضَرُّعِيْ اِلَيْكَ ، وَوَحْشَتِيْ مِنَ النَّاسِ، وَاُنْسِيْ بِكَ
O the Most Generous! O the Most Generous! O the Most Generous!	يَا كَرِيْمُ يَا كَرِيْمُ يَا كَرِيْمُ

Then, place your left cheek on the ground and recite:

There is no god except You, my Lord, truly, truly! O my Lord, I prostrate myself before You as sign of my servitude and humility to You.	لَا اِلٰهَ إِلَّا اَنْتَ رَبِّي حَقّاً حَقّاً، سَجَدْتُ لَكَ يَا رَبِّ تَعَبُّداً وَرِقًّا
O Allāh, certainly, my deeds are feeble; so, please strengthen them for me.	اَللّٰهُمَّ اِنَّ عَمَلِيْ ضَعِيفٌ فَضَاعِفْهُ لِيْ
O the Most Generous! O the Most Generous! O the Most Generous!	يَا كَرِيْمُ يَا كَرِيْمُ يَا كَرِيْمُ

Then, perform sajdah again and recite " شُكراً (Shukran - Thank You)" 100 times. One should seek forgiveness of Allāh as much as possible because this is the place where sins are forgiven. One should also pray for the fulfillment of wishes as this is the place where prayers are accepted.

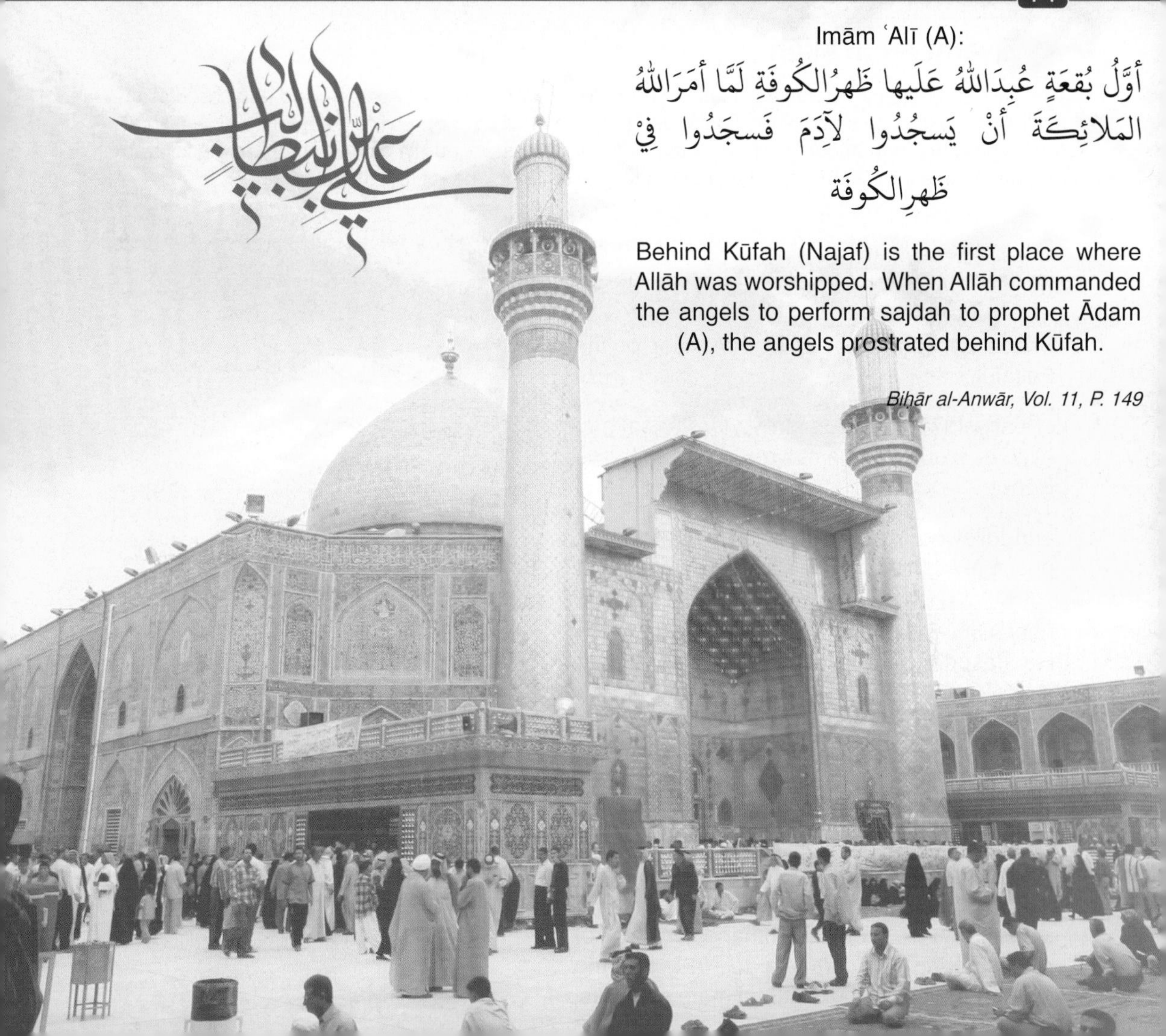

Imām ʿAlī (A):

أَوَّلُ بُقعَةٍ عُبِدَاللهُ عَلَيها ظَهرُالكُوفَةِ لَمَّا أَمَرَاللهُ
المَلائِكَةَ أَنْ يَسجُدُوا لِآدَمَ فَسجَدُوا فِيْ
ظَهرِالكُوفَة

Behind Kūfah (Najaf) is the first place where Allāh was worshipped. When Allāh commanded the angels to perform sajdah to prophet Ādam (A), the angels prostrated behind Kūfah.

Biḥār al-Anwār, Vol. 11, P. 149

Ziyārat Amīn Allāh

This ziyārah is highly estemeed, as is cited in all books of ziyārah. According to Allāmah Majlisī, this is the most reliable and is recommended to recite at all the holy shrines. Jābir ibn ʿAbd Allāh al-Anṣārī narrates from Imām al-Bāqir (A) that when Imām as-Sajjād (A) came to perform the ziyārah of Amīr ul-Muʾminīn (A), he stood near the holy grave, wept, and recited the following:

Peace be upon you, O trustee of Allāh in His lands and proof of Allāh over His servants.	اَلسَّلَامُ عَلَيْكَ يَا اَمِيْنَ اللهِ فِيْ اَرْضِهِ وَحُجَّتَهُ عَلٰى عِبَادِهِ
Peace be upon you, O Commander of the Faithful.	اَلسَّلَامُ عَلَيْكَ يَا اَمِيْرَ الْمُؤْمِنِيْنَ
I bear witness that you strove for the sake of Allāh as it ought to be striven, acted upon His Book,	اَشْهَدُ اَنَّكَ جَاهَدْتَ فِى اللهِ حَقَّ جِهَادِهِ وَعَمِلْتَ بِكِتَابِهِ
and followed the instructions of His Prophet, peace of Allāh be upon him and his household,	وَاتَّبَعْتَ سُنَنَ نَبِيِّهِ صَلَّى اللهُ عَلَيْهِ وَآلِهِ
until Allāh called you to be in His vicinity. So, He grasped you to Him by His will.	حَتّٰى دَعَاكَ اللهُ اِلٰى جِوَارِهِ فَقَبَضَكَ اِلَيْهِ بِاخْتِيَارِهِ
He brought conclusive proofs for all of Allāh's creations, even his enemies.	وَاَلْزَمَ اَعْدَآئِكَ الْحُجَّةَ مَعَ مَالَكَ مِنَ الْحُجَجِ الْبَالِغَةِ عَلٰى جَمِيْعِ خَلْقِهِ
O Allāh, make my soul completely tranquil with Your decrees,	اَللّٰهُمَّ فَاجْعَلْ نَفْسِيْ مُطْمَئِنَّةً بِقَدَرِكَ
satisfied with Your commands, fond of remembering and praying to You, bearing love for the chosen of Your intimate servants,	رَاضِيَةً بِقَضَآئِكَ مُوْلَعَةً بِذِكْرِكَ وَدُعَآئِكَ مُحِبَّةً لِصَفْوَةِ اَوْلِيَآئِكَ

مَحْبُوْبَةً فِيْ اَرْضِكَ وَسَمَآئِكَ صَابِرَةً عَلٰى نُزُوْلِ بَلَائِكَ	(make me) beloved in Your lands and heavens, patient against the affliction of Your tribulations,
شَاكِرَةً لِفَوَاضِلِ نَعْمَآئِكَ ذَاكِرَةً لِسَوَابِغِ آلَائِكَ	thankful for Your graceful bounties, always remembering Your neverending gifts (even if we do not deserve them),
مُشْتَاقَةً اِلٰى فَرْحَةِ لِقَآئِكَ مُتَزَوِّدَةً التَّقْوٰى لِيَوْمِ جَزَآئِكَ	longing for the joy of meeting You, supplied with piety for the day of Your rewarding,
مُسْتَنَّةً بِسُنَنِ اَوْلِيَآئِكَ مُفَارِقَةً لِاَخْلَاقِ اَعْدَائِكَ	pursuing the traditions of Your intimate servants, avoiding the conduct of Your enemies,
مَشْغُوْلَةً عَنِ الدُّنْيَا بِحَمْدِكَ وَثَنَآئِكَ	and distracted from this world by praising and thanking You.

Then, Imām as-Sajjād (A) placed his cheeks against the grave and recited:

اَللّٰهُمَّ اِنَّ قُلُوبَ الْمُخْبِتِيْنَ اِلَيْكَ وَالِهَةٌ	O Allāh, the hearts of those humbling themselves to You are longing to reach You,
وَسُبُلَ الرَّاغِبِيْنَ اِلَيْكَ شَارِعَةٌ وَاَعْلَامَ الْقَاصِدِيْنَ اِلَيْكَ وَاضِحَةٌ	the paths of those desiring You are open, the signs are evident for those turning towards You,
وَاَفْئِدَةَ الْعَارِفِيْنَ مِنْكَ فَازِعَةٌ وَاَصْوَاتَ الدَّاعِيْنَ اِلَيْكَ صَاعِدَةٌ	the hearts of those who recognize You are resorting to You, the voices of those beseeching You are ascending to You,

the doors of responding to them are wide open, the prayer of one who speaks to You confidentially is answered,	وَاَبْوَابَ الْاِجَابَةِ لَهُمْ مُفَتَّحَةٌ وَدَعْوَةَ مَنْ نَاجَاكَ مُسْتَجَابَةٌ
the repentance of one who turns to You modestly is accepted, the tear of one who fears You is granted mercy,	وَتَوْبَةَ مَنْ اَنَابَ اِلَيْكَ مَقْبُوْلَةٌ وَعَبْرَةَ مَنْ بَكٰى مِنْ خَوْفِكَ مَرْحُوْمَةٌ
the one who seeks Your aid is aided, the one who seeks Your help is helped;	وَالْاِغَاثَةَ لِمَنِ اسْتَغَاثَ بِكَ مَوْجُوْدَةٌ وَالْاِعَانَةَ لِمَنِ اسْتَعَانَ بِكَ مَبْذُوْلَةٌ
Your promises to Your servants are fulfilled, the slips of one who seeks Your forgiveness are forgiven,	وَعِدَاتِكَ لِعِبَادِكَ مُنْجَزَةٌ وَزَلَلَ مَنِ اسْتَقَالَكَ مُقَالَةٌ
the deeds of those who act for You are preserved, Your sustenance to Your creatures are descending,	وَاَعْمَالَ الْعَامِلِيْنَ لَدَيْكَ مَحْفُوْظَةٌ وَاَرْزَاقَكَ اِلَى الْخَلَائِقِ مِنْ لَدُنْكَ نَازِلَةٌ
You fulfill and exceed my basic needs to live,	وَعَوَآئِدَ الْمَزِيْدِ اِلَيْهِمْ وَاصِلَةٌ
the sins of those seeking Your forgiveness are forgiven, the requests of Your creatures are granted,	وَذُنُوْبَ الْمُسْتَغْفِرِيْنَ مَغْفُوْرَةٌ وَحَوَآئِجَ خَلْقِكَ عِنْدَكَ مَقْضِيَّةٌ
the rewards of those begging You are provided abundantly, Your gifts exceed my greatest needs,	وَجَوآئِزَ السَّائِلِيْنَ عِنْدَكَ مُوَفَّرَةٌ وَ عَوَآئِدَ الْمَزِيْدِ مُتَوَاتِرَةٌ

وَمَوَآئِدَ الْمُسْتَطْعِمِيْنَ مُعَدَّةٌ
وَمَنَاهِلَ الظِّمَآءِ مُتْرَعَةٌ

those who ask you are given plentiful, continous rewards, and the springs of quenching their thirst are brimful.

اَللَّهُمَّ فَاسْتَجِبْ دُعَآئِيْ وَاقْبَلْ ثَنَآئِيْ
وَاجْمَعْ بَيْنِيْ وَبَيْنَ اَوْلِيَآئِيْ

O Allāh, so respond to my prayer, accept my giving thanks to You, and join me with my masters,

بِحَقِّ مُحَمَّدٍ وَعَلِيٍّ وَفَاطِمَةَ وَالْحَسَنِ
وَالْحُسَيْنِ

by the right of Muḥammad, ʿAlī, Fāṭimah, al-Ḥasan, and al-Ḥusayn.

اِنَّكَ وَلِيُّ نَعْمَآئِيْ وَمُنْتَهٰى مُنَاىَ وَغَايَةُ
رَجَائِيْ فِيْ مُنْقَلَبِيْ وَمَثْوَايَ

Surely, You are the the only source of my furthest desires, the ultimate goal of my wishes, and the target of my hope in my spiritual and material wishes.

اَنْتَ اِلٰهِيْ وَسَيِّدِيْ وَمَوْلَايَ اغْفِرْ
لِأَوْلِيَآئِنَا

You are my God, Leader, and Master. Please forgive me by the sake of Your intimate servants,

وَكُفَّ عَنَّا اَعْدَآئَنَا وَاشْغَلْهُمْ عَنْ
اَذَانَا وَاَظْهِرْ كَلِمَةَ الْحَقِّ

keep our enemies away from us, distract them from harming us, give prevalence to the word of truth

وَاجْعَلْهَا الْعُلْيَا وَاَدْحِضْ كَلِمَةَ الْبَاطِلِ
وَاجْعَلْهَا السُّفْلٰى

and make it the supreme, and refute the word of falsehood and make it the lowest.

اِنَّكَ عَلٰى كُلِّ شَيْءٍ قَدِيْرٌ

Certainly, You are All-Powerful over all things.

Ziyārah of the Holy Head of Imām Ḥusayn (A)

According to historical narrations, the head of Imām Ḥusayn (A) was brought and buried in Najaf for a period of time. According to most scholars, it is most likely buried in Karbalāʿ currently.

Yazīd bin ʿUmar narrates, "One day, when Imām aṣ-Ṣādiq (A) was in Ḥīrah, he asked me, 'Do you want me to fulfill my promise to you and show you the grave of Amīr al-Muʾminīn?' I said 'Yes.' So, Imām aṣ-Ṣādiq (A), his son Ismāʿīl, and I passed a small hill between Ḥīrah and Najaf. The Imām prayed ṣalāh, and Ismāʿīl and I prayed along with him.

Then, he said, 'Rise and say salām to your grandfather Ḥusayn ibn ʿAli.'

I said, 'May I be sacrificed for you! Isn't Imām Ḥusayn (A) in Karbalā?'

The Imām (A) replied, 'Yes, but when they brought his holy head to Shām (Damascus), one of our Shīʿa secretly took the head and buried it next to Amīr al-Muʾminīn.'"

In other reliable aḥādīth from Imām aṣ-Ṣādiq (A), it is said that the graves of Prophet Nūḥ (A), Prophet Ibrāhīm (A), and 370 other Prophets, 600 successors of Prophets, and the best successor of the best Prophet (i.e., Amīr al-Muʾminīn) are located in Kūfah. In the book *Mustadrak*, it is narrated from Muḥammad ibn Mashadī that Imām aṣ-Ṣādiq (A) would perform ziyārah of Imām Ḥusayn (A) next to the head of Imām ʿAlī (A) and offer a four rakaʿāt prayer.

Biḥār al-Anwār, Vol. 45, P. 178

Ziyārah of the Holy Head of Imām Ḥusayn (A)

اَلسَّلَامُ عَلَيْكَ يَا بْنَ رَسُولِ اللهِ، اَلسَّلَامُ
عَلَيْكَ يَا بْنَ اَمِيرِ الْمُؤْمِنِيْنَ

Peace be upon you, O son of Allāh's Messenger. Peace be upon you, O son of the Commander of the Faithful.

اَلسَّلَامُ عَلَيْكَ يَا بْنَ الصِّدِّيْقَةِ الطَّاهِرَةِ
سَيِّدَةِ نِسَاءِ الْعَالَمِيْنَ

Peace be upon you, O son of the truthful and pure leader of the women of the world.

اَلسَّلَامُ عَلَيْكَ يَا مَوْلَايَ يَا اَبَا عَبْدِ اللهِ
وَرَحْمَةُ اللهِ وَبَرَكَاتُهُ

Peace be upon you, O my master, O Abā ʿAbdillāh. May Allāh's mercy and blessings be upon you.

اَشْهَدُ اَنَّكَ قَدْ اَقَمْتَ الصَّلَاةَ، وَآتَيْتَ
الزَّكَاةَ

I bear witness that you certainly established the prayers, gave alms (zakāh),

وَاَمَرْتَ بِالْمَعْرُوْفِ، وَنَهَيْتَ عَنِ
الْمُنْكَرِ

enjoined good, forbade evil,

وَتَلَوْتَ الْكِتَابَ حَقَّ تِلَاوَتِهِ، وَجَاهَدْتَ
فِي اللهِ حَقَّ جِهَادِهِ

recited the Qurʿān as it ought to be recited, strove for the sake of Allāh as it ought to be striven,

and withstood harm for His sake, fulfillfing his responsibility and seeking His reward, until death came to you.	وَصَبَرْتَ عَلَى الْأَذَىٰ فِيْ جَنْبِهِ، مُحْتَسِباً حَتَّىٰ اَتٰيكَ الْيَقِيْنُ
And I bear witness that those who dissented with you, fought against you, disappointed you,	وَاَشْهَدُ اَنَّ الَّذِيْنَ خَالَفُوْكَ وَحَارَبُوْكَ وَاَنَّ الَّذِيْنَ خَذَلُوكَ
and killed you are accursed in the words of the Ummī Prophet	وَالَّذِيْنَ قَتَلُوْكَ مَلْعُوْنُوْنَ عَلَىٰ لِسَانِ النَّبِيِّ الْأُمِّيِّ
And they must be destroyed for their false accusations! May Allāh curse those who oppressed you from the past and future generations, and may He double for them the painful chastisement.	وَقَدْ خَابَ مَنِ افْتَرَىٰ، لَعَنَ اللهُ الظَّالِمِيْنَ لَكُمْ مِنَ الْاَوَّلِيْنَ وَالْآخِرِيْنَ، وَضَاعَفَ عَلَيْهِمُ الْعَذَابَ الْاَلِيْمَ
I have come to visit you, O my master, O the son of Rasūl Allāh, aware of your right,	اَتَيْتُكَ يَا مَوْلَايَ يَا بْنَ رَسُوْلِ اللهِ زَائِراً عَارِفاً بِحَقِّكَ
showing loyalty to your close friends, showing enmity to your enemies, acknowledging the true guidance that you follow,	مُوَالِياً لِاَوْلِيَائِكَ، مُعَادِيًا لِاَعْدَائِكَ، مُسْتَبْصِراً بِالْهُدَى الَّذِيْ اَنْتَ عَلَيْهِ
and understanding that anyone who disagrees with you has deviated. So, please intercede for me with your Lord.	عَارِفاً بِضَلَالَةِ مَنْ خَالَفَكَ، فَاشْفَعْ لِيْ عِنْدَ رَبِّكَ

Farewell Ziyārah of Amīr al-Muʾminīn

May Allāh's peace, mercy, and blessings be upon you.	اَلسَّلَامُ عَلَيْكَ وَرَحْمَةُ اللهِ وَبَرَكَاتُهُ
I entrust you with Allāh and ask Him to keep you under His custody, and I send peace unto you.	اَسْتَوْدِعُكَ اللهَ وَأَسْتَرْعِيكَ وَاَقْرَأُ عَلَيْكَ السَّلَامُ
We have believed in Allāh, the Messengers, and what they have conveyed to us,	آمَنَّا بِاللهِ وَبِالرُّسُلِ وَبِمَا جَاءَتْ بِهِ
and (we believe in) that which they have called and guided us. So please include us with the witnesses.	وَدَعَتْ اِلَيْهِ وَدَلَّتْ عَلَيْهِ فَاكْتُبْنَا مَعَ الشَّاهِدِيْنَ
O Allāh, please do not make this my last visit to him (the Imām),	اَللّٰهُمَّ لَا تَجْعَلْهُ آخِرَ الْعَهْدِ مِنْ زِيَارَتِيْ اِيَّاهُ
and if you cause me to die before that, then I bear witness in my death to the same things that I have born witness to in my lifetime:	فَاِنْ تَوَفَّيْتَنِيْ قَبْلَ ذٰلِكَ فَاِنِّيْ اَشْهَدُ فِيْ مَمَاتِيْ عَلٰى مَا شَهِدْتُ عَلَيْهِ فِيْ حَيَاتِيْ
I bear witness that ʿAlī the Commander of the Faithful, al-Ḥasan,	اَشْهَدُ اَنَّ اَمِيْرَ الْمُؤْمِنِيْنَ عَلِيًّا وَالْحَسَنَ
al-Ḥusayn, ʿAlī ibn al-Ḥusayn, Muḥammad ibn ʿAlī,	وَالْحُسَيْنَ، وَعَلِيَّ بْنَ الْحُسَيْنِ، وَمُحَمَّدَ بْنَ عَلِيٍّ

Jaʿfar ibn Muḥammad, Mūsā ibn Jaʿfar,	وَجَعْفَرَ بْنَ مُحَمَّدٍ، وَمُوْسَىٰ بْنَ جَعْفَرٍ
ʿAlī ibn Mūsā, Muḥammad ibn ʿAlī, ʿAlī ibn Muḥammad,	وَعَلِيَّ بْنَ مُوْسَىٰ، وَمُحَمَّدَ بْنَ عَلِيٍّ وَعَلِيَّ بْنَ مُحَمَّدٍ
al-Ḥasan ibn ʿAlī, and al-Ḥujjah (the proof of Allāh) ibn al-Ḥasan— may Your blessings be upon all of them—are my Imāms (leaders).	وَالْحَسَنَ بْنَ عَلِيٍّ وَالْحُجَّةَ بْنَ الْحَسَنِ صَلَوَاتُكَ عَلَيْهِمْ اَجْمَعِيْنَ اَئِمَّتِيْ
I also bear witness that all of those who have slain and opposed them are polytheists,	وَاَشْهَدُ اَنَّ مَنْ قَتَلَهُمْ وَحَارَبَهُمْ مُشْرِكُوْنَ
and that all of those who reject them shall be in the lowest level of hellfire.	وَمَنْ رَدَّ عَلَيْهِمْ فِيْ اَسْفَلِ دَرْكٍ مِنَ الْجَحِيْمِ
I also bear witness that those who have fought against the Imāms are our enemies and we disassociate from them because they are surely the party of Shayṭān.	وَاَشْهَدُ اَنَّ مَنْ حَارَبَهُمْ لَنَا اَعْدَآءٌ وَنَحْنُ مِنْهُمْ بُرَءَآءُ وَ اَنَّهُمْ حِزْبُ الشَّيْطَانِ
May the curse of Allāh, His angels, and all of mankind be upon those who killed the Imāms,	وَعَلٰى مَنْ قَتَلَهُمْ لَعْنَةُ اللهِ وَالْمَلَآئِكَةِ وَالنَّاسِ اَجْمَعِيْنَ

وَمَنْ شَرِكَ فِيْهِمْ وَمَنْ سَرَّهُ قَتْلُهُمْ

and upon those who had any role in killing them and those who were pleased by their death.

اَللَّهُمَّ اِنِّيْ اَسْاَلُكَ بَعْدَ الصَّلَاةِ
وَالتَّسْلِيْمِ اَنْ تُصَلِّيَ عَلٰى مُحَمَّدٍ وَّعَلِيٍّ

O Allāh, surely I ask you after my prayer and submission that You send blessings upon Muḥammad, ʿAlī,

وَفَاطِمَةَ وَالْحَسَنِ وَالْحُسَيْنِ وَعَلِيٍّ
وَّمُحَمَّدٍ وَّجَعْفَرٍ وَّمُوْسٰى

Fāṭimah, al-Ḥasan, al-Ḥusayn, ʿAlī, Muḥammad, Jaʿfar, Mūsā,

وَعَلِيٍّ وَّمُحَمَّدٍ وَّعَلِيٍّ وَّالْحَسَنِ وَالْحُجَّةِ

ʿAlī, Muḥammad, ʿAlī, al-Ḥasan, and al-Ḥujjah.

وَلَا تَجْعَلْهُ آخِرَ الْعَهْدِ مِنْ زِيَارَتِهِ فَاِنْ
جَعَلْتَهُ فَاحْشُرْنِيْ مَعَ هٰؤُلَاۤءِ الْمُسَمَّيْنَ
الْاَئِمَّةِ

And do not make this my last visit to him, and if you decide so, then please include me with these Imāms who I have named.

اَللَّهُمَّ وَذَلِّلْ قُلُوْبَنَا لَهُمْ بِالطَّاعَةِ
وَالْمُنَاصَحَةِ

O Allāh, cause our hearts to be subservient to them by obeying them, following their advice,

وَالْمَحَبَّةِ وَحُسْنِ الْمُوَازَرَةِ وَالتَّسْلِيْمِ

loving them, supporting them, and submitting to them.

Wādī as-Salām

In our journey towards meeting our Creator, our souls go through many different stages and realms. We first exist in ʿālam al-dhar (the realm of pre-existence), then in ʿālam al-baṭn (the womb) and ʿālam ad-dunyā (this world).

When our souls leave this world, they enter the fourth realm of our journey: barzakh.

According to the Qurʾān and aḥadīth, after we die and our souls enter the realm of barzakh, the souls of the muʾminīn enter Wādī as-Salām, and the evil souls enter the Land of Barāhut (the Land of Uneasiness). Based on these narrations, this is why the graveyard of Wādī as-Salām holds a special significance. It was the tradition of our Imāms and ʿulamā to visit this graveyard to contemplate and reflect. So, as you walk through Wadi as-Salam, think about where we come from, our responsibilities in this world, and our final destination. Imagine your casket being carried out. Reflect on your actions, and ask Allāh to place your soul amongst the muʾminīn in this graveyard.

Some people think they need to be physically buried here for their soul to be here. However, that is not true. Regardless of where you are buried, if you are a true believer, your soul will be transferred here. People also think if they construct houses here, they will be buried here. However this, too, is not necessarily true.

Imām as-Ṣādiq (A): There will be no believer left in the west or the east, except that his soul will be taken to Wādī as-Salām.

According to aḥadīth, the soul of a believer will travel to the River of Kawthar through Wādī as-Salām, and the believers will gather in gardens around this area, drinking delicious beverages and talking to each other. It will be like a piece of heaven!

It is narrated that Imām ʿAlī said, "Whoever enters the graveyard [Wādī as-Salām] and recites the following duʿāʾ, Allāh will reward 50 years worth of blessings and forgive the sins of 50 years for him/her and his/her parents.

With the name of Allāh, the Beneficent, the Merciful	بِسْمِ اللهِ الرَّحْمٰنِ الرَّحِيْمِ
Peace be upon the people who believe that there is no god except Allāh	اَلسَّلَامُ عَلٰى اَهْلِ لَا اِلٰهَ اِلَّا اللهُ
from the people who believe that there is no god except Allāh.	مِنْ اَهْلِ لَا اِلٰهَ اِلَّا اللهُ
O people who believe that there is no god except Allāh,	يَا اَهْلَ لَا اِلٰهَ اِلَّا اللهُ
by the right of there is no god except Allāh,	بِحَقِّ لَا اِلٰهَ اِلَّا اللهُ
how did you find the saying "There is no god except Allāh?"	كَيْفَ وَجَدْتُمْ قَوْلَ لَا اِلٰهَ اِلَّا اللهُ
From there is no god except Allāh!	مِنْ لَا اِلٰهَ اِلَّا اللهُ
O there is no god except Allāh,	يَا لَا اِلٰهَ اِلَّا اللهُ
by the right of there is no god except Allāh,	بِحَقِّ لَا اِلٰهَ اِلَّا اللهُ
forgive whoever says, "There is no god except Allāh."	اِغْفِرْ لِمَنْ قَالَ لَا اِلٰهَ اِلَّا اللهُ
And include us amongst the ones who say, "There is no god except Allāh, Muḥammad is the Messenger of Allāh, and ʿAlī is the close guardian of Allāh."	وَاحْشُرْنَا فِيْ زُمْرَةِ مَنْ قَالَ لَا اِلٰهَ اِلَّا اللهُ مُحَمَّدٌ رَّسُوْلُ اللهِ عَلِيٌّ وَلِيُّ اللهِ

Prophet Hūd (A)

Prophet Hūd (A) was one of the great Prophets of Allāh who lived amongst the tribe of ʿĀd in the land of Aḥqāf (in modern-day Yemen). He was known amongst the people as a great man for his beautiful akhlāq and characteristics. The people of ʿĀd were wealthy and powerful people who lived long lives, had great income, lived in lush lands, and enjoyed many other blessings from Allāh. Unfortunately, they slowly became heedless towards Allāh and began rebelling by worshipping idols. Prophet Hūd (A) was appointed by Allāh to invite the people towards worshipping one God, Allāh, and ceasing their idol worshipping and oppression. Prophet Hūd (A) endeavored for many years to invite the people towards the truth. He would say, "I do not want any reward or money from you, and I am not inviting you for wealth or power. I am inviting you only for your own success." However, the people were oppressive towards Prophet Hūd (A) and persisted in their wrongdoings. They would call him names, such as "crazy" and "liar," and arrogantly taunt him to send the punishment from Allāh if he was indeed speaking the truth. Prophet Hūd (A) continued to advise and guide them, but only a few believed while the rest denied his words and continued in their stubborn ways. Slowly, Allāh's punishments became apparent. A drought took over the land, killing their crops. Then, one day, a cloud appeared in the sky, and the people became happy, but were unaware that this cloud was a cloud of punishment. Soon, Allāh unleashed upon them a vicious storm and ferocious winds. It is said that the wind was so strong that it destroyed the land over the course of seven nights and eight days. By the command of Allāh, everything and everyone on the land was destroyed, except Prophet Hūd (A) and his companions, who were saved by the mercy of Allāh. After this incident, Prophet Hūd (A) migrated towards the land of Ḥaḍramūt.

Prophet Ṣāliḥ (A)

After the tribe of ʿĀd had been destroyed because of their sins, the people of Thamūd settled on that same land and Allāh gave them even more blessings than the people of ʿĀd. They had gardens, groves, and rock houses situated in between the mountains, to protect them from any calamities. Just like the people of ʿĀd, they lived comfortable lives full of blessings, but instead of thanking Allāh and worshipping Him, they, too, began worshipping idols. In order to help them mend their ways, Allāh appointed Prophet Ṣāliḥ (A) to guide them. While a few wise people believed, the others taunted Prophet Ṣāliḥ (A), and asked him to show them a miracle. By the power of Allāh, Prophet Ṣāliḥ (A) granted this request and made a pregnant she-camel appear from inside the mountain. He warned the people not to harm the camel or else Allāh would cast a fierce punishment upon them. Prophet Ṣāliḥ's (A) camel lived peacefully in the land and would eat and drink from the lush land. After witnessing this miracle, some people started to believe, but others persisted in their disbelief. Seeing Prophet Ṣāliḥ's (A) miracle only made them more angry, and they wanted to kill him, but could not do so because they were afraid for their own lives. Instead, they decided to kill the camel. First, the hypocrites cut off her legs and then killed her. They then said to Prophet Ṣāliḥ (A), "If you speak the truth and truly are the Prophet of Allāh, then unleash the punishment that you warned us about." Prophet Ṣāliḥ (A) urged them to seek forgiveness from Allāh, as they only had three days to live before the punishment was sent down. They ignored his warning, however, and continued to taunt him, asking him to make the punishment come sooner. Prophet Ṣāliḥ (A) replied, "How I wish you would ask forgiveness from Allāh so that maybe you would be saved from the punishment." Instead, some of these evil men plotted to kill Prophet Ṣāliḥ (A) and his companions in the middle of the night, but Allāh is the best of planners. Before they could execute their plan, lightning struck from the skies, killing them all while they were in their beds. As Prophet Ṣāliḥ (A) passed by their bodies, he sorrowfully said, "O people, I delivered the message of Allāh to you, but you did not listen because of your arrogance and ignorance."

Ziyārah of Prophet Hūd And Prophet Ṣāliḥ (A)

Peace be upon the close servants of Allāh and His chosen ones,	اَلسَّلَامُ عَلٰى اَوْلِيَآءِ اللهِ وَ اَصْفِيَآئِهِ
Peace be upon the trustees of Allāh and His beloved ones.	اَلسَّلَامُ عَلٰى اُمَنَآءِ اللهِ وَ اَحِبَّائِهِ
Peace be upon the helpers of Allāh and His representatives.	اَلسَّلَامُ عَلٰى اَنْصَارِ اللهِ وَخُلَفَآئِهِ
Peace be upon the source of knowing Allāh.	اَلسَّلَامُ عَلٰى مَحَآلِّ مَعْرِفَةِ اللهِ
Peace be upon the homes of the rememberance of Allāh.	اَلسَّلَامُ عَلٰى مَسَاكِنِ ذِكْرِ اللهِ
Peace be upon the ones who disclose Allāh's orders.	اَلسَّلَامُ عَلٰى مُظْهِرِيْ اَمْرِ اللهِ وَ نَهْيِهِ
Peace be upon those who call towards Allāh.	اَلسَّلَامُ عَلَى الدُّعَاةِ اِلَى اللهِ
Peace be upon the ones who are steadfast in performing what pleases Allāh.	اَلسَّلَامُ عَلَى الْمُسْتَقِرِّيْنَ فِيْ مَرْضَاتِ اللهِ
Peace be upon those who were sincere in their obedience to Allāh.	اَلسَّلَامُ عَلَى الْمُخْلِصِيْنَ فِيْ طَاعَةِ اللهِ
Peace be upon the guides to Allāh.	اَلسَّلَامُ عَلَى الْاَدِلَّاءِ عَلَى اللهِ
Peace be upon them (Prophets Hūd and Ṣāliḥ); the one who is loyal to them is indeed loyal to Allāh.	اَلسَّلَامُ عَلَى الَّذِيْنَ مَنْ وَالَاهُمْ فَقَدْ وَالَى اللهَ

The one who is against them is indeed against Allāh, and the one who knows them indeed knows Allāh.	وَ مَنْ عَادَاهُمْ فَقَدْ عَادَى اللهَ وَ مَنْ عَرَفَهُمْ فَقَدْ عَرَفَ اللهَ
The one who has ignored them has indeed ignored Allāh, and the one who seeks refuge in them has sought refuge in Allāh.	وَ مَنْ جَهِلَهُمْ فَقَدْ جَهِلَ اللهَ وَمَنِ اعْتَصَمَ بِهِمْ فَقَدِ اعْتَصَمَ بِاللهِ
The one who dissassociates from them has indeed dissassociated from Allāh.	وَ مَنْ تَخَلَّى مِنْهُمْ فَقَدْ تَخَلَّى مِنَ اللهِ عَزَّوَجَلَّ
I ask Allāh to bear witness that I declare peace with whomever you were peaceful to, that I declare war against anyone you have declared war against,	وَأُشْهِدُ اللهَ اَنِّي سِلْمٌ لِمَنْ سَالَمْتُمْ وَ حَرْبٌ لِمَنْ حَارَبْتُمْ
that I believe in your secrets and declarations delegating all this to you.	مُؤْمِنٌ بِسِرِّكُمْ وَ عَلَانِيَتِكُمْ مُفَوِّضٌ فِيْ ذٰلِكَ كُلِّهِ اِلَيْكُمْ
May Allāh curse the enemies of Muḥammad and his holy household from among the jin and humans.	لَعَنَ اللهُ عَدُوَّ آلِ مُحَمَّدٍ مِنَ الْجِنِّ وَالِانْسِ
I disassociate from all of them in the presence of Allāh. May Allāh send His blessings upon Muḥammad and his household.	وَاَبْرَءُ اِلَى اللهِ مِنْهُمْ وَ صَلَّى اللهُ عَلٰى مُحَمَّدٍ وَ آلِهِ

Maqām Ṣāḥib az-Zamān (AJ) in Wādī as-Salām

This place is among the oldest places attributed to his eminence, Imām az-Zamān (AJ). Imām aṣ-Ṣādiq (A) used to come here often to offer his prayers and has introduced it as the Miḥrāb of Imām al-Mahdī (AJ).

Imām az-Zamān (AJ) will pass through this spot during the early days of his just government and will head towards the capital of his government: Kūfah.

The Noble Prophet (S) and Imām ʿAlī (A) will meet at this spot during the rajʿat (return).

ʿAllāmah Baḥr al-ʿUlūm who passed away in the year 1212 AH, rebuilt this place[1]. Sayyid Muḥammad Khān, the king of Sanad (British India), tiled the dome and maqām. On 9th Shaʿbān, 1200 AH, the Imām's (AJ) ziyārah was carved on a stone in the miḥrāb.

Muḥadith Nūrī says:
The Maqām of Ṣāḥib az-Zamān (AJ), which contains a ḥaram and dome, is located on the west side of the famous Wādī as-Salām cemetery. The maqām contains a miḥrāb that has been attributed to Imām Mahdī (AJ). The exact history of this miḥrāb and its attribution to Imām Mahdī (AJ) is unclear. It might have been due to him praying there or a miracle that occurred in this place.

Sayyid ʿAbdul Laṭīf Mūsawī Shūshtarī, Tuḥfat al-ʿĀlam, Vol. 1, P. 319

Maqām of Imām Zayn al-'Ābidīn (A)

Every time Imām Zayn al-'Abidīn (A) would go to Najaf to visit his grandfather, Amīr ul-Mu'mineen (A), he would stay in the same place.

Imām al-Bāqir (A):
For several years after the martyrdom of his father, Imām Ḥusayn (A), my father, Imām 'Alī ibn al-Ḥusayn (A), lived in a small house in the outskirts of the city because he did not want to interact with others [those who killed his father]. When he would perform the ziyārah of his grandfather, Imām 'Alī (A), or his father, Imām Ḥusayn (A), he would try to go without people noticing.[1]

Maqām of Amīr ul-Mu'minīn (A)

The Grave of Uthayb Yamānī (known as Sāfī Safā)

Maqām of Amīr ul-Mu'minīn (A) and the gravesite of aṣ-Ṣafā are located on the western side of the holy ḥaram, next to Maqām Imām Zayn al-'Ābidīn (A).

Uthayb Yamānī passed away in the year 37 AH and was buried in Najaf by Amīr ul-Mu'mineen (A).

Its reported that one day, the Imām (A) was sitting in the desert outside of Najaf when he saw a person carrying a body on a camel, heading towards Najaf. As he got closer, the Imām (A) asked him, "Where are you coming from?" The man replied, "Yemen."

The Imām (A) then asked, "Whose body is this?"

He replied, "My father. I have brought him here to bury him in this land.

The Imām (A) asked, "Why didn't you bury him in your own city?"

He replied, "My father's last words were to tell us that a man will be buried here through whose intercession a multitude of people will be forgiven."

The Imām (A) asked, "Do you know who that man is?"

He replied, "No."

The Imām (A) then repeated three times, "By Allāh, I am that man." Then, the Imām (A) stood up and helped bury the body.[2]

1. *Biḥār al-Anwār, Vol. 100, P. 277 & 266*
2. *Ibid, P. 233*

Kumayl ibn Ziyād Nakhaʿī

Kumayl was among the famous companions of Imām ʿAlī (A), known for his bravery and loyalty. He was one of the eight famous pious and ascetic individuals of Kūfah. Imām ʿAlī (A) taught him a special Duʿāʾ, Duʿāʾ al-Khiḍr, which is more commonly known as Duʿāʾ Kumayl, and is recited on Thursday night or the eve of 15th Shaʿbān.

After Imām ʿAlī's (A) martyrdom, Kumayl was a loyal and obedient companion to Imām Ḥasan (A), and one of the few who supported the Imām (A) even during the peace treaty. When Imām Ḥasan (A) was martyred, Kumayl was not in Madīnah, and even during the battle of Karbalā, he was imprisoned until the day after ʿĀshūrāʾ. Once he was released, he began preaching and spreading the news of what happened to the Ahl al-Bayt (A). He also fought alongside Mukhtār and after this, he went into hiding. Nobody knew about his whereabouts, except Imām as-Sajjād (A).

When Ḥajjāj ibn Yūsuf ath-Thaqafī became the governor of Kūfah, he wanted to seek out Kumayl, but since he was in hiding, he seized his tribe's portion of income from the public treasury. Once Kumayl witnessed this, he could not bare the thought of others being oppressed because of him, so he came out of hiding. Ḥajjāj martyred Kumayl in the year 83 AH at the age of 90, just as Imām ʿAlī (A) had foretold him.

Kumayl: ʿAlī ibn Abi Ṭālib (A) took me by my hand to a place called Jabbān. As we reached the desert, he took a deep breath and said, "O Kumayl! These hearts are just like vessels, and the best of them is the one that protects what is in it. O Kumayl! Remember what I tell you:

الناسُ ثلاثةٌ، عالِمٌ ربّانی، و مُتَعلِّمٌ علی سَبیلِ نجاةٍ، وَ
هَمَجٌ رَعاعٌ، لِکُلِّ ناعِقٍ اتباعٌ یمیلونَ مَعَ کُلِّ ریحٍ، لم
یَستَضیئوا بِنُورِ العِلمِ، وَ لَمَ یَلجَوُا إلی رُکنٍ وَثیق

People are of three kinds: mystical scholars, students on the path of salvation, and those who are weak and listen to and obey anyone [the Imām compares these people to flies who sit anywhere and fly off at any change]. These people have not benefited from the light of knowledge and have not sought out a firm pillar [reliable teacher].

یاَ کُمَیل: العِلمُ خیرُ المالِ، العِلمُ یَحرِسُک و أنتَ تَحرُسُ
المالَ و المالُ تَنقُصُهُ النَّفَقَةُ، و الْعِلِمِ یَزکو عَلی الانفاق. ...
یاَ کُمَیل: ماتَ خُزّانُ المالِ، وَالعُلَماءُ باقُونَ مابَقِیَ الدَّهرُ.
اعیاَنُهُم مَفقُودَةٌ وَ أمثالُهُم فِیْ القُلُوبَ مَوجُودَةٌ 1

O Kumayl! Knowledge is better than wealth. Knowledge protects you, whereas you have to protect your wealth. Wealth decreases when you give, yet your knowledge increases when you share it. O Kumayl! Seekers of wealth will vanish, while the scholars will remain as long as the days remain. Even if they are not amongst us physically, they exist within the hearts.

1. Nahjul Balāghah, Saying 147#

Ziyārah of Kumayl ibn Ziyād

Peace be upon Muḥammad, the seal of prophets.	اَلسَّلَامُ عَلىٰ مُحَمَدٍ خَاتِمِ النَّبِيِّيْنْ
Peace be upon ʿAlī, the Commander of the Faithful.	اَلسَّلَامُ عَلىٰ عَلِيٍّ اَمِيْرِالْمُؤْمِنِيْنَ
Peace be upon Fāṭimah az-Zahrāʾ the leader of the women of the worlds.	اَلسَّلَامُ عَلىٰ فَاطِمَةَ الزَّهْرَاء سَيِّدَةِ نِسَاءَ الْعَالَمِيْنَ
Peace be upon Khadījah al-Kubrāh, the mother of the believers.	اَلسَّلَامُ عَلىٰ خَدِيْجَةَ الْكُبْرىٰ أُمِّ الْمُؤْمِنِيْنَ
Peace be upon al-Ḥasan and al-Ḥusayn, the leaders of all the youth of paradise.	اَلسَّلَامُ عَلَى الْحَسَنِ وَالْحُسَيْنِ سَيِّدَيْ شَبَابِ أَهْلِ الْجَنَّةِ مِنَ الْخَلْقِ اَجْمَعِيْنَ
Peace be upon the rest of the Imāms of the Muslims,	اَلسَّلَامُ عَلىٰ سَائِرِ أَئِمَةِالْمُسْلِمِيْنَ
ʿAlī, Muḥammad, Jaʿfar, Mūsā, ʿAlī, Muḥammad, ʿAlī, al-Ḥasan	عَلِيٍّ وَمُحَمّدٍ وَجَعْفَرٍ وَمُوْسَىٰ وَعَلِيٍّ وَمُحَمَّدٍ وَعَلِيٍّ وَالْحَسَنِ
And (al-Mahdī) the successor, the guide, the guided, the one who will fullfill the promise for the believers	وَالْخَلَفِ الْهَادِي الْمَهْدِىِّ مُنْجِزِ وَعْدِ الْمُؤْمِنِيْنَ

Peace be upon the close angels and the righteous servants.	اَلسَّلَامُ عَلٰى مَلَائِكَتِهِ الْمُقَرَّبِيْنَ وَعِبَادِهِ الصَّالِحِيْنَ
Peace be upon the righteous servant, the pious advisor, the God-fearing scholar,	اَلسَّلَامُ عَلَى الْعَبْدِ الصَّالِحِ، الْوَلِيِّ النَّاصِحِ الْعَالِمِ التَّقِيِّ
the one who is buried in the land of Gharī, Kumayl, the son of Ziyād.	الْمَدْفُوْنِ بِأَرْضِ الْغَرِيّ كُمَيْلِ بْنِ زِيَادٍ
Peace be upon you who was guided to perfection by the possessor of perfection (Imām ʿAlī), the commander in war.	اَلسَّلَامُ عَلٰى مَنْ اَكْمَلَهُ الْكَامِلِ فِيْ الصِّفَاتِ وَ الْأَمِيْرِ فِيْ الْغَزَوَاتِ
He entrusted in you the secret and taught you the Duʿāʾ of al-Khiḍr (i.e. Duʿāʾ al-Kumayl),	وَ وَدَّعَهُ السِّرَّ وَعَلَّمَهُ دُعَاءَ الْخِضْرِ
and he informed you about the soul and the reality so you became enlighted.	وَ اَخْبَرَهُ عَنِ النَّفْسِ وَالْحَقِيْقَةِ فَصَارَ فِيْهَا ذَا بَصِيْرَةٍ
I bear witness that you have contributed to the truth,	اَشْهَدُ اَنَّكَ قَدْ اَدَّيْتَ اِلَى الْحَقِّ،

and that you have directed towards the path of truth and guidance and kept away from falsehood and stubbornness.	وَوَجَّهْتَ مِنْهَاجَ الصِّدْقِ وَالرَّشَادِ وَاَعْرَضْتَ عَنِ الْبَاطِلِ وَالْعِنَادِ
Peace be upon one of the disciples of the strong rope of Allāh (Imām ʿAlī),	اَلسَّلَامُ عَلٰى اَحَدِ حَوَارِيِّ حَبْلِ اللهِ الْمَتِيْنِ،
the one who gained the companionship of the leader of the successors and his grandson (Imām Ḥasan).	الْفَائِزِ بِصُحْبَةِ سَيِّدِ الْوَصِيِّيْنَ وَصُحْبَةِ سِبْطِهِ الْأَكْبَرِ
Peace be upon the one who was made aware by the leader of truthful.	اَلسَّلَامُ عَلٰى مَنْ اَخْبَرَهُ بِالْقَوْلِ سَيِّدِالصَّادِقِيْنَ
May Allāh curse your oppressive killer, the wretched and accursed al-Hajjāj bin Yūsuf al-Thaqafī.	لَعَنَ اللهُ قَاتِلَكَ الظَّالِمَ الشَّقِيَّ اللَّعِيْنَ الْحَجَّاجَ بْنِ يُوسُفِ الثَّقَفِيِّ
And peace be upon you O Kumayl bin Ziyād al-Nakhaʿī al-Yamānī.	وَ السَّلَامُ عَلَيْكَ يَا كُمَيْلَ بْنَ زِيَادِ النَّخَعِيِّ الْيَمَانِيِّ
May Allāh's blessings and mercy be upon you.	وَ رَحْمَةُ اللهِ وَ بَرَكَاتُهُ

Now, you may offer a two rakaʿāt prayer and gift it to the soul of Kumayl.

Masjid Ḥannānah

Masjid al-Ḥannānah is located between Najaf and Kūfah, close to the grave of Kumayl ibn Ziyād. It is on this land where the blessed and holy head of Imām Ḥusayn (A) was placed while on the journey towards Kūfah. When this happened, the ground mourned and cried out, and later, a masjid was built as a reminder of this mourning. The word Ḥannānah means "crying."

Ibn Abi ʿUmayr narrates from Mufaḍal:
When Imām aṣ-Ṣādiq (A) came to this place, he offered a two rakaʿāt prayer. When he was asked about the prayer, the Imām (A) said, "This is the place where the blessed head of my grandfather Imām Ḥusayn (A) was placed when they were taking it from Karbalā to ʿUbayd Allāh ibn Ziyād."

ʿAllāmah Majlisī, Tuḥfat az-Zāʾir, P. 106

Masjid Ḥannānah is about 2.5 kilometers away from from the ḥaram of Imām ʿAlī and is near the gravesite of Kumayl

1. Offer a two rakaʿāt prayer with the intention of Taḥṣṣiyat al-Masjid.
2. Recite the ziyārah of the head of Imām Ḥusayn (A) (See P. 76)
3. Recite this duʿāʾ from Imām as-Ṣādiq (A):

O Allāh, surely You see my position and hear my words.	اَللّٰهُمَّ اِنَّكَ تَرٰى مَكَانِيْ، وَتَسْمَعُ كَلَامِيْ
None of my affairs are hidden from You,	وَلَا يَخْفٰى عَلَيْكَ شَيْءٌ مِنْ اَمْرِيْ
and how could they be hidden when You are my Creator and Initiator?	وَكَيْفَ يَخْفٰى عَلَيْكَ مَا اَنْتَ مُكَوِّنُهُ وَبَارِئُهُ
Surely, I have come to You through the intercession of Your Prophet, the Prophet of mercy,	وَقَدْ جِئْتُكَ مُسْتَشْفِعًا بِنَبِيِّكَ نَبِيِّ الرَّحْمَةِ
and am begging You by the successor of Your Prophet. So, I ask You by their right to help me remain steady on the path	وَمُتَوَسِّلًا بِوَصِيِّ رَسُوْلِكَ فَاَسْأَلُكَ بِهِمَا ثَبَاتَ الْقَدَمِ
and for guidance and forgiveness in this world and the hereafter.	وَالْهُدٰى وَالْمَغْفِرَةَ فِي الدُّنْيَا وَالْآخِرَةِ

According to another hadith, whenever Imām as-Ṣādiq (A) would visit Najaf, he would stop and offer prayer in three places:

1. Masjid al-Ḥannānah: the place of Imām Ḥusayn's (A) holy head
2. The Maqām of Imām az-Zamān (AJ) in Wādī as-Salām
3. The holy shrine of Amīr al-Muʿminīn (A)

Tarjumah Kāmil az-Ziyārāt, P. 96

Grand Āyatullāh (Marājiʿ) in the Ḥawza al-ʿIlmīyyah of Najaf

Āyatullāh al-ʿUẓmā Sayyid ʿAlī Sīstānī next to his late teacher, Āyatullāh al-ʿUẓmā Ḥāj Sayyid Abūl Qāsim Khūʾī, who is buried in the ḥaram of Imām ʿAlī (A).

Āyatullāh al-ʿUẓmā Sayyid ʿAlī Sīstānī

Āyatullāh Sīstānī was born on the 9th of Rabiʿ al-Awwal, 1349 AH (4th August, 1930) in Mashhad, Īrān. His family descends from the lineage of Imām Ḥusayn (A) and lived in Iṣfahān during the Safavid empire.

Sultān Ḥusayn Safavī appointed his grandfather, Sayyid Muḥammad, as the Shaykh al-Islām, (representing Shaykh) in Sistān, so his family moved there. Sayyid Sīstānī began his preliminary ḥawza studies after completing the elementary subjects in the year 1360 AH. He attended a series of literature classes by ʿĀdib Neishabūrī and other prominent teachers. After finishing the preliminary and intermediate levels, he began studying philosophical and theological sciences.

In the year 1368 AH, he moved to Qom and attend the fiqh and usūl lessons of Āyatullāh Borūjerdī. In 1371 AH, he moved to Najaf al-Ashraf and benefited from great teachers, such as Āyatullāh Khūʾi, Shaykh Ḥusayn al-Ḥillī, Āyatullāh Ḥakīm, and Āyatullāh Shahrūdī.

In 1380 AH, Āyatullāh Khūʾi and Shaykh al-Ḥillī granted him the permission of ijtihād (deriving laws). Also, Āyatullāh Tehrānī wrote another letter verifying his proficiency in the studies of rijāl and ḥadīth. Since then, Āyatullāh Sīstānī has been teaching the advanced level (Baḥth al-Khārij) of fiqh and usūl (jurisprudence and principles) along with other subjects.

Āyatullāh al-ʿUẓmā Shaykh Bashīr Ḥusayn Najafī

Āyatullāh al-ʿUẓmā Shaykh Muḥammad Isḥāq Fayyāḍ

Āyatullāh al-ʿUẓmā Sayyid Muḥammad Ḥakīm

Āyatullāh Najafī was born in Jalandhar, India in 1942. His father is Ṣādiq ʿAlī, and his grandfather, Muḥammad Ibrahīm Lahore, is one of the well-known shīʿah figures in that region, who migrated to Pakistan. His son, Ṣādiq ʿAlī, continued in the path of his father until he passed away and was buried next to his father.

Āyatullāh Najafī completed his preliminary studies in Pakistan under his grandfather and father, as well as his uncles, Khādim Ḥusayn and Shaykh Akhtar ʿAbbās.

He moved to Najaf in 1965 and studied under great scholars, such as Shaykh Muḥammad Kazim Tabrīzī, Sayyid Muḥammad Rūḥānī, and Āyatullāh Khūʾī. He began teaching in 1968, just as he was teaching before in Jamiʿ al-Lahore. In 1977, he began teaching at an advanced level (dars al-khārij) and has written over 31 books on Fiqh.

Āyatullāh Fayyāḍ was born in 1930 in Soobah, Afghanistan. His father, Muḥammad Riḍa, was a faithful farmer. He completed his preliminary studies in Afghanistan, and after his father passed away, he moved to Mashhad to study under great teachers such as ʿAdib Neishaburi, Sayyid Yūnus Ardabīlī, and Shaykh Kafāi. However, his curious soul was thirsty for the atmosphere of Najaf. With the help of his teacher, Muḥammad ʿAlī Modarres Afghani, he was finally able to move there and benefit from the tutelage of Mirza Kāẓim Tabrīzī, Shāhid Sayyid Asadullāh Madani, Mirza ʿAlī Falsafī, and Sheikh Mujtabā Lankarani. He attended Āyatullāh Khūʾī's classes for 25 years straight and was amongst his elite students. His book Muhāḍirāt, which is published in 10 volumes, is the outcome of those years. He has been teaching dars al-khārij in Jami' al-Najaf since 1978, and currently teaches at Yazdi School.

Āyatullāh Hakīm was born in Najaf in 1935. He is the eldest grandchild of Grand Āyatullāh Sayyid Moḥsin Ḥakīm and was trained by his great father, Āyatullāh Sayyid Muḥammad ʿAlī Hakim, from a young age. He benefited a lot from his grandfather (Sayyid Moḥsin Ḥakīm) and uncle (Sayyid Yūsuf Ḥakīm), as well as from Āyatullāh Khūʾi, Shaykh Ḥusayn al-Ḥilli, and Sayyid ʿAlī Baḥr al-ʿUlūm. He has been teaching advanced levels of Fiqh and Usūl since 1968 AH. From 1983 to 1991, many of his relatives, including his father, brothers, children, and many others were imprisoned or martyred by the Baʿathist regime.

Kūfah

Dear Zāʿir,

According to Qurʾān and aḥadīth, the city of Kūfah is one of the most dignified cities. Know the value of where you are. This city in which you are walking is the same city Imām ʿAlī (A) held his government for years. So take advantage of where you are, and pray for all the Muslims in the world. Donate to help build and expand the Masājid in this city.

There are two primary places you will visit in Kūfah: Masjid al-Kūfah and Masjid al-Saḥlah.

Masjid al-Kūfah is where the Imām (AJ) will establish his government when he returns, and his home will be in Masjid al-Sahla.

The Imāms (A) have identified the significance of Kūfah in several aḥadīth:

Amīr ul-Muʾminīn (A) said:

Kūfah is our city, our neighborhood, and a place for our followers.[1]

Imām Ḥasan al-Mujtabā (A) said:

A footstep in Kūfah is more dear to me than a house in Madināh.

Imām as-Ṣādiq (A) has said:

نَفَقَةُ دِرْهَمٍ بِالْكُوفَةِ تُحْسَبُ بِمِأَةِ دِرْهَمٍ فِيْمَا سِوَاهَا وَ رَكْعَتَانِ فِيْهَا تُحْسَبُ بِمِأَةِ رَكْعَةٍ

Giving one dirham of charity in Kūfah is equal to giving 100 dirhams outside of Kūfah, and two rakaʿāt of prayer offered in Kūfah are equal to 100 rakaʿāt outside Kūfah.

- Aban ibn Taqlab narrates:
  One day, Imām as-Ṣādiq (A) offered a two rakaʿāt prayer behind the gated walls of Kūfah and then said, "This is the spot of al-Qāʿim's (AJ) home."[2]

- Imām as-Ṣādiq (A) said:
  When the Qa'im (AJ) appears, a masjid will be built for him behind Kūfah that contains 1,000 doors, and the houses of Kūfah will be extended so far that it will reach the Euphrates river in Karbalāʾ.

1. Shajarah Tūba, Vol. 1, P. 13
2. Muntakhab al-Athar, P. 488

كوفة
Kūfah

إِنَّ اللهَ تَبارَكَ وَ تَعالَى إِخْتارَ مِنَ الْبُلْدانِ أَرْبَعَةً فَقالَ عَزَّ وَجَلَّ:

وَٱلتِّينِ وَٱلزَّيْتُونِ ﴿١﴾ وَطُورِ سِينِينَ ﴿٢﴾ وَهَٰذَا ٱلْبَلَدِ ٱلْأَمِينِ ﴿٣﴾

فَالتِّيْنُ الْمَدِيْنَةُ وَ الزَّيْتُوْنُ بَيْتُ الْمُقَدِسِ وَ طُوْرُ سِيْنِيْنَ الْكُوْفَةُ وَ هٰذَا الْبَلَدِ الْاَمِيْنُ مَكَّةُ

Prophet Muḥammad (S):
Certainly, Allāh, the Exalted, has selected four cities among others, mentioning this about them: the fig is Madīnah, the olive is Jerusalem, Mount Sinai is Kūfah, and the secure city is Makkāh.[1]

Fig (التِّيْن): Madīnah

Olive (الزَّيْتُوْن): Jerusalem

Mt. Sinai (طُوْرِ سِيْنِيْن): Kūfah

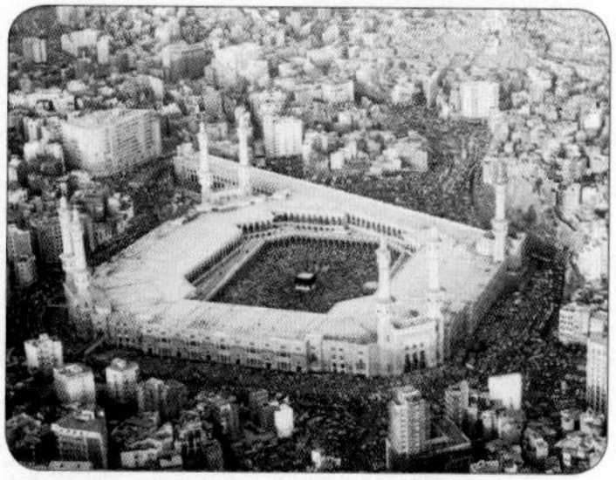

The Secure City (البَلَدِ الأمِيْن): Makkah

Kūfah is one of the four cities where it is permissible for travellers to perform their prayers in full. The specific rulings can be found below according to your Marja'[2]:

Āyatullah Sīstānī & Āyatullah Ḥakīm:
One can perform his/her prayers in full or qasr in the entire city of Kūfah.

Āyatullahs Khumaynī, Lankarānī, Khū'ī, Fāḍil Tabrīzī, Khāmināī, & Makārim Shirāzī:
One can perform his/her prayers in full or qasr in Masjid al-Kūfah, even within the new developments of the Masjid.

Āyatullah Ṣāfī Gulpāygānī:
One can perform his/her prayers in full or qasr in the original part of the Masjid, but one must perform them qasr in the newer developments.

Āyatullah Vaḥīd Khurāsānī:
One can perform his/her prayers in full or qasr in the entire city of Kūfah. It is better to offer qasr prayers outside of Masjid al-Kūfah.

Āyatullah Shubayrī Zanjānī:
Even in the Masjid al-Kūfah, one must perform his/her prayers qasr.

Āyatullah Arākī & Āyatullah Bahjat:
It is ehtiyat wajib to pray qasr even within the Masjid.

1. Nāṣir Makārim Shirāzī, Tafsīr an-Namūnāh, Vol. 27, P. 14
2. Tawḍīḥ al-Masā'il Marājā', Vol. 1, P. 728, Masalah #1356

Entering Kūfah

When you enter the city of Kūfah, say the following:

بِسْمِ اللهِ وَ بِاللهِ وَ فِيْ سَبِيْلِ اللهِ وَعَلَىٰ مِلَّةِ رَسُوْلِ اللهِ صَلَّىٰ اللهُ عَلَيْهِ وَ آلِهِ اَللَّهُمَّ اَنْزِلْنِيْ مُنْزَلًا مُبَارَكًا وَّاَنْتَ خَيْرُ الْمُنْزِلِيْنَ

With the name of Allāh (I begin), in Allāh (I trust), in the path of Allāh, and upon the creed of Rasūl Allāh (I proceed), may Allāh bless him and his household. O Allāh, make this stay blessed for me. Surely, You are the Best Host.

As you head towards Masjid al-Kūfah, say the following as much as you can:

اَللهُ اَكْبَرُ

Allāh is the Greatest

وَلَا اِلٰهَ اِلَّا اللهُ

There is no god except Allāh

وَالْحَمْدُ لِلّٰهِ

All praise is for Allāh

وَسُبْحَانَ اللهِ

And all glory is for Allāh

Masjid al-Kūfah in Aḥadīth

Imām as-Ṣādiq (A) said:

Our wilayāh (guardianship) was presented to the skies, earth, mountains, and cities, but none of them accepted it like the city of Kūfah.

Imam Ali (A) said:

يَأْتِي عَلَيْهِ زَمَانٌ يَكُونُ مُصَلَّى الْمَهْدِيِّ مِنْ وُلْدِي وَمُصَلَّى كُلِّ مُؤْمِنٍ وَلَا يَبْقَى عَلَى الْأَرْضِ مُؤْمِنٌ إِلَّا كَانَ بِهِ، أَوْ حَنَّ قَلْبُهُ إِلَيْهِ

A time will arrive when Masjid al-Kūfah will become the worshipping place of Imām al-Mahdī (AJ) from my progeny, and the worshipping place of every believer. There will not be a believer left in this world except that he or she has come to this masjid, or his or her heart is yearning for this masjid.[1]

1. Man Lā Yahḍuruhu al-Faqīh, Vol.1, P. 150

The Importance of Masjid al-Kūfah

Masjid al-Kūfah was built by Prophet Ādam (A). The structure of the masjid then was much larger than it is today. This masjid is so valuable that the Imāms (A) wanted to show their followers its original vicinity so that they could benefit from its blessings. One day, to show the people how vast the original masjid was, Amīr ul-Muʾminīn stood in front of the door and shot an arrow that landed amongst the date sellers, who were standing further away from the masjid. The Imām (A) then stated that was the original boundary of the masjid and then said:

قَدْ نَقَصَ مِنْ اَسَاسِ الْمِسْجِدِ مِثْلُ مَا نَقَصَ فِيْ تَرْبِيْعَهِ

Today, the masjid has been reduced in size.[1]

Hudhayfa ibn Yamān has said that the original masjid was reduced by 12,000 dhiraʿ (18,000 feet or 5,486 meters).[2]

Mufaḍal narrates, "I was passing through the bazaar with Imām as-Ṣādiq (A). As we passed the saddle shops and reached the oil shops, he dismounted his horse and said:

اِنْزِلْ، فَاِنَّ هَذَا الْمَوْضِعَ كَانَ مَسْجَدَ الْكُوْفَه الْاَوَّلَ الَذِيْ خَطَّهُ آدَمُ وَ اَنَا أَكْرَهُ أَنْ أَدْخُلَهُ رَاكِباً

Come down! This is the beginning of the original Masjid al-Kūfah, which Prophet Ādam (A) had constructed. It is not good to enter [the masjid] on a horse."[3]

Amīr al-Muʿminīn (A) has said:

لَاتُشَدُّ الرِّحَالُ اِلَّا اِلَى ثَلَاثَة مَسَاجِدَ: اَلْمَسْجِدُ الْحَرَامُ، وَمَسْجِدُ رَسُوْلِ اللهِ وَمَسْجِدُ الْكُوْفَة

Do not pack your bags to go anywhere unless it is to these masājid: Masjid al-Harām, Masjid al-Nabī, and Masjid al-Kūfah.[5]

Imām as-Sajjād (A) travelled to Masjid al-Kūfah from Madināh just to offer a prayer. He offered a four rakaʿāt prayer and then rode back to Medina.[6]

Amīr al-Muʿminīn (A) has said:

وَإِنَّ مَسْجِدِكُمْ هٰذَا لَأَحَدُ الْمَسَاجِدِ الْاَرْبَعَة الَّتِيْ اِخْتَارَهَااللهُ لِاَهْلِهَا

Certainly, this masjid of yours [Masjid al-Kūfah] is one of the four masājid that Allāh has picked for His people. Never abandon it. Seek closeness to Allāh by praying in it. To receive answers to your duʿāʾs, pray in it. If people knew what blessings it holds, they would rush towards it from all corners of the earth, even if they had to crawl on the ground in the snow.[7]

Then, Imām ʿAlī (A) placed his holy hand on his chest and said:

مَا دَعَا فِيْهِ مَكْرُوْبٌ بِمَسْأَلَةٍ فِيْ حَاجَةٍ مِنَ الحَوَائِجِ اِلّا أَجَابَهُ اللهُ وَفَرَّجَ عَنْهُ كُرْبَتَهُ

No grieved person will pray for his requests in it [Masjid al-Kūfah] except that Allāh will answer his call and remove his sorrow.[8]

Imām as-Ṣādiq (A) has said:

نِعْمَ الْمَسْجِدُ الْكُوْفَة، صَلَّى فِيْهِ اَلْفُ نَبِيٍّ وَ اَلْفُ وَصِيٍّ

How great is Masjid al-Kūfah! Thousands of Prophets and thousands of their successors have prayed in it![9]

Prophet Muḥammad (S):
Masjid al-Kūfah will intercede for whoever has offered a two rakaʿāt prayer in it on the Day of Judgment.[10]

Imām as-Ṣādiq (A) has said:

إِنَّ الصَّلَاةَ الْمَكْتُوْبَةَ فِيْهِ لَتَعْدِلُ اَلْفَ صَلَاةٍ، وَإِنَّ النَّافِلَةَ فِيْهِ لَتعدِلُ خَمْسَ مِائَةَ صَلَاةٍ وَإِنَّ الْجُلُوْسَ فِيْهِ بِغَيْرِ تَلَاوَةٍ وَ لَاذِكْرٍ لَعِبَادَةٌ

Certainly, one obligatory prayer in Masjid al-Kūfah is equal to 1,000 prayers, and one mustahab prayer is equal to 500 prayers. Even sitting in it without reciting anything is considered worship.

اَلصَّلَاةُ فِيْ مَسْجِدِ الْكُوْفَةِ فَرْداً، أَفْضَلُ مِنْ سَبْعِيْنَ صَلَاةً فِيْ غَيْرِهِ جَمَاعَةً

Performing one set of individuʿāʾl prayers in Masjid al-Kūfah is better than performing 70 congregational prayers in other masājid.[11]

1. Biḥār al-Anwār, Vol. 100, P. 398
2. Ibid, P. 396
3. Uṣūl al-Kāfī, Vol. 8, P. 234
4. Biḥār al-Anwār, Vol. 52, P. 333
5. Wasāʾil ash-Shīʿah, Vol. 5, P. 252
6. Ibid, P. 354
7. Ibid, P. 357
8. Ibid
9. Biḥār al-Anwār, Vol. 100, P. 404
10. Wasāʾil ash-Shīʿah, Vol. 5, P. 239

Imām as-Ṣādiq (A) narrates:

بَيْنَا عَلِيُّ بْنُ أَبِيْ طَالِبٍ عَلَى مِنْبَرِ الْكُوْفَةِ يَخْطُبُ إِذْ أَقْبَلَ ثُعْبَانٌ
مِنْ آخِرِ الْمَسْجِدِ فَوَثَبَ إِلَيْهِ النَّاسُ بِنِعَالِهِمْ فَقَالَ لَهُمْ عَلِيٌّ مَهْلًا
يَرْحَمُكُمُ اللهُ فَإِنَّهَا مَأْمُوْرَةٌ فَكَفَّ النَّاسُ عَنْهَا فَأَقْبَلَ الثُّعْبَانُ إِلَى
عَلِيٍّ حَتَّى وَضَعَ فَاهُ عَلَى أُذُنِ عَلِيٍّ فَقَالَ لَهُ مَا شَاءَ اللهُ أَنْ يَقُوْلَ ثُمَّ إِنَّ
الثُّعْبَانَ نَزَلَ وَ تَبِعَهُ عَلِيٌّ فَقَالَ النَّاسُ يَا أَمِيْرَ الْمُؤْمِنِيْنَ أَلَا تُخْبِرُنَا
بِمَقَالَةِ هَذَا الثُّعْبَانِ فَقَالَ نَعَمْ إِنَّهُ رَسُوْلُ الْجِنِّ قَالَ لِيْ أَنَا وَصِيُّ
الْجِنِّ وَ رَسُوْلُهُمْ إِلَيْكَ يَقُوْلُ الْجِنُّ لَوْ أَنَّ الْإِنْسَ أَحَبُّوْكَ كَحُبِّنَا إِيَّاكَ
وَ أَطَاعُوْكَ كَطَاعَتِنَا لَمَا عَذَّبَ اللهُ أَحَداً مِنَ الْإِنْسِ بِالنَّارِ

One day, Amīr al-Muʿminīn (A) was sitting on the minbar in Masjid al-Kūfah, delivering a sermon, when a serpent appeared from the back of the masjid. People began throwing stones and shoes to scare it away, when the Imām said, "Leave him. He has a purpose to fulfill."

The serpent headed towards the minbar and climbed up to the Imām. He whispered something in his ear and then slithered away.

The people asked, "O Amīr al-Muʿminīn, can you please inform us about what the serpent said?"

Imām ʿAlī (A) said, "Yes. He was a messenger from the jinns. He said, 'I am the messenger of the jinns to you. The jinns said that if the humans loved you the way we love you, and obeyed you the way we obey you, Allāh would not send any humans to the hellfire.'"

After this miracle, this gate became known as Bāb al-Thuʿbān. When Muʿāwiyah heard about this incident, he became very jealous. So, to distract the people from this miracle, he tied an elephant to the gate, and it soon became known as Bāb al-Fīl. However, the gate has been recently restored to its original name, Alḥamdulillāh.

Biḥār al-Anwār, Vol. 93, P. 249

Prayer of Hājāt in Masjid al-Kūfah

قَالَ أَبُوْعَبْدِ الله : «مَنْ كَانَتْ لَه إلىٰ الله حاجة فليَقصد إلىٰ مسجد الكوفة وليسبغ وضوءه وليَصل فيَ المسجد ركعتيَن يقرأ فيَ كل واحدة منهما فاتحة الكتاب وسبع سور معها وهيَ يَا أيها الكافرون ، وإذا جاء نصر الله والفتح، وسبح اسم المعوذتان ، وقل هو الله أحد ، وقل ربك الأعليَ ، وإنا أنزلناه فيَ ليَلة القدر ، فإذا فرغ من الركعتيَن وتشهد وسلم سأل الله حاجته ، فإنها تقضيَ بعون الله إن شاء الله»

Imam as-Sadiq (A):

Whoever offers a two rakaʿāt prayer in Masjid al-Kūfah and in every rakʿah, after reciting Surah al-Hamd, recites Surat an-Nās, al-Falaq, al-Ikhlāṣ, al-Kāfirūn, an-Naṣr, al-Aʿalā and al-Qadr, and then recites a tasbīḥ of Sayyidah Fāṭimah (A) and asks for his or her ḥājāt (wishes), the Almighty will answer all of his needs and requests (that are good for him/her), inshā ʾAllāh!

Biḥār al-Anwār, Vol. 88, P. 346

Entering Masjid al-Kūfah

When you reach the gate of Masjid al-Kūfah, stop and recite:

Peace be upon our leader, the Messenger of Allāh, Muḥammad, son of ʿAbdullāh, may the blessings of Allāh be upon him and his pure progeny.	اَلسَّلَامُ عَلَىٰ سَيِّدِنَا رَسُوْلِ اللهِ مُحَمَّدِ بْنِ عَبْدِ اللهِ صَلَّىٰ اللهُ عَلَيْهِ وَآلِهِ الطَّاهِرِيْنَ
Peace be upon you, O Commander of the Faithful, ʿAlī son of Abī Ṭālib. May the mercy and blessings of Allāh be upon him	اَلسَّلَامُ عَلَىٰ اَمِيْرِ الْمُؤْمِنِيْنَ عَلِيِّ بْنِ أَبِيْ طَالِبٍ وَرَحْمَةُ اللهِ وَبَرَكَاتُهُ
and upon his gatherings, his meeting places, and the places that witnessed his wisdom,	وَعَلَىٰ مَجَالِسِهِ وَمَشَاهِدِهِ وَمَقَامِ حِكْمَتِهِ
and upon the traces of his forefathers Ādam, Nūḥ, Ibrāhīm, Ismāʿīl, and the places that witnessed the displays of his evidence.	وَآثَارِ آبَائِهِ آدَمَ وَنُوْحٍ وَاِبْرَاهِيْمَ وَاِسْمَاعِيْلَ وَتِبْيَانِ بَيِّنَاتِهِ
Peace be upon the wise, just, truthful, great, and fair distinguishing Imām	اَلسَّلَامُ عَلَىٰ الْاِمَامِ الْحَكِيْمِ الْعَدْلِ الصِّدِّيْقِ الْاَكْبَرِ الْفَارُوْقِ بِالْقِسْطِ
through whom Allāh distinguished between the truth and falsehood, disbelief and faith, and polytheism and monotheism	الَّذِيْ فَرَّقَ اللهُ بِهِ بَيْنَ الْحَقِّ وَالْبَاطِلِ وَالْكُفْرِ وَالْاِيْمَانِ وَالشِّرْكِ وَالتَّوْحِيْدِ

so that his enemies would be destroyed or spared based on clear proof and evidence.	لِيَهْلِكَ مَنْ هَلَكَ عَنْ بَيِّنَةٍ وَّيُحْيَا مَنْ حَيَّ عَنْ بَيِّنَةٍ
I bear witness that you are the Commander of the Faithful and the elite of the elite,	اَشْهَدُ اَنَّكَ اَمِيْرُالْمُؤْمِنِيْنَ وَخَاصَّةُ نَفْسِ الْمُنْتَجَبِيْنَ
the adornment of the truthful ones and the most patient of the tested ones.	وَزَيْنُ الصِّدِّيْقِيْنَ وَصَابِرُالْمُمْتَحَنِيْنَ
And certainly you are the judge of Allāh on earth, the judge of His commands, the door to His wisdom, the pledge of His promise,	وَاَنَّكَ حَكَمُ اللهِ فِيْ اَرْضِهِ وَقَاضِيْ اَمْرِهِ وَبَابُ حِكْمَتِهِ وَعَاقِدُ عَهْدِهِ
the spokesman of His promise, the rope that connects Him and His servants, the haven of salvation,	وَالنَّاطِقُ بِوَعْدِهِ، وَالْحَبْلُ الْمَوْصُوْلُ بَيْنَهُ وَبَيْنَ عِبَادِهِ، وَكَهْفُ النَّجَاةِ
the course of God-consciousness, the most elevated rank, and the executor [of the laws] of the Exalted Judge.	وَمِنْهَاجُ التُّقَى، وَالدَّرَجَةُ الْعُلْيَا، وَمُهَيْمِنُ الْقَاضِي الْاَعْلَى
O Commander of the Faithful! Through you, I seek nearness to Allāh!	يَااَمِيْرَالْمُؤْمِنِيْنَ بِكَ اَتَقَرَّبُ اِلَى اللهِ زُلْفَى
You are my guardian, master, and intercessor (to Allāh) in this world and the hereafter.	اَنْتَ وَلِيِّي وَسَيِّدِيْ وَوَسِيْلَتِيْ فِيْ الدُّنْيَا وَالْآخِرَةِ

You may then enter the masjid. It is best to enter from Bāb al-Thu‘bān, and say the following:

Allāh is the Greatest! Allāh is the Greatest! Allāh is the Greatest!	اَللهُ اَكْبَرُ اَللهُ اَكْبَرُ اَللهُ اَكْبَرُ
This is the position of one who seeks refuge in Allāh and in Muḥammad, the beloved of Allāh, may the blessings of Allāh be upon him and his progeny	هٰذَا مَقَامُ الْعَائِذِ بِاللهِ وَبِمُحَمَّدٍ حَبِيْبِ اللهِ صَلَّى اللهُ عَلَيْهِ وَآلِهِ
And in the guardianship of the Commander of the Faithful and the Imāmah of the rightly guided, truthful, representing (verbally), guiding Imāms.	وَبِوِلَايَةِ اَمِيْرِ الْمُؤْمِنِيْنَ وَالْاَئِمَّةِ الْمَهْدِيِّيْنَ الصَّادِقِيْنَ النَّاطِقِيْنَ الرَّاشِدِيْنَ
Those from whom Allāh has kept away all impurity and purified them with a thorough purification	الَّذِيْنَ اَذْهَبَ اللهُ عَنْهُمُ الرِّجْسَ وَطَهَّرَهُمْ تَطْهِيْرًا
I accept them as leaders, guides, and masters. I submit to the command of Allāh and associate none with Him	رَضِيْتُ بِهِمْ اَئِمَّةً وَّهُدَاةً وَّمَوَالِيَّ سَلَّمْتُ لِاَمْرِ اللهِ لَا اُشْرِكُ بِهِ شَيْئاً
And I do not take any guardian other than Allāh. Those who associate partners with Allāh are liars and have strayed into clear error	وَلَا اَتَّخِذُ مَعَ اللهِ وَلِيّاً، كَذَبَ الْعَادِلُوْنَ بِاللهِ وَضَلُّوْا ضَلَالاً بَعِيْدًا
Allāh and the guardians of Allāh are sufficient for me	حَسْبِيَ اللهُ وَاَوْلِيَاءُ اللهِ

I bear witness that there is no god except Allāh alone, without any partners	اَشْهَدُ اَنْ لَّا اِلٰهَ اِلَّا اللّٰهُ وَحْدَهُ لَاشَرِيْكَ لَهُ
And I bear witness that Muḥammad is His servant and messenger, blessings of Allāh be upon him and his family.	وَاَشْهَدُ اَنَّ مُحَمَّداً عَبْدُهُ وَرَسُوْلُهُ صَلَّى اللّٰهُ عَلَيْهِ وَآلِهِ
And that ʿAlī and the rightly guided Imāms from his offspring, peace be upon them, are the guardians and proofs of Allāh over His creation.	وَاَنَّ عَلِيّاً وَّالْاَئِمَّةَ الْمَهْدِيِّيْنَ مِنْ ذُرِّيَّتِهِ عَلَيْهِمُ السَّلَامُ اَوْلِيَآئِيْ وَحُجَّةُ اللّٰهِ عَلَىٰ خَلْقِهِ

Then, offer a two rakaʿāh prayer with the intention of Taḥiyat-e-Masjid.

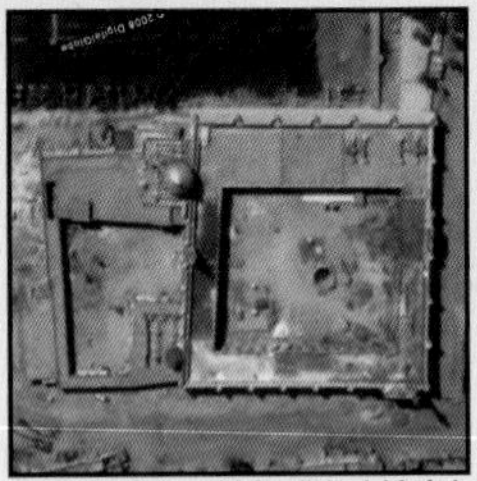

Aerial View of Masjid al-Kūfah

Illustrated Map of Masjid al-Kūfah

1. Maqām of Prophet Ibrāhīm (A)
2. Maqām of Ḥaḍrat Khiḍr (A)
3. Dakkat al-Qaḍā
4. Bayt al-Ṭasht
5. Ark of Prophet Nūḥ
6. Dakkat al-Miʿrāj
7. Maqām of Prophet Ādam (A)
8. Maqām of Jibrāʾīl
9. Maqām of Imām Zayn ul-ʿĀbidīn
10. Bāb al-Faraj Maqām of Prophet Nūḥ
11. Miḥrāb of Shahādah of Imām ʿAlī (A)
12. Maqām and Miḥrāb of Imām as-Ṣādiq (A)
13. Gravesite of Muslim ibn ʿAqīl
14. Gravesite of Mukhtār al-Thaqafī
15. Gravesite of Hānī ibn ʿUrwah

N

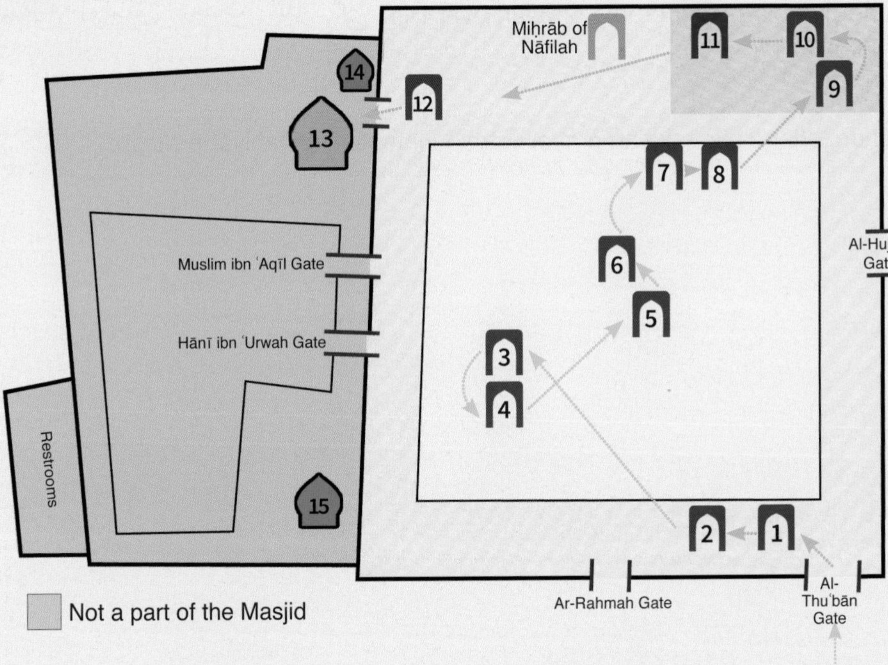

Aʿamāl of Masjid al-Kūfah

The aʿamāl of Masjid al-Kūfah consists of offering several prayers in 12 different spots throughout the masjid, as indicated on the map. These places are:

1. Maqām of Prophet Ibrāhīm (A)
2. Maqām of Ḥaḍrat Khiḍr (A)
3. Dakkat al-Qaḍā (Seat of Judgment)
4. Bayt al-Ṭasht (House of the Washtub)
5. Safīnatun Nūḥ (Ark of Prophet Nūḥ (A))
6. Dakkat al-Miʿrāj (Seat of Miʿrāj)
7. Maqām of Prophet Ādam (A)
8. Maqām of Jibrāʿīl
9. Maqām of Imām Zayn ul-ʿĀbidīn (A)
10. Bāb al-Faraj or Maqām of Prophet Nūḥ (A)
11. Miḥrāb of Shahādah of Imām ʿAlī (A)
12. Maqām and Miḥrāb of Imām as-Ṣādiq (A)

While performing the aʿamāl, keep the following points in mind:

- Place emphasis on quality, not quantity. Perform as much aʿamāl as you can while maintaining sincerity.
- All of the Prophets have also prayed where you are praying. Thus, these are sacred and holy spots.

1. Maqām of Prophet Ibrāhīm

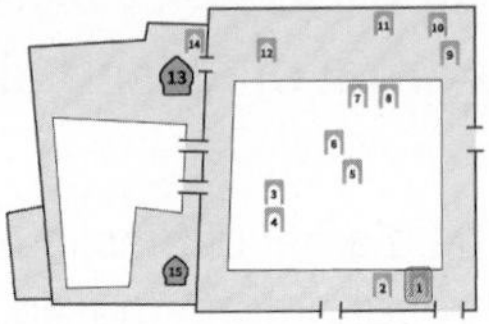

Prophet Ibrahim (A) was born near Kūfāh and lived here for awhile. He also used to worship in Masjid al-Kūfah; thus, this pillar has been named after him. Offer a two raka'āt prayer (reciting Surat al-Fātiḥāh and Ikhlāṣ in both raka'āt) and another two raka'āt prayer (reciting Surat al-Fātiḥāh and Qadr in both raka'āt). Then, recite a tasbīḥ of Fāṭimah az-Zahrā' and the following du'ā':

Peace be upon the righteous, rightly guided servants of Allāh from whom Allāh kept away all impurity and purified thoroughly.	اَلسَّلَامُ عَلَىٰ عِبَادِ اللهِ الصَّالِحِيْنَ الرَّاشِدِيْنَ الَّذِيْنَ اَذْهَبَ اللهُ عَنْهُمُ الرِّجْسَ وَطَهَّرَهُمْ تَطْهِيْراً
And He made them Prophets, messengers, and proofs over all His creations.	وَجَعَلَهُمْ اَنْبِيَاءَ مُرْسَلِيْنَ وَحُجَّةً عَلَىٰ الْخَلْقِ اَجْمَعِيْنَ
And peace be upon the messengers. All praise is for Allāh, the Lord of the worlds. That is the decree of the Almighty, All-Knowing.	وَسَلَامٌ عَلَىٰ الْمُرْسَلِيْنَ، وَالْحَمْدُ لِلهِ رَبِّ الْعَالَمِيْنَ، ذٰلِكَ تَقْدِيْرُ الْعَزِيْزِ الْعَلِيْمِ

Then, repeat seven times:

سَلَامٌ عَلَىٰ نُوْحٍ فِيْ الْعَالَمِيْنَ

Peace be upon Nūh in the worlds.

Then, recite the following:

O Guardian of the believers, we are following the will that you provided to your offspring: the messengers and truthful ones.	نَحْنُ عَلَىٰ وَصِيَّتِكَ يَا وَلِيَّ الْمُؤْمِنِيْنَ الَّتِيْ اَوْصَيْتَ بِهَا ذُرِّيَّتَكَ مِنَ الْمُرْسَلِيْنَ وَالصِّدِّيْقِيْنَ
And we are amongst your followers and the followers of our Prophet Muḥammad, may Allāh's blessings be upon him and his family.	وَنَحْنُ مِنْ شِيْعَتِكَ وَشِيْعَةِ نَبِيِّنَا مُحَمَّدٍ صَلَّى اللهُ عَلَيْهِ وَآلِهِ
And may Allāh's blessings be upon you and all the messengers, Prophets, and truthful ones.	وَعَلَيْكَ وَعَلَىٰ جَمِيْعِ الْمُرْسَلِيْنَ وَالْاَنْبِيَآءِ وَالصَّادِقِيْنَ
And we are upon the creed of Ibrāhīm and the religion of Muḥammad, the unlettered Prophet, and the rightly guided Imāms, and the guardianship of our master, ʿAlī, the Commander of the Faithful.	وَنَحْنُ عَلَىٰ مِلَّةِ اِبْرَاهِيْمَ وَدِيْنِ مُحَمَّدٍ النَّبِيِّ الْاُمِّيِّ وَالْاَئِمَّةِ الْمَهْدِيِّيْنَ وَوِلَايَةِ مَوْلَانَا عَلِيٍّ اَمِيْرِالْمُؤْمِنِيْنَ
Peace be upon the bearer of glad tidings and the warner, may the blessings, pleasure, and mercy of Allāh be upon him	اَلسَّلَامُ عَلَىٰ الْبَشِيْرِ النَّذِيْرِ صَلَوَاتُ اللهِ عَلَيْهِ وَرَحْمَتُهُ وَرِضْوَانُهُ وَبَرَكَاتُهُ
and upon his successor and representative, the witness of Allāh upon His creation after Him, ʿAlī, the Commander of the Faithful, the most truthful, and the clear distinguisher (between truth and falsehood),	وَعَلَىٰ وَصِيِّهِ وَخَلِيْفَتِهِ الشَّاهِدِ للهِ مِنْ بَعْدِهِ عَلَىٰ خَلْقِهِ عَلِيٍّ اَمِيْرِالْمُؤْمِنِيْنَ الصِّدِّيْقِ الْاَكْبَرِ وَالْفَارُوْقِ الْمُبِيْنِ

he to whom you have ordered the people of the worlds to give allegiance.	الَّذِيْ اَخَذْتَ بَيْعَتَهُ عَلَى الْعَالَمِيْنَ
I accept them as guardians, masters, and rulers over myself, my children, my people, my wealth, my providence, my halāl, my harām, my Islām, my religion, my world, my hereafter, my life, and my death.	رَضِيْتُ بِهِمْ اَوْلِيَاءَ وَمَوَالِيَ وَحُكَّاماً فِيْ نَفْسِيْ وَوُلْدِيْ وَاَهْلِيْ وَمَالِيْ وَقِسْمِيْ وَحِلِّيْ وَاِحْرَامِيْ وَاِسْلَامِيْ وَدِيْنِيْ وَدُنْيَايَ وَآخِرَتِيْ وَمَحْيَايَ وَمَمَاتِيْ
You all are the Imāms (leaders) mentioned in the book, the clear leaders in all situations, and the clear judges,	اَنْتُمُ الْاَئِمَّةُ فِيْ الْكِتَابِ وَفَصْلُ الْمَقَامِ وَفَصْلُ الْخِطَابِ
and the eyes of the Ever-Living who never sleeps, and you all are the representing judges of Allāh.	وَاَعْيُنُ الْحَيِّ الَّذِيْ لَا يَنَامُ وَاَنْتُمْ حُكَمَاءُ اللهِ
Through you all, Allāh has judged, and through you all, the right of Allāh is known and recognized.	وَبِكُمْ حَكَمَ اللهُ وَبِكُمْ عُرِفَ حَقُّ اللهِ
There is no god except Allāh, and Muḥammad is the messenger of Allāh.	لَا اِلٰهَ اِلَّا اللهُ مُحَمَّدٌ رَسُوْلُ اللهِ
You all are the light of Allāh in front of and behind us.	اَنْتُمْ نُوْرُ اللهِ مِنْ بَيْنِ اَيْدِيْنَا وَمِنْ خَلْفِنَا
You all are the Godly tradition through whom He has decided all things.	اَنْتُمْ سُنَّةُ اللهِ الَّتِيْ بِهَا سَبَقَ الْقَضَاءُ

O Commander of the Faithful! I submit to you with complete submission. I do not associate anything with Allāh, and I do not take any guardian other than Him.	يَا اَمِيْرَ الْمُؤْمِنِيْنَ اَنَا لَكُمْ مُسَلِّمٌ تَسْلِيْماً لَا اُشْرِكُ بِاللهِ شَيْئاً وَلَا اَتَّخِذُ مِنْ دُوْنِهِ وَلِيًّا
All praise is for Allāh who guided me through you all, and I would not have been guided if Allāh had not guided me.	اَلْحَمْدُ لِلّٰهِ الَّذِيْ هَدَانِيْ بِكُمْ وَمَا كُنْتُ لِاَهْتَدِيَ لَوْلَا اَنْ هَدَانِيَ اللهُ
Allāh is the Greatest, Allāh is the Greatest, Allāh is the Greatest; All praise is for Allāh for that which He has guided us to.	اَللهُ اَكْبَرُ اَللهُ اَكْبَرُ اَللهُ اَكْبَرُ، اَلْحَمْدُ لِلّٰهِ عَلَى مَا هَدَانَا

2. Maqām al-Khiḍr

One day, Imām ʿAlī (A) was praying in this spot and praising Masjid al-Kūfah. One of the virtues he mentioned is that Haḍrat Khiḍr has prayed in this masjid. No specific aʿamāl has been recommended for this maqām. However, one can offer a two rakaʿāt prayer of ḥājāt (wishes) that can also be performed in any other place in the masjid.

3. Dakkat al-Qaḍā (Seat of Judgment)

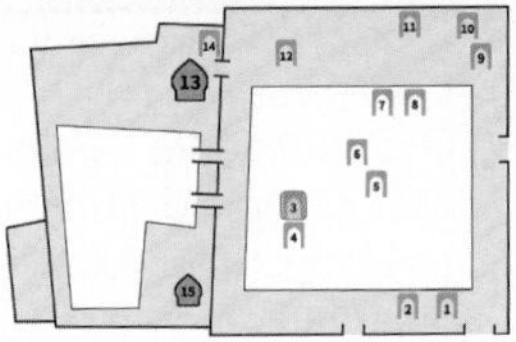

Dakkat al-Qaḍā is the place where Imām ʿAlī (A) used to issue judgments. Offer a two rakaʿāt prayer here, followed by a tasbīḥ and the following duʿāʾ:

O my Master and He who endows me with possessions and encompasses me with great blessings, even though I do not deserve them.	يَا مَالِكِيْ وَمُمَلِّكِيْ وَمُتَغَمِّدِيْ بِالنِّعَمِ الْجِسَامِ مِنْ غَيْرِ اسْتِحْقَاقٍ
My face falls humbly to the earth due to the Mightiness of Your Noble Face.	وَجْهِيْ خَاضِعٌ لِمَا تَعْلُوْهُ الْأَقْدَامُ لِجَلَالِ وَجْهِكَ الْكَرِيْمِ
Do not make my difficulties and efforts (in my path towards You) be in vain (due to my incorrect intentions).	لَا تَجْعَلْ هٰذِهِ الشِّدَّةَ وَلَا هٰذِهِ الْمِحْنَةَ مُتَّصِلَةً بِاسْتِئْصَالِ الشَّأْفَةِ
And grant me from Your bounties without me asking You that which You have never granted anyone.	وَامْنَحْنِيْ مِنْ فَضْلِكَ مَا لَمْ تَمْنَحْ بِهِ اَحَداً مِنْ غَيْرِ مَسْأَلَةٍ
You are the Eternal, the First, who has no beginning or end.	اَنْتَ الْقَدِيْمُ الْاَوَّلُ الَّذِيْ لَمْ تَزَلْ وَلَا تَزَالُ
Send blessings upon Muḥammad and the household of Muḥammad, and forgive me, have mercy upon me, purify my deeds, and bless my lifetime.	صَلِّ عَلَىٰ مُحَمَّدٍ وَآلِ مُحَمَّدٍ وَاغْفِرْ لِيْ وَارْحَمْنِيْ وَزَكِّ عَمَلِيْ وَبَارِكْ لِيْ فِيْ اَجَلِيْ
And place me amongst those whom You release and pardon from the hellfire, by Your mercy, O the Most Merciful!	وَاجْعَلْنِيْ مِنْ عُتَقَائِكَ وَطُلَقَائِكَ مِنَ النَّارِ بِرَحْمَتِكَ يَا اَرْحَمَ الرَّاحِمِيْنَ

Dakkat al-Qaḍā & Bayt at-Ṭasht

Dakkat al-Qaḍā was a shop-like structure in which there was a seat that was used by Imam `Alī (A) for judging. Next to it, there was a short pillar on which the following holy verse was written:

إِنَّ اللهَ يَأْمُرُ بِالْعَدْلِ وَالْإِحْسَانِ

Surely, Allāh enjoins justice and kindness.[1]

Bayt at-Ṭasht is a place where a miracle of Imām ʿAlī (A) took place. There was a girl who had taken a bath in the river, and a leech entered her body and began sucking her blood. The leech slowly grew, causing her stomach to expand. The people began thinking she was carrying a child and wanted Imām ʿAlī (A) to punish her for this. However, the Imām (A) instead ordered the people to set up a tent next to Dakkat al-Qaḍa, and he called a midwife to examine the girl. After the exam, the woman concluded, "This girl is with child." To prove her innocence, the Imām ordered a washtub full of muddy water to be brought and asked the girl to sit in the tub. When the leech smelled the muddy water, it came out of the girl. Through this miracle, the Imām(A) was able to prove her innocence.

1. Sūrat al-Naḥl, Verse 90
2. Al-Anwār al-ʿAlawīyah, P. 110

4. Bayt at-Ṭasht (House of the Washtub)

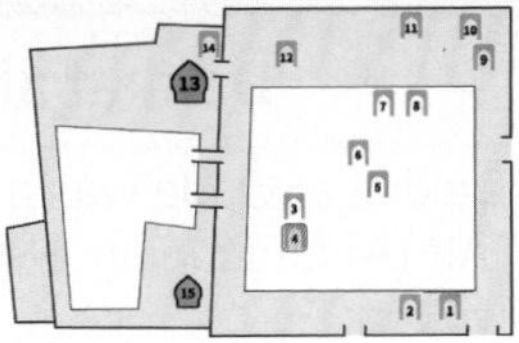

Recite a two rakʿāt prayer, then recite a tasbīḥ and the following duʿāʾ:

O Allāh, surely, I save [the reward of] my submission to Your Oneness, my recognition of You, my sincerity to you, and my confirmation of Your Lordship.	اَللَّهُمَّ اِنِّيْ ذَخَرْتُ تَوْحِيْدِيْ اِ يَّاكَ وَمَعْرِفَتِيْ بِكَ وَاِخْلَاصِيْ لَكَ وَاِقْرَارِيْ بِرُبُوْبِيَّتِكَ
And I save [the reward of] my loyalty to the ones that you have blessed me to recognize from Muḥammad and his progeny, blessings of Allāh be upon them.	وَذَخَرْتُ وِلَايَةَ مَنْ اَنْعَمْتَ عَلَيَّ بِمَعْرِفَتِهِمْ مِنْ بَرِيَّتِكَ مُحَمَّدٍ وَعِتْرَتِهِ صَلَّى اللهُ عَلَيْهِمْ
(I save all that) for the day where I take refuge with You, in this world and the hereafter.	لِيَوْمِ فَزَعِيْ اِلَيْكَ عَاجِلًا وَآجِلًا
Thus, I am now taking refuge with You, O my Master, on this day and on this occasion.	وَقَدْ فَزِعْتُ اِلَيْكَ وَاِلَيْهِمْ يَا مَوْلَايَ فِيْ هٰذَا الْيَوْمِ وَفِيْ مَوْقِفِيْ هٰذَا
I ask You for that which will increase Your blessings and reduce Your punishment, which I fear, and to bless all the sustenance You grant me.	وَسَأَلْتُكَ مَا زَكَىٰ مِنْ نِعْمَتِكَ وَاِزَاحَةَ مَا اَخْشَاهُ مِنْ نِقْمَتِكَ وَالْبَرَكَةَ فِيْمَا رَزَقْتَنِيْهِ
And immunize my heart from all grief, calamities, and disobedience in my religion, in this world and the hereafter, O the Most Merciful.	وَتَحْصِيْنَ صَدْرِيْ مِنْ كُلِّ هَمٍّ وَّجَائِحَةٍ وَّمَعْصِيَةٍ فِيْ دِيْنِيْ وَدُنْيَايَ وَآخِرَتِيْ يَا أَرْحَمَ الرَّاحِمِيْنَ

5. Safīnat an-Nūḥ (The Ark of Nūh (A))

This site is known as Safīnat un-Nūh (The Ark of Nūh). It used to look like a cellar in the middle of the masjid, along with a mihrab. According to narrations, this is where Prophet Nūh (A) built his ship. In addition, the water started bubbling up from the tanoor (underground oven) over here, and this is also where the ship docked.

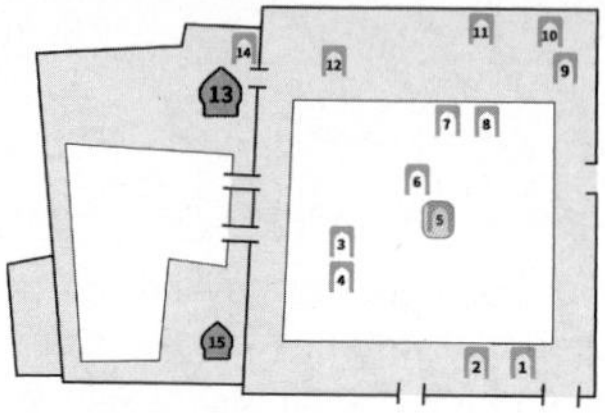

The Quran says that Allāh revealed to Prophet Nūh:

وَاصْنَعِ الْفُلْكَ بِأَعْيُنِنَا وَوَحْيِنَا وَلَا تُخَاطِبْنِي فِي الَّذِينَ ظَلَمُوا إِنَّهُمْ مُغْرَقُونَ

Build the ark before Our eyes and by Our revelation, and do not plead with Me for those who are wrongdoers; they shall certainly be drowned.[1]

Imām as-Ṣādiq (A):

Prophet Nūh (A) was a carpenter. He was the first person to build a ship and guided his people for 950 years, but they would always make fun of him. Prophet Nūh (A) prayed to Allāh to remove them all from this earth. Allāh ordered him to build a ship.

فَعَمِلَ نُوحٌ سَفِينَتَهُ فِي مَسْجِدِ الْكُوفَةِ بِيَدِهِ، فَأَتِيَ بِالْخَشَبِ مِنْ بُعْدٍ حَتَّى فَرَغَ مِنْهَا

So, Prophet Nūh (A) built the ship with his own hands in Masjid al-Kūfah and retrieved wooden planks from far away places until it was complete.[2]

1. Sūrat Hūd, Verse 37
2. Uṣūl al-Kāfī, Vol. 8, P. 234

حَتَّىٰ إِذَا جَاءَ أَمْرُنَا وَفَارَ التَّنُّورُ قُلْنَا احْمِلْ
فِيهَا مِنْ كُلٍّ زَوْجَيْنِ اثْنَيْنِ وَأَهْلَكَ إِلَّا مَنْ سَبَقَ عَلَيْهِ
الْقَوْلُ وَمَنْ آمَنَ وَمَا آمَنَ مَعَهُ إِلَّا قَلِيلٌ

When Our command came and the oven gushed out [a stream of water], We said, 'Carry in it a pair of every kind [of animal], along with your family—except those [of them] against whom the command has already been given—and those who have faith.' And none believed with him except a few.[1]

Imām ʿAlī (A), while mentioning the characteristics of Prophet Nūh (A), said:

فِيْهِ نَجَرَ نُوْحٌ سَفِيْنَتَهُ، وَ فِيْهِ فَارَ التَّنُّوْرُ
وَبِهِ كَانَ بَيْتُ نُوْحٍ وَ مَسْجِدُهُ، وَ فِيْ زَاوِيَتِهِ الْيَمْنِيْ فَارَ
التَّنُّوْرُ

It is in this place that Prophet Nūh (A) built his ark. In this place, the water spurted up from the tanoor (oven) [which was located on the right side of his house]. His house and place of worship were also here.[2]

وَقِيْلَ يَا أَرْضُ ابْلَعِيْ مَاءَكِ وَ يَا سَمَاءُ أَقْلِعِيْ وَغِيْضَ
الْمَاءِ وَقُضِيَ الْأَمْرُ وَاسْتَوَتْ عَلَى الْجُوْدِيِّ وَقِيْلَ بُعْداً
لِّلْقَوْمِ الظَّالِمِيْنَ

Then, it was said, 'O earth, swallow your water! O sky, stop raining!' The waters receded; the command was carried out, and it settled on [Mount] Judi. Then it was said, 'Away with the oppressive ones!'[3]

In the tafsīr of this āyah, Imām as-Ṣādiq (A) says:

فَبَلَعَتْ مَائَهَا مِنْ مَسْجِدِ الْكُوْفَةِ، كَمَا بَدَءَ الْمَاءُ مِنْهُ

When Prophet Nūh's (A) ark reached the center of Masjid al-Kūfah, Allāh ordered the land to absorb the water so the ark could dock. So, the land absorbed its water in Masjid al-Kūfah just as it had made water rise in the beginning.[4]

1. Sūrah Hūd, Verse 40
2. Tafsīr ʿAyāshī, Vol. 2, P. 308
3. Sūrah Hūd, Verse 43
4. Tafsīr ʿAyāshī, Vol. 2, P. 308

6. Dakkat al-Miʿrāj (Seat of Miʿrāj)

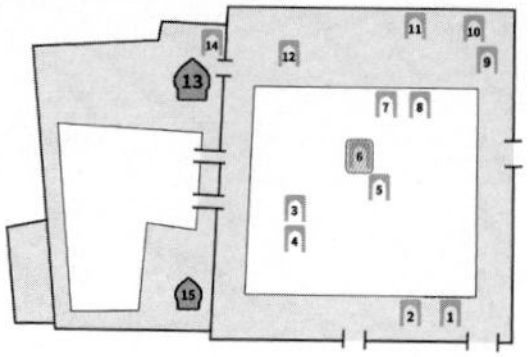

Near the center of the masjid, offer a two rakaʿāt prayer. In the first rakʿah, recite Surat al-Fātiḥāh and Ikhlāṣ. In the second rakʿah, recite Surat al-Fātiḥah and al-Kāfirūn. Then, recite a tasbīḥ and the following duʿāʾ:

اَللّٰهُمَّ اَنْتَ السَّلَامُ وَمِنْكَ السَّلَامُ وَاِلَيْكَ
يَعُوْدُ السَّلَامُ وَدَارُكَ دَارُالسَّلَامِ حَيِّنَا رَبَّنَا
مِنْكَ بِالسَّلَامِ

O Allāh, You are Peace, You are the source of peace, to You belongs peace, and Your abode is the abode of peace. Greet us, our Lord, with peace from You.

اَللّٰهُمَّ اِنِّيْ صَلَّيْتُ هٰذِهِ الصَّلَاةَ ابْتِغَاءَ رَحْمَتِكَ
وَرِضْوَانِكَ وَمَغْفِرَتِكَ وَتَعْظِيْماً لِمَسْجِدِكَ

O Allāh, surely I have offered this prayer seeking Your mercy, pleasure, and forgiveness, and as a sign of esteem for Your masjid.

اَللّٰهُمَّ فَصَلِّ عَلٰى مُحَمَّدٍ وَّآلِ مُحَمَّدٍ وَّارْفَعْهَا فِيْ
عِلِّيِّيْنَ وَتَقَبَّلْهَا مِنِّيْ يَا اَرْحَمَ الرَّاحِمِيْنَ

O Allāh, so please send blessings upon Muḥammad and the family of Muḥammad, and raise my prayer to the highest rank, and accept it from me, O the Most Merciful!

قَالَ الصَّادِقُ:

مَا مِنْ عَبْدٍ صَالِحٍ وَلَا نَبِيٍّ إِلَّا وَقَدْ صَلَّىٰ فِيْ مَسْجِدِ كُوْفَانْ حَتَّىٰ أَنَّ رَسُوْلَ اللهِ لَمَّا أُسْرِيَ بِهِ قَالَ لَهُ جَبْرَئِيْلُ: أَتَدْرِيْ أَيْنَ أَنْتَ يَارَسُوْلَ اللهِ السَّاعَةَ؟ أَنْتَ مُقَابِلُ مَسْجِدِ كُوْفَانْ قَالَ: قُلْتُ فَاسْتَأْذِنْ لِيْ رَبِّيْ حَتَّىٰ آتِيْهِ فَأُصَلِّيْ فِيْهِ رَكْعَتَيْنِ فَاسْتَأْذَنَ اللهُ عَزَّوَجَلَّ فَأَذِنَ لَهُ

Imām as-Ṣādiq (A):

There is no righteous person or Prophet except that he has prayed in Masjid al-Kūfah.

While Rasūl Allāh (S) was ascending to the heavens during Miʿrāj, Jibrāʾīl asked him "Do you know where you are right now? At this moment, you are in front of Masjid al-Kūfah."

The Prophet (S) replied, "Please ask permission from Allāh so that I may offer a two rakaʿāt prayer here."

The Prophet (S) then came down and prayed in Masjid al-Kūfah.

Shaykh Ṭūsī, Tahdhīb al-Ahkām, Vol. 6, P. 32

7. Maqām of Prophet Ādam (A)

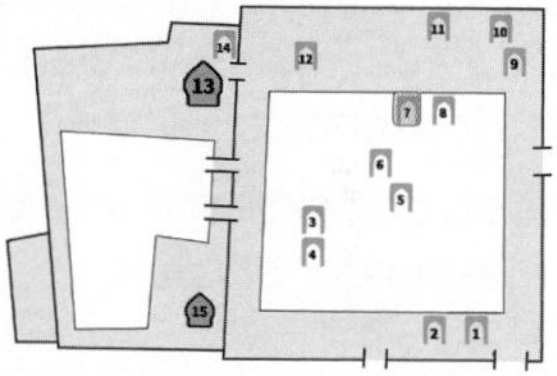

The seventh pillar of Masjid al-Kūfah is known as Maqām Ḥaḍrat Ādam. This is the site where Allāh accepted the tawbah (repentance) of Prophet Ādam (A), as the Qurʿān mentions:

فَتَلَقَّىٰ آدَمُ مِنْ رَبِّهِ كَلِمَاتٍ فَتَابَ عَلَيْهِ إِنَّهُ هُوَ التَّوَّابُ الرَّحِيمُ

Then Ādam received certain words from his Lord, and he turned to Him repentant. Surely, He is the Most Clement (accepting of repentance), the Most Merciful.[1]

In numerous narrations from the Ahl al-Bayt (A), Prophet Ādam (A) interceded through the names of the five best creations: Muḥammad, ʿAlī, Fāṭimah, Ḥasan, and Ḥusayn. It was through these names that Allāh forgave him.[2]

It has been narrated that every night, 60,000 angels descend upon Masjid al-Kūfah and pray at the seventh pillar, and they will not get another chance to return and pray there again until the Day of Resurrection [because there is such a long line of angels waiting to pray there].[3]

1. Sūrat al-Baqarah, Verse 37
2. Nāṣir Makārim Shirāzī, Tafsīr an-Namūnah, Vol. 1, P. 199
3. Wasāʾil ash-Shīʿa, Vol. 5, P. 264

This is the place where Allāh accepted the repentance of Prophet Ādam (A). Face the qiblah and recite the following duʿāʾ:

With the name of Allāh (I begin), in Allāh (I trust), and upon the creed of Rasūl Allāh (I proceed), may Allāh bless him and his Household.	بِسْمِ اللهِ وَبِاللهِ وَعَلَىٰ مِلَّةِ رَسُوْلِ اللهِ صَلَّى اللهُ عَلَيْهِ وَآلِهِ
There is no god except Allāh; Muḥammad is the messenger of Allāh.	وَلَا اِلٰهَ اِلَّا اللهُ، مُحَمَّدٌ رَسُوْلُ اللهِ
Peace be upon our father, Ādam, and our mother, Ḥawwāʾ.	اَلسَّلَامُ عَلَىٰ اَبِيْنَا آدَمَ وَاُمِّنَا حَوَّاءَ
Peace be upon Hābīl, who was killed oppressively and aggressively because he was envied for Allāh's favors and pleasure.	اَلسَّلَامُ عَلَىٰ هَابِيْلَ الْمَقْتُوْلِ ظُلْماً وَّعُدْوَاناً اَلسَّلَامُ عَلَىٰ مَوَاهِبِ اللهِ وَرِضْوَانِهِ
Peace be upon Shayth, the selected one of Allāh, the chosen one and trustee, and upon truthful select ones from his pure progeny, from the first of them and the last.	اَلسَّلَامُ عَلَىٰ شَيْثٍ صَفْوَةِ اللهِ الْمُخْتَارِ الْاَمِيْنِ وَعَلَى الصَّفْوَةِ الصَّادِقِيْنَ مِنْ ذُرِّيَّتِهِ الطَّيِّبِيْنَ اَوَّلِهِمْ وَآخِرِهِمْ
Peace be upon Ibrāhīm, Ismāʿīl, Isḥāq, and Yaʿqūb, and upon their chosen descendants.	اَلسَّلَامُ عَلَىٰ اِبْرَاهِيْمَ وَاِسْمَاعِيْلَ وَاِسْحَاقَ وَيَعْقُوْبَ وَعَلَىٰ ذُرِّيَّتِهِمُ الْمُخْتَارِيْنَ
Peace be upon Mūsā, the one spoken to by Allāh.	اَلسَّلَامُ عَلَىٰ مُوْسَىٰ كَلِيْمِ اللهِ

Peace be upon ʿĪsa, the spirit of Allāh.	اَلسَّلَامُ عَلَىٰ عِيْسَىٰ رُوْحِ اللهِ
Peace be upon Muḥammad, son of ʿAbdullāh, the seal of the Prophets.	اَلسَّلَامُ عَلَىٰ مُحَمَّدِ بْنِ عَبْدِاللهِ خَاتَمِ النَّبِيِّيْنَ
Peace be upon the Commander of the Faithful, and his pure progeny. May the mercy and blessings of Allāh be upon him.	اَلسَّلَامُ عَلَىٰ اَمِيْرِالْمُؤْمِنِيْنَ وَذُرِّيَّتِهِ الطَّيِّبِيْنَ وَرَحْمَةُ اللهِ وَبَرَكَاتُهُ
Peace be upon you in the earlier generations.	اَلسَّلَامُ عَلَيْكُمْ فِي الْاَوَّلِيْنَ
Peace be upon you in the later generations.	اَلسَّلَامُ عَلَيْكُمْ فِي الْآخِرِيْنَ
Peace be upon Fāṭimah az-Zahrāʾ	اَلسَّلَامُ عَلَىٰ فَاطِمَةَ الزَّهْرَاء
Peace be upon the guiding Imāms, the witnesses of Allāh over His creation.	اَلسَّلَامُ عَلَىٰ الْاَئِمَّةِ الْهَادِيْنَ شُهَدَاءِاللهِ عَلَىٰ خَلْقِهِ
Peace be upon the supervisor, the witness over the nations of Allāh, the Lord of the worlds.	اَلسَّلَامُ عَلَىٰ الرَّقِيْبِ الشَّاهِدِ عَلَىٰ الْاُمَمِ لِلّٰهِ رَبِّ الْعَالَمِيْنَ

At this same pillar, offer a four rakaʿāt prayer in two sets of two rakaʿāt. In the first rakʿah, recite Surat al-Fātiḥah and Qadr. In the second rakʿah, recite Surat al-Fātiḥah and Ikhlāṣ. Then, recite a tasbīḥ and the following duʿāʾ:

O Allāh, if I have disobeyed You, then I have certainly also obeyed You in my belief in You.	اَللَّهُمَّ اِنْ كُنْتُ قَدْ عَصَيْتُكَ فَاِنِّيْ قَدْ اَطَعْتُكَ فِيْ الْاِيْمَانِ مِنِّيْ بِكَ
This is Your favor upon me, not a favor from me to You.	مَنّاً مِّنْكَ عَلَيَّ لَا مَنّاً مِنِّيْ عَلَيْكَ
And I have obeyed You in the things You like most: I have not claimed that You have a child, nor have I associated anyone with You.	وَاَطَعْتُكَ فِيْ اَحَبِّ الْاَشْيَاءِ لَكَ لَمْ اَتَّخِذْ لَكَ وَلَداً وَّلَمْ اَدْعُ لَكَ شَرِيْكاً
Still, I have surely disobeyed You in many things, not out of defiance.	وَقَدْ عَصَيْتُكَ فِيْ اَشْيَاءٍ كَثِيْرَةٍ عَلَىٰ غَيْرِ وَجْهِ الْمُكَابَرَةِ لَكَ
Nor to revolt against my servitude to You or out of denial of Your Lordship.	وَلَا الْخُرُوْجِ عَنْ عُبُوْدِيَّتِكَ وَلَا الْجُحُوْدِ لِرُبُوْبِيَّتِكَ
Rather, I have followed my own desires, and Shayṭān has deceived me, although You have had a clear argument against me.	وَلٰكِنِ اتَّبَعْتُ هَوَايَ وَاَزَلَّنِيْ الشَّيْطَانُ بَعْدَ الْحُجَّةِ عَلَيَّ وَالْبَيَانِ
So, if You punish me, it is because of my sins, not because You are being oppressive towards me.	فَاِنْ تُعَذِّبْنِيْ فَبِذُنُوْبِيْ غَيْرَ ظَالِمٍ لِيْ

And if You forgive me and have mercy on me, then this is out of Your Magnanamity and Generosity, O the Most Generous.	وَاِنْ تَعْفُ عَنِّيْ وَتَرْحَمْنِيْ فَبِجُوْدِكَ وَكَرَمِكَ يَا كَرِيْمُ
O Allāh, surely, nothing can stand for my sins except my hope in Your pardon, although my actions have made me unworthy of Your pardon.	اَللّٰهُمَّ اِنَّ ذُنُوْبِيْ لَمْ يَبْقَ لَهَا اِلَّا رَجَاءُ عَفْوِكَ وَقَدْ قَدَّمْتُ آلَةَ الْحِرْمَانِ
So I ask You, O Allāh, for that which I do not deserve, and I seek from You that which I am not worthy.	فَاَنَا اَسْاَلُكَ اللّٰهُمَّ مَا لَااَسْتَوْجِبُهُ وَاَطْلُبُ مِنْكَ مَا لَااَسْتَحِقُّهُ
O Allāh, if You punish me, then it is on account of my sins, and You are never oppressive towards me.	اَللّٰهُمَّ اِنْ تُعَذِّبْنِيْ فَبِذُنُوْبِيْ وَلَمْ تَظْلِمْنِيْ شَيْئاً
And if You forgive me, then You are the best of those who have mercy, O my Master.	وَاِنْ تَغْفِرْلِيْ فَخَيْرُ رَاحِمٍ اَنْتَ يَا سَيِّدِيْ
O Allāh, You are You, and I am me. You are always returning with forgiveness, and I am always returning with sins.	اَللّٰهُمَّ اَنْتَ اَنْتَ وَأَنَا أَنَا اَنْتَ الْعَوَّادُ بِالْمَغْفِرَةِ وَاَنَا الْعَوَّادُ بِالذُّنُوْبِ
You always confer with forebearance, and I always return with impatience.	وَاَنْتَ الْمُتَفَضِّلُ بِالْحِلْمِ وَاَنَا الْعَوَّادُ بِالْجَهْلِ
So I ask you O Allāh, O the Treasure of the weak, O the Supreme Hope,	اَللّٰهُمَّ فَاِنِّيْ اَسْاَلُكَ يَا كَنْزَ الضُّعَفَآءِ، يَا عَظِيْمَ الرَّجَاءِ

O Rescuer of the drowned! O Savior of those who are about to perish! O He who causes the living to die and gives life to the dead. You are Allāh; there is no god except You	يَا مُنْقِذُ الْغَرْقَىٰ يَامُنْجِيَ الْهَلْكَىٰ يَا مُمِيتَ الْاَحْيَآءِ، يَا مُحْيِيَ الْمَوْتَىٰ، اَنْتَ اللّٰهُ لَا اِلٰهَ اِلَّا اَنْتَ
You are the One to whom the ray of the sun, sound of water, rustling of trees, moonlight, darkness of night, light of daytime, and flapping of birds have prostrated	اَنْتَ الَّذِيْ سَجَدَ لَكَ شُعَاعُ الشَّمْسِ وَدَوِيُّ الْمَاءِ وَحَفِيْفُ الشَّجَرِ وَنُوْرُ الْقَمَرِ وَظُلْمَةُ اللَّيْلِ وَضَوْءُ النَّهَارِ وَخَفَقَانُ الطَّيْرِ
I ask you, O Allāh, O the Supreme, by Your right over Muhammad and his truthful family, and by the right of Muhammad and his truthful family over You	أَسْأَلُكَ اللَّهُمَّ يَا عَظِيْمُ بِحَقِّكَ عَلَىٰ مُحَمَّدٍ وَآلِهِ الصَّادِقِيْنَ وَبِحَقِّ مُحَمَّدٍ وَآلِهِ الصَّادِقِيْنَ عَلَيْكَ
And by Your right over Ali, and the right of Ali over You	وَبِحَقِّكَ عَلَىٰ عَلِيٍّ وَبِحَقِّ عَلِيٍّ عَلَيْكَ
And by Your right over Fatimah, and the right of Fatimah over You	وَبِحَقِّكَ عَلَىٰ فَاطِمَةَ وَبِحَقِّ فَاطِمَةَ عَلَيْكَ
And by Your right over Hasan, and the right of Hasan over You	وَبِحَقِّكَ عَلَىٰ الْحَسَنِ وَبِحَقِّ الْحَسَنِ عَلَيْكَ
And by Your right over Husayn, and the right of Husayn over You	وَبِحَقِّكَ عَلَى الْحُسَيْنِ وَبِحَقِّ الْحُسَيْنِ عَلَيْكَ
Surely, their rights over You are amongst Your greatest blessings upon them	فَاِنَّ حُقُوْقَهُمْ عَلَيْكَ مِنْ اَفْضَلِ اِنْعَامِكَ عَلَيْهِمْ

And [I ask you] by the position You have with them, and the position they have with You	وَبِالشَّأْنِ الَّذِيْ لَكَ عِنْدَهُمْ وَبِالشَّأْنِ الَّذِيْ لَهُمْ عِنْدَكَ
Send Your blessings upon them, O my Lord, eternal blessings until they reach Your pleasure	صَلِّ عَلَيْهِمْ يَا رَبِّ صَلَاةً دَائِمَـةً مُنْتَهَىٰ رِضَاكَ
And forgive me, through them, those sins that are between me and You	وَاغْفِرْ لِيْ بِهِمُ الذُّنُوْبَ الَّتِيْ بَيْنِيْ وَبَيْنَكَ
And make Your creatures satisfied with me, and complete Your blessings upon me the same way You completed them upon my ancestors	وَأَرْضِ عَنِّيْ خَلْقَكَ، وَأَتْمِمْ عَلَيَّ نِعْمَتَكَ كَمَا أَتْمَمْتَهَا عَلَىٰ آبَائِيْ مِنْ قَبْلُ
And do not allow any of Your creatures to play any role in these blessings	وَلَا تَجْعَلْ لِأَحَدٍ مِنَ الْمَخْلُوْقِيْنَ عَلَيَّ فِيْهَا امْتِنَاناً
And confer upon me grace the same way You confered upon my ancestors, O Kāf, Hā, Yā, ʿAyn, Ṣād	وَامْنُنْ عَلَيَّ كَمَا مَنَنْتَ عَلَىٰ آبَائِيْ مِنْ قَبْلُ يَا كٓهٰيٰعٓصٓ
O Allāh, the same way You have blessed Muḥammad and his family, answer my duʿāʾ regarding that which I asked you	اَللَّهُمَّ كَمَا صَلَّيْتَ عَلَىٰ مُحَمَّدٍ وَآلِهِ فَاسْتَجِبْ لِيْ دُعَائِيْ فِيْمَا سَأَلْتُ
O the Most Generous, O the Most Generous, O the Most Generous	يَا كَرِيْمُ يَا كَرِيْمُ يَا كَرِيْمُ

Then, go into sajdah and say:

O He who grants the wishes of those who ask through his power, and He knows those inner thoughts of the silent ones.	يَا مَنْ يَقْدِرُ عَلَىٰ حَوَآئِجِ السَّائِلِيْنَ وَيَعْلَمُ مَا فِيْ ضَمِيْرِ الصَّامِتِيْنَ
O He who does not require any explanation (His existence is apparent)!	يَا مَنْ لَا يَحْتَاجُ اِلَىٰ التَّفْسِيْرِ
O He who knows about those eyes that have transgressed and that which is hidden in the chests.	يَا مَنْ يَعْلَمُ خَائِنَةَ الْاَعْيُنِ وَمَا تُخْفِي الصُّدُوْرُ
O He who sent the punishment upon the people of Yūnus and planned to punish them.	يَا مَنْ اَنْزَلَ الْعَذَابَ عَلَىٰ قَوْمِ يُوْنُسَ وَهُوَ يُرِيْدُ اَنْ يُعَذِّبَهُمْ
But they called upon Him humbly, so He relieved their punishment and granted them bounties until now.	فَدَعَوْهُ وَتَضَرَّعُوْا اِلَيْهِ فَكَشَفَ عَنْهُمُ الْعَذَابَ وَمَتَّعَهُمْ اِلَىٰ حِيْنٍ
Surely, You see my position, Your hear my supplication, You know what I conceal, what I declare, and the situation I am in	قَدْ تَرَىٰ مَكَانِيْ وَتَسْمَعُ دُعَائِيْ وَتَعْلَمُ سِرِّيْ وَعَلَانِيَتِيْ وَحَالِيْ
Send blessings upon Muḥammad and the family of Muḥammad, and relieve me from all that which grieves me, regarding the affairs of my religion, my worldly life, and my hereafter	صَلِّ عَلَىٰ مُحَمَّدٍ وَّآلِ مُحَمَّدٍ وَّ اكْفِنِيْ مَا اَهَمَّنِيْ مِنْ اَمْرِ دِيْنِيْ وَدُنْيَايَ وَآخِرَتِيْ

Then, say 70 times: يَا سَيِّدِيْ (*Yā Sayyidī* - O my Master)

Then, raise your head and say the following:

يَا رَبِّ اَسْأَلُكَ بَرَكَةَ هٰذَا الْمَوْضِعِ وَبَرَكَةَ اَهْلِهِ

O my Lord, I ask You for the blessings of this place and the blessings of its people!

وَاَسْأَلُكَ اَنْ تَرْزُقَنِيْ مِنْ رِزْقِكَ رِزْقاً حَلَالًا طَيِّباً تَسُوْقُهُ اِلَيَّ بِحَوْلِكَ وَقُوَّتِكَ

And I ask You to bless me with Your sustenance, sustenance that is lawful and pure, and that You bring it to me through Your Might and Power,

وَاَنَا خَائِضٌ فِيْ عَافِيَةٍ يَا اَرْحَمَ الرَّاحِمِيْنَ

and while I am in good health, O the Most Merciful!

8. Maqām Jibrāʾīl

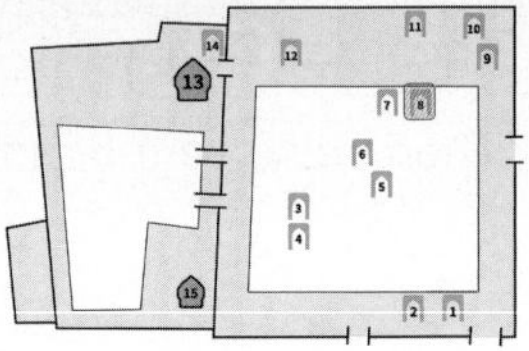

This is the place where Imām ʿAlī (A) said, "Ask me, ask me, before you lose me! Ask me about the paths of the heavens, for surely I know them better than I know the paths of the earth."

A man in the crowd arose and asked, "O Amīr ul-Muʿminīn! Where is Jibrāʾīl right now?"

Imām ʿAlī (A) replied, "Give me a moment." He looked up to the sky, down to the earth, to the right, and to the left. He then said, "You, yourself, are Jibrāʾīl !" Jibrāʾīl said, "You are right!" and then took off to the heavens.

At this time, you could hear the loud takbīrs of the people. They asked, "O Amīr ul-Muʿminīn! How did you know this was Jibrāʾīl?"

He replied, "When I looked towards the seven heavens, seven layers of the earth, the east, and the west and couldn't find him, I knew that this person himself must be Jibrāʾīl!

Bihār al-Anwār, Vol. 39, P. 108

Offer a two rakaʿāt prayer just like Fajr near the pillar. Afterwards, recite a tasbīḥ and the following duʿāʾ:

O Allāh, I ask You by all Your names, those which we know and those we do not know.	اَللّٰهُمَّ اِنِّيْ اَسْاَلُكَ بِجَمِيْعِ اَسْمَآئِكَ كُلِّهَا مَا عَلِمْنَا مِنْهَا وَمَا لَا نَعْلَمُ
And I ask You by Your supreme, greatest name, which You answer to if one calls You by it,	وَاَسْاَلُكَ بِاِسْمِكَ الْعَظِيْمِ الْاَعْظَمِ الْكَبِيْرِ الْاَكْبَرِ الَّذِيْ مَنْ دَعَاكَ بِهِ اَجَبْتَهُ
and if one begs You by it, You will give him.	وَ مَنْ سَأَلَكَ بِهِ اَعْطَيْتَهُ

And if one seeks Your victory by it, You will give him victory.	وَمَنِ اسْتَنْصَرَكَ بِهِ نَصَرْتَهُ
And if one seeks Your forgiveness by it, You will forgive him.	وَمَنِ اسْتَغْفَرَكَ بِهِ غَفَرْتَ لَهُ
And if one seeks Your aid by it, You will aid him.	وَمَنِ اسْتَعَانَكَ بِهِ اَعَنْتَهُ
And if one seeks Your sustenance by it, You will provide sustenance for him.	وَمَنِ اسْتَرْزَقَكَ بِهِ رَزَقْتَهُ
And if one seeks Your help by it, You will help him.	وَمَنِ اسْتَغَاثَكَ بِهِ اَغَثْتَهُ
And if one seeks Your mercy by it, You will grant him mercy.	وَمَنِ اسْتَرْحَمَكَ بِهِ رَحِمْتَهُ
And if one seeks Your refuge by it, You will protect him.	وَمَنِ اسْتَجَارَكَ بِهِ اَجَرْتَهُ
And if one seeks Your trust by it, You will suffice him.	وَمَنْ تَوَكَّلَ عَلَيْكَ بِهِ كَفَيْتَهُ
And if one seeks Your shield by it, You will guard him.	وَمَنِ اسْتَعْصَمَكَ بِهِ عَصَمْتَهُ
And if one asks You for protection from the hellfire by it, You will save him.	وَمَنِ اسْتَنْقَذَكَ بِهِ مِنَ النَّارِ اَنْقَذْتَهُ
And if one asks You for kindness by it, You will be kind to him.	وَمَنِ اسْتَعْطَفَكَ بِهِ تَعَطَّفْتَ لَهُ

And if one hopes in You by it, You will give him.	وَ مَنْ اَمَّلَكَ بِهِ اَعْطَيْتَهُ
That name by which You have taken Ādam as Your chosen one, Nūh as Your confidante, Ibrāhīm as Your friend, Mūsa as the one spoken to by You, ʿĪsā as Your spirit, Muḥammad as Your beloved, and ʿAlī as Your Prophet's successor, Allāh's blessings be upon all of them.	الَّذِيْ اتَّخَذْتَ بِهِ آدَمَ صَفِيّاً، وَ نُوْحاً نَجِيّاً وَاِبْرَاهِيْمَ خَلِيْلاً، وَمُوْسَىٰ كَلِيْماً، وَعِيْسَىٰ رُوْحاً، وَ مُحَمَّداً حَبِيْباً، وَعَلِيّاً وَصِيّاً، صَلَّىٰ اللهُ عَلَيْهِمْ اَجْمَعِيْنَ
(I ask) That You grant me my wishes,	اَنْ تَقْضِيَ لِيْ حَوَآئِجِيْ
overlook my past sins,	وَتَعْفُوَ عَمَّا سَلَفَ مِنْ ذُنُوْبِيْ
and grace me with all that which is befitting of You, as well all the believing men and women, in this world and the hereafter.	وَتَتَفَضَّلَ عَلَيَّ بِمَا اَنْتَ اَهْلُهُ وَلِجَمِيْعِ الْمُؤْمِنِيْنَ وَالْمُؤْمِنَاتِ لِلدُّنْيَآ وَالْآخِرَةِ
O He who dispels the grief of the aggrieved ones! O He who helps the confused ones!	يَا مُفَرِّجَ هَمِّ الْمَهْمُوْمِيْنَ وَ يَاغِيَآثَ الْمَلْهُوْفِيْنَ الْعَالَمِيْنَ
There is no god except You; glory be to You, O Lord of the worlds!	لَا اِلٰهَ اِلَّا اَنْتَ سُبْحَانَكَ يَا رَبَّ الْعَالَمِيْنَ

9. Maqām Imām Zayn ul-ʿĀbidīn (A)

Abū Ḥamzah ath-Thumālī narrates: I was sitting in Masjid al-Kūfāh when someone entered from Bāb al-Ḥujjah. He smelled pure and was wearing a green amāmah, shirt, and slippers. He removed his slippers and went to the 7th pillar and said takbīr. I had goosebumps as he recited the most beautiful four rakaʿāt prayer and duʿāʾ. Then, he went into sajdah and recited "Yā Karīm." When he picked up his head, I looked closely and realized it was Imām as-Sajjād. I kissed his hands and asked, "Why have you come here?" He replied, "To do what you just saw." Offer a two rakaʿāt prayer like Fajr near the pillar. Afterwards, recite a tasbīḥ and the following duʿāʾ:

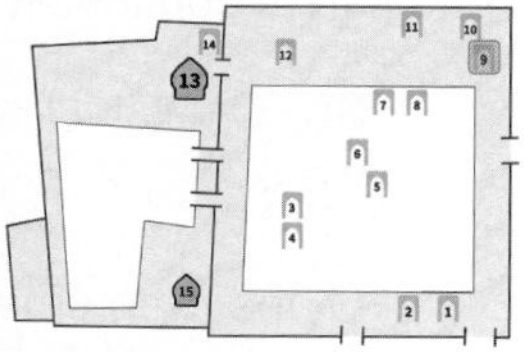

In the Name of Allāh, the Beneficent, the Merciful.	بِسْمِ اللهِ الرَّحْمٰنِ الرَّحِيْمِ
O Allāh, surely, my sins have been increasing, and nothing can stand for them except the hope of Your pardon, even though I have done things for which I do not deserve Your pardon.	اَللّٰهُمَّ اِنَّ ذُنُوْبِيْ قَدْ كَثُرَتْ وَلَمْ يَبْقَ لَهَا اِلَّا رَجَاۤءُ عَفْوِكَ وَقَدْ قَدَّمْتُ آلَةَ الْحِرْمَانِ اِلَيْكَ
Therefore, I ask You, O Allāh, for that which I do not deserve.	فَأَنَا اَسْاَلُكَ اللّٰهُمَّ مَا لَاۤ اَسْتَوْجِبُهُ
And I seek from You that which I do not deserve. O Allāh, If you punish me, then it is on account of my sins and You are never unjust.	وَاطْلُبُ مِنْكَ مَا لَاۤ اَسْتَحِقُّهُ، اَللّٰهُمَّ اِنْ تُعَذِّبْنِيْ فَبِذُنُوْبِيْ وَلَمْ تَظْلِمْنِيْ شَيْئاً
But if You forgive me, then You are already the best of all those who show mercy, O my Leader. O Allāh, You are You and I am me.	وَاِنْ تَغْفِرْ لِيْ فَخَيْرُ رَاحِمٍ اَنْتَ يَا سَيِّدِيْ، اَللّٰهُمَّ اَنْتَ اَنْتَ وَأَنَا أَنَا
You continuously return with forgiveness, and I continuously return with sins.	اَنْتَ الْعَوَّادُ بِالْمَغْفِرَةِ وَاَنَا الْعَوَّادُ بِالذُّنُوْبِ

You always approach me with forbearance, and I continually return with ignorance.	وَاَنْتَ الْمُتَفَضِّلُ بِالْحِلْمِ وَاَنَا الْعَوَّادُ بِالْجَهْلِ
So, O Allāh, I ask You, O Treasure of the weak	اَللَّهُمَّ فَاِنِّيْ اَسْاَلُكَ يَا كَنْزَ الضُّعَفَاءِ
O the Supreme Hope! O Rescuer of the drowned! O Savior of those about to perish! O He who causes the living to die! O He who brings the dead back to life! You are Allāh; there is no god but You.	يَا عَظِيْمَ الرَّجَاءِ، يَا مُنْقِذَ الْغَرْقَىٰ يَا مُنْجِيَ الْهَلْكَىٰ، يَا مُمِيْتَ الْاَحْيَآءِ يَا مُحْيِيَ الْمَوْتَىٰ اَنْتَ اللهُ الَّذِيْ لَا اِلٰهَ اِلاَّ اَنْتَ
You are the one to whom the rays of the sun, the moonlight, the darkness of night, the light of daytime, and the flapping of birds all prostrate.	اَنْتَ الَّذِيْ سَجَدَ لَكَ شُعَاعُ الشَّمْسِ وَنُوْرُ الْقَمَرِ وَظُلْمَةُ اللَّيْلِ، وَضَوْءُ النَّهَارِ وَخَفَقَانُ الطَّيْرِ
So, I ask You, O Allāh, O the Supreme, O the Most Generous, by Your right over Muḥammad and his truthful household, and by the right of Muḥammad and his truthful household over You.	فَأَسْأَلُكَ اللَّهُمَّ يَا عَظِيْمُ بِحَقِّكَ يَا كَرِيْمُ عَلَىٰ مُحَمَّدٍ وَّآلِهِ الصَّادِقِيْنَ وَبِحَقِّ مُحَمَّدٍ وَّآلِهِ الصَّادِقِيْنَ عَلَيْكَ
And by Your right over ʿAlī, and by the right of ʿAlī over You.	وَبِحَقِّكَ عَلَىٰ عَلِيٍّ وَبِحَقِّ عَلِيٍّ عَلَيْكَ
And by Your right over Fāṭimah, and by the right of Fāṭimah over You.	وَبِحَقِّكَ عَلَىٰ فَاطِمَةَ وَبِحَقِّ فَاطِمَةَ عَلَيْكَ
And by Your right over Ḥasan, and by the right of Ḥasan over You.	وَبِحَقِّكَ عَلَى الْحَسَنِ وَبِحَقِ الْحَسَنِ عَلَيْكَ

And by Your right over Ḥusayn, and by the right of Ḥusayn over You. For surely, Your right over them is one of Your greatest blessings upon them.	وَبِحَقِّكَ عَلَى الْحُسَيْنِ وَبِحَقِّ الْحُسَيْنِ عَلَيْكَ، فَاِنَّ حُقُوْقَهُمْ مِنْ اَفْضَلِ اِنْعَامِكَ عَلَيْهِمْ
And (I ask You) by the position that You have with them and by the position that they have with You to bless them, O my Lord, with blessings that are endless until they attain Your pleasure.	وَبِالشَّأْنِ الَّذِيْ لَكَ عِنْدَهُمْ وَبِالشَّأْنِ الَّذِيْ لَهُمْ عِنْدَكَ، صَلِّ يَارَبِّ عَلَيْهِمْ صَلَاةً دائِمَةً مُّنْتَهَى رِضَاكْ
And forgive me, through them, those sins that are between me and You, and complete Your favors upon me in the same way You completed them upon my forefathers. O Kāf Hā Yā ʿAyn Ṣād!	وَاغْفِرْ لِيْ بِهِمْ الذُّنُوْبَ الَّتِيْ بَيْنِيْ وَبَيْنَكَ، وَاَتْمِمْ نِعْمَتَكَ عَلَيَّ كَمَا اَتْمَمْتَهَا عَلَى آبَائِيْ مِنْ قَبْلُ يَا كٓهٰيٰعٓصٓ
O Allāh, just as You have poured blessings upon Muḥammad and the Household of Muḥammad, respond to my prayer and that which I have asked from You.	اَللّٰهُمَّ كَمَا صَلَّيْتَ عَلَى مُحَمَّدٍ وَّآلِ مُحَمَّدٍ فَاسْتَجِبْ لِيْ دُعَائِيْ فِيْمَا سَأَلْتُكَ

Then, perform sajdah and place your right cheek on the ground and recite:

O my Master! O my Master! O my Master! Bless Muḥammad and the Household of Muḥammad, and forgive me. Please, forgive me!	يَا سَيِّدِيْ يَا سَيِّدِيْ يَا سَيِّدِيْ صَلِّ عَلَى مُحَمَّدٍ وَّآلِ مُحَمَّدٍ وَّاغْفِرْ لِيْ وَاغْفِرْ لِيْ

Keep reciting this duʿāʾ with great humility and try to cry. Then, place your left cheek on the ground and repeat these words and ask for your duʿāʾs.

10. Bāb Al-Faraj (Maqām of Prophet Nūḥ (A))

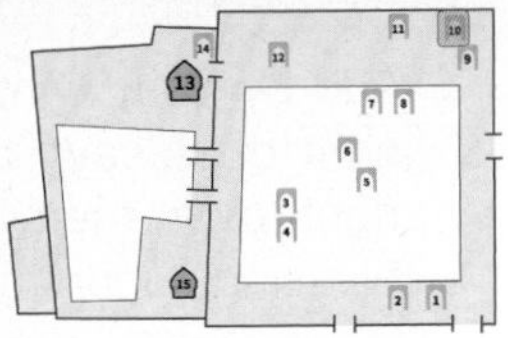

Imām ar-Riḍa (A): Masjid al-Kūfah was the house of Prophet Nūḥ (A). if someone enters it even 100 times, Allāh will forgive 100 of his sins because he is included in the duʿā᾽ of Prophet Nūḥ (A) (71:28). Offer a four rakaʿāt prayer here in two sets of two rakaʿāt, and then recite a tasbīḥ and the following duʿā᾽:

O Allāh, send blessings upon Muḥammad and the Household of Muḥammad, and grant my request.	اَللّٰهُمَّ صَلِّ عَلىٰ مُحَمَّدٍ وَّآلِ مُحَمَّدٍ، وَاقْضِ حَاجَتِيْ
O Allāh! O He who never disappoints one who asks Him and whose gifts are inexhaustible! O Granter of needs! O Responder to the prayers!	يَا اَللّٰهُ يَامَنْ لَايَخِيبُ سَآئِلُهُ وَلَايَنْفَدُ نَائِلُهُ، يَا قَاضِيَ الْحَاجَاتِ، يَا مُجِيبَ الدَّعَوَاتِ
O Lord of the earth and heavens! O Dispeller of grief! O Generous giver of gifts!	يَارَبَّ الْاَرَضِيْنَ وَالسَّمَاوَاتِ، يَا كَاشِفَ الْكُرُبَاتِ، يَاوَاسِعَ الْعَطِيَاتِ
O Defender from hardships! O He who transforms transgressions into good deeds! Look at me with Your bounty, grace, and goodness.	يَادَافِعَ النَّقِمَاتِ، يَا مُبَدِّلَ السَّيِّئَاتِ حَسَنَاتٍ، عُدْ عَلَيَّ بِطَوْلِكَ وَفَضْلِكَ وَاِحْسَانِكَ
And respond to my prayers regarding that which I have asked and sought from You, by the right of Your Prophet, Your Prophet's successor, and Your righteous intimate servants.	وَاسْتَجِبْ دُعَآئِيْ فِيْمَا سَأَلْتُكَ وَطَلَبْتُ مِنْكَ بِحَقِّ نَبِيِّكَ وَوَصِيِّكَ وَاَوْلِيَآئِكَ الصَّالِحِيْنَ

Offer a two raka'āt prayer. Then, recite a tasbīḥ and the following du'ā':

O Allāh, I am enamored with Your essence, completely knowledgable about Your Oneness and Independence, and certain that no one can ever settle my needs except You.	اَللّٰهُمَّ اِنِّيْ حَلَلْتُ بِسَاحَتِكَ لِعِلْمِيْ بِوَحْدَانِيَتِكَ وَصَمَدَانِيَتِكَ، وَاَنَّهُ لَا قَادِرَ عَلٰى قَضَاءِ حَاجَتِيْ غَيْرُكَ
And I know, O my Lord, that the more I witness Your favors upon me, the more I need You. O my Lord, I have been inflicted with grieving matters that You are aware of,	وَقَدْ عَلِمْتُ يَا رَبِّ اَنَّهُ كُلَّمَا شَاهَدْتُ نِعْمَتَكَ عَلَيَّ اشْتَدَّتْ فَاقَتِيْ اِلَيْكَ، وَقَدْ طَرَقَنِيْ يَا رَبِّ مِنْ مُهِمِّ اَمْرِيْ مَا قَدْ عَرَفْتَهُ
because You are the All-knowing who has not been taught. So, I ask You by that Name that when You put it on the heavens, they split, and when You put it on the earth, they spread out,	لِاَنَّكَ عَالِمٌ غَيْرُ مُعَلَّمٍ وَاَسْاَلُكَ بِالْاِسْمِ الَّذِيْ وَضَعْتَهُ عَلَى السَّمَاوَاتِ فَانْشَقَّتْ، وَعَلَى الْاَرَضِيْنَ فَانْبَسَطَتْ
and when You put it on the stars, they diffused, and when You put on the mountains, they settled down,	وَعَلَى النُّجُوْمِ فَانْتَشَرَتْ، وَعَلَى الْجِبَالِ فَاسْتَقَرَّتْ
and I ask You by that Name that You placed with Muḥammad, 'Alī,	وَاَسْاَلُكَ بِالْاِسْمِ الَّذِيْ جَعَلْتَهُ عِنْدَ مُحَمَّدٍ وَّعِنْدَ عَلِيٍّ

al-Ḥasan, al-Ḥusayn, and all the Imāms, may Allāh's blessings be upon them all,	وَعِنْدَ الْحَسَنِ وَعِنْدَ الْحُسَيْنِ وَعِنْدَ الْأَئِمَّةِ كُلِّهِمْ صَلَوَاتُ اللهِ عَلَيْهِمْ اَجْمَعِيْنَ
to bless Muḥammad and the Household of Muḥammad, O my Lord, to grant me all my requests, ease my difficulties,	اَنْ تُصَلِّيَ عَلَىٰ مُحَمَّدٍ وَّآلِ مُحَمَّدٍ وَّاَنْ تَقْضِيَ لِيْ يَا رَبِّ حَاجَتِيْ، وَتُيَسِّرَ عَسِيْرَهَا
relieve my grievances, and unlock for me their locks. If You do all that for me, then all praise be to You!	وَتَكْفِيَنِيْ مُهِمَّهَا، وَتَفْتَحَ لِيْ قُفْلَهَا، فَاِنْ فَعَلْتَ ذٰلِكَ فَلَكَ الْحَمْدُ
and if You do not, then all praise is still for You, for Your judgments are never doubtful or unjust.	وَاِنْ لَمْ تَفْعَلْ فَلَكَ الْحَمْدُ غَيْرَ جَائِرٍ فِيْ حُكْمِكَ وَلَا حَائِفٍ فِيْ عَدْلِكَ

Then, perform sajdah and place your right cheek on the ground and recite:

O Allāh, if Your servant and Prophet, Yūnus, son of Mattā, prayed to You from the belly of the whale, and You responded to him, then I am also praying to You; so, respond to me by the right of Muḥammad and the household of Muḥammad.	اَللّٰهُمَّ اِنَّ يُوْنُسَ بْنَ مَتّىٰ عَلَيْهِ اَلسَّلَامُ عَبْدَكَ وَنَبِيِّكَ دَعَاكَ فِيْ بَطْنِ الْحُوْتِ فَاسْتَجَبْتَ لَهُ وَاَنَا اَدْعُوْكَ فَاسْتَجِبْ لِيْ بِحَقِّ مُحَمَّدٍ وَّآلِ مُحَمَّد

Ask for your wishes. Then, place your left cheek on the ground and recite:

O Allāh, You have certainly commanded us to supplicate to You and You have promised to respond.	اَللَّهُمَّ اِنَّكَ اَمَرْتَ بِالدُّعَآءِ وَتَكَفَّلْتَ بِالْاِجَابَةِ
I am supplicating to You just as You have commanded, so send blessings upon Muḥammad and the household of Muḥammad,	وَاَنَا اَدْعُوْكَ كَمَا اَمَرْتَنِيْ فَصَلِّ عَلٰى مُحَمَّدٍ وَّآلِ مُحَمَّدٍ
and respond to me as You have promised, O the Most Generous!	وَاسْتَجِبْ لِيْ كَمَا وَعَدْتَنِيْ يَا كَرِيْمُ

Then, place your forehead on the ground and recite:

O He who honors all those who are humilated! O He who humiliates all those who are arrogant! You know my agony, so bless Muḥammad and his family, and grant me relief, O the Most Generous!	يَامُعِزَّ كُلِّ ذَلِيْلٍ وَ يَا مُذِلَّ كُلِّ عَزِيْزٍ تَعْلَمُ كُرْبَتِيْ فَصَلِّ عَلٰى مُحَمَّدٍ وَّآلِهِ وَفَرِّجْ عَنِّيْ يَا كَرِيْمُ

The graves in Masjid al-Kūfah tell the message of al-Ḥusayn,
Kufa's every street is a reminder of ʿAlī's pain

Miḥrābs of Masjid al-Kūfaḥ

Miḥrāb of Nāfilah

While facing Qibla, you will see two miḥrābs in the masjid that are both named Miḥrāb of Amīr ul-Muʾminīn. Allāmah Majlisī and Muḥaddith Nūri have concluded that the Imām (A) was most likely struck by the sword in one of the miḥrābs, and the other is the miḥrāb where he used to perform his ibādah, so it is best to receive blessings from both miḥrābs.

1. Mustadrak of Wasāʾil, Vol. 3, P. 469

Miḥrāb of Shahādah

11. Miḥrāb of Amīr al-Mʾuminīn

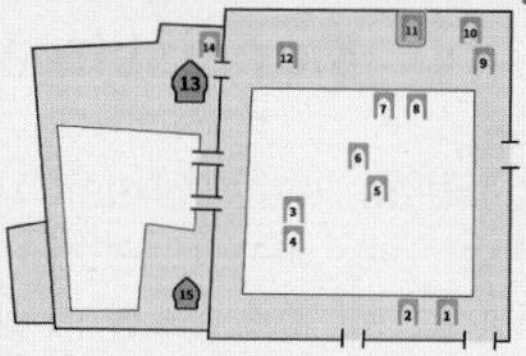

This is the miḥrāb where Imām ʿAlī (A) was struck on the 19th night of Ramaḍān. Offer a two rakaʿāt prayer here. Then, recite a tasbīḥ and the following duʿāʾ:

O He who makes apparent the beautiful and conceals the ugly!	يَا مَنْ اَظْهَرَ الْجَمِيْلَ وَسَتَرَ الْقَبِيْحَ
O He who does not demand submission under duress and does not expose the hidden and unknown!	يَا مَنْ لَمْ يُؤَاخِذْ بِالْجَرِيْرَةِ وَلَمْ يَهْتِكِ السِّتْرَ وَالسَّرِيْرَةَ
O the Supreme Pardoner! O the Best Overlooker! O the Limitless Forgiver!	يَا عَظِيْمَ الْعَفْوِ، يَا حَسَنَ التَّجَاوُزِ، يَا وَاسِعَ الْمَغْفِرَةِ
O He whose hands are expansive with mercy! O He who is a partner in all whispers!	يَا بَاسِطَ الْيَدَيْنِ بِالرَّحْمَةِ، يَا صَاحِبَ كُلِّ نَجْوَى
O the Receiver of all complaints! O He who is generous in clemency! O the Supreme Hope!	يَا مُنْتَهَى كُلِّ شَكْوَى، يَا كَرِيْمَ الصَّفْحِ، يَا عَظِيْمَ الرَّجَاءِ
O my Leader, send blessings upon Muḥammad and the family of Muḥammad, and do with me what is befitting of You, O the Most Generous!	يَاسَيِّدِيْ صَلِّ عَلَى مُحَمَّدٍ وَّآلِ مُحَمَّدٍ وَّافْعَلْ بِيْ مَآ اَنْتَ اَهْلُهُ يَا كَرِيْمُ

Munājāt Imām ʿAlī (A)

O Allāh, surely I ask You for protection on that day when neither wealth nor children will avail, except who comes to Allāh with a free heart	اَللَّهُمَّ إِنِّيْ أَسْأَلُكَ الْأَمَانَ يَوْمَ لَايَنْفَعُ مَالٌ وَّلَابَنُوْنَ إِلَّا مَنْ أَتَى اللهَ بِقَلْبٍ سَلِيْمٍ
And I ask You for protection on that day when the oppressor will bite his nails, saying 'O I wish I had taken a path with the Messenger'	وَأَسْأَلُكَ الْأَمَانَ يَوْمَ يَعَضُّ الظَّالِمُ عَلَىٰ يَدَيْهِ يَقُوْلُ يَا لَيْتَنِيْ اتَّخَذْتُ مَعَ الرَّسُوْلِ سَبِيْلَا
And I ask You for protection on that day then the guilty will be recognized by their marks, so they shall be seized by their heads and feet	وَأَسْأَلُكَ الْأَمَانَ يَوْمَ يُعْرَفُ الْمُجْرِمُوْنَ بِسِيْمَاهُمْ فَيُؤْخَذُ بِالنَّوَاصِيْ وَ الْأَقْدَامِ
And I ask You for protection on that day when neither a father will not satisfy his son, nor will the child satisfy his father. Surely, the promise of Allāh is true	وَ أَسْأَلُكَ الْأَمَانَ يَوْمَ لَايَجْزِيْ وَالِدٌ عَنْ وَّلَدِهِ وَ لَامَوْلُوْدٌ هُوَ جَازٍ عَنْ وَالِدِهِ شَيْئاً إِنَّ وَعْدَ اللهِ حَقٌّ
And I ask You for protection on that day when the oppressors will not benefit from their excuses. And for them is the curse and the evil abode	وَأَسْأَلُكَ الْأَمَانَ يَوْمَ لَايَنْفَعُ الظَّالِمِيْنَ مَعْذِرَتُهُمْ وَلَهُمُ اللَّعْنَةُ وَ لَهُمْ سُوْءُ الدَّارِ
And I ask You for protection on that day when no soul will control another soul. The command on that day will be only for Allāh	وَأَسْأَلُكَ الْأَمَانَ يَوْمَ لَاتَمْلِكُ نَفْسٌ لِّنَفْسٍ شَيْئاً وَّالْأَمْرُ يَوْمَئِذٍ لِلّٰهِ

And I ask You for protection on the day when a man shall flee from his brother, his mother, his father, his spouse, and his children; each one of them on that day will have a concern which will occupy him	وَ أَسْأَلُكَ الْأَمَانَ يَوْمَ يَفِرُّ الْمَرْءُ مِنْ أَخِيْهِ وَأُمِّهِ وَأَبِيْهِ وَصَاحِبَتِهِ وَبَنِيْهِ لِكُلِّ امْرِئٍ مِّنْهُمْ يَوْمَئِذٍ شَأْنٌ يُّغْنِيْهِ
And I ask You for protection on the day when the guilty will wish to redeem himself from the chastisement of that day by (sacrificing) his children, and the near of kin who gave him shelter and all those that are in the earth (wising) that this might deliver him...	وَأَسْأَلُكَ الْأَمَانَ يَوْمَ يَوَدُّ الْمُجْرِمُ لَوْ يَفْتَدِيْ مِنْ عَذَابِ يَوْمِئِذٍ بِبَنِيْهِ وَ صَاحِبَتِهِ وَ أَخِيْهِ وَفَصِيْلَتِهِ الَّتِيْ تُؤْوِيْهِ وَ مَنْ فِيْ الْأَرْضِ جَمِيْعاً ثُمَّ يُنْجِيْهِ
...by no means! Surely, it is a flaming fire, dragging by the head	كَلَّا إِنَّهَا لَظَىٰ نَزَّاعَةً لِلشَّوَىٰ
My Master, O my Master, You are the Master, and I am the servant. And who can have mercy on the servant except the Master?	مَوْلَايَ يَا مَوْلَايَ أَنْتَ الْمَوْلَىٰ وَ أَنَا الْعَبْدُ وَ هَلْ يَرْحَمُ الْعَبْدَ إِلَّا الْمَوْلَىٰ
My Master, O my Master, You are the Owner, and I am the one owned by you. And who can have mercy on the owned except the Owner?	مَوْلَايَ يَا مَوْلَايَ أَنْتَ الْمَالِكُ وَ أَنَا الْمَمْلُوْكُ وَ هَلْ يَرْحَمُ الْمَمْلُوْكَ إِلَّا الْمَالِكُ

My Master, O my Master, You are the Almighty, and I am the lowly. And who can have mercy on the lowly except the Almighty?	مَوْلَايَ يَا مَوْلَايَ أَنْتَ الْعَزِيْزُ وَ أَنَا الذَّلِيْلُ وَ هَلْ يَرْحَمُ الذَّلِيْلَ إِلَّا الْعَزِيْزُ
My Master, O my Master, You are the Creator, and I am the creation. And who can have mercy on the creation except the Creator?	مَوْلَايَ يَا مَوْلَايَ أَنْتَ الْخَالِقُ وَ أَنَا الْمَخْلُوْقُ وَ هَلْ يَرْحَمُ الْمَخْلُوْقَ إِلَّا الْخَالِقُ
My Master, O my Master, You are the Supreme, and I am the miserable. And who can have mercy on the miserable except the Supreme?	مَوْلَايَ يَا مَوْلَايَ أَنْتَ الْعَظِيْمُ وَ أَنَا الْحَقِيْرُ وَ هَلْ يَرْحَمُ الْحَقِيْرَ إِلَّا الْعَظِيْمُ
My Master, O my Master, You are the Powerful, and I am the weak And who can have mercy on the weak except the Powerful?	مَوْلَايَ يَا مَوْلَايَ أَنْتَ الْقَوِيُّ وَ أَنَا الضَّعِيْفُ وَ هَلْ يَرْحَمُ الضَّعِيْفَ إِلَّا الْقَوِيُّ
My Master, O my Master, You are the Wealthy, and I am the poor. And who can have mercy on the poor except the Wealthy?	مَوْلَايَ يَا مَوْلَايَ أَنْتَ الْغَنِيُّ وَ أَنَا الْفَقِيْرُ وَ هَلْ يَرْحَمُ الْفَقِيْرَ إِلَّا الْغَنِيُّ
My Master, O my Master, You are the Bestower, and I am the beggar. And who can have mercy on the beggar except the Bestower?	مَوْلَايَ يَا مَوْلَايَ أَنْتَ الْمُعْطِيْ وَ أَنَا السَّائِلُ وَ هَلْ يَرْحَمُ السَّائِلَ إِلَّا الْمُعْطِيْ
My Master, O my Master, You are the Living, and I am the dead. And who can have mercy on the dead except the Living?	مَوْلَايَ يَا مَوْلَايَ أَنْتَ الْحَيُّ وَ أَنَا الْمَيِّتُ وَ هَلْ يَرْحَمُ الْمَيِّتَ إِلَّا الْحَيُّ

My Master, O my Master, You are the Eternal, and I am the transient. And who can have mercy on the transient except the Eternal?	مَوْلَايَ يَا مَوْلَايَ أَنْتَ الْبَاقِيْ وَ أَنَا الْفَانِيْ وَ هَلْ يَرْحَمُ الْفَانِيْ إِلَّا الْبَاقِيْ
My Master, O my Master, You are the Permanent, and I am the temporary. And who can have mercy on the temporary except the Permanent?	مَوْلَايَ يَا مَوْلَايَ أَنْتَ الدَّآئِمُ وَ أَنَا الزَّائِلُ وَ هَلْ يَرْحَمُ الزَّآئِلَ إِلَّا الدَّآئِمُ
My Master, O my Master, You are the Sustainer, and I am the blessed. And who can have mercy on the blessed except the Sustainer?	مَوْلَايَ يَا مَوْلَايَ أَنْتَ الرَّازِقُ وَ أَنَا الْمَرْزُوْقُ وَ هَلْ يَرْحَمُ الْمَرْزُوْقَ إِلَّا الرَّازِقُ
My Master, O my Master, You are the Generous, and I am the miser. And who can have mercy on the miser except the Generous?	مَوْلَايَ يَا مَوْلَايَ أَنْتَ الْجَوَادُ وَ أَنَا الْبَخِيْلُ وَ هَلْ يَرْحَمُ الْبَخِيْلَ إِلَّا الْجَوَادُ
My Master, O my Master, You are the Healer, and I am the afflicted. And who can have mercy on the afflicted except the Healer?	مَوْلَايَ يَا مَوْلَايَ أَنْتَ الْمُعَافِيْ وَ أَنَا الْمُبْتَلَىٰ وَ هَلْ يَرْحَمُ الْمُبْتَلَىٰ إِلَّا الْمُعَافِيْ
My Master, O my Master, You are the Great, and I am the insignificant. And who can have mercy on the insignificant except the Great?	مَوْلَايَ يَا مَوْلَايَ أَنْتَ الْكَبِيْرُ وَ أَنَا الصَّغِيْرُ وَ هَلْ يَرْحَمُ الصَّغِيْرَ إِلَّا الْكَبِيْرُ
My Master, O my Master, You are the Guide, and I am the straying. And who can have mercy on the straying except the Guide?	مَوْلَايَ يَا مَوْلَايَ أَنْتَ الْهَادِيْ وَ أَنَا الضَّالُّ وَ هَلْ يَرْحَمُ الضَّالَّ إِلَّا الْهَادِيْ

My Master, O my Master, You are the Merciful, and I am the one shown mercy. And who can have mercy on the one shown mercy except the Merciful?	مَوْلَايَ يَا مَوْلَايَ أَنْتَ الرَّحْمٰنُ وَأَنَا الْمَرْحُوْمُ وَ هَلْ يَرْحَمُ الْمَرْحُوْمَ إِلَّا الرَّحْمٰنُ
My Master, O my Master, You are the Authority, and I am the tried. And who can have mercy on the tried except the Authority?	مَوْلَايَ يَا مَوْلَايَ أَنْتَ السُّلْطَانُ وَ أَنَا الْمُمْتَحَنُ وَهَلْ يَرْحَمُ الْمُمْتَحَنَ إِلَّا السُّلْطَانُ
My Master, O my Master, You are the Guide, and I am the confused. And who can have mercy on the confused except the Guide?	مَوْلَايَ يَا مَوْلَايَ أَنْتَ الدَّلِيْلُ وَ أَنَا الْمُتَحَيِّرُ وَ هَلْ يَرْحَمُ الْمُتَحَيِّرَ إِلَّا الدَّلِيْلُ
My Master, O my Master, You are the Forgiving, and I am the sinner. And who can have mercy on the sinner except the Forgiving?	مَوْلَايَ يَا مَوْلَايَ أَنْتَ الْغَفُوْرُ وَ أَنَا الْمُذْنِبُ وَ هَلْ يَرْحَمُ الْمُذْنِبَ إِلَّا الْغَفُوْرُ
My Master, O my Master, You are the Victor, and I am the defeated. And who can have mercy on the defeated except the Victor?	مَوْلَايَ يَا مَوْلَايَ أَنْتَ الْغَالِبُ وَ أَنَا الْمَغْلُوْبُ وَهَلْ يَرْحَمُ الْمَغْلُوْبَ إِلَّا الْغَالِبُ
My Master, O my Master, You are the Nurturer, and I am the nurtured. And who can have mercy on the nurtured except the Nurturer?	مَوْلَايَ يَا مَوْلَايَ أَنْتَ الرَّبُّ وَ أَنَا الْمَرْبُوْبُ وَ هَلْ يَرْحَمُ الْمَرْبُوْبَ إِلَّا الرَّبُّ

My Master, O my Master, You are the High-handed, and I am the humble. And who can have mercy on the humble except the High-handed?	مَوْلَايَ يَا مَوْلَايَ أَنْتَ الْمُتَكَبِّرُ وَ أَنَا الْخَاشِعُ وَ هَلْ يَرْحَمُ الْخَاشِعَ إِلَّا الْمُتَكَبِّرُ
My Master, O my Master, have mercy on me by Your Mercy, and be pleased with me by Your Magnanimity, Generosity, and Grace	مَوْلَايَ يَا مَوْلَايَ اِرْحَمْنِيْ بِرَحْمَتِكَ وَ ارْضَ عَنِّيْ بِجُوْدِكَ وَ كَرَمِكَ وَ فَضْلِكَ
O the Generous, Beneficial, Almighty, and Beneficient. By Your Mercy, O the Most Merciful	يَا ذَا الْجُوْدِ وَ الْإِحْسَانِ وَ الطَّوْلِ وَ الْاِمْتِنَانِ بِرَحْمَتِكَ يَآ أَرْحَمَ الرَّاحِمِيْنَ

By the Lord of the Kaʿbah, I have succeeded!

12. Maqām Imām as-Ṣādiq (A)

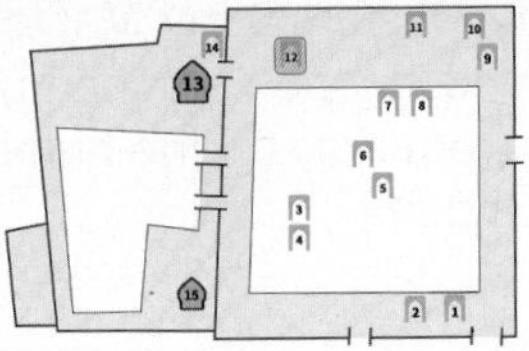

Then go towards Maqām Imām as-Ṣādiq (A). This is where the Imām (A) prayed and made duʿāʾ. Offer a two rakaʿāt prayer here.Then, recite a tasbīḥ and the following duʿāʾ. After the duʿāʾ, recite any duʿāʾ of your choice:

O Designer of all things! O He who fixes all broken things! O He who is present in all sessions! O He who witnesses all whispers!	يَاصَانِعَ كُلِّ مَصْنُوْعٍ، وَيَاجَابِرَ كُلِّ كَسِيْرٍ، وَيَاحَاضِرَ كُلِّ مَلَاءٍ وَيَا شَاهِدَ كُلِّ نَجْوَىٰ
O He who knows about all hidden things! O He who is always present and never absent! O He who always overcomes and is never defeated! O He who is always near and never far! O He who comforts all who are alone!	وَ يَا عَالِمَ كُلِّ خَفِيَّةٍ، وَ يَا شَاهِداً غَيْرَ غَائِبٍ، وَ يَا غَالِباً غَيْرَ مَغْلُوْبٍ، وَ يَا قَرِيْباً غَيْرَبَعِيْدٍ، وَ يَامُوْنِسَ كُلِّ وَحِيْدٍ
O He who existed when nothing else did! O He who brings the dead to life and causes the living to die!	وَ يَا حَيّاً حِيْنَ لَاحَيَّ غَيْرُهُ، يَامُحِيِيَ الْمَوْتَىٰ وَمُمِيْتَ الْأَحْيَاءِ
O He who supports every soul's earnings! There is no god except You. Send blessings upon Muḥammad and the household of Muḥammad.	اَلْقَائِمَ عَلَىٰ كُلِّ نَفْسٍ بِمَا كَسَبَتْ، لَا اِلٰهَ اِلَّا اَنْتَ صَلِّ عَلَىٰ مُحَمَّدٍ وَّآلِ مُحَمَّدٍ

Muslim ibn ʿAqīl

Muslim ibn ʿAqīl grew up amongst the youth of Banī Hāshim, especially his cousins Imām Ḥasan (A) and Imām Ḥusayn (A), and learned the traits of sacrifice and bravery from them. He was a noble young man during the time of Amīr ul-Muʾminīn (A) and married one of the Imām's (A) daughters, Ruqayyah.

During the imāmah of Imām ʿAlī (A), Muslim held an important position in the Imām's army during the years of 36-40 AH.

When the Kūfans sent letters inviting Imām Ḥusayn (A), the Imām (A) replied by sending Muslim as his ambassador. Eighteen thousand people paid their allegiance to Muslim. However, Ibn Ziyād managed to create mass fear and scatter Muslim's followers by threatening and bribing many of them. Soon, Muslim was left all alone in Kūfah to the extent that out of 18,000 people, only 30 people were left by Maghrib time, and at night, not even a single person remained.

Muslim took shelter in the house of a believer named Ṭawʿah. When his hideout was reported to Ibn Ziyād, he sent his troops to capture him. Muslim fought bravely until he was captured and taken to Dār al-Imārah (the governor's court). Here, they beheaded him and threw his body off the roof of the castle. They then sent the heads of Muslim and Hānī to Yazīd.

Muslim ibn ʿAqīl was martyred on the 9th of Dhūl Ḥijjah, 60 AH (day of ʿArafah) and was the first martyr of Imām Ḥusayn's (A) caravan.

Head towards the grave of Muslim ibn ʿAqīl. Before entering, say:

All praise is for Allāh, the Master of the evident truth!	اَلْحَمْدُ لِلّٰهِ الْمَلِكِ الْحَقِّ الْمُبِيْنِ
All the tyrannical oppressors are subservient to His Mightiness.	الْمُتَصَاغِرِ لِعَظَمَتِهِ جَبَابِرَةُ الطَّاغِيْنَ

All the inhabitants of the heavens and the layers of the earth admit His Lordship. All the created beings confess of His Oneness.	الْمُعْتَرِفِ بِرُبُوْبِيَّتِهِ جَمِيْعُ اَهْلِ السَّمَاوَاتِ وَالْاَرَضِيْنَ، الْمُقِرِّ بِتَوْحِيْدِهِ سَائِرُ الْخَلْقِ اَجْمَعِيْنَ
May Allāh send blessings upon the leader of all creations and the people of his household, the noble ones, such blessings that delight them	وَصَلَّى اللّٰهُ عَلَىٰ سَيِّدِ الْأَنَامِ وَاَهْلِ بَيْتِهِ الْكِرَامِ صَلَاةً تَقَرُّ بِهَا اَعْيُنُهُمْ
and humiliate all those amongst the humans and jinns who oppose them.	وَيَرْغَمُ بِهَا اَنْفُ شَانِئِهِمْ مِنَ الْجِنِّ وَالْاِنْسِ اَجْمَعِيْنَ
May the peace of Allāh, the Exalted and Supreme, and the peace of His closest angels, His missioned Prophets, His chosen Imams, His righteous servants, and all the martyrs and truthful ones	سَلَامُ اللّٰهِ الْعَلِيِّ الْعَظِيْمِ وَسَلَامُ مَلَآئِكَتِهِ الْمُقَرَّبِيْنَ وَاَنْبِيَآئِهِ الْمُرْسَلِيْنَ وَاَئِمَّتِهِ الْمُنْتَجَبِيْنَ وَعِبَادِهِ الصَّالِحِيْنَ وَجَمِيْعِ الشُّهَدَآءِ وَالصِّدِّيْقِيْنَ
and all blessings that are pure and delightful, that are coming and going, be upon you, O Muslim, son of ʿAqīl, the son of Abī Ṭālib, and the mercy and blessings of Allāh.	وَالزَّاكِيَاتُ الطَّيِّبَاتُ فِيْمَا تَغْتَدِيْ وَتَرُوْحُ عَلَيْكَ يَا مُسْلِمَ بْنَ عَقِيْلِ بْنِ أَبِيْ طَالِبٍ وَرَحْمَةُ اللّٰهِ وَبَرَكَاتُهُ

I bear witness that you established the prayers, gave alms (zakāt), enjoined good, forbade evil, strove in the way of Allāh in the best manner,	اَشْهَدُ اَنَّكَ اَقَمْتَ الصَّلَاةَ، وَآتَيْتَ الزَّكَاةَ وَاَمَرْتَ بِالْمَعْرُوْفِ، وَنَهَيْتَ عَنِ الْمُنْكَرِ وَجَاهَدْتَ فِيْ اللهِ حَقَّ جِهَادِهِ
and you were slain upon the path of those who strive until you met Allāh, the Lord of Might and Majesty, while He was pleased with you.	وَقُتِلْتَ عَلَى مِنْهَاجِ الْمُجَاهِدِيْنَ فِيْ سَبِيْلِهِ حَتَّىٰ لَقِيْتَ اللهَ عَزَّوَجَلَّ وَهُوَعَنْكَ رَاضٍ
And I bear witness that you fulfilled your oath to Allāh and sacrificed yourself for the sake of supporting Allāh's proof and the son of Allāh's proof (i.e., Imam al-Ḥusayn) until death came to you.	وَاَشْهَدُ اَنَّكَ وَفَيْتَ بِعَهْدِ اللهِ، وَبَذَلْتَ نَفْسَكَ فِيْ نُصْرَةِ حُجَّةِ اللهِ وَابْنِ حُجَّتِهِ حَتَّىٰ اَتَاكَ الْيَقِيْنُ
I bear witness that you submitted and were loyal and sincere to the representative of the Prophet and Messenger,	اَشْهَدُ لَكَ بِالتَّسْلِيْمِ وَالْوَفَاءِ وَالنَّصِيْحَةِ لِخَلَفِ النَّبِيِّ الْمُرْسَلِ
the select grandson (of the Prophet), the guide, the knowledgeable, the Prophet's successor, the conveyor (of his mission), the wronged, and the oppressed Imām.	وَالسِّبْطِ الْمُنْتَجَبِ، وَالدَّلِيْلِ الْعَالِمِ وَالْوَصِيِّ الْمُبَلِّغِ، وَالْمَظْلُوْمِ الْمُهْتَضَمِ

So, may Allāh reward you on behalf of His Messenger, on behalf of the Commander of the Faithful, and on behalf of al-Ḥasan and al-Ḥusayn	فَجَزَاكَ اللهُ عَنْ رَسُوْلِهِ وَعَنْ اَمِيرِ الْمُؤْمِنِيْنَ وَعَنِ الْحَسَنِ وَالْحُسَيْنِ
with the best of rewards that befits your steadfastness, reliance (on Allāh), and assistance. How excellent is the final abode!	اَفْضَلَ الْجَزَآءِ بِمَا صَبَرْتَ وَاحْتَسَبْتَ وَاَعَنْتَ فَنِعْمَ عُقْبَى الدَّارِ
May Allāh curse He who murdered you, He who ordered your murder, and whoever oppressed you.	لَعَنَ اللهُ مَنْ قَتَلَكَ، وَلَعَنَ اللهُ مَنْ اَمَرَ بِقَتْلِكَ، وَلَعَنَ اللهُ مَنْ ظَلَمَكَ
May Allāh curse He who forged lies against you, who ignored your rights, and belittled your sanctity.	وَلَعَنَ اللهُ مَنِ افْتَرَىٰ عَلَيْكَ، وَلَعَنَ اللهُ مَنْ جَهِلَ حَقَّكَ وَاسْتَخَفَّ بِحُرْمَتِكَ
May Allāh curse those who cheated you after they had sworn allegiance to you, those who disappointed and let you down, and those who allied against you instead of assisting you.	وَلَعَنَ اللهُ مَنْ بَايَعَكَ وَغَشَّكَ وَخَذَلَكَ وَاَسْلَمَكَ وَمَنْ اَلَبَّ عَلَيْكَ وَمَنْ لَمْ يُعِنْكَ
All praise is for Allāh, who made the hellfire an eternal abode for such people. Woeful indeed will be the place where they are led!	اَلْحَمْدُلِلّٰهِ الَّذِيْ جَعَلَ النَّارَ مَثْوَاهُمْ وَبِئْسَ الْوِرْدُ الْمَوْرُوْدُ

I bear witness that you were killed oppressively and that Allāh shall fulfill His promise to you.	اَشْهَدُ اَنَّكَ قُتِلْتَ مَظْلُوماً وَاَنَّ اللهَ مُنْجِزٌ لَكُمْ مَا وَعَدَكُمْ
I have come to visit you, aware of your rights, submissive to you, following your traditions.	جِئْتُكَ زَائِراً عَارِفاً بِحَقِّكُمْ مُسَلِّماً لَكُمْ تَابِعاً لِسُنَّتِكُمْ
I am preparing myself to support you until Allāh judges, and He is the best of judges.	وَنُصْرَتِي لَكُمْ مُعَدَّةٌ حَتَّىٰ يَحْكُمَ اللهُ وَهُوَ خَيْرُ الْحَاكِمِينَ
So, I am always with you and never with your enemies.	فَمَعَكُمْ مَعَكُمْ لَا مَعَ عَدُوِّكُمْ
May Allāh's peace be upon you and upon your souls and bodies and upon the present and absent ones among you.	صَلَوَاتُ اللهِ عَلَيْكُمْ وَعَلَىٰ اَرْوَاحِكُمْ وَاَجْسَادِكُمْ وَشَاهِدِكُمْ وَغَائِبِكُمْ
May Allāh's peace, mercy, and blessings be upon you.	وَالسَّلَامُ عَلَيْكُمْ وَرَحْمَةُ اللهِ وَبَرَكَاتُهُ
May Allāh kill the nation that has killed you with deeds and words.	قَتَلَ اللهُ اُمَّةً قَتَلَتْكُمْ بِالْاَيْدِي وَالْاَلْسُنِ

Then, enter and say the following:

Peace be upon you, O righteous servant of Allāh, who was obedient to His messenger, the Commander of the Faithful, Ḥasan, and Ḥusayn, peace be upon them.	اَلسَّلَامُ عَلَيْكَ اَيُّهَا الْعَبْدُ الصَّالِحُ الْمُطِيْعُ لِلّٰهِ وَلِرَسُوْلِهِ وَلِاَمِيْرِ الْمُؤْمِنِيْنَ وَالْحَسَنِ وَالْحُسَيْنِ عَلَيْهِمُ السَّلَامُ
All praise is for Allāh, and peace be upon His chosen servants, Muḥammad and his household.	اَلْحَمْدُ لِلّٰهِ وَسَلَامٌ عَلٰى عِبَادِهِ الَّذِيْنَ اصْطَفٰى مُحَمَّدٍ وَّآلِهِ

May Allāh's peace, mercy, blessings, and forgiveness be upon you, your soul, and your body.	وَالسَّلَامُ عَلَيْكُمْ وَرَحْمَةُ اللهِ وَبَرَكَاتُهُ وَمَغْفِرَتُهُ وَعَلَىٰ رُوْحِكَ وَبَدَنِكَ
I bear witness that you died for the same principles for which the martyrs of Badr, those who strove in Allāh's way, died	اَشْهَدُ اَنَّكَ مَضَيْتَ عَلَىٰ مَامَضَىٰ عَلَيْهِ الْبَدْرِيُّوْنَ الْمُجَاهِدُوْنَ فِيْ سَبِيْلِ اللهِ
and did their best in struggling against Allāh's enemies and in supporting Allāh's intimate servants.	الْمُبَالِغُوْنَ فِيْ جِهَادِ اَعْدَآئِهِ وَنُصْرَةِ اَوْلِيَآئِهِ
So, may Allāh reward you with the best, most abundant, most affluent reward that He grants to anyone who has fulfilled their allegiance to Him,	فَجَزَاكَ اللهُ اَفْضَلَ الْجَزَآءِ، وَاَكْثَرَ الْجَزَآءِ، وَاَوْفَرَ جَزَآءِ اَحَدٍ مِّمَّنْ وَفَىٰ بِبَيْعَتِهِ
responded to His invitation, and obeyed His representatives.	وَاسْتَجَابَ لَهُ دَعْوَتَهُ، وَاَطَاعَ وُلَاةَ اَمْرِهِ
I bear witness that you exerted all efforts in acting sincerely and you put forth all possible endeavors until Allāh raised you with the martyrs,	اَشْهَدُ اَنَّكَ قَدْ بَالَغْتَ فِيْ النَّصِيْحَةِ وَاَعْطَيْتَ غَايَةَ الْمَجْهُوْدِ حَتَّىٰ بَعَثَكَ اللهُ فِيْ الشُّهَدَآءِ
placed your soul with the souls of the delighted ones,	وَجَعَلَ رُوْحَكَ مَعَ اَرْوَاحِ السُّعَدَآءِ

and decided for you the most spacious abode in the gardens of His Paradise	وَاَعْطَاكَ مِنْ جِنَانِهِ اَفْسَحَهَا مَنْزِلاً
and the best rooms therein, and raised your name to the ʿillīyīn (the loftiest place),	وَاَفْضَلَهَا غُرَفاً، وَرَفَعَ ذِكْرَكَ فِي الْعِلِّيِّيْنَ
and added you to the group of the Prophets, the truthful ones, the martyrs, and the righteous ones. How excellent is the company of these people!	وَحَشَرَكَ مَعَ النَّبِيِّيْنَ وَالصِّدِّيْقِيْنَ وَالشُّهَدَآءِ وَالصَّالِحِيْنَ وَحَسُنَ اُولٰئِكَ رَفِيْقاً،
I bear witness that you never neglected or avoided your responsibilties	اَشْهَدُ اَنَّكَ لَمْ تَهِنْ وَلَمْ تَنْكُلْ
and that you died with insight regarding the commands you were given and following and emulating the path of the righteous ones and Prophets.	وَاَنَّكَ قَدْ مَضَيْتَ عَلَىٰ بَصِيْرَةٍ مِنْ اَمْرِكَ مُقْتَدِياً بِالصَّالِحِيْنَ وَمُتَّبِعاً لِّلنَّبِيِّيْنَ
So, may Allāh gather us with you and His Messenger and intimate servants in the abodes of the modest ones. Surely, He is the Most Merciful.	فَجَمَعَ اللهُ بَيْنَنَا وَبَيْنَكَ وَبَيْنَ رَسُوْلِهِ وَاَوْلِيَآئِهِ فِيْ مَنَازِلِ الْمُخْبِتِيْنَ فَاِنَّهُ اَرْحَمُ الرَّاحِمِيْنَ

1. Offer a two rakaʿāt prayer and gift it to Ḥaḍrat Muslim.
2. Recite the duʿāʾ that is recited after the ziyārah of Ḥaḍrat Abbās (See Karbalāʾ section).
3. When you are bidding farewell, recite the same farewell you recite for Ḥaḍrat Abbās, but instead of saying "قبر ابن اخي رسولك", say "قبر مسلم بن عقيل"– the grave of Muslim ibn ʿAqīl.

Mukhtār ibn Abī ʿUbaydah al-Thaqafī

Mukhtār ibn Abī ʿUbaydah al-Thaqafī was born in the first year of Hijrah. He was a young boy during the time of Imām Ali (A), and grew up in his presence. Although he was a devout shīʿāh, he was unable to participate in the battle of Karbalā', as he was imprisoned. Mukhtār was imprisoned twice by Ibn Ziyād. He was first imprisoned on the day of 'Ashura and again on the day of the Ṭawwābīn uprising.

After he was released from prison, he launched a campaign to avenge the killing of Imām Ḥusayn (A). After another unsuccessful uprising of the Ṭawwābīn, Mukhtār laid the foundation for the shīʿāh to rise up again. His army was called the Red Army and comprised of many other shīʿāh. Mukhtār's army was led by Ibrāhīm ibn Malik al-Ashtar. He knew that in order for such a movement to succeed, it would either need to be led by one of the Ahl al-Bayt (A) or at least be approved by them.

So, Mukhtār wrote letters to Imām as-Sajjād (A) and Muḥammad ibn Hanafiyya, the son of Imām ʿAlī (A). Imām as-Sajjād (A) had seen the lack of loyalty from the people and knew, based on his father's sayings, that these people only wanted the religion as long as it did not negatively interfere with their lives. Therefore, he did not directly answer the letter. So, Mukhtar went ahead with the uprising and was able to take revenge. When he sent the head of Ubaydullah ibn Ziyād to the Imām, the Imām fell into sajdah and said:

اَلْحَمْدُ لِلهِ الَّذِيْ أَدْرَكَ لِيْ ثَارِيْ مِنْ أَعْدَائِيْ وَ جَزَىٰ اللهُ الْمُخْتَارَ خَيْراً[1]

All praise is for Allāh who helped take revenge from my enemies, and may Allāh reward Mukhtār with the best.

Additionally, Minhāl ibn ʿAmr reports, "One year, I went to Hajj and saw ʿAlī ibn Ḥusayn (A). He asked me, 'What has happened to Ḥurmalah ibn Kāhil?' I replied, 'I have seen him alive in Kūfah.' Upon hearing this, the Imām (A) raised his hands and said, 'O Allāh! Make him feel the pain of burning metal!' When I returned to Kūfah, they had brought Ḥurmalah to Mukhtār. He ordered for his hands and legs to be cut off, and then burnt his body."[2]

Amongst our scholars, there is a difference of opinion in regard to Mukhtār and his uprising. Whereas some of our earlier scholars did not hold a good opinion about him, our more recent scholars, such as Allāmah Ḥillī, Muqaddas Ardabīlī, Shaykh Abbas Qumī, Allāmah Amīnī, and Ayatullah Khuī, mention his name with honor.

For many years, the public did not know the exact location of his grave until Allāmah Abdul Ḥusayn Tehranī ordered a search for the grave of Mukhtār. Under the supervision of Allāmah Sayyid Mahdī Baḥr al-ʿUlūm and Allāmah Tehranī, they dug up the eastern side of the old wall of Masjid al-Kūfah until they reached a plaque that said:

هَذَا قَبْرَالْمُخْتَارُ بْنَ اَبِیْ عُبَيْدَ ثَقَفِیْ

This is the grave of Mukhtār, son of Abī ʿUbaydah al-Thaqafī

1. Shaykh Ṭūsī, Ikhtiyār Maʿarifat al-Rijāl, Vol. 1, P. 341
2. Ibn Shahr Āshūb, Manāqib, Vol. 4, P. 331

Peace be upon you O righteous servant!	اَلسَّلَامُ عَلَيْكَ أَيُّهَا الْعَبْدُ الصَّالِحُ
Peace be upon you O sincere guardian!	اَلسَّلَامُ عَلَيْكَ أَيُّهَا الْوَلِيُّ النَّاصِحُ
Peace be upon you O Abā Isḥāq al-Mukhtār!	اَلسَّلَامُ عَلَيْكَ يَا أَبَا إِسْحَاقَ الْمُخْتَارِ
Peace be upon you who took revenge and fought the disobedient disbelievers!	اَلسَّلَامُ عَلَيْكَ أَيُّهَا الْآخِذُ بِالثَّارِ الْمُحَارِبُ لِلْكَفَرَةِ الْفُجَّارِ
Peace be upon you, O one who is sincere in obedience to Allāh and in loving Imām Zayn ul-ʿĀbidīn (A).	اَلسَّلَامُ عَلَيْكَ أَيُّهَا الْمُخْلِصُ لِلّٰهِ فِيْ طَاعَتِهِ وَ لِزَيْنِ الْعَابِدِيْنَ فِيْ مَحَبَّتِهِ
Peace be upon you, He who pleased the chosen Prophet, the judge between heaven and hell, and the one who dispels hardships and troubles,	اَلسَّلَامُ عَلَيْكَ يَا مَنْ رَضِيَ عَنْهُ النَّبِيُّ الْمُخْتَارُ وَ قَسِيْمُ الْجَنَّةِ وَ النَّارِ وَ كَاشِفُ الْكَرْبِ وَالْغُمَّةِ
And [the Prophet] who reached a status that none of the Imāms were able to reach.	قَائِماً مَقَاماً لَمْ يَصِلْ إِلَيهِ أَحَدٌ مِنَ الْأُمَّةِ
Peace be upon you, He who sacrificed himself to please the Imāms in aiding the pure progeny [of Prophet Muḥammad],	اَلسَّلَامُ عَلَيْكَ يَا مَنْ بَذَلَ نَفْسَهُ فِيْ رِضَاءِ الْأَئِمَّةِ فِيْ نُصْرَةِ الْعِتْرَةِ الطَّاهِرِيْنَ
and the one who took revenge for them from the cursed, transgressing gang.	وَالْآخِذُ بِثَارِهِمْ مِنَ الْعِصَابَةِ الْمَلْعُوْنَةِ الْفَاجِرَةِ
So may Allāh reward you on behalf of the Prophet and his holy household, peace be upon them.	فَجَزَاكَ اللّٰهُ عَنِ النَّبِيِّ وَ عَنْ أَهْلِ بَيْتِهِ عَلَيْهِمُ اَلسَّلَام

Mūsūʿah Ziyārat al-Maʿṣūmīn, Vol. 2, P. 361

The ḍarīḥ of Hānī ibn ʿUrwah

Hānī ibn ʿUrwah

Hānī ibn ʿUrwah was a close companion of Amīr ul-Muʾminīn (A) and among the elders of Kūfah, who was in charge of the Banī Murād tribe.

When Muslim ibn ʿAqīl came to Kūfah, he stayed with Hānī, who helped him gather weapons and an army. When ʿUbaydullāh ibn Ziyād began searching for Muslim and found out he was hiding in Hānī's house, he became very angry and asked for Hānī.

Hānī eventually confessed to housing Muslim, but refused to turn him in. Ibn Ziyād struck his head and face with his cane, breaking his nose.

Even though Hānī was the respected leader of his tribe, they dragged him across the floor, and ultimately, Hānī ibn ʿUrwah was beheaded on the 9th of Dhūl Ḥijjah, 60 AH, along with Muslim.

The news of their martyrdom reached Imām Ḥusayn (A) as he was headed to Kūfah with his caravan.

Stand next to the grave of Hānī ibn ʿUrwah and send your salām upon the Prophet (S) and recite:

May the peace and blessings of Allāh, the Supreme, be upon you, Hānī, the son of ʿUrwah.	سَلَامُ اللهِ الْعَظِيْمِ وَصَلَوَاتُهُ عَلَيْكَ يَا هَانِيَ بْنَ عُرْوَةَ
Peace be upon you, O righteous servant (of Allāh), who acted sincerely for the sake of Allāh, His Messenger, the Commander of the Faithful, al-Ḥasan, and al-Ḥusayn, peace be upon them.	اَلسَّلَامُ عَلَيْكَ اَيُّهَا الْعَبْدُ الصَّالِحُ النَّاصِحُ لِلّٰهِ وَلِرَسُوْلِهِ وَلِاَمِيْرِالْمُؤْمِنِيْنَ وَالْحَسَنِ وَالْحُسَيْنِ عَلَيْهِمُ السَّلَامُ
I bear witness that you were oppressively killed. So, may Allāh curse those who killed you and dared to shed your blood, and may He fill their graves with fire.	اَشْهَدُ اَنَّكَ قُتِلْتَ مَظْلُوْماً فَلَعَنَ اللهُ مَنْ قَتَلَكَ وَاسْتَحَلَّ دَمَكَ وَحَشَىٰ قُبُوْرَهُمْ نَاراً
I bear witness that you met Allāh while He was pleased with Your actions and sincerity.	اَشْهَدُ اَنَّكَ لَقِيْتَ اللهَ وَهُوَ رَاضٍ عَنْكَ بِمَا فَعَلْتَ وَنَصَحْتَ
And I bear witness that you have attained the rank of the martyrs and that your soul has been included with the souls of the delighted ones, for you strove sincerely for Allāh and His Messenger,	وَاَشْهَدُ اَنَّكَ قَدْ بَلَغْتَ دَرَجَةَ الشُّهَدَاءِ وَجَعَلَ رُوْحَكَ مَعَ اَرْوَاحِ السُّعَدَاءِ بِمَا نَصَحْتَ لِلّٰهِ وَلِرَسُوْلِهِ مُجْتَهِداً

and sacrificed yourself for the sake and pleasure of Allāh.	وَبَذَلْتَ نَفْسَكَ فِيْ ذَاتِ اللهِ وَمَرْضَاتِهِ
So, may Allāh have mercy upon you and be pleased with you, and may He include you with Muḥammad and his pure household,	فَرَحِمَكَ اللهُ وَرَضِيَ عَنْكَ وَحَشَرَكَ مَعَ مُحَمَّدٍ وَآلِهِ الطَّاهِرِيْنَ
and may He gather us with you and them in the Blissful Abode. May Allāh's peace, mercy, and blessings be upon you.	وَجَمَعَنَا وَإِيَّاكُمْ مَعَهُمْ فِيْ دَارِ النَّعِيْمِ وَسَلَامٌ عَلَيْكَ وَرَحْمَةُ اللهِ وَبَرَكَاتُهُ

Then, offer a two rakaʿāt prayer and gift it to Ḥaḍrat Hānī and ask for your wishes. Next, recite the duʿāʾ that is recited after the ziyārah of Ḥaḍrat Abbās. When you are bidding farewell, recite the same farewell you recite for Ḥaḍrat Abbās, but instead of saying "قبر ابن اخي رسولك", say "قبر هانيَ بن عروه."

Maytham al-Tammār

Maytham, son of Yahyā, was a slave from the Banī Asad tribe in the land of Nihrawān.[1] Some also consider him to be Iranian. Amīr ul-Mu'minīn (A) purchased and set him free. He was given the title al-Tammār, which means the one who sells dates, as this was his job.

When Imām ʿAlī (A) asked him for his name, he replied, "Salīm."

The Imām (A) then told him, "The Noble Prophet (S) has told me that your real name is Maytham (the name which was given to you by your parents).

Maytham replied, "The Noble Prophet (S) and Imām ʿAlī (A) speak the truth. My name is Maytham."

Then, the Imām (A) replied, "Indeed, your original name is better for you."[2]

Maytham was among the special companions of Imām ʿAlī (A) and learned many things based on his capacity. The Imām (A) also informed him of many secrets and hidden realities, as well as future

Shrine of Maytham at-Tammār

events to the point that even Ibn ʿAbbās took lessons from Maytham.

The author of al-Qarat writes, "Abū Khālid al-Tammār said, 'I was companying Maytham on a ship that was carrying pomegranates on the Euphrates River. He told us that Muʿāwiyah has just passed away. It was on Friday when the news of him passing away reached us. So, I did some research and figured out that the actual day and time of his departure was the time when Maytham had told us."[3]

Maytham was imprisoned by Ibn Ziyād at the same time as Mukhtār ibn Abī ʿUbayd ath-Thaqafī.

Shaykh al-Mufīd writes, "Maytham told Mukhtār in prison, 'You will rise up to seek revenge for Ḥusayn ibn ʿAlī (A) and will kill this person who wants to kill you now.' When Ibn Ziyād was about to kill Mukhtār, he received a letter from Yazīd to set Mukhtār free.'"[4]

One day, Imām ʿAlī (A) called Maytham and asked him, "O Maytham! If Ibn Ziyād summons you and asks you to abandon me, what will you do?"

Maytham replied, "O Amīr ul-Muʾminīn (A) I will never abandon or disassociate from you."

The Imām (A) said, "They will kill you and hang you from your date palm."

He said, "I will be patient."

Imām ʿAlī (A) said, "In this case, you will be with me in the hereafter."[5]
Many historians have reported that Imām ʿAlī (A) told Maytham how he

1. Nihrawān is a place in ʿIrāq located between Wāsit and Baghdād; it used to be part of Irān, and was captured by the Muslims on their first attack.
2. Ibn Ḥajar Asqalānī, al-Iṣābah, Vol. 6, P. 249
3. Thaqafī Kūfī, al-Ghārāt, P. 572
4. Shaykh al-Mufīd, al-Irshād, Vol. 1, P. 32
5. Thaqafī Kūfī, al-Ghārāt, P. 572

would be martyred:

"Once I am gone, they will capture you and hang you. On the third day, blood will flow from your nose and mouth and will dye your beard; you will be among those ten people who will be hung in front of Amr ibn Hārith's house. Your tree will be the shortest one." Then, the Imām (A) actually showed him the palm tree and said, "You will be hung from this tree."

After the martyrdom of Imām ʿAlī (A), Maytham used to come by that palm tree and would pray and talk with the tree. He would tell Amr ibn Hārith, "Soon, I will be your neighbor. Be a good neighbor for me."

Amr didn't know what he was talking about and asked him, "Do you want to buy Ibn Masʿūd's house or Ibn Ḥakīm's?"[6]

Maytham performed Hajj during his last year of life, and went to visit Umm Salamah in Madīnah. When he asked for news of Imām Ḥusayn (A), she told him, "I have heard the Noble Prophet (S) mention you to Amīr ul-Muʾminīn (A) many times, and Imām Ḥusayn (A) would mention you a lot as well."

When Maytham returned to Kūfah, Ubaydullāh ibn Ziyād captured him. This was 10 days before Imām Ḥusayn (A) entered the land of Karbalāʾ.

He asked Maytham, "Where is your Allāh?"

Maytham replied, "He is on the watch for the oppressors, and you are one of them."[7]

Finally, he was hung, just as Imām ʿAlī (A) had foretold, but even as they hung him, he wouldn't stop praising the Ahl al-Bayt (A) or stop mentioning the evil conduct of Banī Umayyah. Therefore, Ibn Ziyād ordered his men to cut off his tongue and kill him. He was the first Muslim to be martyred in such a manner.

6. Ibn Ḥajar Asqalānī, al-Iṣābah, Vol. 6, P. 250
7. Ibid

Ziyārah of Maytham at-Tammār

Peace be upon you, O Messenger of Allāh.	اَلسَّلَامُ عَلَيْكَ يَارَسُوْلَ اللهِ
Peace be upon you, O Commander of the Faithful.	اَلسَّلَامُ عَلَيْكَ يَاأَمِيْرَالْمُؤْمِنِيْنَ
Peace be upon you, O Fāṭimah az-Zahrā᾿, leader of the women of the worlds.	اَلسَّلَامُ عَلَيْكِ يَافَاطِمَةُ الزَّهْرَاءَ سَيِّدَةَ نِسَاءِ الْعَالَمِيْنَ
Peace be upon you, O Ḥasan and Ḥusayn, leaders of the youth of paradise.	اَلسَّلَامُ عَلَى الْحَسَنِ وَالْحُسَيْنِ سَيِّدَيْ شَبَابِ أَهْلِ الْجَنَّةِ
Peace be upon all the Imāms from the lineage of al-Ḥusayn. May Allāh's peace, mercy, and blessings be upon him.	اَلسَّلَامُ عَلَى الْأَئِمَةِ مِنْ ذُرِيَّةِ الْحُسَيْنِ عَلَيْهِمُ السَّلَامُ وَ رَحْمَةُ اللهِ وَ بَرَكَاتُهُ
Peace be upon you, O righteous servant, O Maytham, son of Yahyā, at-Tammār (the date seller),	اَلسَّلَامُ عَلَيْكَ اَيُّهَا الْعَبْدُ الصَّالِحُ يَا مَيْثَمُ بْنُ يَحْيَى التَّمَارِ

one who was obedient to Allāh, His messenger, the Commander of the Faithful, Fāṭimah, Ḥasan, and Ḥusayn.	الْمُطِيْعُ لِلّٰهِ وَلِرَسُوْلِهِ وَلْأَمِيْرِالْمُؤْمِنِيْنَ وَلِفَاطِمَةَ وَالحَسَنِ وَ الحُسَيْنِ
I bear witness that you established the prayer, gave charity (zakāh), enjoined the good, forbade the evil, and strove for the sake of Allāh is it ought to be striven,	أَشْهَدُ انَّكَ قَدْ أَقَمْتَ الصَّلٰوةَ وَ آتَيْتَ الزَّكَاةَ وَ أَمَرْتَ بِالْمَعْرُوْفِ وَ نَهَيْتَ عَنِ الْمُنْكَرِ وَجَاهَدْتَ فِيْ اللهِ حَقَّ جِهَادِهِ
and that you acted according to His book, taking the righteous as leaders and following the footsteps of the Prophets.	وَعَمِلْتَ بِكِتَابِهِ مُقْتَدِياً بِالصَّالِحِيْنَ وَ مُتَّبِعاً لِلنَّبِيِّيْنَ
And I bear witness that you were killed in a state of oppression,	وَ أَشْهَدُ انَّكَ قُتِلْتَ مَظْلُوْماً
so may Allāh curse whoever oppressed you, treated you ill, and commanded your murder.	فَلَعَنَ اللهُ مَنْ ظَلَمَكَ وَمَنْ اِفْتَرَىٰ عَلَيْكَ وَمَنْ أَمَرَ بِقَتْلِكَ
And may Allāh remove His mercy from whoever laid the grounds for your enmity and hatred until the Day of Judgment.	وَ لَعَنَ اللهُ مَنْ نَصَبَ لَكَ الْعَدَاوَةَ وَالْبَغْضَاءَ اِلَىٰ يَوْمِ الْقِيَامَةِ

And may Allāh fill their graves with fire and punish them with a severe punishment.	وَ حَشَا اللّٰهُ قُبُوْرَهُمْ نَاراً وَ أَعَدَّ لَهُمْ عَذَاباً أَلِيْماً
I have come to you, O righteous servant of Allāh, visiting your grave while acknowledging your right and recognizing your virtues.	جِئْتُكَ اَيُّهَا الْعَبْدُ الصَّالِحُ زَائِراً قَبْرَكَ مُقِرًّا بِحَقِّكَ مُعْتَرِفاً بِفَضْلِكَ
So, I ask Allāh by the honorable standing that you have with Him that He sends His blessings upon Muḥammad and the household of Muḥammad,	فَأَسْأَلُ اللّٰهَ بِالشَّأْنِ الَّذِيْ لَكَ عِنْدَهُ أَنْ يُصَلِّيَ عَلَىٰ مُحَمَّدٍ وَّ آلِ مُحَمَّدٍ
and that He grants us our wishes in this world and the hereafter.	وَ أَنْ يَقْضِيَ لَنَا حَوَائِجَنَا فِيْ الدُّنْيَا وَ الْآخِرَةِ
May the mercy and blessings of Allāh be upon you	وَ رَحْمَةُ اللّٰهِ وَبَرَكَاتُهُ

You may then recite a two rakaʿāt salāh and gift it to the soul of Maytham.

Dār al-Imārah

Dār al-Imārah, the governor's court, was built by Sa'd ibn Abī Waqqas in the year 17 AH. It is the oldest Islamic structure in ʿIrāq, after building the Masjid al-Kūfah. It is 100 m^2, and some of its original pillars and walls still remain today. Muslim ibn ʿAqīl was martyred in this castle, and the holy heads of Imām Ḥusayn (A) and the martyrs of Karbalāʾ were displayed here as well. Later, after Mukhtār's uprising, the heads of the killers of Imām Ḥusayn (A) and his progeny were displayed here. This castle is an excellent example for those who reflect. As the Qurʾān says:

فَاعْتَبِرُوا يَا أُولِي الْأَبْصَارِ

So take a lesson, O you who have insight! (59:2)

When Moṣʿab ibn Zubayr martyred Mukhtār, ʿAbd al-Malik ibn Marwān came to ʿIrāq and defeated him, and then entered the Dār al-Imārah. When they presented the head of Moṣʿab to him, a man named Abū Muslim Nakhaʿī stood and said to ʿAbd al-Malik, "I was in this Dār al-Imārah when the head of Imām Ḥusayn (A) was presented Ibn Ziyād, and after some time, the head of Ibn Ziyād was presented to Mukhtār, and later I saw Mukhtār's head presented to Moṣʿab and, now I see Moṣʿab's head presented to you!"

When ʿAbd al-Malik heard of this irony, he became frightened and ordered for Dār al-Imārah to be destroyed.

60 AH: Martyrdom of Muslim ibn ʿAqīl
61 AH: Martyrdom of Imām Ḥusayn (A)
66 AH: Death of Ubaydullah ibn Ziyād
67 AH: Martyrdom of Mukhtār al-Thaqafī
71 AH: Death of Muṣʿab ibn Zubayr
73 AH: Death of ʿAbdullah ibn Zubayr
86 AH: Death of ʿAbd al-Malik ibn Marwān

مسجد سهله

Masjid al-Sahlah

Illustrated Map of Masjid al-Sahlah

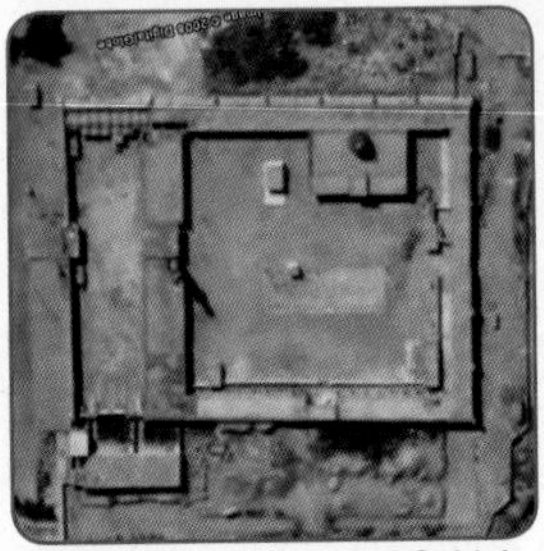

Aerial View of Masjid al-Sahlah

1 Maqām Imām as-Ṣādiq (A)

2 Maqām Prophet Ibrāhīm (A)

3 Maqām and House of Prophet Idrīs

4 Maqām Ḥaḍrat Khiḍr

5 Maqām of Ṣāliḥīn and Nabīyyīn

6 Maqām Imām Zayn ul-ʿĀbidīn (A)

7 Maqam Imām az-Zamān

Masjid Zayd ibn Ṣawḥān

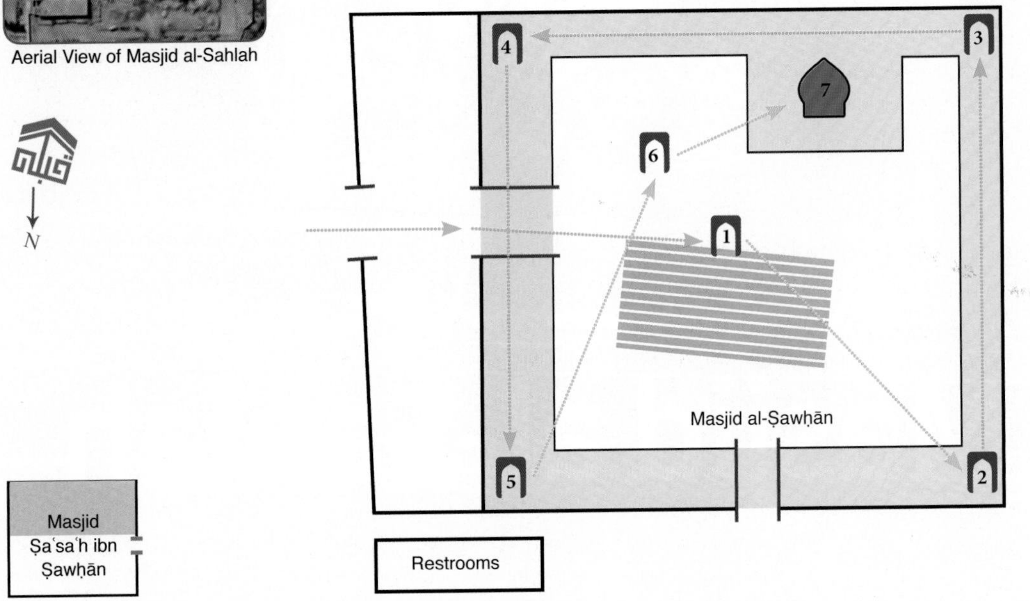

Masjid al-Sahlah

Masjid al-Sahlah is located about 2 kilometers northwest of Masjid al-Kūfah and was built by Arab tribes during the first century of hijrah. Some say it has been named after its builder, Saheel. The Masjid was built on the land where the Abdul Qays tribe lived, and Banī Zafar is a branch of this tribe. Therefore, it is also sometimes referred to as Masjid as-Saheel, Banī Zafar, and Abdul Qays.

Ibn al-Faqih narrates that Imām ʿAlī (A) said, "There are four places in Kūfah where four masaajid have been built." When asked about those four masaajid, the Imām (A) replied, "One of them is the Masjid of Zafar or Masjid al-Sahla."

The Virtues of Masjid al-Sahlah

After Masjid al-Kūfah, there is no other masjid as virtuous as Masjid al-Sahlah. Imām as-Ṣādiq (A) mentions some of its virtues below:

- It contains the houses of Prophet Idrīs (A), Prophet Ibrāhīm (A), and Ḥaḍrat Khiḍr (A)
- Imām az-Zamān (AJ) will live here with his family
- All 124,000 Prophets have prayed in this masjid
- Residing in this masjid is like residing in the tent of the Noble Prophet (S)
- Whoever sincerely recites du'ā' in this masjid will receive his/her answer (if it is khayr)

Then, Imām as-Ṣādiq (A) said, "If I were closer to this masjid, I would perform all my prayers in it. The virtues of this masjid are far greater than what I have told you."

Abū Baṣīr replied, "May my life be sacrificed for you! Will Imām az-Zamān (AJ) always reside in this masjid?"

The Imām (A) answered, "Yes. This masjid is among those places where Allāh likes to be worshipped."

According to Imām as-Ṣadiq (A), there is not a day or night that passes by where angels are not worshipping in this masjid.

Additionally, many of the 'ulama have met Imam al-Mahdī (AJ) in this masjid.

Imām as-Sadiq (A):

مَنْ صَلَّى فِي مَسْجِدِ السَّهْلَةِ رَكْعَتَيْنِ زادَ اللهُ فِي عُمْرِهِ سَنَتَيْنِ

If someone offers a two raka'āt prayer in Masjid al-Sahlah, Allāh will extend his life by two years.[1]

Prayer of Ḥājāt

It is a tradition of the Prophets and Imāms to offer a two raka'āt prayer in Masjid al-Sahlah between Maghrib and Isha prayers. It has been narrated by Imām as-Ṣādiq (A) that if anyone who is grieved performs such a prayer and then makes du'ā', Allāh will remove his pain and sadness.

1. Biḥār al-Anwār, Vol. 97, P. 436, Ḥadith #6
2. Ibid, P. 439
3. Ibid, P. 436

Āʿamāl of Masjid al-Sahlah

Before entering the Masjid, stand at the gate and recite:

With the Name of Allāh (I begin), in Allāh (I trust), from Allāh (I derive power), and to Allāh (I direct my affairs). Only that which Allāh wills shall happen, and the best names belong to Allāh.	بِسْمِ اللهِ وَبِاللهِ وَمِنَ اللهِ وَإِلَى اللهِ وَمَا شَآءَ اللهُ وَخَيْرُ الْاَسْمَآءِ لِلّٰهِ
I rely upon Allāh. There is no might or power except with Allāh, the Exalted, the Supreme.	تَوَكَّلْتُ عَلَى اللهِ وَلَاحَوْلَ وَلَاقُوَّةَ اِلَّا بِاللهِ الْعَلِيِّ الْعَظِيْمِ
O Allāh, place me amongst those who construct Your masājid and houses.	اَللَّهُمَّ اجْعَلْنِيْ مِنْ عُمَّارِ مَسَاجِدِكَ وَبُيُوْتِكَ
O Allāh, I direct my attention towards You, through Muḥammad and the household of Muḥammad, and I present them with my requests.	اَللَّهُمَّ اِنِّيْ اَتَوَجَّهُ اِلَيْكَ بِمُحَمَّدٍ وَّآلِ مُحَمَّدٍ وَّأُقَدِّمُهُمْ بَيْنَ يَدَيْ حَوَآئِجِيْ
So, O Allāh, by their right, make me worthy of Your regard in this world and the hereafter, and amongst those who are near to You.	فَاجْعَلْنِيْ اَللَّهُمَّ بِهِمْ عِنْدَكَ وَجِيْهاً فِيْ الدُّنْيَا وَالْآخِرَةِ وَمِنَ الْمُقَرَّبِيْنَ

O Allāh, by their right, accept my prayers, forgive my sins, increase my sustenance,	اَللَّهُمَّ اجْعَلْ صَلَاتِيْ بِهِمْ مَقْبُوْلَةً، وَذَنْبِيْ بِهِمْ مَغْفُوْراً، وَرِزْقِيْ بِهِمْ مَبْسُوْطاً
respond to my supplications, grant all my requests, and look at me with Your noble face so mercifully that I attain Your honor.	وَدُعَائِيْ بِهِمْ مُسْتَجَاباً، وَحَوَآئِجِيْ بِهِمْ مَقْضِيَةً، وَانْظُرْ اِلَيَّ بِوَجْهِكَ الْكَرِيْمِ نَظْرَةً رَّحِيْمَةً اَسْتَوْجِبُ بِهَا الْكَرَامَةَ عِنْدَكَ
And never turn it away from me, through Your mercy, O the Most Merciful. O the turner of hearts and sights, make my heart firm in following Your religion and the religion of Your Prophet and close guardian.	ثُمَّ لَا تَصْرِفْهُ عَنِّيْ اَبَداً بِرَحْمَتِكَ يَا اَرْحَمَ الرَّاحِمِيْنَ يَا مُقَلِّبَ الْقُلُوْبِ وَالْأَبْصَارِ ثَبِّتْ قَلْبِيْ عَلَىٰ دِيْنِكَ وَدِيْنِ نَبِيِّكَ وَوَلِيِّكَ
And do not cause my heart to deviate after You have guided me. And grant me mercy from You, for You are the most liberal Giver.	وَلَا تُزِغْ قَلْبِيْ بَعْدَ اِذْ هَدَيْتَنِيْ، وَهَبْ لِيْ مِنْ لَدُنْكَ رَحْمَةً اِنَّكَ اَنْتَ الْوَهَّابُ
O Allāh, I direct my attention towards You, seeking Your pleasure,	اَللّٰهُمَّ إِلَيْكَ تَوَجَّهْتُ، وَ مَرْضَاتَكَ طَلَبْتُ
desiring Your reward, having full faith in You, and relying on You completely.	وَ ثَوَابَكَ ابْتَغَيْتُ وَ بِكَ آمَنْتُ وَ عَلَيْكَ تَوَكَّلْتُ
So, O Allāh, turn Your face towards me and allow me to turn my face towards You.	اَللّٰهُمَّ فَاقْبِلْ بِوَجْهِكَ اِلَيَّ وَ اقْبِلْ بِوَجْهِيْ إِلَيْكَ

Then, recite Āyat ul-Kursī, Sūrat an-Falaq, and Sūrat al-Nās. Next, recite the following dhikr seven times:

All glory is due to Allāh. All praise is for Allāh. There is no god except Allāh. Allāh is the Greatest!	سُبْحَانَ اللهِ وَ أَلْحَمْدُ لِلّٰهِ وَ لَآ اِلٰهَ اِلَّا اللهُ وَ اللهُ اَكْبَرُ

Then, recite the following duʿāʾ:

O Allāh, all praise is for You, for You have guided me. All praise is for You, for You have favored me.	اَللَّهُمَّ لَكَ الْحَمْدُ عَلَىٰ مَا هَدَيْتَنِيْ وَلَكَ الْحَمْدُ عَلَىٰ مَا فَضَّلْتَنِيْ
All praise is for You, for You have honored me. All praise is for You for all the beneficial trials that You have bestowed upon me.	وَلَكَ الْحَمْدُ عَلَىٰ مَا شَرَّفْتَنِيْ، وَلَكَ الْحَمْدُ عَلَىٰ كُلِّ بَلَآءٍ حَسَنٍ ابْتَلَيْتَنِيْ
O Allāh, accept my prayer and supplication, purify my heart, expand my capacity, and accept my repentance.	اَللَّهُمَّ تَقَبَّلْ صَلَاتِيْ وَدُعَآئِيْ، وَطَهِّرْ قَلْبِيْ، وَاشْرَحْ لِيْ صَدْرِيْ وَتُبْ عَلَيَّ
Surely, You are the One who continuously accepts repentance and the Most Merciful.	اِنَّكَ اَنْتَ التَّوَّابُ الرَّحِيْمُ

1. Maqām Imām as-Ṣādiq (A)

Bashār Makārī narrates:
One day, I went to visit Imām Jaʿfar as-Ṣādiq (A) in Kūfah. The Imām (A), who was busy eating dates, said to me, "O Bashār! Come closer and enjoy some dates, too."
I replied, "Please, you enjoy. On my way here, I saw a scene that hurt my heart and made me lose my appetite."

However, the Imām (A) insisted that I eat some dates, so I began eating, too. Then, the Imām asked me, "What did you see while coming here that made you so upset?"

I said, "I saw that soldiers of the Sulṭān were beating a woman and dragging her to prison. She was begging for help, but no one was helping her."

The Imām asked, "Why were they hitting her?"

I said, "I heard from people that she had said. 'O Fāṭimah! May Allāh curse those who oppressed you!'"

When the Imām heard this, he stopped eating and started crying so much that his blessed beard and handkerchief became soaked. Then, he said to me, "O Bashār! Let's go to Masjid al-Sahlah and pray to Allāh for the release of that woman."

As we headed towards the Masjid, some shīʿah were also going to Dār al-Khilāfah to see what would happen to that woman.

When we reached the Masjid, each one of us offered a two rakāʿat of prayer in the corner. Afterwards, Imām as-Ṣādiq (A) raised his hands and recited this duʿāʾ:

أَنْتَ اللهُ لَآ إِلٰهَ إِلَّا أَنْتَ مُبْدِيْءُ الْخَلْقِ وَ مُعِيْدُهُمْ...

You are Allāh; there is no god except You. You initiated creation and will resurrect them...

Then, the Imām went into sujūd and recited a dhikr that I could not hear. Then, he lifted his head and said, "Get up! The woman has just been released."

We came out of the Masjid and came across someone who was returning from Dār al Khilāfah.

The Imām asked him, "What is the news of the woman?"

The man replied, "She was released!"

The Imām asked, "Why did they release her?"

He replied, "I didn't understand, but I was standing at the door of Dār al-Khilāfah when a guard came out and asked the woman, 'What did you say?'

The woman replied, 'I mistakenly said, 'O Fāṭimah! May Allāh curse those who oppressed you!''

The guard took out 20 dirhams and told the woman, 'Take this and ask the Sulṭān for forgiveness.'

The woman refused to take the money. When the guard saw this, he went back to Dār al-Khilāfah. After some time, he came out and told the woman that she was free and could go home, so the woman returned to her home."

Imām as-Ṣādiq (A) asked, "The woman refused to take the 20 dirham from him?"

The man replied, "Yes, by Allāh, even though she was in need of that money."

The Imām (A) handed me seven dirhams from his pocket and said, "Go to her home and convey my salām to her, and give her this money, too."

So, we went to her home and conveyed the Imām's salām to her. The woman replied, "I ask you by Allāh, did the Imām (A) really send his salām upon me?"

I replied, "I swear by Allāh, Imām as-Ṣadiq (A) sent his salām to you."

At this time, she gasped and fainted. We waited for her to regain consciousness. She then said, "What did you say? Can you repeat it?"

We repeated the message three times and then gave her the money and told her that the Imām (A) sent it for her.

The woman took the money and said, "Please ask the Imām to ask Allāh to forgive my sins. There is no better intercessor than him and his grandfathers!"

When I returned to Imām as-Ṣadiq (A) and told him what happened, the Imām made duʿāʾ for her while crying.

Muḥammad bin Jaʿfar Mashhadī, Al Mazār al-Kabīr, P. 136-140

Sayyid bin Ṭāwūs said: Go to Masjid al-Sahlah on Tuesday night because it is better than any other times. After reciting Maghrib prayers and its nawāfil, go to the middle of the Masjid (Maqām Imām as-Ṣādiq (A)) and offer a two rakaʿāt prayer with the intention of taḥiyyat al-Masjid. Then, raise your hand and recite the following duʿāʾ:

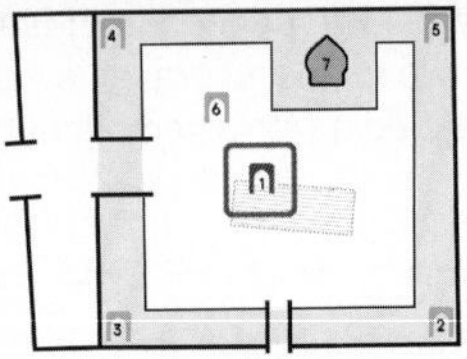

You are Allāh; there is no god except You. You are the Originator of creation and its repeater.	اَنْتَ اللّٰهُ لَا اِلٰهَ اِلَّا اَنْتَ مُبْدِئُ الْخَلْقِ وَمُعِيْدُهُمْ
You are Allāh; there is no god except You. You are the Creator of creatures and their Sustainer.	وَاَنْتَ اللّٰهُ لَا اِلٰهَ اِلَّا اَنْتَ خَالِقُ الْخَلْقِ وَرَازِقُهُمْ
You are Allāh; there is no god except You. You are the Straightener and the Expander. You are Allāh; there is no god except You. You are the Director of all affairs	وَاَنْتَ اللّٰهُ لَا اِلٰهَ اِلَّا اَنْتَ الْقَابِضُ الْبَاسِطُ، وَاَنْتَ اللّٰهُ لَا اِلٰهَ اِلَّا اَنْتَ مُدَبِّرُ الْاُمُوْرِ
and the Resurrector of those who are in graves. You are the Inheritor of the earth and whoever is on it. I ask You by Your Name: the Treasured,	وَبَاعِثُ مَنْ فِي الْقُبُوْرِ، اَنْتَ وَارِثُ الْاَرْضِ وَمَنْ عَلَيْهَا، اَسْاَلُكَ بِاسْمِكَ الْمَخْزُوْنِ،
the Concealed, the Ever-living, and the Self-subsistent. You are Allāh; there is no god except You. You are the Knower of secrets and what is hidden.	الْمَكْنُوْنِ الْحَيِّ الْقَيُّوْمِ وَاَنْتَ اللّٰهُ لَا اِلٰهَ اِلَّا اَنْتَ عَالِمُ السِّرِّ وَاَخْفَى

I ask you by that Name that You respond to when one calls You by it and You give to one who asks You by it.	اَسْاَلُكَ بِاسْمِكَ الَّذِيْ اِذَا دُعِيْتَ بِهِ اَجَبْتَ، وَاِذَا سُئِلْتَ بِهِ اَعْطَيْتَ
And I ask You by Your right over Muḥammad and his household and by their right over You, which You have made incumbent upon Yourself, to send blessings upon Muḥammad and the household of Muḥammad,	وَاَسْاَلُكَ بِحَقِّكَ عَلَىٰ مُحَمَّدٍ وَّاَهْلِ بَيْتِهِ وَبِحَقِّهِمُ الَّذِيْ اَوْجَبْتَهُ عَلَىٰ نَفْسِكَ اَنْ تُصَلِّيْ عَلَىٰ مُحَمَّدٍ وَّآلِ مُحَمَّدٍ
and that you grant me my requests in this very hour! In this very hour! O the Hearer of prayers! O my Leader! O my Master! O my Aide!	وَاَنْ تَقْضِيَ لِيْ حَاجَتِيْ السَّاعَةَ السَّاعَةَ، يَا سَامِعَ الدُّعَاءِ، يَا سَيِّدَاهُ يَامَوْلَاهُ يَا غِيَاثَاهُ
I ask You by all the Names that You use for Yourself and the Names that You take exclusively for Yourself in Your unseen knowledge that You send blessings upon Muḥammad and the household of Muḥammad,	اَسْاَلُكَ بِكُلِّ اِسْمٍ سَمَّيْتَ بِهِ نَفْسَكَ اَوِ اسْتَأْثَرْتَ بِهِ فِيْ عِلْمِ الْغَيْبِ عِنْدَكَ اَنْ تُصَلِّيْ عَلَىٰ مُحَمَّدٍ وَّآلِ مُحَمَّدٍ
And that you hasten our relief in this very hour. O the turner of hearts and sights! O the Hearer of prayers!	وَاَنْ تُعَجِّلَ فَرَجَنَا السَّاعَةَ، يَا مُقَلِّبَ الْقُلُوْبِ وَالْأَبْصَارِ، يَاسَمِيْعَ الدُّعَاءِ

Then, perform sajdah with humility and make duʿāʾ. Then, go towards Maqām Ibrāhīm.

2. Maqām Prophet Ibrāhīm (A)

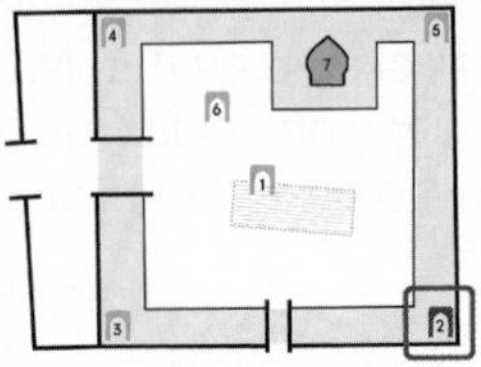

Go to the northwest corner of the masjid. This was where the house of Prophet Ibrāhīm (A) was. Offer a two rakaʿāt prayer here, followed by a tasbīḥ and the following duʿāʾ:

O Allāh, I ask you by the right of this sacred area and He who used to worship You here.	اَللّٰهُمَّ بِحَقِّ هٰذِهِ الْبُقْعَةِ الشَّرِيْفَةِ، وَبِحَقِّ مَنْ تَعَبَّدَ لَكَ فِيْهَا
Surely, You know my needs,	قَدْ عَلِمْتَ حَوَائِجِيْ
So send blessings upon Muḥammad and the household of Muḥammad and settle them (my needs) for me.	فَصَلِّ عَلٰى مُحَمَّدٍ وَّآلِ مُحَمَّدٍ وَّاقْضِهَا
And surely, you have accounted for my sins, so send blessings upon Muḥammad and the household of Muḥammad and forgive them.	وَقَدْ اَحْصَيْتَ ذُنُوْبِيْ فَصَلِّ عَلٰى مُحَمَّدٍ وَّآلِ مُحَمَّدٍ وَّاغْفِرْهَا
O Allāh, please only keep me alive as long as life is better for me, and cause me to die if death is better for me. And cause me to die while I am loyal to Your intimate servants and averse to Your enemies,	اَللّٰهُمَّ اَحْيِنِيْ مَا كَانَتِ الْحَيَاةُ خَيْراً لِيْ، وَاَمِتْنِيْ اِذَا كَانَتِ الْوَفَاةُ خَيْراً لِّيْ عَلٰى مُوَالَاةِ اَوْلِيَآئِكَ وَمُعَادَاةِ اَعْدَآئِكَ
and deal with me in the way that is befitting of You, O the Most Merciful!	وَافْعَلْ بِيْ مَا اَنْتَ اَهْلُهُ يَا اَرْحَمَ الرَّاحِمِيْنَ

3. Maqām & House of Prophet Idrīs (A)

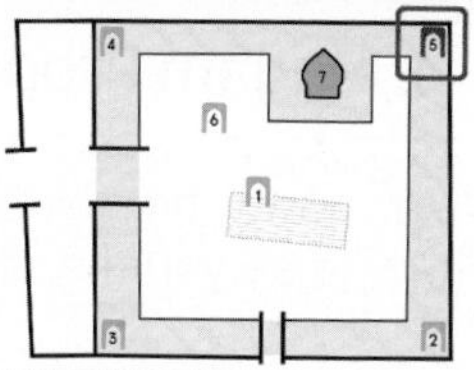

Next, go to the southwest corner and recite a two rakaʿāt prayer. Then, raise your hands and recite the following duʿāʾ:

O Allāh, I have offered this prayer seeking Your pleasure,	اَللّٰهُمَّ اِنِّيْ صَلَّيْتُ هٰذِهِ الصَّلَاةَ ابْتِغَاءَ مَرْضَاتِكَ
wishing for Your gift, and hoping for Your bounties and rewards.	وَطَلَبَ نَائِلِكَ وَرَجَاءَ رِفْدِكَ وَجَوَائِزِكَ
So, send blessings upon Muḥammad and the household of Muḥammad, and accept it (the prayer) from me in the best way.	فَصَلِّ عَلَىٰ مُحَمَّدٍ وَّآلِ مُحَمَّدٍ وَّتَقَبَّلْهَا مِنِّيْ بِاَحْسَنِ قَبُوْلٍ
And deliver my hopes to me, out of Your mercy,	وَبَلِّغْنِيْ بِرَحْمَتِكَ الْمَأْمُوْلَ
and deal with me in the way that is befitting of You, O the Most Merciful!	وَافْعَلْ بِيْ مَا اَنْتَ اَهْلُهُ يَا اَرْحَمَ الرَّاحِمِيْنَ

Next, go into sajdah, humbly place your cheeks on the turbah, and recite any dhikr.

4. Maqām Prophet Khiḍr (A)

Next, go to the southeast corner and offer a two rakaʿāt prayer. Then, raise your hands and recite the following duʿāʾ:

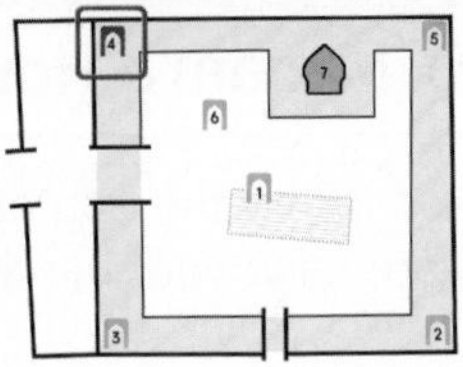

O Allāh, if my sins and faults have ruined Your image of me and hindered my voice from reaching You,	اَللّٰهُمَّ اِنْ كَانَتِ الذُّنُوْبُ وَالْخَطَايَا قَدْ اَخْلَقَتْ وَجْهِيْ عِنْدَكَ فَلَمْ تَرْفَعْ لِيْ اِلَيْكَ صَوْتاً
and they have prevented You from responding to my prayers, then I ask You in Your Name, O Allāh, for surely, there is nothing like You.	وَلَمْ تَسْتَجِبْ لِيْ دَعْوَةً فَاِنِّيْ اَسْاَلُكَ بِكَ يَا اللّٰهُ فَاِنَّهُ لَيْسَ مِثْلَكَ اَحَدٌ
And I seek the intercession of Muḥammad and his household to You, and I ask You to send blessings upon Muḥammad and the household of Muḥammad,	وَاَتَوَسَّلُ اِلَيْكَ بِمُحَمَّدٍ وَآلِهِ وَاَسْاَلُكَ اَنْ تُصَلِّيَ عَلَىٰ مُحَمَّدٍ وَّآلِ مُحَمَّدٍ
and to welcome me with Your Noble Face, to accept me turning my face towards You, not to let me down when I supplicate You,	وَاَنْ تُقْبِلَ اِلَيَّ بِوَجْهِكَ الْكَرِيْمِ وَتُقْبِلَ بِوَجْهِيْ اِلَيْكَ وَلَا تُخَيِّبْنِيْ حِيْنَ اَدْعُوْكَ
and not to deprive me (of Your response) when I please You. O the Most Merciful!	وَلَا تَحْرِمْنِيْ حِيْنَ اَرْجُوْكَ يَا اَرْحَمَ الرَّاحِمِيْنَ

5. Maqām as-Ṣāliḥīn & Anbīyyā᾽ (A)
The Station of the Righteous Ones and Prophets

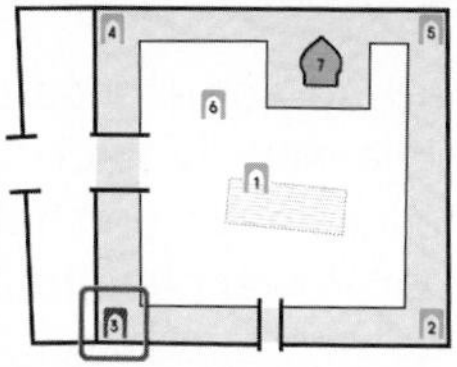

Go to the northeast corner of the masjid and perform a two rakaʿāt prayer, recite a tasbīḥ, and then recite the following duʿā᾽:

O Allāh, I ask You by Your Name, O Allāh, to send blessings upon Muḥammad and the household of Muḥammad,	اَللّٰهُمَّ اِنِّيْ اَسْاَلُكَ بِاِسْمِكَ يَا اَللّٰهُ اَنْ تُصَلِّيَ عَلَىٰ مُحَمَّدٍ وَّآلِ مُحَمَّدٍ
and cause the last days of my life to be the best of them, the last deeds of my life to be the best them, and the best of my days to be the day on which I meet You. Surely, You are Powerful over all things.	وَاَنْ تَجْعَلَ خَيْرَ عُمْرِيْ آخِرَهُ، وَخَيْرَ اَعْمَالِيْ خَوَاتِيْمَهَا وَخَيْرَ اَيَّامِيْ يَوْمَ اَلْقَاكَ فِيْهِ اِنَّكَ عَلَىٰ كُلِّ شَيْءٍ قَدِيْرٌ
O Allāh, accept my prayer and listen to my confidential speech. O the Exalted! O the Supreme! O the All-Powerful! O the Capable! O He who is Everliving and never dies!	اَللّٰهُمَّ تَقَبَّلْ دُعَائِيْ وَاسْمَعْ نَجْوَايَ يَا عَلِيُّ يَا عَظِيْمُ يَا قَادِرُ يَا قَاهِرُ يَا حَيًّا لَا يَمُوْتُ
Send blessings upon Muḥammad and the household of Muḥammad, and forgive those sins that are between me and You.	صَلِّ عَلَىٰ مُحَمَّدٍ وَّآلِ مُحَمَّدٍ وَّاغْفِرْ لِيَ الذُّنُوْبَ الَّتِيْ بَيْنِيْ وَبَيْنَكَ

And do not expose me in the presence of witnesses, protect me with Your Eye that never sleeps, and have mercy upon me with Your Power over me. O the Most Merciful!	وَلَاتَفْضَحْنِيْ عَلَىٰ رُؤُوْسِ الْأَشْهَادِ وَاحْرُسْنِيْ بِعَيْنِكَ الَّتِيْ لَاتَنَامُ وَارْحَمْنِيْ بِقُدْرَتِكَ عَلَيَّ يَا اَرْحَمَ الرَّاحِمِيْنَ
May Allāh send blessings upon our leader, Muḥammad, and his purified household. O Lord of the worlds!	وَصَلَّى اللّٰهُ عَلَىٰ سَيِّدِنَا مُحَمَّدٍ وَّآلِهِ الطَّاهِرِيْنَ يَا رَبَّ الْعَالَمِيْنَ

O my savior, O my guide
Where is it that you abide?
In this time that's darker than night,
you're my hope and my light

6. Maqām Imām Zayn ul-ʿĀbidīn (A)

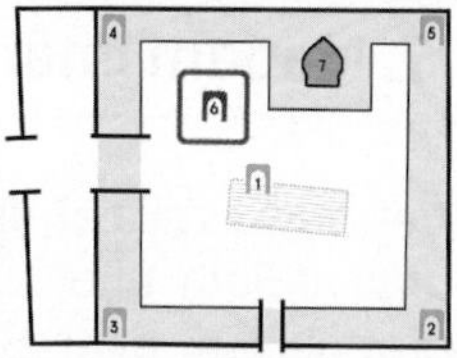

There is a house in the middle of the Masjid. Here, offer a two rakaʿāt prayer. Then, recite a tasbīḥ and the following duʿāʾ:

O He who is closer to me than my jugular vein! O He who does that which He wills! O He who intervenes between man and his heart!	يَا مَنْ هُوَ اَقْرَبُ اِلَيَّ مِنْ حَبْلِ الْوَرِيْدِ يَا فَعَّالًا لِّمَا يُرِيْدُ يَا مَنْ يَّحُوْلُ بَيْنَ الْمَرْءِ وَقَلْبِهِ
Send blessings upon Muḥammad and his household, and intervene between us and those who intend harm to us, through Your might and power. O He who is sufficient over all things and none is sufficient without Him.	صَلِّ عَلَى مُحَمَّدٍ وَّآلِهِ، وَحُلْ بَيْنَنَا وَبَيْنَ مَنْ يُّؤْذِيْنَا بِحَوْلِكَ وَقُوَّتِكَ يَا كَافِيْ مِنْ كُلِّ شَيْءٍ وَّلَا يَكْفِيْ مِنْهُ شَيْءٌ
Relieve us from those affairs that worry us in this world and the hereafter. O the Most Merciful!	اِكْفِنَا الْمُهِمَّ مِنْ اَمْرِالدُّنْيَا وَالْآخِرَةِ يَا اَرْحَمَ الرَّاحِمِيْنَ

Next, go into sajdah, humbly place your cheeks on the turbah, and ask for your wishes.

7. Maqām Imām al-Mahdī (AJ)

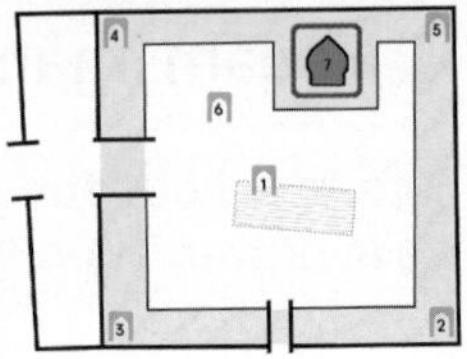

Offer a two rakaʿāt prayer (in the first rakʿah, it is better to recite Sūrat al-Fatḥ after Sūrat al-Fātiḥah, and in the second rakʿah, Sūrat al-Naṣr after Sūrat al-Fātiḥah). Then, stand and recite the following duʿāʾ:

May the most perfect, comprehensive and general salutation from Allāh,	سَلَامُ اللهِ الْكَامِلُ التَّامُّ الشَّامِلُ الْعَامُّ
and His eternal mercy and complete blessings be upon Allāh's proof and guardian in His land and countries and His representative over His creation and servants.	وَصَلَوَاتُهُ الدَّائِمَةُ وَبَرَكَاتُهُ الْقَائِمَةُ التَّامَّةُ عَلَىٰ حُجَّةِ اللهِ وَوَلِيِّهِ فِيْ اَرْضِهِ وَبِلَادِهِ وَخَلِيْفَتِهِ عَلَىٰ خَلْقِهِ وَعِبَادِهِ
And upon the offspring of prophethood and the remainder of the elite and chosen ones, the master of the time and the manifestation of faith,	وَسُلَالَةِ النُّبُوَّةِ وَبَقِيَّةِ الْعِتْرَةِ وَالصَّفْوَةِ، صَاحِبِ الزَّمَانِ وَمُظْهِرِ الْإِيْمَانِ
the teacher of the rules of the Qurʾān, the one who will purify the earth and will spread justice all over the world,	وَمُلَقِّنِ اَحْكَامِ الْقُرْآنِ، وَمُطَهِّرِ الْأَرْضِ وَنَاشِرِ الْعَدْلِ فِيْ الطُّوْلِ وَالْعَرْضِ
the upright proof, the guided, the awaited, pleased leader.	وَالْحُجَّةِ الْقَائِمِ الْمَهْدِيْ الْإِمَامِ الْمُنْتَظَرِ الْمَرْضِيْ

The son of the purified Imāms, the successor son of the pleased successors, the infallible guide and son of the infallible, guiding Imāms.	وَابْنِ الْأَئِمَّةِ الطَّاهِرِيْنَ الْوَصِيِّ ابْنِ الْأَوْصِيَاءِ الْمَرْضِيِّيْنَ الْهَادِيْ الْمَعْصُوْمِ ابْنِ الْأَئِمَّةِ الْهُدَاةِ الْمَعْصُوْمِيْنَ
Peace be upon you, O the one who will honor the oppressed believers! Peace be upon you, O the one who will dishonor the arrogant, oppressive infidels!	اَلسَّلَامُ عَلَيْكَ يَا مُعِزَّ الْمُؤْمِنِيْنَ الْمُسْتَضْعَفِيْنَ، اَلسَّلَامُ عَلَيْكَ يَا مُذِلَّ الْكَافِرِيْنَ الْمُتَكَبِّرِيْنَ الظَّالِمِيْنَ
Peace be upon you my master, O master of the time! Peace be upon you, O son of the Rasūl Allāh!	اَلسَّلَامُ عَلَيْكَ يَا مَوْلَايَ يَا صَاحِبَ الزَّمَانِ، اَلسَّلَامُ عَلَيْكَ يَا بْنَ رَسُوْلِ اللهِ
Peace be upon you, O son of the Commander of the Faithful! Peace be upon you, O son of Fātimah az-Zahrā', the leader of the women of the world!	اَلسَّلَامُ عَلَيْكَ يَا بْنَ اَمِيْرِالْمُؤْمِنِيْنَ، اَلسَّلَامُ عَلَيْكَ يَابْنَ فَاطِمَةَ الزَّهْرَاءِ سَيِّدَةِ نِسَآءِ الْعَالَمِيْنَ
Peace be upon you O son of the infallible proofs and Imāms, and the Imām of all of creation.	اَلسَّلَامُ عَلَيْكَ يَا بْنَ الْأَئِمَّةِ الْحُجَجِ الْمَعْصُوْمِيْنَ وَالْإِمَامِ عَلَى الْخَلْقِ اَجْمَعِيْنَ

Peace be upon you O my master, a salutation from one who is sincere in his/her loyalty to you. I bear witness that you are the guided Imam, both in words and actions,	اَلسَّلَامُ عَلَيْكَ يَا مَوْلَايَ سَلَامَ مُخْلِصٍ لَكَ فِيْ الْوِلَايَةِ، اَشْهَدُ اَنَّكَ الْإِمَامُ الْمَهْدِيُّ قَوْلاً وَفِعْلاً
and that you are the one who will fill the earth with peace and justice after it has been filled with oppression and injustice. May Allāh hasten your relief (reappearance), make your advent easy, bring your time near, increase your followers and helpers,	وَاَنْتَ الَّذِيْ تَمْلَأُ الْأَرْضَ قِسْطاً وَعَدْلاً بَعْدَ مَا مُلِئَتْ ظُلْماً وَجَوْراً، فَعَجَّلَ اللهُ فَرَجَكَ وَسَهَّلَ مَخْرَجَكَ وَقَرَّبَ زَمَانَكَ وَكَثَّرَ اَنْصَارَكَ وَاَعْوَانَكَ
and fulfill what He promised you, as He is the most truthful, who said: "And We wanted to confer favor upon those who were oppressed in the land and make them leaders and make them inheritors."	وَاَنْجَزَ لَكَ مَاوَعَدَكَ فَهُوَ اَصْدَقُ الْقَائِلِيْنَ وَنُرِيْدُ اَنْ نَمُنَّ عَلَى الَّذِيْنَ اسْتُضْعِفُوْا فِيْ الْأَرْضِ وَنَجْعَلَهُمْ اَئِمَّةً وَنَجْعَلَهُمُ الْوَارِثِيْنَ
O my master, O master of the time, O son of the Rasūl Allāh, my request/wish is...	يَا مَوْلَايَ يَاصَاحِبَ الزَّمَانِ يَابْنَ رَسُوْلِ اللهِ حَاجَتِيْ

Ask for your wishes here and continue to recite the duʿāʾ:

So intercede for me to attain my wish, for surely, I am turning towards you with my request knowing that your intercession is accepted and you have a praiseworthy position with Allāh.	فَاشْفَعْ لِيْ فِيْ نَجَاحِهَا فَقَدْ تَوَجَّهْتُ اِلَيْكَ بِحَاجَتِيْ لِعِلْمِيْ اَنَّ لَكَ عِنْدَ اللهِ شَفَاعَةً مَقْبُوْلَةً وَمَقَاماً مَحْمُوْداً
So, I ask you by the sake of He who singled you out [to execute] His commands and accepted you to keep His secret, and by your honorable status that is between you and Allāh,	فَبِحَقِّ مَنِ اخْتَصَّكُمْ بِاَمْرِهِ وَارْتَضَاكُمْ لِسِرِّهِ ، وَبِالشَّأْنِ الَّذِيْ لَكُمْ عِنْدَ اللهِ بَيْنَكُمْ وَبَيْنَهُ
Please ask Allāh, the Exalted, to grant my wish, answer my duʿā', and relieve my hardship.	سَلِ اللهَ تَعَالَى فِيْ نُجْحِ طَلِبَتِيْ وَ اِجَابَةِ دَعْوَتِيْ وَكَشْفِ كُرْبَتِيْ

Ask for your wishes and duʿā's.

Masjid Ṣaʿṣaʿah ibn Ṣawḥān & Masjid Zayd ibn Ṣawḥān

Ṣawḥān was a famous companion of Imām ʿAlī (A). A look at the life of Ṣawḥān and his sons depicts a clear picture of obedience and devotion to Imām ʿAlī (A).

These two old masājid are located close to Masjid al-Sahlah and are named after two loyal and sincere companions of Amīr ul-Muʾminīn (A).

Ṣawḥān had four sons who were all among the loyal companions of Amīr ul-Muʾminīn (A): Zayd, Ṣaʿṣaʿah, ʿAbdullah, and Sayḥān.

Ṣawḥān was a Jew who lived in Khaybar. Upon witnessing the Imām (A) lift the gate during the Battle of Khaybar, his son, Ṣaʿṣaʿah was amazed and embraced Islām. Ṣawḥān became very upset by this and said, "O my son! He is only able to lift the gate because he is a magician!" Still, Ṣaʿṣaʿah knew the truth and become a loyal companion of the Imām (A).

A few years later, Ṣawḥān travelled to Medina, looking for his son, Ṣaʿṣaʿah, whom he still loved very much. At this time, the Prophet (S) had died, and there was a struggle for the khilāfah. At this time, Ṣawḥān saw Imām ʿAlī (A) being dragged through the streets in chains. When he saw this, he immediately accepted Islām.

Ṣaʿṣaʿah asked, "O Father, what has made you accept Islām now?"

His father replied, "When I saw his miracle at Khaybar, I though he was a magician. But now that I have seen him stay silent, despite his great strength and power, in order to defend the truth, it is clear to me that he is the true leader. All the signs in our book clearly apply to him."

Ṣaʿṣaʿah ibn Ṣawḥān

Gravesite of Ṣaʿṣaʿah ibn Ṣawḥān

According to Imām as-Ṣādiq (A), "None of Imām ʿAlī's (A) companions recognized his rights the way Ṣaʿṣaʿah and his companions did.

Ṣaʿṣaʿah participated in all three battles with Imām ʿAlī (A). During the Battle of Jamal, after Sayḥān and Zayd were martyred, Ṣaʿṣaʿah upheld flag. During the Battle of Ṣiffīn, when Muʿāwiyah blocked the water for Imām ʿAlī's (A) army, the Imām (A) sent Ṣaʿṣaʿah to negotiate with Muʿāwiyah. He was also a negotiator during the Battle of Nihrawān.

Additionally, Ṣaʿṣaʿah was one of the only companions who carried the janāzah of Imām ʿAlī (A). After the Imām's death, Muʿāwiyah tried to have Ṣaʿṣaʿah curse Imām ʿAlī (A), but he refused and instead cursed Muʿāwiyah. Thus, he was exiled to Bahrain and passed away there in the year 56 AH. His grave is located south of Manama and is often visited by the believers.

Masjid al-Ṣaʿṣaʿah is a place where he used to perform ibādah. From our traditions, we also understand that Imām ʿAlī (A) prayed here, as well as Imām al-Mahdī (AJ), who also recited the special duʿāʾ of Rajab here.

Upon entering this masjid, one should offer two rakaʿāt of Taḥiyat-e-Masjid, recite the special duʿāʾ of this masjid, and recite the duʿāʾ for the month of Rajab.

Zayd ibn Ṣawḥān

Gravesite of Zayd ibn Ṣawḥān

It has been narrated that the Noble Prophet (S) had told Zayd, "A part of you will go to heaven before you." Sure enough, during the time of the third khalīfah, Zayd was exiled to Damascus, and his left hand was cut off during the conquest of Nahavand, a city in Irān. He was martyred in the Battle of Jamal.

It has been narrated from Imām as-Ṣādiq (A) that when Zayd fell on the ground during the battle, Imām ʿAlī (A) went to his side and cried out:

يَازَيْدَا! رَحِمَكَ اللهُ كُنْتَ خَفِيفَ الْمَؤْنَهِ عَظِيمَ الْمَعُونَةِ

O Zayd! May Allāh have mercy on you! You asked for so little, but gave so much.

Masjid al-Zayd has now become a part of Masjid al-Sahlah. The recommended aʿamāl for this masjid is two offer two-rakaʿāt of Taḥiyat-e-Masjid and recite the special duʿāʾ for the masjid.

قال رسول الله صلى الله عليه وآله

حسين مني وأنا من حسين

كَرْبَلَاء

Karbalāʾ

Karbalāʾ

Dear Zāʾir,

Welcome to heaven on Earth. Welcome to the sanctuary over which the angels fight to visit. Welcome to the land that witnessed the salvation of Islām. Welcome to the land whose tragedy will be avenged only with the advent of the Awaited Savior. As you tread these lands, let one of your main duʿās be for the return of the Imām and to be included amongst his companions, just like the 72.

Although many stores and hotels have been constructed in this area, and it may be different to one's imagination, remember that you are still walking in the same lands that Imām Ḥusayn (A) did.

In this city, you will find three primary landmarks:

- The holy shrine of Imām Ḥusayn (A)
- The holy shrine of Ḥaḍrat ʿAbbās
- Mukhayyam (Tent site)
- Till az-Zaynabīya (Hill of Zaynab)
- Sites of martyrdom
- Other holy landmarks

Inside the ḥaram of Imām Ḥusayn (A), you will find:

- The six-cornered ḍarīḥ, which contains:
    - The grave of Imām Ḥusayn (A)
    - The grave of Ḥaḍrat ʿAlī Akbar
    - The grave of Ḥaḍrat ʿAlī Asghar
- The ḍarīḥ of the companions
- The ḍarīḥ of Ḥabīb ibn Maẓahir (Men's side)
- The ḍarīḥ of Ibrāhīm al-Mujāb (Women's side)
- The Madhbah (Site of martyrdom)

Karbalāʾ

Karbalāʾ is located on the western side of the Euphrates River, about 67 miles (108 km) from Baghdād. Its history dates back to Babylonian times. Some historians assert that the word "Karbalāʾ" has been derived from the ancient Babylonian language and means "closeness to God"(قرب الله).

Other people date its history back to ancient civilizations, due to the various remains and ancient temples in the city. The word Karbalāʾ is a compound word of two Assyrian words: "karb" — meaning shrine — and "ill" — meaning God; hence, the combination results in "Shrine of God."

More famously, Karbalāʾ comes from the two words "Karb" (hardships) and "Balāʾ" (difficulties) beacuse when Imām Ḥusayn (A) reached this land, he asked what it was called. Upon hearing the name "Karbalāʾ," he said the following:

اَللَّهُمَّ إِنِّيْ أَعُوْذُ بِكَ مِنَ الْكَرْبِ وَ الْبَلَاء

O Allāh! Certainly, I seek refuge with You from the hardships and difficulties.

Other names for Karbalāʾ are "Tif" and "Hira" (known as "Hāʾir" today), which means "the land which refused to allow water into it." It was given this name because when the ʿAbbāsid khalīfah Mutawakkil ordered the holy shrine to be destroyed and flooded, the water miraculously stopped when it reached the holy grave, and instead went around it. This land was just a barren desert until the year 61 AH. However, after the tragedy of Karbalāʾ and construction of the holy shrines, it has become the center of pilgrimage in ʿIrāq.

رُويَ أنِ الإمامَ الحُسينَ (عليهِ السَّلام) اشترى النواحيَ
التي فيهَا قبرُهُ مِن أهلِ نينوا وَ الغاضريَّة بستينَ ألفَ دِرهم،
و تصدق بها عليهم، وَ شرطَ عليهم أن يرشدوا إلى قبره وَ
يُضيِّفوا من زارَه ثلاثاً

Imām Ḥusayn (A) and his caravan arrived in Karbalā᾿ on the 2nd of Muharram, 61 AH. According to some narrations, Imām Ḥusayn (A) bought a small piece of land, about 36 km² in size (about 14 mi²), for 6,000 dirhams from the people of Naynavā and Ghāziriyah. In the contract, he placed a condition that the sellers must guide the pilgrims in performing ziyārah of his grave and host them for three days. Today, that land is where Imām Ḥusayn (A) and his companions are buried.

Majma῾ al-Baḥrayn,Vol.4P.32, Ṭarīḥī

Today, the city of Karbalāʾ is about 43 km^2 (about 16 mi^2), and the barren desert that was once filled with sand and rocks has been replaced with buildings and gardens that are watered by the Euphrates River. There are two main roads leading into the city: one from Najaf and another from Baghdād, which is 97 km long (about 60 miles) and goes through the city of Musayyab.

Karbalāʾ can be divided into two parts: the older Karbalāʾ and the new Karbalāʾ (based on construction). The new Karbalāʾ contains tall buildings, wide roads, and most of the government buildings, religious schools, and other infrastructure.

The most well-known neighborhoods are Bāb as-Salālimah, Bāb at-Ṭāq, Bāb al-Baghdād, Bāb al-Khān, Mukhayyim, Bāb an-Najaf, and Eastern and Western ʿAbbāsiyah.

New provinces have also been added, such as the provinces of al-Ḥusayn (A), Muʿʿ Alīmān, al-ʿAbbās (A), an-Naqīb, Inqilāb, Ḥurr, and Ramaḍān.

Imām Ḥusayn (A): The Third Imām

Name:	Ḥusayn (A)
Kunyah:	Abū ʿAbdillāh
Title:	Sayyid ash-Shuhadāʾ
Parents:	Imām ʿʿAlī (A) & Sayyidah Fāṭimah az-Zahrāʾ(A)
Birthday:	3rd Shaʿbān, 4 AH
Birthplace:	Madīnah
Ring inscription:	إِنَّ اللهَ بَالِغُ أَمْرِهِ Certainly Allāh delivers His command
Number of children:	6
Duration of Imāmah:	10 years
Date of martyrdom:	10th Muharram (ʿĀshūrāʾ), 61 AH
Place of martyrdom:	Karbalāʾ
Cause of martyrdom:	Battle against army of Yazīd ibn Muʿāwiyah (May Allāh remove His mercy from them)
Life span:	57 years old
Holy shrine:	Karbalāʾ, ʿIrāq
Eras of his life:	■ Approximately 6.5 years during the Prophethood of Rasūl Allāh (S) ■ Approximately 31 years during the imāmah of Imām ʿAlī (A) ■ Approximately 9.5 years during the Imāmah of Imām Ḥasan (A) ■ Approximately 10 years during his own Imāmah

The Ṣalāh (Prayer) of Imām Ḥusayn (A)

Each Maʿṣūm has a special ṣalāh that can be found in Mafātiḥ al-Jinān.

The prayer of Imām Ḥusayn (A) consists of four rakaʿāt with two salāms (like two sets of Fajr prayers). In each rakʿah:

- Recite Sūrat al-Fātiḥah and Sūrat al-Ikhlāṣ 50 times each in qiyām (standing).
- Then, go into rukūʿ and recite each sūrah 10 times.
- Then, stand from rukūʿ, and recite each sūrah 10 times.
- Then, perform sajdah and recite each sūrah 10 times.
- Then, sit up in julūs, and recite each sūrah 10 times.
- Then, perform sajdah again, and recite each sūrah 10 times.
- Repeat this method in all four rakaʿāt.

After completing the prayer, recite the accompanying duʿāʾ, which can be found in Mafātiḥ al-Jinān.

History of the Shrine

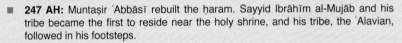

- **61 AH:** The Banī Asad tribe buried the holy bodies of Imām Ḥusayn (A), Ḥaḍrat ʿAbbās (A), and the other martyrs and built a shrine over them, under the guidance of Imām as-Sajjād (A).
- **65 AH:** Mukhtār ath-Thaqafī built a dome over the holy grave using bricks and plaster, and placed two gates around it.
- **132 AH:** Abū al-ʿAbbās Safāḥ expanded the haram by creating an adjacent annex next to the Imām's (A) holy grave.
- **146 AH:** Abū Jaʿfar Manṣūr destroyed the annex.
- **158 AH:** Mahdī ʿAbbāsī rebuilt the annex.
- **171 AH:** Harūn ar-Rashīd destroyed the entire shrine and cut down the cedar tree next to it.
- **193 AH:** ʾAmīn ʿAbbāsī rebuilt the shrine.
- **236 AH:** Mutawakkil ʿAbbāsī destroyed the shrine of Imām Ḥusayn (A) and plowed its land.
- **247 AH:** Muntaṣir ʿAbbāsī rebuilt the ḥaram. Sayyid Ibrāhīm al-Mujāb and his tribe became the first to reside near the holy shrine, and his tribe, the ʿAlavian, followed in his footsteps.
- **273 AH:** Muḥammad ibn Muḥammad ibn Zayd, the leader of the Tabarestan movement, gradually rebuilt the haram.
- **280 AH:** Dāʿī ʿAlavī built a dome over the holy grave.
- **367 AH:** ʿAḍud ad-Dawlah daylamī built a dome with four porches and a ḍarīḥ made of tusk, as well as towers and other construction in the city.
- **372 AH:** A 2,870 square yard (about 2400 m^2) wall was built around the city.
- **397 AH:** ʿImrān ibn Shāhīn built a masjid named after him next to the porches.
- **407 AH:** After two candles fell, the shrine was set on fire, but the minister of the time, Ḥasan ibn al Faḍl, rebuilt the shrine.
- **412 AH:** Ḥasan ibn al-Faḍl, the state minister of the time, built a second wall

around the city with four metal gates.

- **479 AH:** Mālik Shāh Saljūqī rebuilt the wall around the shrine.
- **620 AH:** Al-Nāṣir li-Dīnillāh ʿAbbāsī built a ḍarīḥ for the shrine.
- **767 AH:** Sulṭān ʾUways Jalāʾirī built the internal dome and a porch.
- **786 AH:** Sulṭān ʾAḥmad ibn ʾUways built two golden minarets and extended the shrine's courtyard.

- **914 AH:** Shāh Ismāʿīl Ṣafawī gilded the shrine's surroundings and gifted 12 golden lamps to the haram.
- **920 AH:** Shāh Ismāʿīl Ṣafawī constructed a box out of teakwood for the ḍarīḥ.
- **932 AH:** Shāh Ismāʿīl II gifted a beautiful silver ḍarīḥ to the ḥaram.
- **941 AH**: Shāh ʿAbbās Ṣafawī performed a pilgrimage to Karbalāʾ. During this time, he dredged the river and rebuilt the shrine of Imām Ḥusayn (A).
- **953 AH:** Shāh Suleymān Qānūnī made further repairs to the shrine and transformed the sandy lands around the area into gardens.
- **983 AH:** ʿAlī Pāshā renovated the dome.
- **1032 AH:** Shāh ʿAbbās Ṣafawī built a copper ḍarīḥ and tiled the dome.
- **1048 AH:** Sulṭān Murād IV ordered for the dome to be plastered from the outside.
- **1135 AH:** Nādir Shāh's wife donated significant funds for the renovation and extension of the holy shrine.
- **1155 AH**: Nādir Shāh ʾAfshār adorned the existing buildings and donated expensive gifts to the shrine.
- **1211 AH:** Āghā Muḥammad Khān Qājār ordered the dome to be covered in gold.
- **1216 AH:** Wahhabis attacked Karbalāʾ, destroying the ḍarīḥ and the courtyard, and stole its properties. After the attack, an Indian ruler built beautiful homes and bazaars (shops) in Karbalāʾ. He also built a stronger wall around the city.
- **1217 AH:** Sayyid ʿAlī Tabātabāʿi, author of *Al-Riyāḍ*, built a fourth wall around the city with six gates.
- **1227 AH:** Fatḥʿalī Shāh Qājār ordered for the haram to be renovated and replaceds the golden plates atop the dome.
- **1232 AH:** Fatḥʿalī Shāh Qājār built a silver ḍarīḥ and gilded the courtyard.
- **1250 AH:** Fatḥʿalī Shāh Qājār renovated the dome and the courtyard and constructed the dome of Ḥaḍrat ʿAbbās's (A) shrine as well.
- **1273 AH:** Nāṣir ad-Dīn Shāh renovated the dome of the shrine of Imām Ḥusayn (A) and part of its gildings.
- **1276 AH:** Telegraph lines were established in Karbalāʾ, connecting it to the rest of the world.

- **1285 AH:** Midḥat Pāshā set up government buildings and expanded the city.
- **1333 AH:** After World War I, the city of Karbalāʾ was extended with new buildings and wider roads.
- **1418 AH:** Due to the Intifāḍah, many people took refuge in the shrine, but the tyrant Saddam Hussein fired a cannon at the holy dome, destroying a part of its gilding. He then opened fire on people, causing mass bloodshed. The bullet holes are still visible inside the holy shrine.
- **1428 AH:** In order to enhance the usage of the courtyard and protect the pilgrims from harsh weather, a roof was built over the courtyard.
- **1431 AH:** The minarets of the shrine of Ḥaḍrat ʿAbbās (A) were gilded.

Intifāḍah Shaʿbāniyah

The Intifāḍah Shaʿbāniyah, which took place in 1991, was a very significant event for the ʿIrāqi peple. From 1979 to 2003, ʿIrāq was ruled by the evil tyrant Saddam Hussein, who brutally tortured many Muslims, especially the Shīʿah. In the year 1991, Saddam attacked Kuwait, but was defeated.

Several days after the army was defeated in Kuwait and left in a vulnerable state, the ʿIrāqi people decided to revolt against his oppressive regime. The Shīʿah were quickly able to gain control over many cities, such as Kirkuk, and the Baʿth regime was very close to being overthrown.

US politicians grew worried about the Shīʿah gaining power, and thus granted the Baʿth regime access to American helicopters. Through this action, they essentially gave them the green light to destroy the Shīʿah uprising. In addition to the helicopters, Saddam's army also used tanks to suppress the revolts. Even from within the Shīʿah, some turned against them and joined the Ba'athists.

During the Intifāḍah, tens of thousands of Shīʿah within the deserts, cities, and prisons were martyred. This event is marked as a "Day of Resistance" in ʿIrāq and served as a catalyst in overthrowing the oppressive regime of Saddam Hussein.

➢ Al-Qiblah Gate of the shrine of Ḥaḍrat ʿAbbās (A)

After destroying the shrine and killing Shīʿah, the army of Saddam Hussein take photos of their destruction.

Holy Sites and Map of Karbalāʾ

1 Holy Shrine of Imām Ḥusayn (A)

2 Holy Shrine of Ḥaḍrat ʿAbbās (A)

3 The Hill of Zaynab (A) (التِّلّ الزَّيْنَبِي)

4 Tent Site (مُخَيَّم)

5 Maqām of al-ʿAbbās's Left Hand (الكَفّ العَبّاس)

6 Maqām of al-ʿAbbās's Right Hand (الكَفّ العَبّاس)

7 Lion of Lady Fiḍḍah

8 Maqām of Ṣāḥib az-Zamān

9 Meeting Spot of Imām Ḥusayn (A) & ʿUmar ibn Sāʿad

10 Maqām of ʿAlī al-Akbar

11 Maqām of ʿAlī al-Aṣghar

12 Ibn Ḥamzah Shrine

13 Maqām of Imām aṣ-Ṣādiq (A)

14 Ibn Fahad al-Ḥilli shrine

15 Maqām of Imām Mūsā al-Kāẓim (A)

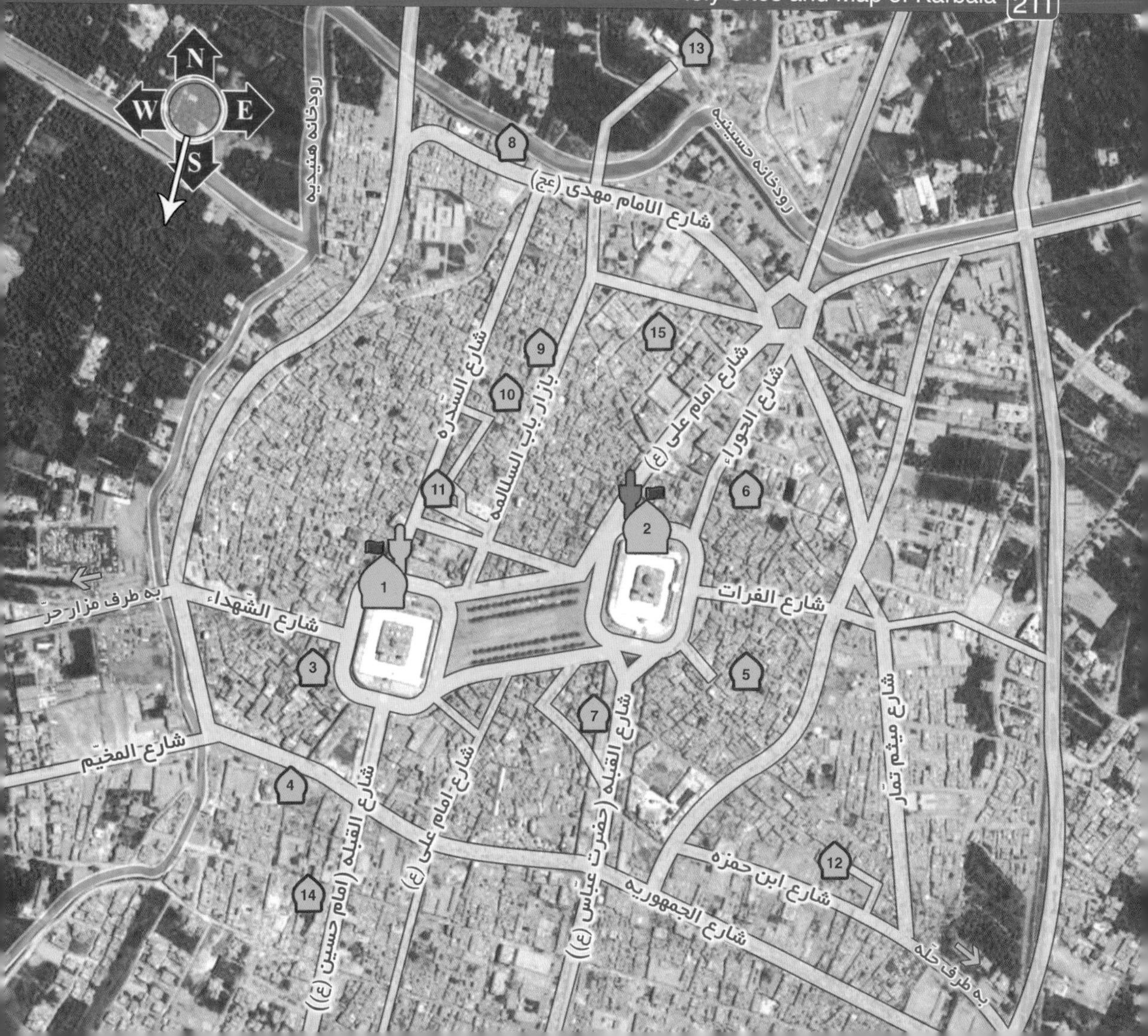
N
W
E
S
رودخانه هندیه
رودخانه حسینیه
شارع الامام مهدی (عج)
13
8
15
9
10
11
6
2
1
3
5
7
4
12
14
شارع السدره
بازار باب السلامه
شارع امام علی (ع)
شارع الحوراء
شارع الفرات
به طرف مزار حرّ
شارع الشّهداء
شارع المخیّم
شارع القبله (امام حسین (ع))
شارع امام علی (ع)
شارع القبله (حضرت عبّاس (ع))
شارع میثم تمّار
شارع ابن حمزه
شارع الجمهوریه
به طرف حلّه

Map of the Holy Shrine of Imām Ḥusayn (A)

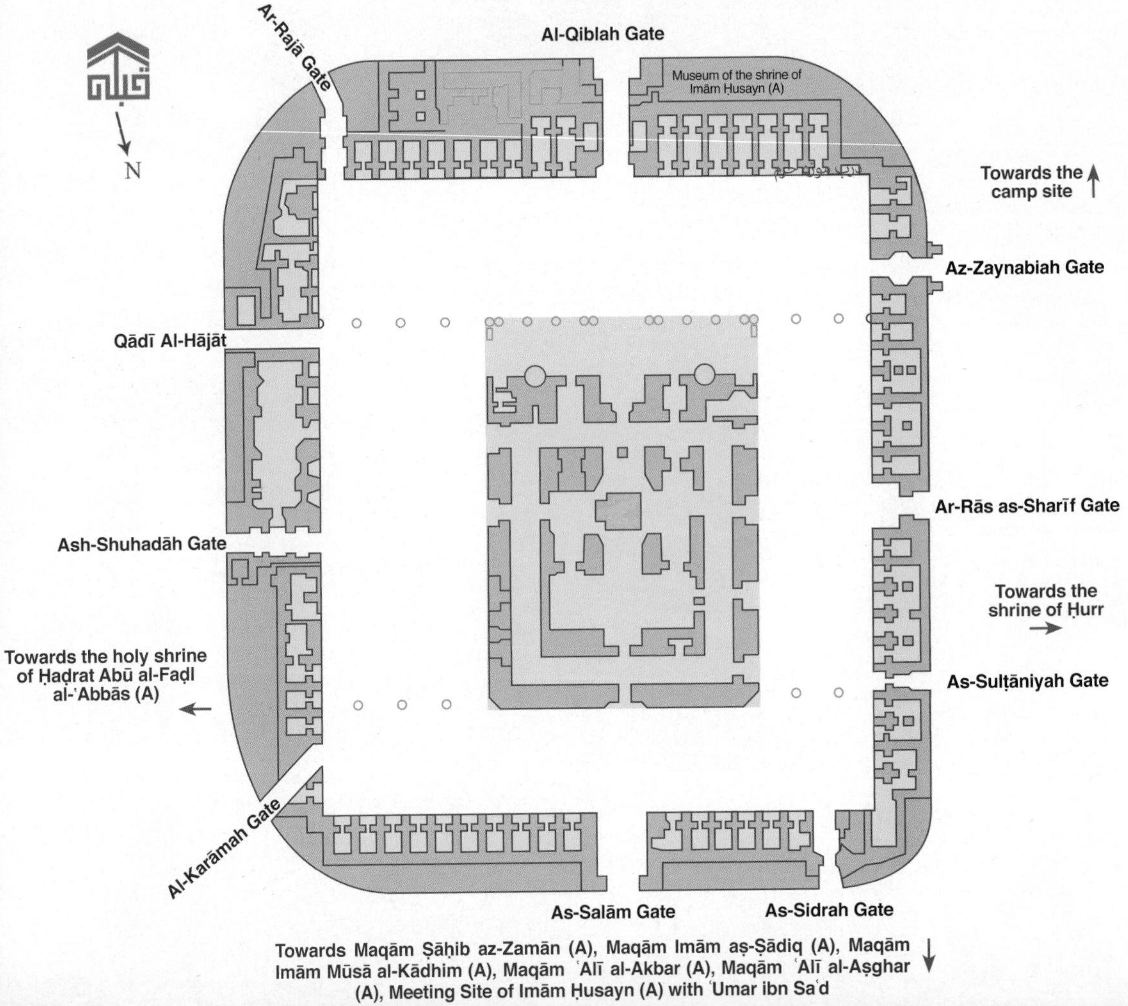
N
Ar-Rajā Gate
Al-Qiblah Gate
Museum of the shrine of Imām Ḥusayn (A)
Towards the camp site
Az-Zaynabiah Gate
Qādī Al-Ḥājāt
Ar-Rās as-Sharīf Gate
Ash-Shuhadāh Gate
Towards the shrine of Ḥurr
Towards the holy shrine of Ḥaḍrat Abū al-Faḍl al-ʿAbbās (A)
As-Sulṭāniyah Gate
Al-Karāmah Gate
As-Salām Gate
As-Sidrah Gate
Towards Maqām Ṣāḥib az-Zamān (A), Maqām Imām aṣ-Ṣādiq (A), Maqām Imām Mūsā al-Kādhim (A), Maqām ʿAlī al-Akbar (A), Maqām ʿAlī al-Aṣghar (A), Meeting Site of Imām Ḥusayn (A) with ʿUmar ibn Saʿd

Gates of the Holy Shrine of Imām Ḥusayn (A)

Qāḍī Al-Ḥājāt Gate
بَاب قَاضِي الحاجَات

Ar-Rajāʾ Gate
بَاب الرَّجَاء

Al-Qiblah Gate
بَاب القِبْلَة

Az-Zaynabiyyah Gate
بَاب الزَّيْنَبِيَّة

Ar-Rās as-Sharīf Gate
بَاب الرَّأس الشَّرِيف

As-Sulṭāniyyah Gate
بَاب السُّلْطَانِيَّة

As-Sidrah Gate
بَاب السِّدْرَة

As-Salām Gate
بَاب السَّلَام

Al-Karāmah Gate
بَاب الكَرَامَة

Ash-Shuhadāʾ Gate
بَاب الشُّهَدَاء

قَالَ رَسُولُ اللهِ ﷺ: «إِنَّ الْحُسَيْنَ بْنَ عَلِيٍّ فِي السَّمَاءِ أَكْبَرُ مِنْهُ فِي الْأَرْضِ وَإِنَّهُ لَمَكْتُوبٌ عَنْ يَمِينِ عَرْشِ اللهِ عَزَّ وَجَلَّ مِصْبَاحُ هُدًى وَسَفِينَةُ نَجَاةٍ»

Prophet Muḥammad (S):
Indeed, Ḥusayn ibn ʿAlī (A) is greater in the heavens than on the earth. Indeed, it is written on the right side of the ʿarsh (throne) that Ḥusayn (A) is the lantern of guidance and the ark of salvation.

الحسين مصباح الهدى وسفينة النجاة

Bāb as-Sidrah

عَنْ يَحْيَ بْنِ الْمُغِيْرَةِ الرَّازِيِّ : قَالَ : كُنْتُ عِنْدَ جَرِيْرِ بْنِ عَبْدِ الْحَمِيْدِ إِذْ جَاءَهُ رَجُلٌ مِنْ أَهْلِ الْعِرَاقِ فَسَأَلَهُ جَرِيْرٌ عَنْ خَبَرِ النَّاسِ فَقَالَ تَرَكْتُ الرَّشِيْدَ وَ قَدْ كَرَبَ قَبْرَالْحُسَيْنِ وَ أَمَرَ أَنْ تُقْطَعَ السِّدْرَةُ الَّتِيَ فِيْهِ فَقُطِعَتْ.

قَالَ فَرَفَعَ جَرِيْرٌ يَدَيْهِ وَ قَالَ اللهُ أَكْبَرُ جَاءَنَا فِيهِ حَدِيْثٌ عَنْ رَسُولِ اللهَ أَنَّهُ قَالَ : (لَعَنَ اللهُ قَاطِعَ السِّدْرَةِ) ثَلَاثاً فَلَمْ نَقِفْ عَلَى مَعْنَاهُ حَتَّى الْآنَ لِأَنَّ الْقَصْدَ بِقَطْعِهِ تَغْيِرُ مَصْرَعِ الْحُسَيْنِ حَتَّى لَايَقِفَ النَّاسُ عَلَى قَبْرِهِ.

Yaḥyā ibn al-Mughīrah ar-Rāzī has narrated:

I was near Jarīr ibn ʿAbd al-Ḥamīd, when a person from ʿIrāq entered.

Jarīr asked, “What is the latest news in ʿIrāq?”

It was replied, “Hārūn ar-Rashīd has ordered for the cedar tree of Karbalāʾ to be cut down.”

Jarīr replied, “Allāhu Akbar! There is a narration from the Prophet (S) where he said three times, ‘May the curse of Allāh be upon the one who cuts down the cedar tree!’ Now we understand the meaning of this ḥadīth.”[1]

The cedar tree marked the grave of Abā ʿAbd Allāh and was located near Bāb as-Sidrah. Hārūn ar-Rashīd cut down the tree because he did not want anyone to visit the grave of Abā ʿAbd Allāh.

[1] Al-Amālī, P. 325, Shaykh at-Ṭūsī

Interior Map of the Shrine of Imām Ḥusayn (A)

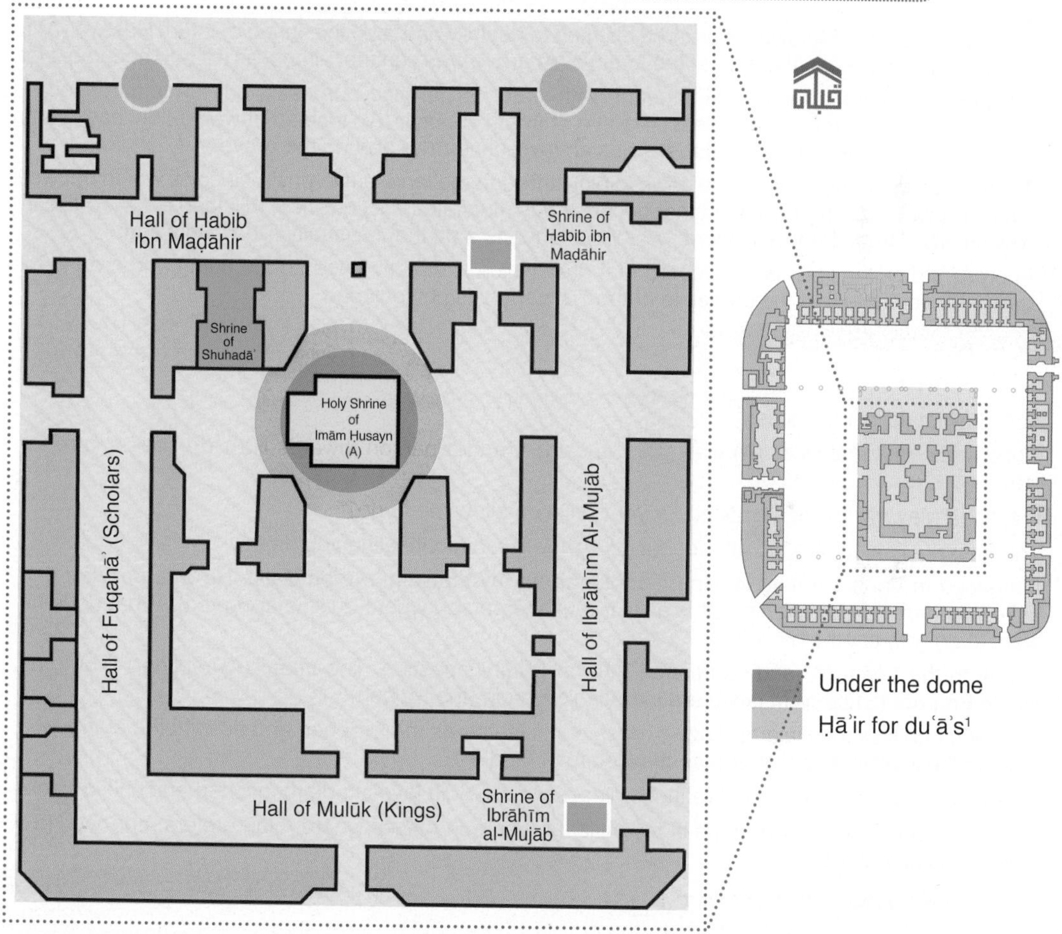

[1]According to some narrations, the Hā'ir encompasses the entire room where the ḍarīḥ is; thus, it is good to recite du'ā's in the entire room. However, for performing ṣalāh, please refer to the rulings of your marja'.

Hā̓ir al-Ḥusaynī: A Place Where Du̒ā̓s Are Accepted

In the year 236 AH, Mutawakkil ordered his men to destroy and raze the shrine of Imām Ḥusayn (A) to the ground. As a result, the area of the Imām's (A) grave was sunken, almost as if it had become a pit.

He then commanded them to till the land with water for farming purposes, but to his surprise, the water would not enter into the blessed grave of Imām Ḥusayn (A); instead, it would flow backwards or around the grave, almost as if there was an invisible barrier around the grave.

Then, he ordered them to release cows to plow through the land, but even those cows would not walk over the grave.[1] Some have said that because this miraculous occurrence, this land is called "Ḥā'ir", which comes from the Arabic word "حَيْر", which means a pit that is usually filled with water.[2]

In present day, the Ḥā'ir is considered that area which is directly beneath the dome and around the ḍarīḥ. Please note that the gravesite of the 72 martyrs is not included.

1. Biḥār al-Anwār Vol. 98, P. 117
2. Ṣaḥāḥ al-Lughah wa Miṣbāḥ al-Munīr

Abū Hāshim Ja̒farī narrates:

Once, while Imām al-Hādī (A) was sick, he said, "Send a person towards Hā'ir (to seek a cure for me)."

I replied, "May my life be sacrificed for you! Will you allow me to go?"

The Imām (A) said, "Yes, go ahead, but go with *taqīyah* (concealing your faith)."

I intended to go, but before leaving, I spoke about my trip with ̒Alī ibn Balāl. He was puzzled and asked, "Imām al-Hādī (A) himself is a Hā̓ir (a place/person where du̒ā̓ is accepted). What does he want to do with another Hā̓ir?"

I went to the Imām (A) and mentioned ̒Alī ibn Balāl's question. The Imām (A) replied, "Didn't the Noble Prophet (S) perform tawāf around Allāh's House (the Ka̒bah)?

And didn't he kiss the Ḥajar al-Aswad, despite his status as the Prophet, and despite the status of a Mu̓min (believer) being higher than the House of God?!

Know that places like Karbalā̓ are those places where Allāh loves to be mentioned and called upon.

Likewise, I prefer for people to seek my shifā̓ and cure in places where Allāh prefers, and the Hā̓ir Ḥusaynī is one of them."

Kāmil az-Ziyārah, Ch. 90, Ḥadīth #1

Can a Visitor Offer Full Prayers in the Shrine of Imām Ḥusayn (A)?

Karbalāʾ (Ḥāʾir al-Ḥusaynī) is one of the four places where a traveller may choose to offer his/her Ṣalāh in full or qasr.

In Karbalāʾ, the only area where you may perform your prayers in full is in the vicinity of the Ḥāʾir. If you are unsure of its vicinity, then practice iḥtiyāṭ (caution) by praying qasr.

Pilgrims can act according to their Marjaʿs fatwā below:

Āyatullahs Khumaynī, Fāḍil Lankarānī, and Khāminiʾī: it is permissible to perform your prayers in full within 37.7 feet of the holy grave.

Āyatullahs Sīstānī and Subḥānī: it is permissible to perform your prayers within 36 feet of the holy grave; out of precaution, it is better to prayer qasr further out from the ḍarīḥ.

Āyatullah Waḥīd Khurāsānī: it is permissible to perform your prayers in full within the entire haram.

Āyatullahs Khūʾī, Bahjat, Makārim, and Tabrīzī: it is permissible to perform your prayers in full around the holy ḍarīḥ (Hā'ir) and iḥtiyāṭ wājib to perform qasr prayers further out from the ḍarīḥ.

Āyatullah Ṣāfī Gulpāygānī: it is permissible to perform your prayers in full within the entire haram.

Āyatullah Arākī and Shubayrī Zanjānī: a traveller must offer qasr prayer even in the Ḥāʾir.

Tawḍīʿ al-Masāʾil Marājiʿ, Vol.1, P.753, Rule 1356

Imām Ḥusayn (A) and the Pigeons

Dawūd ibn Farqad narrates:

I was sitting in the house of Imām aṣ-Ṣādiq (A) and noticed a pigeon that was busy reciting something.

The Imām looked at me and asked, "O Dawūd, do you know what this bird is saying?"

I replied, "May I be sacrificed for you. I don't know."

The Imām replied, "He is asking Allāh to withhold His mercy from the killers of Ḥusayn ibn ʿAlī (A). It is good to keep these birds in your homes [as pets]."

Kāmil al-Ziyārah, Ibn Qulawayh

He who knows not your love, O Ḥusayn, has verily lived in vain

Ziyārah of Imām Ḥusayn (A)

As you leave your home, keep reciting the following dhikr with humility:

There is no god except Allāh! Allāh is the Greatest! All praise is for Allāh!	لَا إِلَهَ إِلَّا اللهُ وَاللهُ أَكْبَرُ وَالْحَمْدُ لِلهِ

When you enter Karbalāʾ:

- Enter humbly, with a broken heart.
- A pilgrim of Karbalāʾ is like a pilgrim of Mecca; hence, maintain honor, dignity, and patience, and be a good travel partner for others.
- Protect your gaze, tongue, and hands from forbidden acts. Avoid arguing and holding grudges against one another. If you maintain such etiquettes, then the rewards of Ḥajj and ʿUmrah will be written for you, inshā'Allāh.
- If you come across other pilgrims on the way who need help, assist them if you can.
- While in Karbalāʾ, consume simple food and avoid meat and lavish food.
- When you reach the Euphrates, recite the following 100 times each:
  - Allāhu Akbar
  - Lā ilāha illallāh
  - Ṣalawāt
- Wear clean clothes and perform ghusl. Then, recite the following duʿāʾ:

In the name of Allāḥ and with (the help) of Allāh,	بِسْمِ اللهِ وَبِاللهِ
O Allāh, please make it [the water] a light, purifier, protector, and cure from all diseases, illnesses, injuries, and disabilities.	اَللَّهُمَّ اجْعَلْهُ نُوْراً وَطَهُوْراً وَحِرْزاً وَشِفَاءً مِنْ كُلِّ دَاءٍ وَسُقْمٍ وَآفَةٍ وَعَاهَةٍ
O Allāh, through this water, purify my heart, expand my chest, and make my affair easy.	اَللَّهُمَّ طَهِّرْ بِهِ قَلْبِيْ وَاشْرَحْ بِهِ صَدْرِيْ وَسَهِّلْ لِيْ بِهِ اَمْرِيْ

As you head towards the holy shrine:

- Talk less and remember Allāh abundantly.
- Start by praising Allāh and reciting ṣalawāt as you walk slowly, with complete tranquility.
- Walk modestly and with humility, just as servants and companions would.
- Enter the shrine in the same condition that you entered the city — tired, thirsty, hungry, sad, etc. and ask for your wishes.
- Offer many prayers and recite abundant ṣalawāts
- Before entering the shrine, recite the Idhn ad-Dukhūl (Permission to Enter)

Inside the ḥaram:

- When you enter the ḥaram, head towards Ḥāʾir al-Ḥusaynī and ask for your duʿās, because this is the place of istijābah (acceptance of duʿāʾs).
- Try to offer your obligatory prayers, as well as recommended prayers, by the Imām's (A) grave since it is accepted there. The rewards for performing a wājib (mandatory) prayer there is equal to performing Ḥajj, and a nāfilah prayer (recommended) is equal to performing ʿUmrah.
- Ibn Qulawayh narrates from Imām al-Bāqir (A), "Whenever you have a *ḥājah* (request), go to the holy grave of Imām Ḥusayn (A) and offer a four rakaʿāt prayer (in two sets of two rakaʿāt), and then ask for your request."
- Among the recommended deeds is reciting ṣalawāt upon him and his holy family.
- Stand behind the head and recite ṣalawāt upon the Noble Prophet (S) and his beloved family and Imām Ḥusayn (A).
- Recite the tasbīḥ of Amīr al-Muʾminīn 1,000 times by the holy head (If you're facing qiblah, the head is located in the furthest part of the ḍarīḥ on your right).
- Recite the tasbīḥ of Sayyidah Faṭimah (A) 1,000 times by the Imām's (A) foot.
- It is recommended to offer a two rakaʿāt prayer by the holy head in which you recite Sūrat al-Fātiḥah and Sūrat ar-Raḥmān in the first rakʿah and Sūrat al-Fātiḥah and Sūrat al-Mulk in the second rakʿah. The reward of this prayer is equal to 25 accepted Ḥajj alongside the Prophet (S).

> It is narrated from Imām aṣ-Ṣādiq (A) that whoever walks to perform the ziyārah of Imām Ḥusayn (A), for each step, Allāh will give him/her the reward of 1,000 good actions, forgive 1,000 sins, and elevate his/her status by 1,000 levels.

Tasbīḥ of Amīr al-Mu᾿minīn (A)

Glory be to Him whose treasures never diminish!	سُبْحَانَ الَّذِيْ لَا تَنْفَدُ خَزَائِنُهُ
Glory be to Him, whose signs can never be erased!	سُبْحَانَ الَّذِيْ لَا تَبِيْدُ مَعَالِمُهُ
Glory be to Him; that which He has can never be annihilated	سُبْحَانَ الَّذِيْ لَا يَفْنَىٰ مَا عِنْدَهُ
Glory be to Him who never takes a partner in His judgment!	سُبْحَانَ الَّذِيْ لَا يُشْرِكُ اَحَداً فِيْ حُكْمِهِ
Glory be to Him, whose honor never decreases	سُبْحَانَ الَّذِيْ لَا اضْمِحْلَالَ لِفَخْرِهِ
Glory be to Him whose duration is never terminated! Glory be to He besides whom there is no god!	سُبْحانَ الَّذِيْ لَا انْقِطَاعَ لِمُدَّتِهِ، سُبْحَانَ الَّذِيْ لَا اِلٰهَ غَيْرُهُ

Tasbīḥ of Sayyidah Fāṭimah (A)

Glory be to the Owner of majesty and exalted greatness!	سُبْحَانَ ذِى الْجَلَالِ الْبَاذِخِ الْعَظِيْمِ
Glory be to the Owner of honor and sublime authority!	سُبْحَانَ ذِى الْعِزِّ الشَّامِخِ الْمُنِيْفِ

Glory be to the Owner of the splendid and eternal kingdom!	سُبْحَانَ ذِيْ الْمُلْكِ الْفَاخِرِ الْقَدِيْمِ
Glory be to the Owner of splendor and beauty!	سُبْحَانَ ذِيْ الْبَهْجَةِ وَالْجَمَالِ
Glory be to Him who is clad in light and dignity!	سُبْحَانَ مَنْ تَرَدَّىٰ بِالنُّوْرِ وَالْوِقَارِ
Glory be to Him who sees the footprints of the ant on the stone and the exact time of the bird dipping down in the air!	سُبْحَانَ مَنْ يَرَىٰ اَثَرَ النَّمْلِ فِيْ الصَّفَا وَوَقْعَ الطَّيْرِ فِيْ الْهَوَاءِ

Ziyārah of Imām Ḥusayn (A)

When you reach the gate of the holy shrine, stop and recite the following:

Allāh is the Greatest! All praise is due to Allāh! All glory be to Allāh day and night!	اَللهُ اَكْبَرُ كَبِيْراً، وَالْحَمْدُ لِلّٰهِ كَثِيْراً، وَسُبْحَانَ اللهِ بُكْرَةً وَاَصِيْلاً،
All praise be to Allāh, who guided us to this, and we would not have been guided if He had not guided us.	اَلْحَمْدُ لِلّٰهِ الَّذِيْ هَدَانَا لِهٰذَا وَمَا كُنَّا لِنَهْتَدِيَ لَوْ لَا اَنْ هَدَانَا اللهُ
Certainly, the Prophets of our Lord brought the truth.	لَقَدْ جَاءَتْ رُسُلُ رَبِّنَا بِالْحَقِّ

Then, say:

Peace be upon you, O Messenger of Allāh	اَلسَّلَامُ عَلَيْكَ يَا رَسُوْلَ اللهِ
Peace be upon you, O Prophet of Allāh	اَلسَّلَامُ عَلَيْكَ يَا نَبِيَّ اللهِ
Peace be upon you, O Seal of the Prophets	اَلسَّلَامُ عَلَيْكَ يَا خَاتَمَ النَّبِيِّيْنَ
Peace be upon you, O Leader of the Prophets	اَلسَّلَامُ عَلَيْكَ يَا سَيِّدَ الْمُرْسَلِيْنَ
Peace be upon you, O Beloved of Allāh	اَلسَّلَامُ عَلَيْكَ يَا حَبِيْبَ اللهِ
Peace be upon you, O Commander of the Faithful	اَلسَّلَامُ عَلَيْكَ يَا اَمِيْرَالْمُؤْمِنِيْنَ
Peace be upon you, O Chief of the Prophet's successors	اَلسَّلَامُ عَلَيْكَ يَا سَيِّدَ الْوَصِيِّيْنَ
Peace be upon You O Leader of the illuminated faces	اَلسَّلَامُ عَلَيْكَ يَا قَائِدَ الْغُرِّ الْمُحَجَّلِيْنَ
Peace be upon you, O son of Fāṭimah, the leader of the women of the worlds	اَلسَّلَامُ عَلَيْكَ يَا بْنَ فَاطِمَةَ سَيِّدَةِ نِسَاءِ الْعَالَمِيْنَ

Peace be upon you and the Imāms from your lineage	اَلسَّلَامُ عَلَيْكَ وَعَلَى الْاَئِمَّةَ مِنْ وُلْدِكَ
Peace be upon you, O Successor of Amīr al-Muʾminīn	اَلسَّلَامُ عَلَيْكَ يَا وَصِيَّ اَمِيْرِالْمُؤْمِنِيْنَ
Peace be upon you, O truthful martyr	اَلسَّلَامُ عَلَيْكَ اَيُّهَا الصِّدِيْقُ الشَّهِيْدُ
Peace be upon you, O angels of Allāh who reside in this noble place	اَلسَّلَامُ عَلَيْكُمْ يَا مَلَائِكَةَ اللهِ الْمُقِيْمِيْنَ فِيْ هٰذَا الْمَقَامِ الشَّرِيْفِ
Peace be upon you, O angels of my Lord who surround the grave of al-Ḥusayn	اَلسَّلَامُ عَلَيْكُمْ يَامَلَائِكَةَ رَبِّي الْمُحْدِقِيْنَ بِقَبْرِالْحُسَيْنِ
Peace be upon you as long as I exist, and as long as the day and night exist	اَلسَّلَامُ عَلَيْكُمْ مِنِّيْ اَبَداً مَا بَقِيْتُ وَبَقِيَ اللَّيْلُ وَالنَّهَارُ

Then, say:

Peace be upon you, O Abā ʿAbd Allāh!	اَلسَّلَامُ عَلَيْكَ يَا اَبَا عَبْدِاللهِ،
Peace be upon you, O son of Rasūl Allāh!	اَلسَّلَامُ عَلَيْكَ يَا بْنَ رَسُوْلِ اللهِ،

Peace be upon you, O son of Amīr ul-Muʾminīn!	اَلسَّلَامُ عَلَيْكَ يَا بْنَ اَمِيْرِالْمُؤْمِنِيْنَ
My father, my mother, and I are all your servants.	عَبْدُكَ وَابْنُ عَبْدِكَ وَابْنُ اَمَتِكَ
I affirm that I am your servant and refuse to oppose you.	الْمُقِرُّ بِالرِّقِ وَالتَّارِكُ لِلْخِلَافِ عَلَيْكُمْ
I am a friend of your friends and enemy of your enemies.	وَالْمُوَالِيْ لِوَلِيِّكُمْ وَالْمُعَادِيْ لِعَدُوِّكُمْ
I have intended to come to your sanctuary and seek refuge in your shrine, and I seek nearness to you.	قَصَدَ حَرَمَكَ وَاسْتَجَارَ بِمَشْهَدِكَ، وَتَقَرَّبَ اِلَيْكَ بِقَصْدِكَ
May I enter, O Messenger of Allāh?	أَأَدْخُلُ يَا رَسُوْلَ اللهِ
May I enter, O Prophet of Allāh?	أَأَدْخُلُ يَا نَبِيَّ اللهِ
May I enter, O Commander of the Faithful?	أَأَدْخُلُ يَا اَمِيْرَالْمُؤْمِنِيْنَ
May I enter, O Chief of the Prophet's successors?	أَأَدْخُلُ يَا سَيِّدَ الْوَصِيِّيْنَ

May I enter, O Fatimah, Leader of the women of the worlds?	أَأَدْخُلُ يَا فَاطِمَةَ سَيِّدَةَ نِسَاءِ الْعَالَمِيْنَ
May I enter, O my master, O Abā ʿAbd Allāh?	أَأَدْخُلُ يَا مَوْلَايَ يَا ابَا عَبْدِاللهِ
May I enter, O my master, O son of Rasūl Allāh?	أَأَدْخُلُ يَا مَوْلَايَ يَابْنَ رَسُوْلِ اللهِ

Then, if your heart has become soft and tears come into your eyes, it means you have received permission to enter. Enter the shrine and say:

All praise is for Allāh the One, the Unique, the Matchless, The Eternal One, who guided me to your guardianship,	اَلْحَمْدُ لِلّٰهِ الْوَاحِدِ الْأَحَدِ الْفَرْدِ الصَّمَدِ الَّذِيْ هَدَانِيْ لِوَلَايَتِكَ
chose me to visit you,	وَخَصَّنِيْ بِزِيَارَتِكَ
and made my journey to you easy.	وَسَهَّلَ لِيْ قَصْدَكَ

Then, go to the door of the tomb and stand by the head of the grave and say:

Peace be upon you, O inheritor of Ādam, the chosen one of Allāh.	اَلسَّلَامُ عَلَيْكَ يَا وَارِثَ آدَمَ صَفْوَةِ اللهِ

Peace be upon you, O inheritor of Nūh, the Prophet of Allāh.	اَلسَّلَامُ عَلَيْكَ يَا وَارِثَ نُوْحٍ نَبِيِّ اللهِ
Peace be upon you, O inheritor of Ibrahīm, the intimate friend of Allāh.	اَلسَّلَامُ عَلَيْكَ يَا وَارِثَ اِبْرَاهِيْمَ خَلِيْلِ اللهِ
Peace be upon you, O inheritor of Mūsa, the one spoken to by Allāh.	اَلسَّلَامُ عَلَيْكَ يَا وَارِثَ مُوْسَىٰ كَلِيْمِ اللهِ
Peace be upon you, O inheritor of Īsa, the spirit of Allāh.	اَلسَّلَامُ عَلَيْكَ يَا وَارِثَ عِيْسَىٰ رُوْحِ اللهِ
Peace be upon you, O inheritor of Muhammad, the beloved of Allāh.	اَلسَّلَامُ عَلَيْكَ يَا وَارِثَ مُحَمَّدٍ حَبِيْبِ اللهِ
Peace be upon you, O inheritor of the Commander of the Faithful.	اَلسَّلَامُ عَلَيْكَ يَا وَارِثَ اَمِيْرِالْمُؤْمِنِيْنَ
Peace be upon you, O son of Muhammad, the chosen one.	اَلسَّلَامُ عَلَيْكَ يَا بْنَ مُحَمَّدٍ الْمُصْطَفَىٰ
Peace be upon you, O son of ʿAlī, the well-pleased.	اَلسَّلَامُ عَلَيْكَ يَا بْنَ عَلِيٍّ الْمُرْتَضَىٰ
Peace be upon you, O son of Fāṭimah az-Zahrā᾽.	اَلسَّلَامُ عَلَيْكَ يَا بْنَ فَاطِمَةَ الزَّهْرَاءِ

Peace be upon you, O son of Khadījah, the great lady.	اَلسَّلَامُ عَلَيْكَ يَا بْنَ خَدِيْجَةَ الْكُبْرٰى
Peace be upon you, O avenger of Allāh, son of His avenger, and the one who was left alone without supporters.	اَلسَّلَامُ عَلَيْكَ يَا ثَارَاللهِ وَابْنَ ثَارِهِ وَالْوِتْرَ الْمَوْتُوْرَ
I bear witness that you established the prayers, gave alms,	اَشْهَدُ اَنَّكَ قَدْ اَقَمْتَ الصَّلَاةَ وَآتَيْتَ الزَّكَاةَ
enjoined the right, forbade evil,	وَاَمَرْتَ بِالْمَعْرُوْفِ وَنَهَيْتَ عَنِ الْمُنْكَرِ
and obeyed Allāh and His Messenger until certainty (death) came to you.	وَاَطَعْتَ اللهَ وَرَسُوْلَهُ حَتّٰى اَتَاكَ الْيَقِيْنُ
So, may Allāh curse the people who killed you, and may Allāh curse the people who oppressed you.	فَلَعَنَ اللهُ اُمَّةً قَتَلَتْكَ، وَلَعَنَ اللهُ اُمَّةً ظَلَمَتْكَ
May Allāh curse the people who were pleased when they had heard about it.	وَلَعَنَ اللهُ اُمَّةً سَمِعَتْ بِذٰلِكَ فَرَضِيَتْ بِهِ
O my Master, O Abā ʿAbd Allāh!	يَا مَوْلَايَ يَا اَبَاعَبْدِاللهِ

I bear witness that you were light in the sublime loins and purified wombs.	اَشْــــهَدُ اَنَّكَ كُنْــتَ نُــوْراً فِى الْاَصْلَابِ الشَّامِخَةِ، وَالْاَرْحَامِ الْمُطَهَّرَةِ،
The impurities of ignorance could not touch you,	لَمْ تُنَجِّسْكَ الْجَاهِلِيَّةُ بِاَنْجَاسِهَا
nor could it dress you in its murky clothes.	وَلَمْ تُلْبِسْكَ مِنْ مُدْلَهِمَّاتِ ثِيَابِهَا
I also bear witness that you are one of the mainstays of the religion and the pillars of the believers.	وَاَشْهَدُ اَنَّكَ مِنْ دَعَائِمِ الدِّيْنِ، وَاَرْكَانِ الْمُؤْمِنِيْنَ
I also bear witness that you are the pious, God-conscious, pleased, purified, guiding, and well-guided Imām.	وَاَشْهَدُ اَنَّكَ الْاِمَامُ الْبَرُّ التَّقِيُّ الرَّضِيُّ الزَّكِيُّ الْهَادِىَ الْمَهْدِيُّ
And (I bear witness) that the Imāms from your progeny are the spokesmen of piety,	وَاَشْهَدُ اَنَّ الْاَئِمَّةَ مِنْ وُلْدِكَ كَلِمَةُ التَّقْوَىٰ
the signs of guidance, the firmest handle (of Islam), and the proofs upon the inhabitants of the world.	وَاَعْلَامُ الْهُدَىٰ، وَالْعُرْوَةُ الْوُثْقَىٰ، وَالْحُجَّةُ عَلَىٰ اَهْلِ الدُّنْيَا
And I bear witness to Allāh, His angels, His Prophets, and His Messenger,	وَاُشْهِدُ اللّٰهَ وَمَلَائِكَتَهُ وَاَنْبِيَاءَهُ وَرُسُلَهُ

that I believe in you all and your return, have full confidence in the laws of my religion, which is affirmed by my deeds.	اَنِّي بِكُمْ مُؤْمِنٌ وَبِا يَابِكُمْ مُوْقِنٌ بِشَرَايِعِ دِيْنِيْ وَخَوَاتِيْمِ عَمَلِيْ
My heart is at peace with you all,	وَقَلْبِيْ لِقَلْبِكُمْ سِلْمٌ
and all my affairs are based on your commands.	وَاَمْرِيْ لِاَمْرِكُمْ مُتَّبِعٌ،
May Allāh's blessings be upon you and your souls,	صَلَوَاتُ اللهِ عَلَيْكُمْ وَعَلَىٰ اَرْوَاحِكُمْ
your bodies, your forms,	وَعَلَىٰ اَجْسَادِكُمْ وَعَلَىٰ اَجْسَامِكُمْ
upon the present of you and the absent from you,	وَ عَلَىٰ شَاهِدِكُمْ وَعَلَىٰ غَائِبِكُمْ
and the apparent and the invisible from you.	وَعَلَىٰ ظَاهِرِكُمْ وَعَلَىٰ بَاطِنِكُمْ

Then, throw yourself on the grave, kiss it, and say:

May my father and mother be sacrificed for you, O son of the Messenger of Allāh!	بِاَبِيْ اَنْتَ وَاُمِّيْ يَا بْنَ رَسُوْلِ اللهِ
May my father and mother be sacrificed for you, O Abā ʿAbd Allāh!	بِاَبِيْ اَنْتَ وَاُمِّيْ يَا اَبَاعَبْدِاللهِ
Extremely insufferable was the calamity and astounding is the misfortune that you suffered for us and for all the inhabitants of the heavens and the earth.	لَقَدْ عَظُمَتِ الرَّزِيَّةُ وَجَلَّتِ الْمُصِيْبَةُ بِكَ عَلَيْنَا وَ عَلٰى جَمِيْعِ اَهْلِ السَّمَاوَاتِ وَالْاَرْضِ
Therefore, may Allāh curse the people who saddled up, gave rein to their horses, and prepared themselves to kill you,	فَلَعَنَ اللهُ اُمَّةً اَسْرَجَتْ وَاَلْجَمَتْ وَتَهَيَّأَتْ لِقِتَالِكَ
O my Master, O Abā ʿAbd Allāh!	يَا مَوْلَايَ يَا اَبَا عَبْدِاللهِ
I have moved towards your sanctuary and come to your shrine,	قَصَدْتُ حَرَمَكَ وَاَتَيْتُ اِلٰى مَشْهَدِكَ
asking Allāh by the standing that you enjoy with Him and the position you occupy with Him	اَسْأَلُ اللهَ بِالشَّأْنِ الَّذِيْ لَكَ عِنْدَهُ وَبِالْمَحَلِّ الَّذِيْ لَكَ لَدَيْهِ
to send blessings on Muḥammad and on the household of Muḥammad,	اَنْ يُصَلِّيْ عَلٰى مُحَمَّدٍ وَّآلِ مُحَمَّدٍ
and to place me with you in this world and in the hereafter.	وَاَنْ يَجْعَلَنِيْ مَعَكُمْ فِي الدُّنْيَا وَالْآخِرَةِ

Then, offer a two rakaʿāt prayer by the holy head, just like Fajr. There is also a recommended two rakaʿāt prayer that is performed in the following method: in the first rakʿah, recite Sūrat al-Fātiḥah and Sūrat ar-Raḥmān, and in the second, recite Sūrat al-Fātiḥah and Sūrat al-Mulk. The reward of this prayer is equal to 25 accepted Ḥajj alongside the Prophet (S). Then, recite the following:

O Allāh! Surely I have prayed, bowed, and prostrated to You. You are One, without any partners,	اَللَّهُمَّ اِنِّيْ صَلَّيْتُ وَرَكَعْتُ وَسَجَدْتُ لَكَ وَحْدَكَ لَا شَرِيْكَ لَكَ
for surely, prayers, bowing, and prostration are not for anyone except You,	لِاَنَّ الصَّلَاةَ وَالرُّكُوْعَ وَالسُّجُوْدَ لَا تَكُوْنُ اِلَّا لَكَ
and You are Allāh; there is no God except You.	لِاَنَّكَ اَنْتَ اللهُ لَا اِلٰهَ اِلَّا اَنْتَ
O Allāh, bless Muḥammad and the household of Muḥammad,	اَللَّهُمَّ صَلِّ عَلٰى مُحَمَّدٍ وَّآلِ مُحَمَّدٍ
and convey to them from me the best of peace and greetings,	وَاَبْلِغْهُمْ عَنِّيْ اَفْضَلَ السَّلَامُ وَالتَّحِيَّةِ
and return unto me their peace.	وَارْدُدْ عَلَيَّ مِنْهُمُ السَّلَامَ
O Allāh! These two rakaʿāt are a gift from me to my master, Ḥusayn, son of ʿAlī, peace be on both of them.	اَللَّهُمَّ وَهَاتَانِ الرَّكْعَتَانِ هَدِيَّةٌ مِنِّيْ اِلَى مَوْلَايَ الْحُسَيْنِ بْنِ عَلِيٍّ عَلَيْهِمَا السَّلَامُ
O Allāh! Bless Muḥammad and him [Ḥusayn],	اَللَّهُمَّ صَلِّ عَلٰى مُحَمَّدٍ وَّعَلَيْهِ

and accept from me and reward me more than my hopes and expectations from You and Your guardian, O the Guardian of the believers!	وَتَقَبَّلْ مِنِّيْ وَأْجُرْنِيْ عَلَىٰ ذٰلِكَ بِاَفْضَلِ اَمَلِيْ وَرَجَائِيْ فِيْكَ وَفِيْ وَلِيِّكَ يَا وَلِيَّ الْمُؤْمِنِيْنَ

Then, go to the footside of the grave and stand near the head of ʿAlī ibn Ḥusayn (A) and say:

Peace be upon you, O son of the Messenger of Allāh.	اَلسَّلَامُ عَلَيْكَ يَا بْنَ رَسُوْلِ اللهِ
Peace be upon you, O son of the Prophet of Allāh.	اَلسَّلَامُ عَلَيْكَ يَابْنَ نَبِيِّ اللهِ
Peace be upon you, O son of the Commander of the Faithful.	اَلسَّلَامُ عَلَيْكَ يَا بْنَ اَمِيْرِ الْمُؤْمِنِيْنَ
Peace be upon you, O son of al-Ḥusayn, the martyr.	اَلسَّلَامُ عَلَيْكَ يَا بْنَ الْحُسَيْنِ الشَّهِيْدِ
Peace be upon you, O martyr.	اَلسَّلَامُ عَلَيْكَ اَيُّهَا الشَّهِيْدُ
Peace be upon you, O the oppressed and the son of the oppressed.	اَلسَّلَامُ عَلَيْكَ اَيُّهَا الْمَظْلُوْمُ وَابْنُ الْمَظْلُوْمِ
May Allāh curse those who killed you.	لَعَنَ اللهُ اُمَّةً قَتَلَتْكَ
May Allāh curse those who oppressed you.	وَلَعَنَ اللهُ اُمَّةً ظَلَمَتْكَ،
May Allāh curse those who heard about this event and were pleased with it.	وَلَعَنَ اللهُ اُمَّةً سَمِعَتْ بِذٰلِكَ فَرَضِيَتْ بِهِ

Then, throw yourself on the grave, kiss it, and say:

Peace be upon you, O guardian of Allāh and the son of His guardian.	اَلسَّلَامُ عَلَيْكَ يَا وَلِيَّ اللهِ وَابْنَ وَلِيِّهِ
The misfortune and calamity that you suffered was astounding and extremely unbearable for us and all the Muslims.	لَقَدْ عَظُمَتِ الْمُصِيْبَةُ وَجَلَّتِ الرَّزِيَّةُ بِكَ عَلَيْنَا وَعَلَىٰ جَمِيْعِ الْمُسْلِمِيْنَ
So, may Allāh remove His Mercy from those who killed you.	فَلَعَنَ اللهُ اُمَّةً قَتَلَتْكَ،
I dissociate from them in the presence of Allāh and in your presence.	وَأَبْرَأُ اِلَى اللهِ وَاِلَيْكَ مِنْهُمْ

Then, go near the door that is by the footside of ʿAlī ibn Ḥusayn (A), and turn towards the shrine of the other martyrs and say:

Peace be upon all of you, O intimate servants of Allāh and His beloved ones.	اَلسَّلَامُ عَلَيْكُمْ يَا اَوْلِيَآءَ اللهِ وَاَحِبَّائَهُ
Peace be upon all of you, O chosen ones of Allāh and His sincere servants	اَلسَّلَامُ عَلَيْكُمْ يَا اَصْفِيَآءَ اللهِ وَاَوِدَّاءَهُ
Peace be upon all of you, O supporters of Allāh's religion.	اَلسَّلَامُ عَلَيْكُمْ يَا اَنْصَارَ دِيْنِ اللهِ
Peace be upon all of you, O supporters of the Messenger of Allāh.	اَلسَّلَامُ عَلَيْكُمْ يَا اَنْصَارَ رَسُوْلِ اللهِ
Peace be upon all of you, O supporters of the Commander of the Faithful	اَلسَّلَامُ عَلَيْكُمْ يَا اَنْصَارَ اَمِيْرِ الْمُؤْمِنِيْنَ

Peace be upon all of you, O supporters of Fāṭimah, the leader of the women of the worlds.	اَلسَّـــلَامُ عَلَيْكُمْ يَا اَنْصَارَ فَاطِمَةَ سَيِّدَةِ نِسَاءِ الْعَالَمِيْنَ،
Peace be upon all of you, O supporters of Abī Muḥammad, al-Ḥasan, the son of ʿAlī, the sincere guardian.	اَلسَّلَامُ عَلَيْكُمْ يَا اَنْصَارَ أَبِيْ مُحَمَّدٍ الْحَسَنِ بْنِ عَلِيٍّ الْوَلِيِّ النَّاصِحِ،
Peace be upon all of you, O supporters of Abī ʿAbd Allāh.	اَلسَّلَامُ عَلَيْكُمْ يَا اَنْصَارَ اَبِيْ عَبْدِاللهِ،
May my father and mother be sacrificed for you. Surely, you all are pure, and pure is the land in which you are buried.	بِاَبِيْ اَنْتُمْ وَاُمِّيْ طِبْتُمْ وَطَابَتِ الْأَرْضُ الَّتِيْ فِيْهَا دُفِنْتُمْ،
And you attained great success! O how I wish that I were with you so that I could also attain great success!	وَفُزْتُـــمْ فَـــوْزاً عَظِيْماً، فَيَا لَيْتَـــنِيْ كُنْتُ مَعَكُمْ فَاَفُوْزَ مَعَكُمْ

Then, come back to the head side of Imām Ḥusayn (A) and pray for yourself, your family, parents, brothers, and sisters because all invocations and supplications are accepted in this shrine.

Ziyārat ʿĀshūrāʾ

Sāliḥ ibn ʿUqbah and Sayf ibn ʿUmayrah have reported that ʿAlqamah ibn Muḥammad al-Ḥaḍramī once asked Imām al-Bāqir (A) to teach him a prayer he could recite when he would visit Imām Ḥusayn's (A) shrine on the day of ʿĀshūrāʾ.

He also asked the Imām (A) to teach him another prayer that he could recite from his own home when he would be unable to visit the shrine on ʿĀshūrāʾ, after which he would point to the shrine and send greetings to Imām Ḥusayn (A).

The Imām (A) said, "O ʿAlqamah! After you salute Imām Ḥusayn (A) with greetings and offer the two-unit prayer, you may say "Allāhu Akbar" and then recite the following ziyārah. If you do so, you will have recited the prayer that is recited by the angels who visit Imām Ḥusayn (A).

You will also be raised 100 million ranks to be included with those who were martyred with him. Moreover, you will be granted the reward of visiting all the Prophets, as well as the reward of all the visitors of Imām Ḥusayn (A) since the day of his martyrdom."

Peace be upon you, O Abā ʿAbd Allāh.	اَلسَّلَامُ عَلَيْكَ يَا أَبَا عَبْدِ اللهِ
Peace be upon you, O son of Allāh's Messenger.	اَلسَّلَامُ عَلَيْكَ يَا ابْنَ رَسُوْلِ اللهِ
Peace be upon you, O son of the Commander of the Faithful and the chief of the Prophet's successors.	اَلسَّلَامُ عَلَيْكَ يَا ابْنَ أَمِيرِ الْمُؤْمِنِيْنَ وَ ابْنَ سَيِّدِ الْوَصِيِّيْنَ
Peace be upon you, O son of Fāṭimah, the leader of the women of the worlds.	اَلسَّلَامُ عَلَيْكَ يَا ابْنَ فَاطِمَةَ سَيِّدَةِ نِسَاءِ الْعَالَمِيْنَ

Peace be upon you, O avenger of Allāh, son of His avenger, and the one who was left alone without supporters.	اَلسَّلَامُ عَلَيْكَ يَا ثَارَ اللهِ وَ ابْنَ ثَارِهِ وَ الْوِتْرَ الْمَوْتُوْرَ
Peace be upon you and upon the souls that reside in your courtyard.	اَلسَّلَامُ عَلَيْكَ وَ عَلَى الْأَرْوَاحِ الَّتِيْ حَلَّتْ بِفِنَائِكَ
May the peace of Allāh be upon all of you, from me, for as long as I exist, and as long as there are day and night.	عَلَيْكُمْ مِنِّيْ جَمِيْعاً سَلَامُ اللّٰهِ أَبَداً مَا بَقِيْتُ وَ بَقِيَ اللَّيْلُ وَ النَّهَارُ
O Abā ʿAbd Allāh! Unbearable is the sorrow,	يَا أَبَا عَبْدِ اللهِ لَقَدْ عَظُمَتِ الرَّزِيَّةُ
and excruciating and unbearable is the misfortune you suffered for us	وَجَلَّتْ وَعَظُمَتِ الْمُصِيْبَةُ بِكَ عَلَيْنَا
and for all the people of Islām.	وَ عَلَى جَمِيْعِ أَهْلِ الْإِسْلَامُ
Your tragedy has been excruciating and unbearable in the heavens and for all the inhabitants of the heavens.	وَجَلَّتْ وَعَظُمَتْ مُصِيْبَتُكَ فِيْ السَّمَاوَاتِ عَلَى جَمِيْعِ أَهْلِ السَّمَاوَاتِ
So, may Allāh curse the people who laid the basis of oppression and injustice against you, O Ahlul Bayt.	فَلَعَنَ اللهُ أُمَّةً أَسَّسَتْ أَسَاسَ الظُّلْمِ وَ الْجَوْرِ عَلَيْكُمْ أَهْلَ الْبَيْتِ
May Allāh curse the people who removed you from your position	وَ لَعَنَ اللهُ أُمَّةً دَفَعَتْكُمْ عَنْ مَقَامِكُمْ

and lowered you from the ranks that Allāh placed you in.	وَأَزَالَتْكُمْ عَنْ مَرَاتِبِكُمُ الَّتِيْ رَتَّبَكُمُ اللهُ فِيْهَا
May Allāh curse the people who murdered you.	وَ لَعَنَ اللهُ أُمَّةً قَتَلَتْكُمْ
and those who paved the way for them to do so and who made it possible for them to fight against you.	وَ لَعَنَ اللهُ الْمُمَهِّدِيْنَ لَهُمْ بِالتَّمْكِيْنِ مِنْ قِتَالِكُمْ
I disassociate from them in the presence of Allāh and You, and I disassociate from their devotees, followers, and friends.	بَرِئْتُ إِلَى اللهِ وَإِلَيْكُمْ مِنْهُمْ وَ مِنْ أَشْيَاعِهِمْ وَ أَتْبَاعِهِمْ وَأَوْلِيَاءِهِمْ
O Abā ʿAbd Allāh! Surely, I am at peace with those who are at peace with you, and I am at war with those who have fought against you until the Day of Judgment.	يَا أَبَا عَبْدِ اللهِ إِنِّيْ سِلْمٌ لِمَنْ سَالَمَكُمْ وَحَرْبٌ لِمَنْ حَارَبَكُمْ إِلَى يَوْمِ الْقِيَامَةِ
May Allāh also curse the families of Ziyād and Marwān.	فَلَعَنَ اللهُ آلَ زِيَادٍ وَ آلَ مَرْوَانَ
May Allāh also curse all the descendants of Umayyah.	وَ لَعَنَ اللهُ بَنِيْ أُمَيَّةَ قَاطِبَةً
May Allāh also curse the son of Marjānah, ʿUmar, the son of Saʿd, and Shimr.	وَ لَعَنَ اللهُ ابْنَ مَرْجَانَةَ وَ لَعَنَ اللهُ عُمَرَ بْنَ سَعْدٍ وَ لَعَنَ اللهُ شِمْراً

May Allāh also curse the people who saddled up, gave reins to their horses and masked their faces in preparation for fighting against you.	وَ لَعَنَ اللهُ أُمَّةً أَسْرَجَتْ وَأَلْجَمَتْ وَ تَنَقَّبَتْ لِقِتَالِكَ
May my father and mother be sacrificed for you! Surey, my grief for you is extremely insufferable!	بِأَبِيْ أَنْتَ وَ أُمِّيْ لَقَدْ عَظُمَ مُصَابِيْ بِكَ
So, I ask Allāh, who has honored your position and honored me through you,	فَأَسْأَلُ اللهَ الَّذِيْ أَكْرَمَ مَقَامَكَ وَأَكْرَمَنِيْ بِكَ
that He provides me the chance to avenge you with the divinely appointed Imām from the household of Muḥammad, peace of Allāh be upon him and his household.	أَنْ يَرْزُقَنِيْ طَلَبَ ثَارِكَ مَعَ إِمَامٍ مَنْصُوْرٍ مِنْ أَهْلِ بَيْتِ مُحَمَّدٍ صَلَّى اللهُ عَلَيْهِ وَآلِهِ
O Allāh, make me illustrious in Your sight by the right of Ḥusayn, peace be upon him, in this world and in the hereafter.	اللّٰهُمَّ اجْعَلْنِيْ عِنْدَكَ وَجِيْهاً بِالْحُسَيْنِ عَلَيْهِ اَلسَّلَامُ فِيْ الدُّنْيَا وَ الْآخِرَةِ
O Abā ʿAbd Allāh!	يَا أَبَا عَبْدِ اللهِ
Surely, I seek nearness to Allāh, to His Messenger, to the Commander of the Faithful, to Fāṭimah, to al-Ḥasan, and to you	إِنِّيْ أَتَقَرَّبُ إِلَى اللهِ وَإِلَى رَسُوْلِهِ وَ إِلَى أَمِيْرِالْمُؤْمِنِيْنَ وَإِلَى فَاطِمَةَ وَإِلَى الْحَسَنِ وَإِلَيْكَ

through my loyalty to you and by disassociating from those who killed you and incurred your hostility, and by disassociating with those who laid the basis of oppression and injustice against you all.	بِمُوَالَاتِكَ وَ بِالْبَرَاءَةِ مِمَّنْ قَاتَلَكَ وَ نَصَبَ لَكَ الْحَرْبَ وَ بِالْبَرَاءَةِ مِمَّنْ أَسَّسَ أَسَاسَ الظُّلْمِ وَالْجَوْرِ عَلَيْكُم
In the presence of Allāh and His Messenger, I also disassociate from those who laid the basis for this, established their foundations on it, and continued in oppressing and persecuting you and your followers.	وَأَبْرَأُ إِلَى اللهِ وَإِلَى رَسُوْلِهِ مِمَّنْ أَسَّسَ أَسَاسَ ذٰلِكَ وَبَنَىٰ عَلَيْهِ بُنْيَانَهُ وَ جَرَىٰ فِيْ ظُلْمِهِ وَ جَوْرِهِ عَلَيْكُمْ وَ عَلَىٰ أَشْيَاعِكُمْ
I disassociate from them in the presence of Allāh and you all, and I seek nearness to Allāh and you all, by declaring loyalty to you and to your loyalists and by disassociating from your enemies, those who incur your animosity, and their adherents and followers.	بَرِئْتُ إِلَى اللهِ وَ إِلَيْكُمْ مِنْهُمْ وَأَتَقَرَّبُ إِلَى اللهِ ثُمَّ إِلَيْكُمْ بِمُوَالَاتِكُمْ وَ مُوَالَاةِ وَلِيِّكُمْ وَ بِالْبَرَاءَةِ مِنْ أَعْدَائِكُمْ وَالنَّاصِبِيْنَ لَكُمُ الْحَرْبَ وَبِالْبَرَاءَةِ مِنْ أَشْيَاعِهِمْ وَأَتْبَاعِهِمْ
Surely, I am at peace with those who are at peace with you;	إِنِّيْ سِلْمٌ لِمَنْ سَالَمَكُمْ
I am at war against those who are at war against you;	وَحَرْبٌ لِمَنْ حَارَبَكُمْ
I am a friend to your friends;	وَوَلِيٌّ لِمَنْ وَالَاكُمْ

and I am an enemy of your enemies.	وَعَدُوٌّ لِمَنْ عَادَاكُمْ
So, I ask Allāh who has granted me the honor of recognizing you all and your intimate servants,	فَأَسْأَلُ اللهَ الَّذِيْ أَكْرَمَنِيْ بِمَعْرِفَتِكُمْ وَمَعْرِفَةِ أَوْلِيَائِكُمْ
and who granted me disassociation from your enemies,	وَرَزَقَنِي الْبَرَاءَةَ مِنْ أَعْدَائِكُمْ
to include me with you in this world and in the hereafter,	أَنْ يَجْعَلَنِيْ مَعَكُمْ فِيْ الدُّنْيَا وَالْآخِرَةِ
and to grant me a firm foothold of honesty with you in this world and in the hereafter.	وَأَنْ يُثَبِّتَ لِيْ عِنْدَكُمْ قَدَمَ صِدْقٍ فِيْ الدُّنْيَا وَ الْآخِرَةِ
I also ask Him to make me attain the praiseworthy status that you enjoy with Allāh,	وَ أَسْأَلُهُ أَنْ يُبَلِّغَنِي الْمَقَامَ الْمَحْمُوْدَ لَكُمْ عِنْدَ اللهِ
and to grant me the chance to take vengeance with the rightly guided Imām, the spokesperson of the truth.	وَ أَنْ يَرْزُقَنِيْ طَلَبَ ثَارِيْ مَعَ إِمَامٍ هُدًيٍ (مَهْدِيٍّ) ظَاهِرٍنَاطِقٍ بِالْحَقِّ مِنْكُمْ
I also ask Allāh by your right and by the standing that you all have with Him	وَ أَسْأَلُ اللهَ بِحَقِّكُمْ وَبِالشَّأْنِ الَّذِيْ لَكُمْ عِنْدَهُ

That He bestows me, in return for my grief for you, with the greatest compensation that He has ever given for misfortunes that have afflicted anyone.	أَنْ يُعْطِيَنِيْ بِمُصَابِيْ بِكُمْ أَفْضَلَ مَا يُعْطِيْ مُصَاباً بِمُصِيْبَتِهِ
Your misfortune has been so astounding and so catastrophic for Islām,	مُصِيْبَةً مَا أَعْظَمَهَا وَ أَعْظَمَ رَزِيَّتَهَا فِيْ الْإِسْلَامِ
and for all the heavens and earth.	وَفِيْ جَمِيْعِ السَّمَاوَاتِ وَ الْأَرْضِ
O Allāh, please make me in this current situation one of those who receive Your blessings, mercy, and forgiveness	اَللّٰهُمَّ اجْعَلْنِيْ فِيْ مَقَامِيْ هٰذَا مِمَّنْ تَنَالُهُ مِنْكَ صَلَوَاتٌ وَرَحْمَةٌ وَمَغْفِرَةٌ
O Allāh, please make me live my life the same way Muḥammad and his household lived, and make me die upon the same principles that Muḥammad and his household died.	اَللّٰهُمَّ اجْعَلْ مَحْيَايَ مَحْيَا مُحَمَّدٍ وَّ آلِ مُحَمَّدٍ وَّ مَمَاتِيْ مَمَاتَ مُحَمَّدٍ وَّ آلِ مُحَمَّدٍ
O Allāh, this day was considered a blessed day by the descendants of Umayyah,	اَللّٰهُمَّ إِنَّ هٰذَا يَوْمٌ تَبَرَّكَتْ بِهِ بَنُوْأُمَيَّةَ
and by the son of the liver-eating woman, the accursed and son of the accursed, as said by You and Your Prophet, may Allāh's peace be upon him and his household,	وَابْنُ آكِلَةِ الْأَكْبَادِ اللَّعِيْنُ ابْنُ اللَّعِيْنِ عَلَىٰ لِسَانِكَ وَلِسَانِ نَبِيِّكَ صَلَّىٰ اللهُ عَلَيْهِ وَآلِهِ
on every occasion and in every situation that Your Prophet (S) attended.	فِيْ كُلِّ مَوْطِنٍ وَمَوْقِفٍ وَقَفَ فِيْهِ نَبِيُّكَ صَلَّىٰ اللهُ عَلَيْهِ وَآلِهِ

O Allāh, pour curses upon Abū Sufyān, Muʿāwiyah, and Yazīd son of Muʿāwiyah.	اَللَّهُمَّ الْعَنْ أَبَا سُفْيَانَ وَمُعَاوِيَةَ وَيَزِيْدَ بْنَ مُعَاوِيَةَ
May Your curse be upon them incessantly and eternally.	عَلَيْهِمْ مِنْكَ اللَّعْنَةُ أَبَدَ الْآبِدِيْنَ
This is the day on which the family of Ziyād and the family of Marwān gloated,	وَهٰذَا يَوْمٌ فَرِحَتْ بِهِ آلُ زِيَادٍ وَآلُ مَرْوَانَ
because they killed al-Ḥusayn, may Allāh's blessings be upon him.	بِقَتْلِهِمُ الْحُسَيْنَ صَلَوَاتُ اللهِ عَلَيْهِ
So, O Allāh, pour frequent curses upon them and increase for them the painful chastisement.	اَللَّهُمَّ فَضَاعِفْ عَلَيْهِمُ اللَّعْنَ مِنْكَ وَالْعَذَابَ (الأَلِيْمَ)
O Allāh, surely, I seek nearness to You on this day, on this occasion, and on all the days of my life, by disassociating from them and invoking Your curses upon them,	اَللَّهُمَّ إِنِّيْ أَتَقَرَّبُ إِلَيْكَ فِيْ هٰذَا الْيَوْمِ وَفِيْ مَوْقِفِيْ هٰذَا وَأَيَّامِ حَيَاتِيْ بِالْبَرَاءَةِ مِنْهُمْ وَاللَّعْنَةِ عَلَيْهِمْ
and by declaring loyalty to Your Prophet and Your Prophet's Household, peace be upon him and them.	وَبِالْمُوَالَاةِ لِنَبِيِّكَ وَآلِ نَبِيِّكَ عَلَيْهِ وَعَلَيْهِمُ اَلسَّلَامُ

- According to Imām al-Hādī (A),reciting اَللَّهُمَّ الْعَنْهُمْ جَمِيْعاً 100 times is equivalent to reciting the entire laʿan 100 times.
- Additionally, reciting the last three salāms 100 times is equivalent to reciting the entire salām 100 times.

Then, say 100 times:

O Allāh, pour curses upon the first oppressor who usurped the rights of Muḥammad and his household and the last follower who approves of this.	اَللّٰهُمَّ الْعَنْ أَوَّلَ ظَالِمٍ ظَلَمَ حَقَّ مُحَمَّدٍ وَّآلِ مُحَمَّدٍ وَّآخِرَ تَابِعٍ لَهُ عَلىٰ ذٰلِكَ
O Allāh, pour curses upon the gang that fought against al-Ḥusayn,	اَللّٰهُمَّ الْعَنِ الْعِصَابَةَ الَّتِيْ جَاهَدَتِ الْحُسَيْنَ
and who supported each other against him, paid homage to his enemies, and participated in killing him.	وَشَايَعَتْ وَبَايَعَتْ وَتَابَعَتْ عَلىٰ قَتْلِهِ
O Allāh, pour curses upon all of them	اَللّٰهُمَّ الْعَنْهُمْ جَمِيْعاً

Then, say 100 times:

Peace be upon you, O Abā ʿAbd Allāh	اَلسَّلَامُ عَلَيْكَ يَا أَبَا عَبْدِ اللهِ
and upon the souls that gathered in your courtyard.	وَعَلىٰ الْأَرْوَاحِ الَّتِيْ حَلَّتْ بِفِنَائِكَ
May the peace of Allāh be upon you from me for as long as I exist and as long as there are day and night.	عَلَيْكَ مِنِّيْ سَلَامُ اللهِ اَبَداً مَا بَقِيْتُ وَبَقِيَ اللَّيْلُ وَالنَّهَارُ
May Allāh not make this my last visit to you all.	وَلَا جَعَلَهُ اللهُ آخِرَ الْعَهْدِ مِنِّيْ لِزِيَارَتِكُمْ
Peace be upon al-Ḥusayn,	اَلسَّلَامُ عَلىٰ الْحُسَيْنِ

upon ʿAlī, the son of al-Ḥusayn,	وَعَلَىٰ عَلِيِّ بْنِ الْحُسَيْنِ
upon the children of al-Ḥusayn,	وَعَلَىٰ أَوْلَادِ الْحُسَيْنِ
and upon the companions of al-Ḥusayn.	وَعَلَىٰ أَصْحَابِ الْحُسَيْنِ

Then, say:

O Allāh, pour special curses on the first oppressor and begin with him first,	اَللَّهُمَّ خُصَّ أَنْتَ أَوَّلَ ظَالِمٍ بِاللَّعْنِ مِنِّيْ وَابْدَا بِهِ أَوَّلاً
and then remove Your mercy from the second, the third, and the fourth.	ثُمَّ الْعَنِ الثَّانِيَ وَالثَّالِثَ وَالرَّابِعَ
O Allāh, curse Yazīd, the fifth,	اَللَّهُمَّ الْعَنْ يَزِيْدَ خَامِساً
and curse ʿUbayd Allāh the son of Ziyād and the son of Marjānah, ʿUmar ibn Saʿd, Shimr,	وَالْعَنْ عُبَيْدَ اللهِ بْنَ زِيَادٍ وَابْنَ مَرْجَانَةَ وَعُمَرَ بْنَ سَعْدٍ وَشِمْراً
the family of Abī Sufyān, the family of Ziyād, and the family of Marwān until the Day of Judgment.	وَآلَ أَبِيْ سُفْيَانَ وَآلَ زِيَادٍ وَآلَ مَرْوَانَ إِلَىٰ يَوْمِ الْقِيَامَةِ

Then, go into sajdah and say:

O Allāh, all praise is for You, the praise of those who thank You for their misfortunes.	اَللَّهُمَّ لَكَ الْحَمْدُ حَمْدَ الشَّاكِرِيْنَ لَكَ عَلَىٰ مُصَابِهِمْ
All praise be to Allāh for my great grief.	اَلْحَمْدُ لِلّٰهِ عَلَىٰ عَظِيْمِ رَزِيَّتِيْ
O Allāh, grant me the intercession of al-Ḥusayn on the day of coming (to You).	اَللَّهُمَّ ارْزُقْنِيْ شَفَاعَةَ الْحُسَيْنِ يَوْمَ الْوُرُوْدِ
And make by foostep steadfast	وَثَبِّتْ لِيْ قَدَمَ صِدْقٍ عِنْدَكَ
with al-Ḥusayn and the companions of al-Ḥusayn,	مَعَ الْحُسَيْنِ وَأَصْحَابِ الْحُسَيْنِ
who sacrificed their souls in defense of al-Ḥusayn, peace be upon him.	الَّذِيْنَ بَذَلُوْا مُهَجَهُمْ دُوْنَ الْحُسَيْنِ عَلَيْهِ السَّلَامُ

Ḥabīb ibn Maḍāhir

Ḥabīb ibn Maḍāhir Asadī was a Kūfi from the Banī Asad tribe, as well as a revered companion of the Noble Prophet (S). In addition to participating in all three battles of Jamal, Ṣiffīn, and Nihrawān, he was also a sincere student of Amīr ul-Muʾminīn (A) to the extent that the Imām (A) had taught him the knowledge of "Manāyā & Balāyā," which is knowledge of the inner self.[1]

Ḥabīb was part of a special unit of the Imām's (A) army, called "Shurṭat al-Khamīs." Ḥabīb was amongst the Shīʿah leaders of Kūfah who sent letters to Imām Ḥusayn (A). When Muslim ibn ʿAqīl came to Kūfah, Ḥabīb offered his allegiance and also tried to collect allegiance from others. Imām Ḥusayn (A) wrote him a letter after the martyrdom of Muslim ibn ʿAqīl, asking him to join him in Karbalāʾ.

Ḥabīb had a high status in the eyes of Imām Ḥusayn (A), and when he joined Imām Ḥusayn (A) in Karbalāʾ, he was placed as the commander of the army's left wing. He also attempted to recruit some men from the Banī Asad to join the Imām's (A) army, but the Yazīdi army prevented that from happening.[2]

Ḥabīb was 75 years at the time of his martyrdom, and his head was placed on a spear, along with others, and paraded through Kūfah. His grave is apart from the 72 companions because similar to Ḥurr, his tribe came and buried his body. His darīḥ is located on the men's side.

[1] Al-Ḥusayn (A) fī Ṭarīqah Ilā ash-Shahādah, P.6
[2] Anṣār al-Ḥusayn, P.66

Peace be upon you, O righteous and obedient servant of Allāh, His Messenger, Amīr al-Muʾminīn, Fāṭimah az-Zahrāʾ, Ḥasan and Ḥusayn (peace be upon them).	اَلسَّلَامُ عَلَيْكَ اَيُّهَا الْعَبْدُ الصَّالِحُ الْمُطِيعُ لِلّٰهِ وَلِرَسُولِهِ وَلِاَمِيرِالْمُؤْمِنِينَ وَلِفَاطِمَةَ الزَّهْرَاءِ وَالْحَسَنِ وَالْحُسَيْنِ عَلَيْهِمُ السَّلَامُ
O displaced and intimate friend!	الْغَرِيبِ الْمُوَاسِي

I bear witness that you strove in the path of Allāh,	اَشْهَدُ اَنَّكَ جاهَدْتَ فِيْ سَبِيْلِ اللهِ
and helped Ḥusayn, the son of the daughter of the Messenger of Allāh,	وَنَصَرْتَ الحُسَيْنَ بْنَ بِنْتِ رَسُوْلِ اللهِ
defended him and gave your life to protect him.	وَوَاسَيْتَ بِنَفْسِكَ، وَبَذَلْتَ مُهْجَتَكَ
So, may the complete peace of Allāh be upon you.	فَعَلَيْكَ مِنَ اللهِ السَّلَامُ التَّامُّ
Peace be upon you, O bright moon!	اَلسَّلَامُ عَلَيْكَ أَيُّهَا الْقَمَرُ الزَّاهِرُ
Peace be upon you, O Ḥabīb ibn Maẓāhir al-Asadī, and also the mercy and blessings of Allāh.	اَلسَّلَامُ عَلَيْكَ يَا حَبِيْبَ بْنَ مُظَاهِرِ الْأَسَدِيْ وَ رَحْمَةُ اللهِ وَ بَرَكَاتُهُ

Ibrāhīm al-Mujāb

The grave of Sayyid Ibrāhīm al-Mujāb is located on the women's side. Sayyid Ibrāhīm al Mujāb was the son of Sayyid Muḥammad ʿĀbid, who was the son of Imām Mūsā al-Kāḍim (A). He came to Karbalāʾ in the year 247 AH and settled there. During that time, Muḥammad Muntaṣir, the son of Mutawakkil, was the ʿAbbāsid cʿAlīph in power. He was very offended by how his father used to treat the Shīʿah and therefore took a different approach by allowing them to perform ziyārah to the shrine of Imām Ḥusayn (A).

During this time, Sayyid Ibrāhīm came to Karbalāʾ for Ziyārah. When he reached the Imām's (A) holy shrine, he faced the holy grave and greeted him:

اَلسَّلَامُ عَلَيْكَ يَا جَدَّا

Peace be upon you, O Grandfather

A reply was heard coming out of the grave:

وَ عَلَيْكَ السَّلَامُ يَا وَلَدِي

And peace be upon you, O Grandson

Since then, he has been known as Sayyid Ibrāhīm al Mujāb (the one who was answered).

Peace be upon you, O pure leader, immaculate guardian, and generous caller!	اَلسَّلَامُ عَلَيْكَ اَيُّهَا السَّيِّدُ الزَّكِيُّ الطَّاهِرُ الْوَلِيُّ وَالدَّاعِيْ الْحَفِيُّ
I bear witness that you spoke the truth, spoke honestly, and called [others] towards my master and your master, Ḥusayn, both publicly and in secret.	اَشْهَدُ اَنَّكَ قُلْتَ حَقًّا وَنَطَقْتَ صِدْقاً وَدَعَوْتَ اِلَى مَوْلَايَ وَمَوْلَاكَ الْحُسَيْنِ عَلَانِيَةً وَسِرّاً
Those who followed you have won; those who have believed in you are saved; and those who rejected and opposed you are disappointed and have lost. O my leader and son of my leader, O my master and son of my master,	فَازَ مُتَّبِعُكَ وَنَجَا مُصَدِّقُكَ وَخَابَ وَخَسِرَ مُكَذِّبُكَ وَالْمُتَخَلِّفُ عَنْكَ، يَا سَيِّدِيْ وَابْنَ سَيِّدِيْ وَ يَامَوْلَايَ وَ ابْنَ مَوْلَايَ
Bear witness to my testimony next to you, so that I may attain success by recognizing you, obeying you, believing you, and following you.	اِشْهَدْ لِيْ بِهٰذِهِ الشَّهَادَةِ لِاَكُوْنَ مِنَ الْفَائِزِيْنَ بِمَعْرِفَتِكَ وَطَاعَتِكَ وَتَصْدِيْقِكَ وَاتِّبَاعِكَ،
Peace be upon you, O Sayyid Ibrāhīm Al-Mujāb, son of Mūhammad Al-ʿĀbid, son of Mūsā, the son of Jaʿfar, and also the mercy and blessings of Allāh.	وَالسَّلَامُ عَلَيْكَ يَاسَيِّدُ اِبْرَاهِيْمُ الْمُجَابُ ابْنُ الْمُحَمَّدِ الْعَابِدِ بْنِ الْإِمَامِ مُوْسَى بْنِ جَعْفَرٍ وَّرَحْمَةُ اللهِ وَبَرَكَاتُهُ

Madhbaḥ: The Place of Martyrdom

And whoever is killed unjustly,
We have given his heir authority
(17:33)

This is the place where the head of Imām Ḥusayn (A) was severed from his body. This area is covered by a ḍarīḥ to mark its significance. For men, there is a silver door leading to this room, and the sister's entrance is through the courtyard. This room is southwest of Ḥabīb ibn Maḍāhir's grave.

The Smell of Apple

Fital Nishapūrī narrates the following story from Umm Salmah:

One day, the Prophet (S) was sitting next to Umm Salmah when Angel Jibrāʾīl descended. The two of them were talking, when Ḥasan ibn ʿAlī (A) knocked on the door. She went to open the door and saw that Ḥusayn was also with him. The two of them entered and saw their grandfather talking to Jibrāʾīl, who looked like Daḥiyah Kalbī, one of the good companions of the Prophet (S). The boys began walking in circles around him.

Jibrāʾīl said, "O Rasūl Allāh, what are these children doing?" The Prophet (S) replied, "They are seeing you in the form Daḥiyah Kalbī." Then, Jibrāʾīl pretended to reach into his pocket and suddenly pulled out an apple, quince, and pomegranate and handed them to Imām Ḥasan. Again, he pulled out the same three fruits and gave them to Imām Husayn (A). The two of them happily showed the fruits to their grandfather. The Prophet (S) took the fruits, smelled them, and then gave them back. He said to the boys, "Take these fruits and go to your mother. And if you go to your father first, then that is better."

The two young Imāms followed the Prophet's (S) instructions and went home without eating the fruits. Some time later, the Prophet (S) went to visit them and saw that the fruit was still there. He said, "O ʿAlī, why didn't you eat from the fruit and give it to your wife and children?" He then told them the story behind where the fruit came from, and then the Prophet (S), Imām ʿAlī, Sayyidah Fāṭimah (A), Imām Ḥasan, Imām Ḥusayn (A), and Umm Salmah all ate from the fruit. But even as they ate, the fruit did not diminish. Regardless of how much they ate, the fruit remained intact until after the Prophet (S) died. Imām Ḥusayn has said that after Fāṭimah (A) died, the pomegranate disappeared. Then, when Imām ʿAlī was martyred, the quince disappeared.

السلام عليك يابن أمير المؤمنين
MARJAEYAT TV

Now, only the apple remained. When Imām Ḥusayn (A) and his companions were under siege and forbidden water, Imām Ḥusayn (A) said that every time he was thirsty, he would smell the apple, and his extreme thirst would subside. When his thirst became unbearable and his martyrdom was approaching, he finally bit into the apple.

Imām as-Sajjād (A) has said that when the Imām was martyred, the fragrance of the apple arose from the spot of his martyrdom. Imām as-Sajjād (A) looked for the apple, but could not find anything; yet, the smell of the apple remained. The Imām (A) visited his grave and could smell the apple from his grave.

So when the shiʿahs go for ziyārah, if they want to smell the apple, they should go to the ḍarīh near sahar time, and if they are sincere, they will smell it, inshāAllāh.

Farewell Ziyārah of Imām Ḥusayn (A)

Peace be on you, O my master.	اَلسَّلَامُ عَلَيْكَ يَا مَوْلَايَ
Peace be on you, O the proof of Allāh.	اَلسَّلَامُ عَلَيْكَ يَا حُجَّةَ اللهِ
Peace be on you, O the chosen one of Allāh.	اَلسَّلَامُ عَلَيْكَ يَا صَفْوَةَ اللهِ
Peace be on you, O the pure one of Allāh.	اَلسَّلَامُ عَلَيْكَ يَا خَالِصَةَ اللهِ
Peace be on you, O he who was killed thirsty.	اَلسَّلَامُ عَلَيْكَ يَا قَتِيلَ الظَّمَاءِ
Peace be on you, O stranger in a strange land.	اَلسَّلَامُ عَلَيْكَ يَا غَرِيبَ الْغُرَبَاءِ
Peace be on you, the farewell salutations of one who is neither tired of nor averse to [your ziyārah].	اَلسَّلَامُ عَلَيْكَ سَلَامُ مُوَدِّعٍ لَا سَئِمٍ وَلَا قَالٍ
If I leave, it is not because I am tired [of your ziyārah], and if I remain here, it is not because I doubt your acceptance of my ziyārah and duʿāʾs, which Allāh has promised the patient ones.	فَإِنْ اَمْضِ فَلَا عَنْ مَلَالَةٍ وَإِنْ أُقِمْ فَلَا عَنْ سُوْءِ ظَنٍ بِمَا وَعَدَ اللهُ الصَّابِرِيْنَ
May Allāh not make this my last visitation to you,	لَاجَعَلَهُ اللهُ آخِرَ الْعَهْدِ مِنِّيْ لِزِيَارَتِكَ
and may He grant me the opportunity to return to your shrine,	وَرَزَقَنِيْ اللهُ الْعَوْدَ اِلَىٰ مَشْهَدِكَ

and a place in your courtyard and [a chance] to stand in your sanctuary.	وَالْمَقَامَ بِفِنَآئِكَ وَالْقِيَامَ فِيْ حَرَمِكَ
I beseech only Him that He makes me fortunate through you	وَاِيَّاهُ اَسْئَلُ اَنْ يُسْعِدَنِيْ بِكُمْ
And places me with you in this world and the hereafter.	وَيَجْعَلَنِيْ مَعَكُمْ فِيْ الدُّنْيَا وَالْاٰخِرَةِ

Turbah of Imām Ḥusayn (A)

Prophet Muḥammad (S):

أَلَا وَإِنَّ الْإِجَابَةَ تَحْتَ قُبَّتِهِ، وَالشِّفَاءَ فِيْ تُرْبَتِهِ، وَالْأَئِمَّةَ عَلَيْهِمَ السَّلَام مِنْ وُلْدِهِ

Know that the answer [to prayers] lies under his holy dome, and the cure [for illnesses] lies in his dust and the Imāms (A) of his lineage.

Mustadrak al-Wasāil, Vol. 10, P. 335

In a ḥadīth foretelling his own death, Imām Mūsā al-Kāẓim (A) said:

وَلَا تَأْخُذُوْا مِنْ تُرْبَتِيْ شَيْئاً لِتَبَرَّكُوْا بِهِ فَإِنَّ كُلَّ تُرْبَةٍ لَنَا مُحَرَّمَةٌ إِلَّا تُرْبَةُ جَدِّيَ الْحُسَيْنِ بْنِ عَلِيٍّ (عَلَيْهِمَا السَّلَامْ) فَإِنَّ اللهَ عَزَّوَجَلَّ جَعَلَهَا شِفَاءً لِشِيْعَتِنَا وَ أَوْلِيَائِنَا

Do not take any dirt from my grave as tabarruk (blessing), for certainly, all dirt is ḥarām (to eat) except for the dirt (turbah) of my grandfather, Ḥusayn ibn ʿAlī (A), in which the Almighty has placed (cure) for our Shīʿah and intimate servants.

Jāmiʿ Ahādith as-Shīʿah, Vol. 12, P. 533

Aḥkām and Effects of Soil from Imām Ḥusayn's (A) Grave

- It is mustaḥab (recommended) to prostrate on the turbah of Imām Ḥusayn (A) during ṣalāh and leads to greater rewards (than without sajdah).[1]
- Eating any sort of turbah (soil) is ḥarām (forbidden), except for the turbah of Imām Ḥusayn (A), which you are allowed to have a little of with the intention of attaining cure (shifāʾ).[2]
- Giving a taste of turbah of Imām Ḥusayn (A) to newborns is mustaḥab.[3]
- It is necessary to respect the turbah; any sort of disrespectful act towards it is ḥarām, such as:
    - Making it najis (ritually impure)
    - Throwing it where it is disrespectful (if it falls somewhere disrespectful, it must be removed)
- It is mustaḥab to place some turbah with a mayyit (dead body) and also mix some into his/her hunūt[4] as well.
- It is mustaḥab to include some turbah with presents being sent to others, such as the mahr (wedding dowry).
- It is mustaḥab to smell, kiss, and rub the turbah of Imām Ḥusayn (A) over the eyes, hands, and even over other parts of your body.
- It can be concluded that one's entire life should be accompanied by the turbah of Imām Ḥusayn (A).

[1]Al-ʿUrwah al-Wuthqā Vol.1, Fi Masjid al-Jibha, P.646
[2]Tawḍīʿ al Masāʾil, Rule 2628
[3]Taḥrīr al Wasīlah Vol.2, P.310, Rule #2
[4]Hunut is a small amount of camphor that is placed on the following seven parts of sajdah after ghusl al-mayyit: the forehead, palms of both hands, both knees, and the tips of both big toes.

Tasbīḥ of Turbah

History of the Tasbiḥ of Turbah

After the Noble Prophet (S) gifted and taught the famous tasbīḥ of Fāṭimah az-Zahrā (A) to his daughter, she made her own tasbīḥ using a wool thread with ties.

After the martyrdom of Ḥamzah in the battle of Uḥud, she replaced the knots in her tasbīḥ with dirt from his grave and used that for her dhikr. Many followed her lead and did the same.

When Imām Ḥusayn (A) was martyred in Karbalā, due to his unique status and high virtue, his turbah replaced all prior ones.

Imām Mūsā al-Kāẓim (A): Our Shīʿah are not without need of five things: a toothbrush, comb, prayer rug, turbah tasbīḥ, and ʿaqīq (agate) ring[1].

Imām ʿAlī ar-Riḍā (A): Whoever recites the following dhikr with a tasbiḥ made of turbah, with every bead of the tasbīḥ, the Almighty will record for him/her 6,000 good acts, erase 6,000 sins, elevate him/her 6,000 levels, and write for him/her 6,000 cures[2]:

سُبْحَانَ اللهِ وَالْحَمْدُلِلّٰهِ وَلَا إِلٰهَ إِلَّا اللهُ وَ اللهُ أَكْبَر

All glory be for Allāh, all praise is for Allāh, and there is no god except Allāh; God is Great!

[1]Biḥār al-Anwār Vol.83 P.334
[2]Miṣbāḥ al-Mutahajjid P.678

Madīnah: the pure soil of Sayyid ash-Shuhadā Ḥamzah ibn ʿAbd al Muṭṭʿalīb (uncle of the Prophet) and the martyrs of the battle of Uḥud

Karbalā: the pure soil of Abā ʿAbd Allāh al-Ḥusayn

Reciting dhikr using a tasbīḥ made out of the turbah of Imām Ḥusayn (A) and even just carrying it has greats rewards.

مَن كانَ مَعَهُ سُبحَةٌ مِن طِينِ قَبرِ الحُسَينِ عَلَيهِ السَّلامِ كُتِبَ مُسَبِّحاً و إن لَم يُسَبِّح بِها

Imām aṣ-Ṣādiq (A):

Whoever carries a tasbīḥ made from the turbah of Imām Ḥusayn (A) will be counted as someone who is glorifying Allāh, even if he is not saying anything.

Biḥār al-Anwār, Vol. 83, P. 332

Imām Ḥusayn's (A) Turbah

Even though we have many aḥādīth that say where the turbah should be taken from, the closer the soil is to the grave of Imām Ḥusayn (A), the better it is.

طِيْنُ قَبْرِ الْحُسَيْنِ عَلَيْهِ السَّلَام فِيْهِ شَفَاءٌ وَ إِنْ أُخْذَ عَلَىٰ رَأْسِ مِيْلٍ

Imām aṣ-Ṣādiq (A) said: There is cure in Imām Ḥusayn's (A) turbah even if it is within 1,800 meters [from his grave].

Wasā'il as-Shī'ah, Vol. 14, P. 513, H.19718

Some pilgrims came to ʿIrāq and said to Imām aṣ-Ṣādiq (A), "We know that the turbah of Imām Ḥusayn (A) cures every ailment, but does it also protect and give safety from fear?" The Imām (A) replied, "Yes, anytime someone wants to find peace and security from what they fear, they should hold onto the turbah and recite the following duʿāʾ three times:

O Allāh, I have begun this morning clinging to Your covenant (divine fiṭrah) and in Your high presence, which cannot be shortened or changed,	اَصْبَحْتُ اللّٰهُمَّ مُعْتَصِماً بِذِمَامِكَ وَجِوَارِكَ الْمَنِيْعِ الَّذِيْ لَا يُطَاوَلُ وَلَا يُحَاوَلُ،
(seeking protection) from the evil of all forceful and domineering ones from amongst Your creations, both the silent and speaking ones,	مِنْ شَرِّ كُلِّ غَاشِمٍ وَطَارِقٍ مِنْ سَائِرِ مَنْ خَلَقْتَ وَمَا خَلَقْتَ مِنْ خَلْقِكَ الصَّامِتِ وَالنَّاطِقِ
being covered from all terrifying things in a blessed covering and protected shield	فِيْ جُنَّةٍ مِنْ كُلِّ مَخُوْفٍ بِلِبَاسٍ سَابِغَةٍ حَصِيْنَةٍ
which is the guardianship of household of Your Prophet Muḥammad, may Allāh bless him and his Household.	وَهِيَ وَلَاءُ اَهْلِ بَيْتِ نَبِيِّكَ مُحَمَّدٍ صَلَّى اللهُ عَلَيْهِ وَآلِهِ

I am guarding myself against all those who intend harm upon me behind the impenetrable wall, which is my sincere profession of their true leadership and my adherence to their rope,	مُحْتَجِزاً مِنْ كُلِّ قَاصِدٍ لِيْ اِلَىٰ اَذِيَّةٍ بِجِدَارٍ حَصِيْنٍ الْإِخْلَاصِ فِي الْإِعْتِرَافِ بِحَقِّهِمْ وَالتَّمَسُّكِ بِحَبْلِهِمْ جَمِيْعاً
and I bear with certainty that the truth is for them, with them, from them, in them, and amid them.	مُوْقِناً اَنَّ الْحَقَّ لَهُمْ وَمَعَهُمْ وَمِنْهُمْ وَفِيْهِمْ وَبِهِمْ
I thus love those whom they love, hate those who hate them, and disocciate from those who disocciate from them.	اُوَالِي مَنْ وَالَوا وَاُعَادِيْ مَنْ عَادَوا وَ اُجَانِبُ مَنْ جَانَبُوا
So, send blessings upon Muḥammad and his household.	فَصَلِّ عَلَىٰ مُحَمَّدٍ وَّ آلِهِ
O Allāh, protect me, through them, against the evil of all that which I fear.	وَاَعِذْنِيْ اَللّٰهُمَّ بِهِمْ مِنْ شَرِّ كُلِّ مَا اَتَّقِيْهِ
O the Supreme! I am restraining the enemies against me through the Originator of the heavens and the earth,	يَا عَظِيْمُ حَجَزْتُ الْأَعَادِيَ عَنِّيْ بِبَدِيْعِ السَّمَاوَاتِ وَالْأَرْضِ
"Certainly We have set a barrier before them and a barrier behind them, and have covered them so they do not see."	اِنَّا جَعَلْنَا مِنْ بَيْنِ اَيْدِيْهِمْ سَدًّا وَ مِنْ خَلْفِهِمْ سَدًّا فَاَغْشَيْنَاهُمْ فَهُمْ لَا يُبْصِرُوْنَ

Then, kiss the turbah, rub it over your eyes, and say:

O Allāh, I ask You by the right of this blessed dust,	اَللّٰهُمَّ إِنِّيْ أَسْأَلُكَ بِحَقِّ هٰذِهِ التُّرْبَةِ الْمُبَارَكَةِ
by the right of its owner,	وَبِحَقِّ صَاحِبِهَا
by the right of his grandfather,	وَبِحَقِّ جَدِّهِ
by the right of his father,	وَبِحَقِّ أَبِيْهِ
by the right of his mother,	وَبِحَقِّ أُمِّهِ
by the right of his brother,	وَبِحَقِّ أَخِيْهِ
and by the right of his purified sons,	وَبِحَقِّ وُلْدِهِ الطَّاهِرِيْنَ
to make it a cure for every ailment,	اَجْعَلْهَا شِفَاءً مِنْ كُلِّ دَاءٍ
security against every fear,	وَأَمَاناً مِنْ كُلِّ خَوْفٍ
and safeguard against every evil.	وَحِفْظاً مِنْ كُلِّ سُوْءٍ

The Land of Karbalāʾ and the Land of Makkah

عَــنْ أَبِيْ عَبْدِاللهِ قَالَ:إِنَّ أَرْضَ الْكَعْبَةِ قَالَتْ: مَــنْ مِثْلِيْ وَ قَدْ بُنِيَ بَيْتُ اللهِ عَلَيَّ ظَهْرِيْ
يَأْتِيْنِيْ النَّاسُ مِنْ كُلِ فَجٍ عَمِيْقٍ وَجُعِلْتُ حَرَمُ اللهِ وَأَمْنِهِ. فَأَوْحي اللهُ إِلَيْهَا أَنْ كُفِّي وَقَرِّي
مَــا فَضْلُ مَا فُضِّلْتِ بِهِ فِيْمَا أَعْطَيْتُ أَرْضَ كَرْبَلَاءَ إِلَّا بِمَنْزِلَةِ الْإِبْرَةِ غُرِسَــتْ فِيْ الْبَحْرِ
فَحَمَلَــتْ مِنْ مَاءِ الْبَحْرِ وَ لَوْلَا تُرْبَةُ كَرْبَلَاءَ مَا فَضَّلْتُكِ وَلَوْلَا مَنْ تَضَمَّنَهُ أَرْضُ كَرْبَلَاءَ
مَا خَلَقْتُكِ وَخَلَقْتُ البَيْــتِ الَّذِيْ بِهِ افْتَخَرْتِ فَقَرِّيْ وَاسْــتَقَرِّيْ وَكُوْنِيْ ذَنْباً مُتَوَاضِعاً
ذَلِيْلاً مُهِيْناً غَيْرَمُسْتَنْكِفٍ وَلَامُسْــتَكْبِرٍلِأَرْضِ كَرْبَلَاءَ وَإِلَّاسُخْتُ بِكِ وَهَوَيْتُ بِكِ فِيْ
نَارِ جَهَنَّمَ.

Imām aṣ-Ṣādiq (A):

The land of the Kaʿbah once said, "Who has the same value as me?! Allāh has built His house upon my land, and people from all over the world come to me. Allāh has made me His sanctuary."

Allāh revealed to it, "Your virtue compared to the virtue that I have granted to the land of Karbalāʾ is like a drop of water on a needle dipped in the sea. If it were not for the dust of Karbalāʾ, I would not have honored you. If it were not for that which is held within the land of Karbalāʾ, I would have not created you, nor would I have created the house about which you boasted.Therefore, become humbled before the land of Karbalāʾ."

Biḥār al-Anwār Vol.101, P.106

Indeed, it was through Imām Ḥusayn (A) and his sacrifice that Allāh is known as He should be. Thus, if there were no Karbalāʾ, there would be no Kaʿbah.

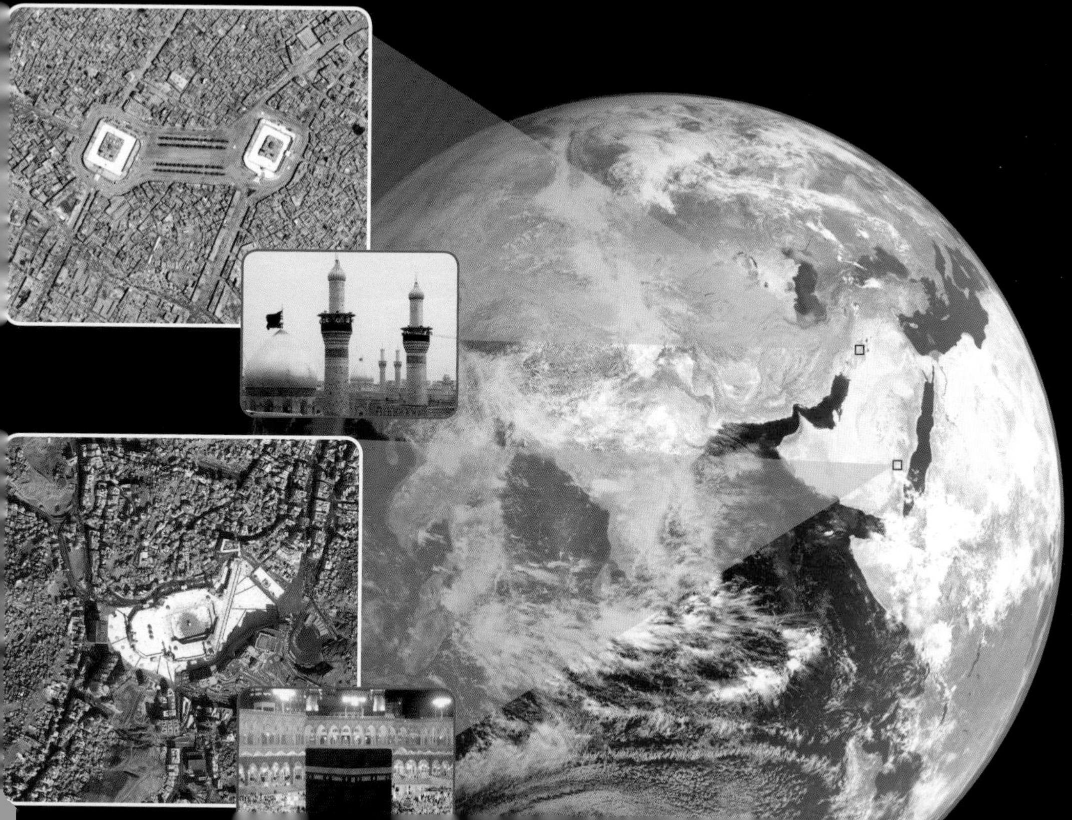

Kaʿbah & Zamzam; Karbalā᾿ & Euphrates

Imām aṣ-Ṣādiq (A): Indeed Allāh, the Blessed and Exalted, has elevated some lands and bodies of water above others. Some of them boasted to others and some transgressed, and they were punished for not being humble to Allāh. Because of its transgressions, polytheists took over (the land of) Kaʿbah and changed the taste of the zamzam water. Indeed, the land of Karbalā᾿ and Euphrates River were the first land and body of water that glorified Allāh, the Blessed and Exalted.

So, Allāh blessed them and said to the Land of Karbalā᾿, "Speak of that with which the Almighty Allāh has honored you, for indeed the lands and the waters have boasted to one another."

The Land of Karbalā᾿ said:

أَنَا أَرْضُ اللهِ الْمُقَدَّسَةِ الْمُبَارَكَةِ. الشِّفَاءُ فِيْ تُرْبَتِيْ وَ مَائِيْ وَلَافَخْرَ بَلْ خَاضِعَةٌ ذَلِيْلَةٌ لِمَنْ فَعَلَ بِيْ وَلَافَخْرَ عَلَى مَنْ دُوْنِيْ بَلْ شُكْراً لِلهِ

I am the sacred and blessed land of Allāh. Cure has been placed in my dust and water, and I am not arrogant. Rather, I am humble and humiliated before He who has blessed me. I do not boast to those who are lower than me in rank. On the contrary, I am thankful to Allāh.

So, Allāh honored it, increased His blessings upon it for its humility, and rewarded it with by burying in its land Imām Ḥusayn (A) and his companions. Imām aṣ-Ṣādiq (A) added:

مَنْ تَوَاضَعَ لِلَّهِ رَفَعَهُ اللهُ وَ مَنْ تَكَبَّرَ وَضَعَهُ اللهُ تَعَالَى

"Allāh elevates those who humble themselves before Him and He degrades those who are arrogant."

Kāmil al-Ziyārah, P. 821, Ibn Qulawayh

Baynul Ḥaramayn & Ṣafā and Marwah

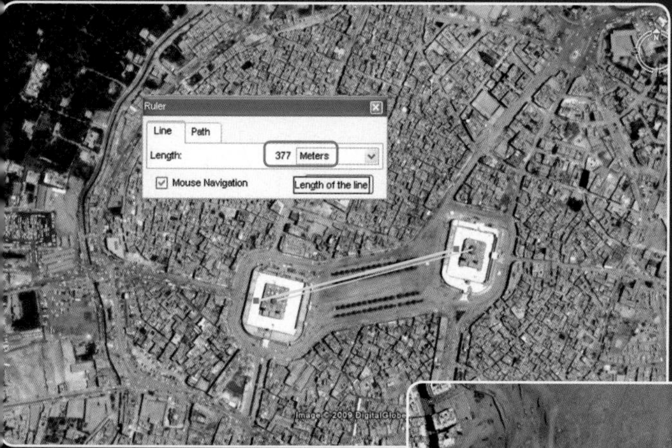

There is a distance of 377 meters (412 yards) between the mountains of Ṣafā and Marwah, where pilgrims perform their Saʿī.

This is the same distance that is between the shrines of Imām Ḥusayn (A) and Ḥaḍrat ʿAbbās (A).

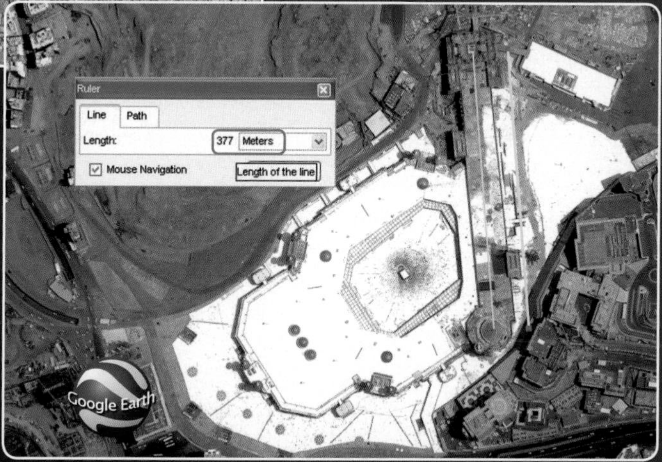

السلام عليك يا قمر العشيره

Ḥaḍrat Abū al-Faḍl al-ʿAbbās

Name:	ʿAbbās
Kunyah:	Abū al-Faḍl
Title:	Qamar Banī Hāshim (The moon of the tribe of Hāshim), Sāqī (Waterbearer), Bāb al-Ḥawāʾij (The Door to Wishes)
Parents:	Imām ʿAlī (A) & Fāṭimah Umm al-Banīn
Birthday:	4th Shaʿbān, 26 AH
Birthplace:	Madīnah
Number of children:	Four sons and one daughter
Date of martyrdom:	10th Muharram (ʿĀshūrāʾ), 61 AH
Place of martyrdom:	Karbalāʾ
Cause of martyrdom:	Battle against army of Yazīd (May Allāh remove His mercy from him)
Life span:	34 years
Holy shrine:	Karbalāʾ, ʿIrāq

كَانَ عَمُّنَا الْعَبَّاسِ بْنِ عَلِيٍّ نَافِذَ الْبَصِيْرَةِ صُلْبَ الْاِيْمَانِ جَاهَدَ مَعَ أَبِيْ عَبْدِاللهِ وَأَبلَا بَلَاءً حَسَناً وَ مَضَى شَهِيْداً

Imām aṣ-Ṣādiq (A)

Our uncle ʿAbbās ibn ʿAlī had great wisdom, insight, and strong faith. He sacrificed his life in the presence of Abā ʿAbd Allāh (A) and achieved martyrdom.

ʿUmdah aṭ-Ṭālib Fī Ansāb Āli Abī Ṭālib, P. 653, Ibn ʿAnbah

Map of the Holy Shrine of Ḥaḍrat ʿAbbās (A)

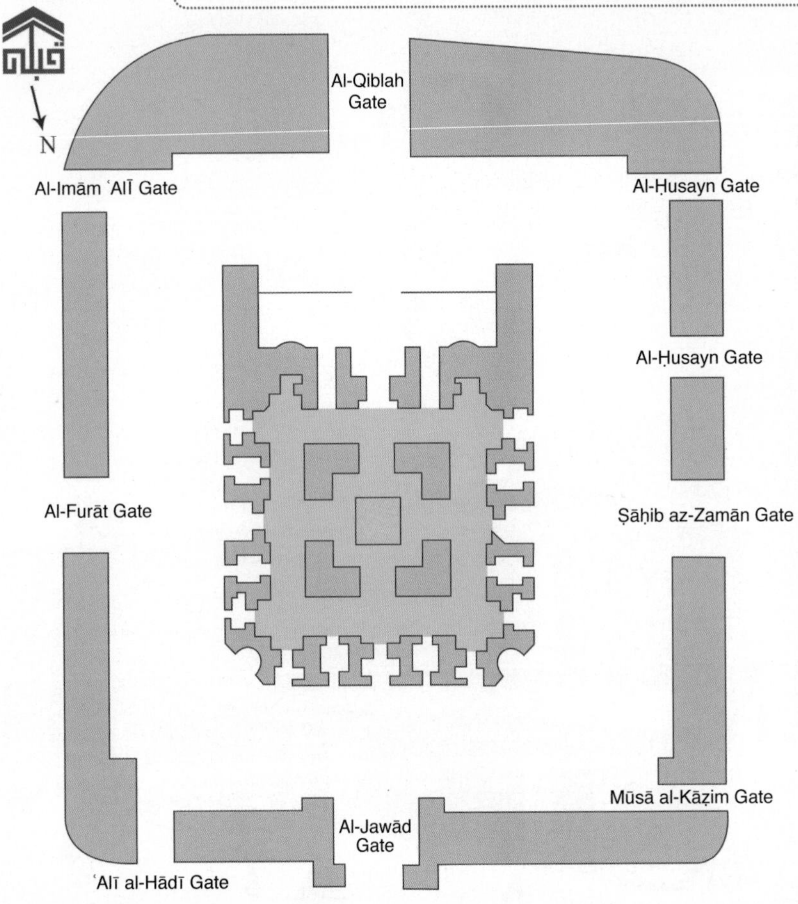

رَحِمَ اللهُ عَمِّيَ الْعَبَّاس فَلَقَدْ آثَرَ وَ أَبْلَى
وَ فَدَىٰ أَخَاهُ بِنَفْسِهِ حَتَّى قُطِعَتْ يَدَاهُ
فَأَبْدَلَهُ اللهُ بِهِمَا جَنَاحَيْنِ يَطِيْرُ بِهِمَا مَعَ
الْمَلَائِكَةِ فِيْ الْجَنَّةِ كَمَا جَعَلَ لِجَعْفَرَ
بْنَ أَبِيْ طَالِبٍ وَ إِنَّ لِلْعَبَّاسِ عِنْدَاللهِ
مَنْزِلَةً يَغْبِطُهُ بِهَا جَمِيْعُ الشُّهَدَاءِ يَوْمَ
الْقِيَامَةِ

Imām Sajjād (A):

May Allāh bless my uncle ʿAbbās, who sacrificed himself and gave up his life to save his brother to the point that his arms were cut off his body, and Allāh granted him two wings instead by which he could fly to Heaven, just as He did for Jaʿfar ibn Abī Ṭālib. Know that ʿAbbās has such a unique place that all the martyrs will envy his position on the Day of Judgment.

ʿUmdah aṭ-Ṭālib Fī Ansāb Āli Abī Ṭālib, P. 653, Ibn ʿAnbah

Etiquette of Ziyārah of Ḥaḍrat ʿAbbās (A)

The status of infallibility is manifested completely within the 14 Maʿṣūmīn, while others have been able to reach it to some extent, such as Sayyidah Zaynab, ʿAlī Akbar, Sayyidah Maʿsūmah, and Ḥaḍrat ʿAbbās (A).

Ḥaḍrat ʿAbbās (A) is a personality that has reached a very high level of ʿiṣmah (infallibility). In fact, he has reached such a high level that some of the aḥkām, etiquettes, and mustaḥabāt of his ziyārah and ḥaram are similar to those of the 14 Maʿṣūmīn.

- Just as we perform ziyārah of the Maʿṣūmīn,for the ziyarah of Ḥaḍrat ʿAbbās it is also recommended to stand with your back towards the qiblah and your front towards the ḍarīḥ.
- Ṣalāt ul-Ziyārah (a two rakaʿāt prayer after reciting ziyārah), which is recommended for the 14 Maʿṣūmīn, is also recommended for Ḥaḍrat ʿAbbās.
- It is highly recommended for those who are in the state of janābah or ḥaydh not to enter the shrine of Ḥaḍratʿ Abbās (A), just as with the 14 Maʿsūmīn.

Beneficial Āʿmāl for Ḥājāt

The following āʿmāl are proven to be effective:

- In the ḥaram, recite the following tasbīḥ 133 times in one sitting. InshaʿAllāh, Allāh will grant your needs.

يَاكَاشِفَ الْكَرْبِ عَنْ وَجْهِ الْحُسَيْنِ اِكْشِفْ كَرْبِي بِحَقِّ أَخِيْكَ الْحُسَيْنِ

Yā Kāshifa-l-karbi ʿan wajhi-l-Ḥusayn (A), ikshif karbī biḥaqqi akhīka-l-Ḥusayn (A)

O Dispeller of grief from the face of Ḥusayn (A), dispell my grief, by the right of Ḥusayn's (A) brother.

- Ṣalāh of tawassul to Ḥaḍrat ʿAbbās:

  The revered scholar al-Kalbāsī has recommended the following Salāh of tawassul to Recite a two rakaʿāt prayer; in each rakʿah, recite Surat al-Fātihah once and *"Ya Ḥayyu, Ya Qayyūm"* 100 times. After the ṣalāh, recite 100 times:

  "As-salāmu ʿalayka yā ʿAbbās ibn Amīru-l-muʾminīn"

In Rememberance of Umm al-Banīn

Even though Umm al-Banīn was not in Karbalāʾ, many pilgrims do the following when they want to exit the hall after performing the ziyārah of ʿAbbās (A). They stand by the western door next to the minaret, take the name of Umm al-Banīn, and take blessings from that doorway, as if to say, "O Umm al-Banīn, we will never forget your sacrifices! All praise be upon you and your brave children!" This is why this door has been named the Door of Umm al-Banīn.

O ʿAbbas, so few understand your name!
The understanding of your greatness my soul cannot retain!

Ziyārah of Ḥaḍrat ʿAbbās (A)

Imām aṣ-Ṣādiq (A): When you want to perform the Ziyārah of al-ʿAbbās (A), stand at the door to the ḍarīḥ and recite the following:

May the peace of Allāh and His closest angels, commissioned Prophets, righteous servants, all the martyrs, and all the truthful (ones),	سَلَامُ اللهِ وَسَـلَامُ مَلَآئِكَتِهِ الْمُقَرَّبِيْنَ وَاَنْبِيَآئِهِ الْمُرْسَلِيْنَ وَعِبَادِهِ الصَّالِحِيْنَ وَجَمِيْعِ الشُّهَدَاءِ وَالصِّدِّيْقِيْنَ

and also pure, true blessings that come and go, be upon you, O son of the Commander of the Faithful!	وَالزَّاكِيَاتُ الطَّيِّبَاتُ فِيْمَا تَغْتَدِيْ وَتَرُوْحُ عَلَيْكَ يَا بْنَ اَمِيْرِ الْمُؤْمِنِيْنَ
I bear witness to your submission, honesty, loyalty, and sincerity to the descendants of the Prophet, may Allāh's blessings be upon him and his household,	اَشْهَدُ لَكَ بِالتَّسْلِيْمِ وَالتَّصْدِيْقِ وَالْوَفَآءِ وَالنَّصِيْحَةِ لِخَلَفِ النَّبِيِّ صَلَّى اللهُ عَلَيْهِ وَآلِهِ الْمُرْسَلِ
the chosen grandson (of the Prophet), the knowledgeable guide (to the true religion), the conveying successor, and the wrongfully oppressed one.	وَالسِّبْطِ الْمُنْتَجَبِ، وَالدَّلِيْلِ الْعَالِمِ، وَالْوَصِيِّ الْمُبَلِّغِ، وَالْمَظْلُوْمِ الْمُهْتَضَمِ
So, may Allāh reward you on behalf of His Messenger, the Commander of the Faithful, al-Ḥasan, and al-Ḥusayn, may Allāh's peace be upon them,	فَجَزَاكَ اللهُ عَنْ رَسُوْلِهِ وَعَنْ اَمِيْرِ الْمُؤْمِنِيْنَ وَعَنِ الْحَسَنِ وَالْحُسَيْنِ صَلَوَاتُ اللهِ عَلَيْهِمْ
with the best reward for your steadfastness, dedication (to the sake of God), and support (for the right party). Surely, the reward of the eternal life is great!	اَفْضَلَ الْجَزَاءِ بِمَا صَبَرْتَ وَاحْتَسَبْتَ وَاَعَنْتَ فَنِعْمَ عُقْبَى الدَّارِ
May Allāh curse he who killed you, ignored your rights, and violated your sanctity.	لَعَنَ اللهُ مَنْ قَتَلَكَ وَلَعَنَ اللهُ مَنْ جَهِلَ حَقَّكَ وَاسْتَخَفَّ بِحُرْمَتِكَ

May Allāh's curse be upon he who blocked you from the water of the Euphrates.	وَلَعَنَ اللهُ مَنْ حَالَ بَيْنَكَ وَبَيْنَ مَاءِ الْفُرَاتِ
I bear witness that you were killed oppressively,	اَشْهَدُ اَنَّكَ قُتِلْتَ مَظْلُوماً
and that Allāh will surely fulfill His promise to you.	وَاَنَّ اللهَ مُنْجِزٌ لَكُمْ مَاوَعَدَكُمْ
O son of the Commander of the Faithful, I have come to you with loyalty.	جِئْتُكَ يَا بْنَ اَمِيرِ الْمُؤْمِنِيْنَ وَافِداً اِلَيْكُمْ
My heart is submissive to you and follows you,	وَقَلْبِيْ مُسَلِّمٌ لَكُمْ وَتَابِعٌ
and I am your follower, ready to support you until Allāh judges, and He is the best of Judges!	وَاَنَالَكُمْ تَابِعٌ وَنُصْرَتِيْ لَكُمْ مُعَدَّةٌ حَتّىٰ يَحْكُمَ اللهُ وَهُوَخَيْرُالْحَاكِمِيْنَ
I am with you, not with your enemy. Surely, I believe in you and your return,	فَمَعَكُمْ مَعَكُمْ لَا مَعَ عَدُوِّكُمْ اِنِّيْ بِكُمْ وَبِاِيَابِكُمْ مِنَ الْمُؤْمِنِيْنَ
and I deny your opposers and killers.	وَبِمَنْ خَالَفَكُمْ وَقَتَلَكُمْ مِنَ الْكَافِرِيْنَ
Certainly, I believe in you and your return and reject those who opposed and killed you.	إِنِّيْ بِكُمْ وَ بِإِيَابِكُمْ مِنَ الْمُؤْمِنِيْنَ وَ بِمَنْ خَالَفَكُمْ وَ قَتَلَكُمْ مِنَ الْكَافِرِيْنَ
May Allāh kill the group who killed you with their hands and tongues.	قَتَلَ اللهُ اُمَّةً قَتَلَتْكُمْ بِالْاَيْدِيْ وَالْاَلْسُنِ

Then, enter, fall upon the grave, face the qiblah, and recite the following:

Peace be upon you, O righteous servant, who was obedient to Allāh, His Messenger,	اَلسَّلَامُ عَلَيْكَ اَيُّهَا الْعَبْدُ الصَّالِحُ الْمُطِيْعُ لِلّٰهِ وَلِرَسُوْلِهِ
the Commander of the Faithful, al-Ḥasan, and al-Ḥusayn, peace and blessings of Allāh be upon them.	وَلِاَمِيْرِ الْمُؤْمِنِيْنَ وَالْحَسَنِ والْحُسَيْنِ صَلَّى اللهُ عَلَيْهِمْ وَسَلَّمَ،
May Allāh's peace, mercy, blessings, forgiveness, and pleasure be upon you, your soul, and your body.	اَلسَّلَامُ عَلَيْكَ وَرَحْمَةُ اللهِ وَبَرَكَاتُهُ وَمَغْفِرَتُهُ وَرِضْوَانُهُ وَعَلٰى رُوْحِكَ وَبَدَنِكَ،
I bear witness, and call Allāh to witness, that you abided by the same course that was taken by the warriors of (the battle of) Badr and those who strove for Allāh's sake,	اَشْهَدُ وَاُشْهِدُ اللهَ اَنَّكَ مَضَيْتَ عَلٰى مَا مَضٰى بِهِ الْبَدْرِيُّوْنَ وَالْمُجَاهِدُوْنَ فِيْ سَبِيْلِ اللهِ
who sincerely served Him in the battlefields against His enemies, did their best to support His disciples, and defended His beloved ones.	الْمُنَاصِحُوْنَ لَهُ فِيْ جِهَادِ اَعْدَائِهِ الْمُبَالِغُوْنَ فِيْ نُصْرَةِ اَوْلِيَآئِهِ الذَّآبُّوْنَ عَنْ اَحِبَّآئِهِ
So, Allāh may reward you with the best, most abundant, and most complete rewards,	فَجَزَاكَ اللهُ أَفْضَلَ الْجَزَآءِ وَأَكْثَرَ الْجَزَآءِ وَأَوْفَرَ الْجَزَآءِ
and the most conclusive reward that He may give to anyone who fulfills His homage, answers His call, and obeys His guardians.	وَاَوْفٰى جَزَآءِ اَحَدٍ مِمَّنْ وَفٰى بِبَيْعَتِهِ وَاسْتَجَابَ لَهُ دَعْوَتَهُ وَاَطَاعَ وُلَاةَ اَمْرِهِ

I bear witness that you acted sincerely and exerted all your efforts (in this regard).	اَشْهَدُ اَنَّكَ قَدْ بالَغْتَ فِيْ النَّصِيْحَةِ وَاَعْطَيْتَ غايَةَ الْمَجْهُوْدِ
May Allāh resurrect you with the martyrs,	فَبَعَثَكَ اللهُ فِيْ الشُّهَدَآءِ،
place your soul with the souls of the felicitous ones,	وَجَعَلَ رُوْحَكَ مَعَ اَرْوَاحِ السُّعَدَآءِ،
grant you the largest abode and greatest room in His Paradise,	وَاَعْطَاكَ مِنْ جِنانِهِ اَفْسَحَها مَنْزِلاً وَاَفْضَلَها غُرَفاً،
exalt your praise to the highest levels,	وَرَفَعَ ذِكْرَكَ فِيْ عِلِّيِّيْنَ
and join you with the Prophets, the truthful ones, the martyrs, and the righteous ones. How excellent is the companionship of such ones!	وَحَشَرَكَ مَعَ النَّبِيِّيْنَ وَالصِّدِّيْقِيْنَ وَالشُّهَدَآءِ وَالصَّالِحِيْنَ وَحَسُنَ اُوْلٰئِكَ رَفِيْقاً،
I bear witness that you did not lag behind or turn away,	اَشْهَدُ اَنَّكَ لَمْ تَهِنْ وَلَمْ تَنْكُلْ
and that you left this life with full insight of the truth, following the examples of the righteous ones, and following the Prophets.	وَاَنَّكَ مَضَيْتَ عَلٰى بَصِيْرَةٍ مِنْ اَمْرِكَ مُقْتَدِياً بِالصَّالِحِيْنَ وَمُتَّبِعاً لِّلنَّبِيِّيْنَ
So, may Allāh gather us with you, in the abodes of His Messenger and His intimate servants, who enjoy the status of the humble ones.	فَجَمَعَ اللهُ بَيْنَنا وَبَيْنَكَ وَبَيْنَ رَسُوْلِهِ وَاَوْلِيَآئِهِ فِيْ مَنازِلِ الْمُخْبِتِيْنَ،

Certainly, He is the Most Merciful!	فَاِنَّهُ اَرْحَمُ الرَّاحِمِيْنَ

Offer a two rakaʿāt prayer by the holy head and then say:

O Allāh, send blessings upon Muḥammad and the household of Muḥammad,	اَللّٰهُمَّ صَلِّ عَلٰى مُحَمَّدٍ وَّآلِ مُحَمَّدٍ
and do not leave for me, in this honored place and glorified shrine, any sin except that You forgive it,	وَلَاتَدَعْ لِيْ فِيْ هٰذَا الْمَكَانِ الْمُكَرَّمِ وَالْمَشْهَدِ الْمُعَظَّمِ ذَنْباً اِلَّا غَفَرْتَهُ،
any grief except that You relieve it, any illness except that You cure it, any defect except that You cover it up,	وَلَاهَمّاً اِلَّافَرَّجْتَهُ، وَلَامَرَضاً اِلَّاشَفَيْتَهُ، وَلَاعَيْباً اِلَّاسَتَرْتَهُ،
any sustenance except that You expand it, any fear except that You pacify it, any disunity except that You reunify it,	وَلَا رِزْقاً اِلَّا بَسَطْتَهُ، وَلَاخَوْفاً اِلَّاآمَنْتَهُ، وَلَاشَمْلاً اِلَّا جَمَعْتَهُ،
any absent one except that You guard him and bring him near to me,	وَلَاغَائِباً اِلَّا حَفِظْتَهُ وَاَدْنَيْتَهُ،
and any single need in this world or the hereafter, whose settlement achieves your gratification and my goodness, except that You grant it. O the Most Merciful!	وَلَاحَاجَةً مِنْ حَوَآئِجِ الدُّنْيَا وَالْآخِرَةِ لَكَ فِيْهَا رِضًى وَّلِيَ فِيْهَاصَلَاحٌ اِلَّا قَضَيْتَهَا يَا اَرْحَمَ الرَّاحِمِيْنَ.

Then, turn towards the ḍarīḥ and standing at the footside, say:

Peace be upon you, O Abū al-Faḍl al-ʿAbbās, the son of the Commander of the Faithful.	اَلسَّلَامُ عَلَيْكَ يَا اَبَا الْفَضْلِ الْعَبَّاسَ ابْنَ اَمِيرِالْمُؤْمِنِيْنَ،
Peace be upon you, O son of the chief of the successors (of the Prophets).	اَلسَّلَامُ عَلَيْكَ يَا بْنَ سَيِّدِالْوَصِيِّيْنَ
Peace be upon you, O son of the foremost to Islam, the first to believe,	اَلسَّلَامُ عَلَيْكَ يَا بْنَ اَوَّلِ الْقَوْمِ اِسْلَاماً وَاَقْدَمِهِمْ اِيْمَاناً
the best to have served the religion of Allāh,	وَاَقْوَمِهِمْ بِدِيْنِ اللهِ
and the most precise (in practicing ther responsibilities in) Islām.	وَاَحْوَطِهِمْ عَلَى الْاِسْلَامِ
I bear witness that you served Allāh, His Messenger, and your brother sincerely. You were the most excellent self-sacrificing brother.	اَشْهَدُ لَقَدْ نَصَحْتَ لِلّٰهِ وَلِرَسُوْلِهِ وَلِاَخِيْكَ فَنِعْمَ الْاَخُ الْمُوَاسِيْ،
So, may Allāh's curse be on the group who killed you,	فَلَعَنَ اللهُ اُمَّةً قَتَلَتْكَ،
may Allāh's curse be on the group who oppressed you.	وَلَعَنَ اللهُ اُمَّةً ظَلَمَتْكَ،
Allāh's curse be on the group who violated your sanctitiy,	وَلَعَنَ اللهُ اُمَّةً اِسْتَحَلَّتْ مِنْكَ الْمَحَارِمَ،
and violated the sanctity of Islam.	وَانْتَهَكَتْ حُرْمَةَ الْاِسْلَامِ،

You were the most excellent steadfast fighter, protector, supporter, and brother who defended his brother,	فَنِعْمَ الصَّابِرُ الْمُجاهِـــدُ الْمُحَامِيْ النَّاصِرُ وَالْاَخُ الدَّافِعُ عَنْ اَخِيْهِ،
responded to the obedience to his Lord,	الْمُجِيْبُ اِلَىٰ طَاعَةِ رَبِّهِ،
and worked desirably for gaining the abundant reward and a beautiful tribute, which others refused.	الرَّاغِبُ فِيْمَا زَهِـــدَ فِيْهِ غَيْرُهُ مِنَ الثَّوَابِ الْجَزِيْلِ وَالثَّنَاءِ الْجَمِيْلِ،
So, may Allāh include you in the rank of your fathers in the gardens of bliss.	وَاَلْحَقَــكَ اللّٰهُ بِدَرَجَةِ آبائِــكَ فِيْ جَنَّاتِ النَّعِيْمِ،
O Allāh, I have visited Your intimate servants out of my desire for gaining your reward	اَللَّهُمَّ اِنِّيْ تَعَرَّضْتُ لِزِ يَارَةِ اَوْلِيَائِكَ رَغْبَةً فِيْ ثَوَابِكَ
and hoping for Your forgiveness and Your greatest benevolence.	وَرَجَآءً لِمَغْفِرَتِكَ وَجَزِيْلِ اِحْسَانِكَ،
So, I ask You to send blessings upon Muḥammad and his immaculate household,	فَاَسْـــاَلُكَ اَنْ تُصَـــلِّيْ عَلَىٰ مُحَمَّـــدٍ وَّآلِهِ الطَّاهِرِيْنَ،
and to make my sustenance flow, make my life delightful,	وَاَنْ تَجْعَلَ رِزْقِيْ بِهِمْ دَارًّا وَعَيْشِيْ بِهِمْ قَارًّا
accept my ziyāarah, and make my life pure through them	وَزِ يَارَتِيْ بِهِمْ مَقْبُوْلَةً وَحَيَاتِيْ بِهِمْ طَيِّبَةً

and raise my rank to the rank of the honored ones, make me one of those who changes and becomes successful and prosperous, upon returning from visiting the shriness of Your beloved ones,	وَاَدْرِجْـــنِيْ اِدْرَاجَ الْمُكْرَمِـــيْنَ، وَاجْعَلْنِيْ مِمَّنْ يَنْقَلِبُ مِنْ زِ يَارَةِ مَشَاهِدِ اَحِبَّائِكَ مُفْلِحاً مُنْجِحاً،
and deserve forgiveness of sins, covering up of defects, and relief of disasters.	قَدِ اسْتَوْجَبَ غُفْرَانَ الذُّنُوْبِ وَسَتْرَ الْعُيُوْبِ وَكَشْفَ الْكُرُوْبِ،
Certainly, You are the Lord of piety and forgiveness.	اِنَّكَ اَهْلُ التَّقْوٰى وَاَهْلُ الْمَغْفِرَةِ.

Farewell Ziyārah of Ḥaḍrat ʿAbbās (A)

This duʿāʾ was narrated from Abū Ḥamzah ath-Thumālī; scholars also recommend to recite it when you bid farewell:

I entrust you in Allāh's care and ask to keep you under His guard, and invoke peace upon you.	اَسْـــتَوْدِعُكَ اللهَ وَاَسْتَرْعِيْكَ وَاَقْرَأُ عَلَيْكَ اَلسَّلَامَ
We have believed in Allāh, in His Messenger, in His Book, and in that which he conveyed from Allāh.	آمَنَّا بِاللهِ وَبِرَسُوْلِهِ وَبِكِتَابِهِ وَبِمَاجَاءَ بِهِ مِنْ عِنْدِاللهِ،

O Allāh, record our names with the witnesses. O Allāh, do not decide this pilgrimage to the tomb of the son of Your Messenger's brother to be the last one of mine. Peace be upon him and upon his Household.	اَللّٰهُمَّ فَاكْتُبْنَا مَعَ الشَّاهِدِيْنَ، اَللّٰهُمَّ لَا تَجْعَلْهُ آخِرَ الْعَهْدِ مِنْ زِيَارَتِيْ قَبْرَ ابْنِ اَخِيْ رَسُوْلِكَ صَلَّى اللهُ عَلَيْهِ وَآلِهِ
Grant me opportunities to visit him so long as You keep me ʿAlīve, join me to him and to his fathers in the gardens of Paradise,	وَارْزُقْنِيْ زِيَارَتَهُ اَبَداً مَّا اَبْقَيْتَنِيْ وَاحْشُرْنِيْ مَعَهُ وَمَعَ آبَائِهِ فِيْ الْجِنَانِ
and introduce me to him, to Your Messenger, and to Your guardians.	وَعَرِّفْ بَيْنِيْ وَبَيْنَهُ وَبَيْنَ رَسُوْلِكَ وَاَوْلِيَائِكَ،
O Allāh, send Your blessings to Muḥammad and the Household of Muḥammad,	اَللّٰهُمَّ صَلِّ عَلَىٰ مُحَمَّدٍ وَّآلِ مُحَمَّدٍ
and take me to You while I have faith in You	وَتَوَفَّنِيْ عَلَى الْإِيْمَانِ بِكَ
certifying Your Messenger,	وَالتَّصْدِيْقِ بِرَسُوْلِكَ
being loyal to ʿAlī, son of Abū Ṭālib, and the Imāms from his progeny, and dissociating from their enemies.	وَالْوِلَايَةِ لِعَلِيِّ بْنِ اَبِيْ طَالِبٍ وَالْأَئِمَّةِ مِنْ وُلْدِهِ وَالْبَرَاءَةِ مِنْ عَدُوِّهِمْ
My Lord, surely, I am please with this.	فَاِنِّيْ قَدْ رَضِيْتُ يَا رَبِّيْ بِذٰلِكَ،
Allāh may send blessings upon Muḥammad and the Household of Muḥammad.	وَصَلَّى اللهُ عَلَىٰ مُحَمَّدٍ وَّآلِ مُحَمَّدٍ

The Maqām of al-ʿAbbās's Right Hand

Ibn Shahr Āshūb said: ʿAbbās (A) was the Sāqī (water bearer), Qamar Banī Hāshim (Moon of Banī Hāshim), and the flagbearer of Imām Ḥusayn (A). He came to get water, and they attacked him and he confronted them saying:

لاأرهب الموت إذ الموت رقىَ حتّىَ أوارىَ في المصاليت لقا
نفسي لنفس المصطفىَ الطّهر وقا إنّي أنا العبّاس أغدوا بالسّقا
و لاأخاف الشرّ يوم الملتقي

I never fear death when it comes around.
May my life be sacrificed for the life of the pure Muṣṭafā!
I am al-ʿAbbās, the Saqqā, who has no fear of the evil and I will make the enemy scatter.

Zayd ibn Warqā was hiding behind a palm tree. Along with Hakīm ibn Tufayl, he struck the right hand of ʿAbbās (A). So,ʿAbbās switched the sword and waterbag to his left and chanted:

إنّي أُحامي أبداً عن ديني والله إن قطعتم يميني
نجل النّبيّ الطّاهر الأمين و عن إمام صادق اليقين

By Allāh! If you cut off my right hand,
I shall not cease defending my religion!
An Imām true to his conviction do I defend,
A son of the pure and trustworthy Prophet, whom Allāh did send.

Place of the right hand of Ḥaḍrat ʿAbbās
Towards the northeast and southeast of Ḥaḍrat ʿAbbās's courtyard, there are two places where the blessed hands of Ḥaḍrat ʿAbbās (A) were severed.

The Maqām of al-ʿAbbās's Left Hand

Ḥaḍrat ʿAbbās (A) continued to fight. Meanwhile, Hakīm ibn Tufayl, who was hiding behind another palm tree, came out and stuck the left arm of Ḥaḍrat ʿAbbās (A), who then said:

يَا نفس لا تخشي من الكفّار
و أبشري برحمة الجبّار
مع النّبيّ السّيّد المختار
قدقطعوا ببغيهم يساري   فأصلهم يَا ربّ حرّ النّار

O Self, do not fear the infidels!
And be glad [to receive] the Mercy of the Almighty
With the Prophet, the master of chosen ones
Along with the masters and pure ones
They have cut off my left [arm] with their tyranny
So burn them, O Lord, with the heat of the fire

Alas, ʿAbbās (A) was struck with a metal club and fell to the sands of Karbalā᾽. Imām Ḥusayn (A) rushed towards his brother and found him lying on the ground by the Euphrates River. He cried out:

تعدّيتم يَاشرّ قوم بفعلكم   و خالفتم قول النّبيّ محمّد
أما كان خير الرّسل وصّاكم بنا   أما نحن من نسل النّبيّ المسدّد
أما كانت الزّهراء أمّيَ دونكم أما كان من خير البريّة أحمد
لعنتم و أخزيتم بما قدجنيتم   فسوف تلاقوا حرّ نار توقد

O the worst of people! You have opposed the orders of the Prophet (S) with this tyrannical and oppressive act. Didn't the best of messengers advise you to love and obey us? Are we not from the lineage of the chosen Prophet (S) that have been chosen? Is Fāṭimah az-Zahrā᾽ (A) your mother or ours? Was she not the best of creations from Aḥmad? You have been cursed and disgraced due to this act you have committed. You will soon taste the heat of the fire and its scorching flames.

Maqām of Ṣāḥib az-Zamān (AJ)

The Maqām of Ṣāḥib az-Zamān (AJ) is located on the path to Imām aṣ-Ṣādiq's (A) maqām and contains a high level of spirit and hope for those hearts seeking to reconnect with the Imām of the time, and who are awaiting his blissful return. It is widely believed that Imām Mahdī (AJ) was present here, and thus, this place holds a certain blessing. It is recommended to come here and pray for his reappearance. May Allāh the Almighty illuminate our eyes through his blissful return. There is a river next to the maqām that is connected to the Euphrates.

Oldest picture of Maqām Ṣāḥib az-Zamān (AJ)

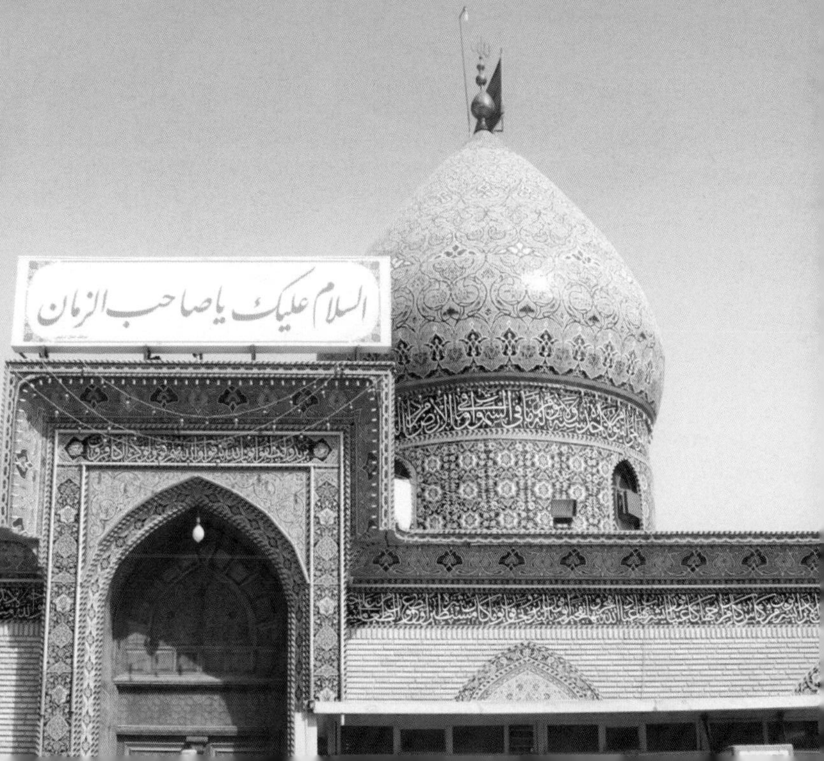
السلام عليك يا صاحب الزمان

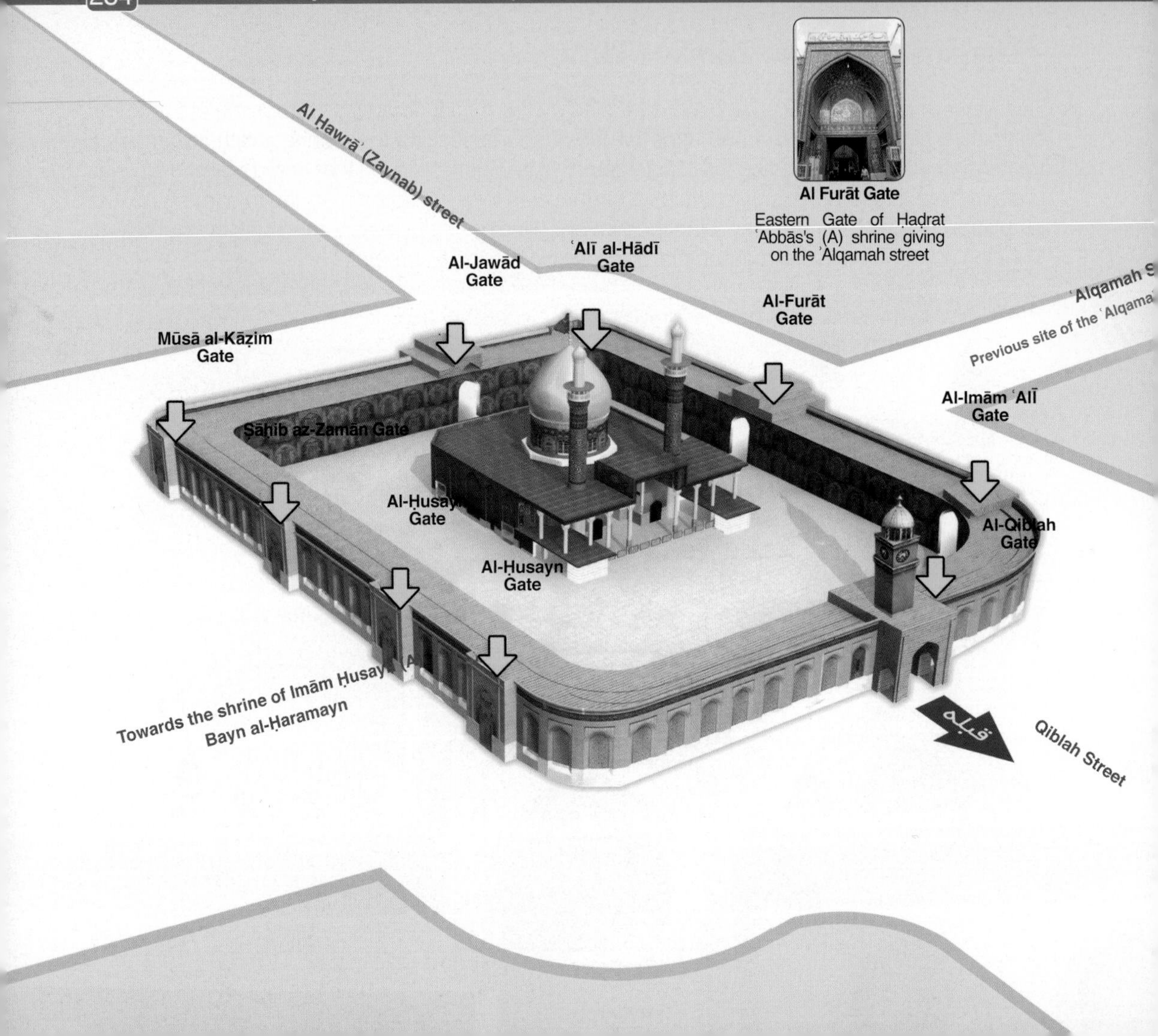
Al Furāt Gate
Eastern Gate of Ḥaḍrat ʿAbbās's (A) shrine giving on the ʾAlqamah street
Al Ḥawrāʾ (Zaynab) street
ʿAlqamah S
Previous site of the ʿAlqama
Al-Jawād Gate
ʿAlī al-Hādī Gate
Al-Furāt Gate
Mūsā al-Kāẓim Gate
Al-Imām ʿAlī Gate
Ṣāḥib az-Zamān Gate
Al-Ḥusayn Gate
Al-Qiblah Gate
Al-Ḥusayn Gate
Towards the shrine of Imām Ḥusay
Bayn al-Ḥaramayn
قبلة
Qiblah Street

The Euphrates River

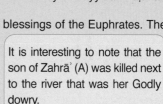

The supreme event of Karbalāʾ occurred near the Euphrates River (Furāt). Today, this river is 20 km east of Karbalāʾ. According to narrations, the water of the Furāt has many virtues and blessings, some of which are mentioned below:

- Drinking from it is always mustaḥab, whether or not it is for cure.
- It is mustaḥab to give newborns a taste of the water of furāt and turbah of Abā ʿAbd Allāh.
- Whoever performs ghusl with water from the Euphrates River, it is as if he or she is reborn and cleansed of all sins before they perform their ziyarah.
- According to some narrations, the Euphrates River was the Islamic dowry of Sayyidah Fāṭimah (A).
- Reminder: You don't have to go into the actual river to get the blessings of the Euphrates. The tap water in Karbalāʾ is from the Euphrates, so insha ʾAllāh using the tap water has the same bounties and blessings.
- The ʿAlqamah River is a branch of the Euphrates that flows from Karbala ʾ to Kūfah. It used to be on the eastern part of Ḥaḍrat ʿAbbās's ḥaram, but has now dried up, which is why that street is known as ʿAlqamah Street.

It is interesting to note that the son of Zahrāʾ (A) was killed next to the river that was her Godly dowry.

Al-Mukhayyam: The Campsite

When Imām Ḥusayn (A) reached Karbalāʾ on 2nd Muharram, 61 AH, he ordered his men to set up their tents in a place known as al-Mukhayyam, Khaymagah, or the campsite.

This location was away from the actual battlefield, and the Imām (A) had dug a trench behind it, blocking the enemies from attacking the tents.

The Imām's (A) family, along with Sayyidah Zaynab, and all the Banī Hāshim stayed within these tents.[1]

The location of every single tent was very carefully thought out. The Imām's (A) tent, along with Sayyidah Zaynab's, was in the center while the tents of Banī Hāshim were surrounding them.[2]

Other features of those tents include:

- Tents were formed in a horseshoe shape for better management and protection against the enemy.
- Some of the tents were used as supplies tents to gather food and water.
- Despite the lack of people, everything was very well-organized. For example, some tents were designated to store weapons.
- There was a tent designated exclusively for the bodies of the martyrs.

Some of the Tents of Imām Ḥusayn (A)

- Commander's tent
- Medical tent
- Tent of water provision
- Tent of shuhadāʾ
- Storage tent
- Strategizing tent
- Tent of Imām as-Sajjād (A)
- Tent of companions
- Tent of Banī Hāshim
- Family tent
- Tent of Sayyidah Zaynab (A)

- After the shahādah of Imām Ḥusayn, the enemies attacked the tents, looted everything they could find, and set fire on them.

Today, al-Mukhayyam has a symbolic structure resembling the exact position of the tents back then. One can see the tents of the Imām and his family, such as the tent of Imām Ḥusayn (A) and his miḥrāb, the tent of Imām as-Sajjād (A), and the tent of Qāsim.

[1]Ḥayāh al-Imām al Ḥusayn, Vol.3, P.93
[2]The Life of Sayyid ash-Shuhadā' P.329, Ḥusayn 'Imād Zādih

Till az-Zaynabiyyah

Till az-Zaynabiyyah (The Hill of Zaynab) is located southwest of the holy shrine. It has been written in the book of *Tārikh wa Jughrāfiyā Karbalāʾ*:

"On the day of ʿĀshūrāʾ, Sayyidah Zaynab used to stand on this hill and oversee the maqtal (battlefield) and would follow every step of her brother, Imām Ḥusayn (A), with her eyes. Many times, she went up the hill in a state of fear, and it has been reported that she mourned and expressed her grief for many incidents from atop that hill."

How difficult it must have been to witness all of those heinous acts that the son of Amīr al-Muʾminīn (A) and Sayyidah Fāṭimah az-Zahrāʾ (A) was suffering from! Indeed, she was given divine tolerance when Imām Ḥusayn put his hand over her chest and recited duʿāʾ in order to help her bear witnessing such scenes.

اَلسَّلَامُ عَلَيْكِ يَا بِنْتَ سَيِّدِ الْأَنْبِيَاءِ

Peace be upon you, O daughter of the Leader of the Prophets.

اَلسَّلَامُ عَلَيْكِ يَا بِنْتَ صَاحِبِ الْحَوْضِ وَاللِّوَاءِ

Peace be upon you, O daughter of the Master of the heavenly pond and the flag.

اَلسَّلَامُ عَلَيْكِ يَا بِنْتَ مَنْ عُرِجَ بِهِ إِلَى السَّمَاءِ وَوَصَلَ إِلَى مَقَامِ قَابِ قَوْسَيْنِ أَوْ أَدْنَى

Peace be upon you, O daughter of he who was taken to the skies and who reached the position of the distance between two parenthes or even closer.

اَلسَّلَامُ عَلَيْكِ يَا بِنْتَ نَبِيِّ الْهُدَى وَسَيِّدِ الْوَرَى وَمُنْقِذِ الْعِبَادِ مِنَ الرَّدَى

Peace be upon you, O daughter of the Prophet of true guidance, the leader of (all) human beings, and the savior of the servants from being destroyed.

اَلسَّلَامُ عَلَيْكِ يَا بِنْتَ صَاحِبِ الْخُلُقِ الْعَظِيمِ وَالشَّرَفِ الْعَمِيمِ وَالْآيَاتِ وَالذِّكْرِ الْحَكِيمِ

Peace be upon you, O daughter of the master of supreme morality, encompassing nobility, and the signs and wise remembrance of Allāh (i.e., the Qurʾān).

اَلسَّلَامُ عَلَيْكِ يَا بِنْتَ صَاحِبِ الْمَقَامِ الْمَحْمُودِ وَالْحَوْضِ الْمَوْرُودِ وَاللِّوَاءِ الْمَشْهُودِ

Peace be upon you, O daughter of the master of the honorable position, the pond from which people shall drink (on the Resurrection Day), and the flag, which shall be witnessed by everybody.

اَلسَّلَامُ عَلَيْكِ يَا بِنْتَ مَنْهَجِ دِينِ الْإِسْلَامِ وَصَاحِبِ الْقِبْلَةِ وَالْقُرْآنِ وَعَلَمِ الصِّدْقِ وَالْحَقِّ وَالْإِحْسَانِ

Peace be upon you, O daughter of the path of Islām and the master of the qiblah and Qurʾān, and the banner of honesty, truth, and goodness.

An old picture of Till az-Zaynabiyyah before reconstruction

Even with all of her greatness, unfortunately, no narrated ziyārah of Sayyidah Zaynab has reached us today. Ziyārāt that exist today are pieces put together from history. If a pilgrim wants to recite a ziyārah at this location for her, it is recommended they recite the ziyārah of Sayyidah Maʿṣūmah found in Mafātih al-Jinān.

Maqām Imām aṣ-Ṣādiq (A)

Maqām of Imām aṣ-Ṣādiq (A) is located on the northern side of Imām Ḥusayn's (A) shrine, as you pass the Nahr al-Ḥusayniyyah and walk through gardens known as Jaʿfariyyāt. Thirty meters in, you will reach this place where it is said Imām Ja'far aṣ-Ṣādiq (A) used to reside. He would perform ghusl with the water of the Euprhates and then go towards the ḥaram to perform ziyārah.

The maqām used to be a hexagon shaped building with a green dome on top. However, after the Intifāḍah Shaʿbāniyya of 1991, Saddam began destroying religious monuments and masājid. During this time, this maqām was also leveled to the ground.

One of the neighboring landlords rebuilt it in 1994, but it was left without a caretaker due to security precautions, as it was too close to a military base. This strategic placement allowed Saddam's forces to prevent any locals or pilgrims from visiting this place.

Today, this maqām has expanded by 600 meters². There is a beautiful gate at the entrance, as well as a large courtyard where pilgrims rest.

Ḥurr: The Free

Ḥurr, the son of Yazīd ibn al-Nājīya al-Tamīmī al-Rīyāḥī was from the tribe of Banī Tamīm. He was well-known in his tribe and in Kūfah. In the year 60 AH, he was appointed by ʿUbaydullāh ibn Ziyād as the commander of 30,000 militants from the Banī Tamīm and Hamdan tribes. After ʿUmar ibn Saʿad, he was the most important figure of the Kufan Army in the battle of Karbalā᾽ and was tasked with the mission to block the path of Imām Ḥusayn (A).

As he and his men reached the Imām's (A) caravan, the Imām (A) ordered his men to provide water for Ḥurr and his troops, and the Imām (A) himself even brought some water to Ḥurr. This compassion shown by the Imām (A) awakened Ḥurr's soul, leading to a shift in his behavior to such an extent that on the 8th of Muḥarram, ibn Saʿad repositioned him further from the Imām.

But the touch of an Infallible (A) did not stop there. Once the Truth sheds some light on the heart of a believer who has the capacity to bear the Truth, it will work its charm. So, on the day of ʿĀshūrā᾽, he finally made up his mind and used the excuse of watering his horse to break away from ibn Saʿad's army and joined Imām Ḥusayn (A). The minute he was pardoned from the Imām (A), he asked for permission to be the first one in the battlefield. He tried to talk with the people of Kūfah and warn them about conducting the biggest mistake of their lives. A group of the enemies were moved by his speech and wanted to end the war, but the rest of the army began launching arrows at him. After a great battle, Ayyūb ibn Musarraḥ martyred al-Ḥurr.

Imām Ḥusayn (A) rushed towards him As Ḥurr was taking his last few breaths, the Imām placed Ḥurr's head on his lap, and said:

أَنْتَ حُرٌّ كَمَا سَمَّتكَ أُمُّكَ وَ أَنْتَ حُرٌّ فِي الدُّنْيَا وَ أَنْتَ حُرٌّ فِي الأَخِرَة

You are Ḥurr (free) just as your mother named you— free in this world and free in the hereafter.

The Imām then closed Ḥurr's eyes and tied the wound on his head with a piece of cloth.

Location of Ḥurr's Shrine

Ḥurr's tomb is located in a place called Harbah, approximately four miles northwest of Imām Ḥusayn's shrine. He is this far away because when his tribesmen heard that the army of ʿUmar ibn Saʿad wanted to trample the bodies, they took his body and buried him in a place called Nawāmis.

His shrine was first built upon the order of Shāh Ismāʿīl Ṣafawī. He ordered his grave to be opened, and they found his body untouched, just as if he had been killed yesterday, and the handkerchief which Imām Ḥusayn (A) had tied around his head was there, as well. Shāh Ismāʿīl opened the handkerchief, and fresh blood started flowing down and would not stop with any other handkerchief. So, they had to return the very same handkerchief to his head. It was right then that Shāh Ismāʿīl Ṣafawī ordered for his shrine to be built.

Imām az-Zamān (AJ) has sent his salāms upon Ḥurr twice: once in ziyārah ar-Rajabiyyah and the other in ziyārah an-Nāḥiyyah al-Muqaddasah.

Muntakhab at-Tawārīkh, P. 310

Ziyārah of Ḥurr

Peace be upon you O righteous servant!	اَلسَّلَامُ عَلَيْكَ اَيُّهَا الْعَبْدُ الصَّالِحُ
Peace be upon you, O he who strives sincerely!	اَلسَّلَامُ عَلَيْكَ اَيُّهَا الْمُجَاهِدُ النَّاصِحُ
Peace be upon you, O he who was loyal to the happiness that was to come!	اَلسَّلَامُ عَلَيْكَ يَا مَنْ وَفَىٰ بِالسَّعَادَةِ الرَّابِحَةِ

Peace be upon you, O he who broke his allegiance to Yazīd and sacrificed his soul for Ḥusayn, the martyr!	اَلسَّـــلَامُ عَلَيْكَ يَامَنْ نَكَثَ بَيْعَةَ يَزِيْدَ وَفَدَى بِرُوْحِهِ لِلْحُسَيْنِ الشَّهِيْدِ
Peace be upon you, O brave hero!	اَلسَّلَامُ عَلَيْكَ اَيُّهَا الْبَطَلُ الصِّنْدِيْدُ
Peace be upon you, O valiant horseman!	اَلسَّلَامُ عَلَيْكَ اَيُّهَا الْفَارِسُ الشُّجَاعُ
Peace be upon you, O he who blocked the enemies!	اَلسَّلَامُ عَلَيْكَ اَيُّهَا الْبَطَلُ الْمَنَّاعُ
Peace be upon you who abandoned tyranny,	اَلسَّلَامُ عَلَيْكَ يا مَنْ تَرَكَ الطُّغْيَانَ
and obeyed the foremost in religion,	وَ اَطَاعَ الْوَاحِدَ الدَّيَّانَ
and entered into the obedience of the Most Merciful,	وَدَخَلَ فِيْ طَاعَةِ الرَّحْمٰنِ
and sacrificed his soul for Ḥusayn, the thirsty martyr in a strange land,	وَفَدَى بِرُوْحِهِ لِلْحُسَـيْنِ الشَّهِيْدِ الْغَرِيْبِ الْعَطْشَانِ
and fought aggression,	وَصَالَ عَلَى الْعُدْوَانِ
and fell from his horse on the soil, and was rewarded with glory and heaven.	وَ هَوَى صَرِيْعاً عَلَى التُّرْبَانِ وَ حَظِيَ بِالْخُلْدِ وَ الْجِنَانِ
May the mercy and blessings of Allāh be upon you!	وَرَحْمَةُ اللهِ وَبَرَكَاتُهُ،

Peace be upon you, O he who sacrificed his own soul for the son of the Prophet (S).	اَلسَّـــلَامُ عَلَيْكَ يَـــا مَنْ فَدَىٰ بِنَفْسِـــهِ لِاِبْنِ الرَّسُوْلِ،
Peace be upon you, O he who strove to defend the son of al-Batūl.	اَلسَّلَامُ عَلَيْكَ يَا مُجَاهِداً دُوْنَ ابْنِ الْبَتُوْلِ،
Peace be upon you, O he who was steady and courageous against the stabbing and beating of the swords.	اَلسَّـــلَامُ عَلَيْكَ يَا مَنْ ثَبَـــتَ لِلطَّعْنِ وَ ضَرْبِ السُّيُوْفِ،
Peace be upon you and upon your slain offspring.	اَلسَّلَامُ عَلَيْكَ وَ عَلَىٰ وَلَدِكَ الْمَقْتُوْلِ
Peace be upon you for whom Ḥusayn (A) cried,	اَلسَّلَامُ عَلَيْكَ يَا مَنْ بَكَاهُ الْحُسَيْنُ عَلَيْهِ السَّلَامُ
and he said, "Your mother was not mistaken when she named you Ḥurr, for you are Ḥurr (free) in this world and the hereafter."	وَ قَالَ :مَا أَخْطَأَتْ أُمُّكَ إِذْ سَـــمَّتْكَ الْحُرَّ، فَاَنْتَ حُرٌّ فِيْ الدُّنْيَا وَ سَعِيْدٌ فِيْ الْآخِرَةِ
O how I wish I could be with you so I could attain success with you just how you were successful with Ḥusayn and the companions of Ḥusayn	فَيَا لَيْتَنِيْ كُنْتُ مَعَكَ فَاَفُـــوْزُ مَعَكَ كَمَا فُزْتَ مَعَ الْحُسَيْنِ وَاَصْحَابِ الْحُسَيْنِ
Peace be upon you O Ḥurr, son of Yazīd ar-Riyāḥī, and the mercy and blessings of Allāh!	وَالسَّلَامُ عَلَيْكَ يَا حُرَّ بْنَ يَزِيْدَ الرِّيَاحِيْ وَ رَحْمَةُ اللهِ وَبَرَكَاتُهُ

The Adab (Etiquette) of Ḥaḍrat ʿAbbās towards his Imām (A)

This is an aerial picture of Ḥaḍrat ʿAbbās's (A) ḥaram's in relation to Imām Ḥusayn's (A) haram. You can see that Ḥaḍrat ʿAbbās's (A) grave is positioned behind Imām Ḥusayn's (A) grave, just as you would see an Imām stands in front of the followers in congregational prayers.

Rewards of Performing Ziyārah on Foot

Performing ziyārah of Imām Ḥusayn (A) on foot has many rewards, which is why our scholars place great emphasis on it.

مَنْ خَرَجَ مِنْ مَنْزِلِهِ يُرِيْدُ زِيَارَةَ قَبْرِ الْحُسَيْنِ بْنِ عَلِيٍّ عَلَيْهِمَاالسَّلَام إِن كَانَ مَاشِيَا كُتِبْتُ لَهُ بِكُلِّ خُطْوَةٍ حَسَنَةٌ و مَحَاعَنْهُ سَيِّئَة[1]

Imām aṣ-Ṣādiq (A): When one leaves his/her house to perform the ziyārah of Imām Ḥusayn (A) by foot, one good act will be written and one sin will be removed for every step he/she takes.

Muʿāwiyah ibn Wahāb, a companion of Imām aṣ-Ṣādiq (A), narrates: I went to visit Imām aṣ-Ṣādiq (A). He was sitting in his prayer spot and talking to Allāh after completing his ṣalāh, and he was reciting the following prayer for the pilgrims of Imām Ḥusayn (A):

اِغْفِرْلِيْ وَ لِإِخْوَانِيْ وَ زُوَّارِ قَبْرِ أَبِي الْحُسَيْنِ بْنِ عَلِيْ صَلَوَاتُ اللهِ عَلَيْهِمَا الَّذِيْنَ أَنْفِقُوْا أَمْوَالَهُمْ وَ اشَخَصُوا أبدانَهُم رَغبَةً فِی بِرِّنا

Forgive me and my brothers, and the pilgrims to the grave of my father, Ḥusayn ibn ʿAlī (A), those who spend their wealth and give their bodies, yearning for our goodness.

فارحَم تلكَ الوُجوه التِیَ غيَّرتها الشَّمسُ و ارحَم تلكَ الخُدُودَ الَّتِیَ تُقَلَّبُ علیَ قَبرِ أبِیَ عبدالله و ارحَم تلكَ الأعیُنَ الَّتِیَ جرت دُمُوعُها رَحمَةً لنا

Then, have mercy upon those faces which the sun has changed in color, and have mercy upon those faces that have turned towards the grave of Abā ʿAbd Allāh (A), and have mercy upon those eyes that have shed tears for the sake of our love.

اَللّٰهُمَّ إِنِّيْ اَسْتَوْدِعُكَ تِلْكَ الْأَنْفُسَ وَ تِلْكَ الْأَبْدَانَ حَتّٰى تُرَوِّيَهُمْ مِنَ الْحَوْضِ يَوْمَ الْعَطَشْ[2]

O Allāh, surely, I entrust You with these souls and bodies until we reunite at the fountain of Kawthar on the day of thirst.

[1] Biḥār al-Anwār Vol.89 P.82

[2] Thawāb al-Aʿmāl P.95, Shaykh Ṣadūq

Some Great Scholars Walking to Karbalāʾ

Late Āyatullah Khūʾī in his youth

Late Āyatullah Mīrzā Jawād Tabrīzī

Āyatullah Sayyid Muḥammad Saʿīd Ḥakīm

The tradition of performing ziyārah on foot has been practiced since the time of the Maʿṣūmīn (A). The reward for this action cannot even be measured. Faḍil Darbandī writes:

The act of walking to perform ziyārah is either due to a lack of money, which shows the pilgrim's level of enthusiasm and passion, or it is due to the pilgrim viewing him or herself humbly in comparison to the role model of martyrdom. In either of these situations, the pilgrim will be able to tolerate every little pain and hardship during such a journey, and both cases are extremely precious.[3]

It has been the tradition in ʿIrāq for individuals, groups, and caravans to walk from various cities, such as Najaf, Baṣrah, and Baghdād, towards Karbalāʾ. The walk is done more frequently during peak times, such as Arbaʿīn, the week of ʿĀshūrāʾ, 15th Shaʿbān, and 1st Rajab.

Many of our great scholars have participated in this tradition as well. This walk would provide many new tabligh opportunities, while people were mourning and reciting poems on the path.

During the regime of Saddam, such walks themselves were viewed as a movement against the regime, especially while walking on the unofficial path through the palm tree lands by the Euphrates River. In the year 1397 AH, while this walk was taking place, an intense battle erupted between the army and the pilgrims, leaving many pilgrims wounded or killed. This event is known as the "Arbaʿīn of Bloodshed."

[3]Isrār ash-shahādah, Vol.89 P.631, Fāḍil Darbandī

Shahīd Sayyid Muḥammad Taqī Jalālī

Shahīd Āyatullāh Sayyid Muṣṭafā Khumaynī

Shahīd Sayyid ʿAbd aṣ-Ṣāḥib and Shahīd Sayyid Muḥammad Ḥusayn Ḥakīm

Oldest picture of the walk to Karbalāʾ (1916)

After the downfall of Saddam, the Shīʿah had a fervent desire to establish the tradition of walking from Najaf to Karbalāʿ, so they started building mawākib (resting areas) on the path from Najaf to Karbalāʾ.

Madinah al-Imām ʿAlī for pilgrims 8 km south of Karbalāʾ

Ḥaḍrat ʿAbbās's guesthouse 13 km south of Karbalāʾ

Imām Ḥusayn's guesthouse 15 km south of Karbalāʾ

Shīʿah and Sunnī hand in hand on the walk to Karbalāʾ

ʿIrāqi Christans walk to Karbalāʾ

People walk with wheelchairs and strollers

A cyclist travels from Northern Irān to Karbalāʾ

Ziyārat Arbaʿīn

Shaykh Ṭūsī in *Tahzīb* and *Miṣbāḥ* narrates this ḥadīth of Imām Ḥasan al-ʿAskarī (A):

The signs of a mu’min (believer) are five:

- Reciting 51 rakaʿāt everyday, out of which 17 rakaʿāt are mandatory and 34 are nāfilah (recommended)
- Reciting Ziyārat al-Arbaʿīn
- Wearing a ring on the right hand
- Placing one’s forehead on the soil (during sajdah)
- Reciting بِسْمِ اللهِ الرَّحْمٰنِ الرَّحِيْمِ out loud

On the 20th of Safar, the caravan of Imām Ḥusayn (A) arrived in Karbala, returning from Damascus. On this day, Jābir ibn ʿAbd Allāh al-Anṣārī performed the first visit to the grave of Imām Ḥusayn. Therefore, it is recommended to visit the holy shrine of Imām Ḥusayn (A) on this day. The following ziyārah is narrated by Ṣafwān Jamāl from Imām aṣ-Ṣādiq (A):

On the day of Arbaʿīn, recite the following a few hours before ẓuhr:

Peace be upon the close guardian of Allāh and His most beloved.	اَلسَّلَامُ عَلَىٰ وَلِيِّ اللهِ وَحَبِيْبِهِ
Peace be upon the friend of Allāh and His elite.	اَلسَّلَامُ عَلَىٰ خَلِيْلِ اللهِ وَنَجِيْبِهِ
Peace be upon the choice of Allāh and son of His choice.	اَلسَّلَامُ عَلَىٰ صَفِيِّ اللهِ وَابْنِ صَفِيِّهِ
Peace be upon al-Ḥusayn, the wronged and martyred.	اَلسَّلَامُ عَلَى الْحُسَيْنِ الْمَظْلُوْمِ الشَّهِيْدِ
Peace be upon the prisoners of agony and victims who were killed as their family members watched tearfully.	اَلسَّلَامُ عَلَىٰ أَسِيرِ الْكُرُبَاتِ وَقَتِيْلِ الْعَبَرَاتِ،

O Allāh, I bear witness that he is Your guardian and the son of Your guardian, Your chosen one and the son of Your chosen one, and the one who is successful through Your Honor.	اَللَّهُمَّ إِنِّيْ أَشْهَدُ أَنَّهُ وَلِيُّكَ وَابْنُ وَلِيِّكَ وَصَفِيُّكَ وَابْنُ صَفِيِّكَ الْفَآئِزُ بِكَرَامَتِكَ
You have honored him with martyrdom and endued him with happiness,	أَكْرَمْتَهُ بِالشَّهَادَةِ وَحَبَوْتَهُ بِالسَّعَادَةِ
privileged him with a pure birth,	وَاجْتَبَيْتَهُ بِطِيْبِ الْوِلَادَةِ
made him one of the chiefs,	وَجَعَلْتَهُ سَيِّداً مِنَ السَّادَةِ
one of the leaders,	وَقَائِداً مِنَ الْقَادَةِ
and one of the defenders (of Your religion),	وَذَائِداً مِنَ الذَّادَةِ
gave him the inheritances of the Prophets,	وَأَعْطَيْتَهُ مَوَارِيْثَ الْأَنْبِيَاءِ
and chose him as a proof upon Your creations from the Prophets' successors	وَجَعَلْتَهُ حُجَّةً عَلَىٰ خَلْقِكَ مِنَ الْأَوْصِيَاءِ
So, he called to you flawlessly, gave advice,	فَأَعْذَرَ فِي الدُّعَاءِ وَمَنَحَ النُّصْحَ
and sacrificed his soul to save Your servants from ignorance and confusion of misguidance.	وَبَذَلَ مُهْجَتَهُ فِيْكَ لِيَسْتَنْقِذَ عِبَادَكَ مِنَ الْجَهَالَةِ وَحَيْرَةِ الضَّلَالَةِ
Yet, those who were seduced by this worldly life,	وَقَدْ تَوَازَرَ عَلَيْهِ مَنْ غَرَّتْهُ الدُّنْيَا

who sold their share (of reward) with the lowliest and meanest,	وَبَاعَ حَظَّهُ بِالْأَرْذَلِ الْأَدْنَىٰ
sold their hereafter for the lowest price,	وَشَرَىٰ آخِرَتَهُ بِالثَّمَنِ الْأَوْكَسِ
and acted arrogantly, perished because they followed their desires,	وَتَغَطْرَسَ وَتَرَدَّىٰ فِيْ هَوَاهُ
brought upon themselves Your wrath and the wrath of Your Prophet,	وَأَسْخَطَكَ وَأَسْخَطَ نَبِيَّكَ،
and obeyed the worst and hypocritical of Your servants, and the bearers of the burdens (of sins) who deserve Hellfire—all those supported each other against him.	وَأَطَاعَ مِنْ عِبَادِكَ أَهْلَ الشِّقَاقِ وَالنِّفَاقِ وَحَمَلَةَ الْأَوْزَارِ الْمُسْتَوْجِبِيْنَ النَّارَ
However, he fought against them painstakingly with steadfastness, expecting Your reward until his blood was shed on account of his obedience to You, and his women were violated.	فَجَاهَدَهُمْ فِيْكَ صَابِراً مُحْتَسِباً حَتَّىٰ سُفِكَ فِيْ طَاعَتِكَ دَمُهُ وَاسْتُبِيْحَ حَرِيْمُهُ
So, O Allāh, pour upon them heavy and punish them with a painful chastisement.	اَللَّهُمَّ فَالْعَنْهُمْ لَعْناً وَبِيْلاً وَعَذِّبْهُمْ عَذَاباً أَلِيْماً
Peace be upon you, O son of Allāh's Messenger.	اَلسَّلَامُ عَلَيْكَ يَا بْنَ رَسُوْلِ اللهِ
Peace be upon you, O son of the chief of the Prophets' successors.	اَلسَّلَامُ عَلَيْكَ يَا بْنَ سَيِّدِ الْأَوْصِيَاءِ
I bear witness that you are the trustee of Allāh and the son of His trustee.	أَشْهَدُ أَنَّكَ أَمِيْنُ اللهِ وَابْنُ أَمِيْنِهِ

You lived felicitously, lived your life with praiseworthiness, and died while unrecognized, oppressed, and martyred.	عِشْتَ سَعِيْداً وَمَضَيْتَ حَمِيْداً وَمُتَّ فَقِيْداً مَظْلُوْماً شَهِيْداً
I also bear witness that Allāh will fulfill His promise to You,	وَأَشْهَدُ أَنَّ اللهَ مُنْجِزٌ مَا وَعَدَكَ
exterminate those who disappointed you,	وَمُهْلِكٌ مَنْ خَذَلَكَ
and punish those who killed you.	وَمُعَذِّبٌ مَنْ قَتَلَكَ
I also bear witness that you fulfilled your pledge to Allāh and strove hard in His way until death came to you,	وَأَشْهَدُ أَنَّكَ وَفَيْتَ بِعَهْدِ اللهِ وَجَاهَدْتَ فِيْ سَبِيْلِهِ حَتَّىٰ أَتَاكَ الْيَقِيْنُ
So, may Allāh curse those who killed you.	فَلَعَنَ اللهُ مَنْ قَتَلَكَ
May Allāh curse those who wronged you.	وَلَعَنَ اللهُ مَنْ ظَلَمَكَ
May Allāh curse the people who were pleased when they heard about it.	وَلَعَنَ اللهُ أُمَّةً سَمِعَتْ بِذٰلِكَ فَرَضِيَتْ بِهِ
O Allāh, I ask You to bear witness that I am a friend of his friends and an enemy of his enemies. May my father and mother be sacrificed for you, O son of Rasūl Allāh.	اَللّٰهُمَّ إِنِّيْ أُشْهِدُكَ أَنِّيْ وَلِيٌّ لِمَنْ وَالَاهُ وَعَدُوٌّ لِمَنْ عَادَاهُ بِأَبِيْ أَنْتَ وَأُمِّيْ يَا بْنَ رَسُوْلِ اللهِ

I bear witness that you were light in the sublime loins and purified wombs,	أَشْهَدُ أَنَّكَ كُنْتَ نُوراً فِي الْأَصْلَابِ الشَّامِخَةِ وَالْأَرْحَامِ الْمُطَهَّرَةِ
the impurities of ignorance could not subject you to filth, nor could its murky clothes dress you,	لَمْ تُنَجِّسْكَ الْجَاهِلِيَّةُ بِأَنْجَاسِهَا وَلَمْ تُلْبِسْكَ الْمُدْلَهِمَّاتُ مِنْ ثِيَابِهَا
I also bear witness that you are one of the mainstays of the religion, the pillars of Muslims, and the haven of the believers.	وَأَشْهَدُ أَنَّكَ مِنْ دَعَائِمِ الدِّيْنِ وَأَرْكَانِ الْمُسْلِمِيْنَ وَمَعْقِلِ الْمُؤْمِنِيْنَ
I also bear witness that you are the pious, God-fearing, content, pure, guiding, and well-guided Imām.	وَأَشْهَدُ أَنَّكَ الْإِمَامُ الْبَرُّ التَّقِيُّ الرَّضِيُّ الزَّكِيُّ الْهَادِى الْمَهْدِيُّ
And I bear witness that the Imāms from your progeny are the spokesmen of piety, the signs of guidance, the firmest handle (of Islam),	وَأَشْهَدُ أَنَّ الْأَئِمَّةَ مِنْ وُلْدِكَ كَلِمَةُ التَّقْوَىٰ وَأَعْلَامُ الْهُدَىٰ وَالْعُرْوَةُ الْوُثْقَىٰ
and the decisive proofs upon the inhabitants of the world.	وَالْحُجَّةُ عَلَىٰ أَهْلِ الدُّنْيَا
I also bear witness that I believe in you all and in your return, and I have full confidence in the laws of my religion as can be affirmed by my deeds.	وَأَشْهَدُ أَنِّيْ بِكُمْ مُؤْمِنٌ، وَبِإِيَابِكُمْ مُوْقِنٌ بِشَرَايِعِ دِيْنِيْ وَخَوَاتِيمِ عَمَلِيْ

My heart is at peace with you all, I follow your commands, and my support for you all is set until Allāh permits.	وَقَلْبِيْ لِقَلْبِكُمْ سِلْمٌ وَأَمْرِيْ لِأَمْرِكُمْ مُتَّبِعٌ وَنُصْرَتِيْ لَكُمْ مُعَدَّةٌ حَتَّىٰ يَأْذَنَ اللهُ لَكُمْ
So, I am with you, I am with you, not with your enemies.	فَمَعَكُمْ مَعَكُمْ لَامَعَ عَدُوِّكُمْ
May Allāh's blessings be upon you,	صَلَوَاتُ اللهِ عَلَيْكُمْ
upon your souls, upon your bodies,	وَعَلَىٰ أَرْوَاحِكُمْ وَأَجْسَادِكُمْ
upon the present and absent ones amongst you, and upon the apparent and invisible ones amongst you.	وَشَاهِدِكُمْ وَغَائِبِكُمْ وَظَاهِرِكُمْ وَبَاطِنِكُمْ
Respond to us, O Lord of the Worlds.	آمِيْنَ رَبَّ الْعَالَمِيْنَ

Offer a two rakaʿāt ṣalāh of ziyārah and ask for your wishes

Imām Ḥusayn's (A) Ziyārah on the 15th of Shaʿbān

مَنْ أَحَبّ أَنْ يُصَافِحَهُ مِائَةُ أَلْفِ نَبِيّ وَ أَرْبَعَةٌ وَعِشْرُونَ أَلْفَ نَبِيٍّ فَلْيَزُرْ قَبْرَ أَبِي عَبْدِ اللهِ (عليه اَلسَّلَام) الْحُسَيْنِ بْنِ عَلِيّ (عليهما اَلسَّلَام) فِي النِّصْفِ مِنْ شَعْبَانَ فَإِنّ أَرْوَاحَ النَّبِيِّينَ: يَسْتَأْذِنُونَ اللهَ فِي زِيَارَتِهِ فَيُؤْذَنُ لَهُمْ مِنْهُمْ خَمْسَةٌ أُولُو الْعَزْمِ مِنَ الرُّسُلِ قُلْنَا مَنْ هُمْ؟

قَالَ: نُوحٌ وَإِبْرَاهِيمُ وَ مُوسَىَ وَ عِيسَىَ وَ مُحَمّدٌ (صلى الله عليه و آله و سلّم)

قُلْنَا لَهُ: مَا مَعْنَىَ أُولُو الْعَزْمِ؟

قَالَ: بُعِثُوا إِلَىَ شَرْقِ الْأَرْضِ وَ غَرْبِهَا جِنِّهَا وَ إِنْسِهَا

It has been narrated from Imām aṣ-Ṣādiq and Imām ʿAlī ibn al-Ḥusayn (A) that:

"One who wishes to greet all 124,000 Prophets should visit the grave of Imām Ḥusayn ibn ʿAlī (A) on the 15th of Shaʿbān because the souls of the Prophets have taken permission from Allāh to perform the ziyārah of the Imām (A) on that night, and the Almighty granted their request. Five of them are the Ūlūl ʿAẓm Prophets."

It was asked, "Who are they?"

The Imām replied, "Prophets Nūḥ, Ibrāhīm, Mūsā, ʿĪsā, and Muḥammad (S)"

We asked, "What is the meaning of Ūlūl ʿAzm?"

The Imām (A) replied, "Those prophets who have been raised to guide everyone in the west and the east from among the jinns and human beings."

Kāmil az-Ziyārah, P. 594

إذا كان النّصفُ من شعبانَ نادىٰ مُنادٍ مِنَ الأفُقِ الأعلىٰ زائِرِیَ الحُسينِ ارجِعوا مغفُوراً لَكُم ثَوابُكُم علَى اللهِ رَبِّكُم و مُحمّدٍ نَبيِّكُم

Imām Jaʿfar aṣ-Ṣādiq (A):

On the 15th of Shaʿbān, a caller announces from the highest horizon, "O visitors of Ḥusayn (A), return [to your homes] forgiven; your rewards will be given by Allāh, your Lord, and by Muḥammad (S), your Prophet."

Kāmil az-Ziyārah, P. 593

من زار الحسين عليه اَلسَّلام ليلةَ النصف من شعبان غفرَاللهُ له ماتقدّمَ من ذنوبه و ما تأخَّرَ و من زارَهُ يومَ عرفةَ كَتَبَ اللهُ له ثوابَ ألفِ حَجّةٍ مُتَقَبَّلَةٍ و ألفَ عُمرَةٍ مَبرُورةٍ ومَن زارَهُ يَومَ عاشُوراء فَكَأنّما زارَاللهَ فوقَ عرشِهِ

Imām Jaʿfar aṣ-Ṣādiq (A):

Whoever visits the grave of Imām Ḥusayn (A) on the eve of the 15th of Shaʿbān, Allāh will forgive his past and future sins; and whoever visits him on the day of ʿArafah, Allāh will write for him the rewards of 1,000 accepted Ḥajj and 1,000 accepted ʿUmrah; and whoever visits him on the day of ʿĀshūrāʾ, it will be like he is visiting Allāh at His throne.

Kāmil az-Ziyārah, P. 599

من زار قبر الحسين بن عليٍ عليهما اَلسَّلَام ليلةً من ثلاث ليَالٍ غفرَاللهُ لَهُ ماتقدَّمَ مِن ذَنبِهِ و ما تأخّرَ قال قلتُ أيّ اللّيالي جُعلتُ فِداكَ قالَ ليلةَ الفِطرِ أو ليلةَ الأضحَىٰ أو ليلةَ النّصفِ من شعبانَ

Imām Jaʿfar aṣ-Ṣādiq (A):

Allāh will forgive the past and future sins of anyone who visits Ḥusayn ibn ʿAlī (A) on one of three eves. I humbly asked, "May I be sacrificed for you. What are those three eves?" The Imām (A) replied, "The eve of ʿĪd al-Fiṭr, the eve of ʿĪd al-Aḍḥā, and the eve of 15th Shaʿbān."

Kāmil az-Ziyārah, P. 596

زائرُ الحسين عليه اَلسَّلَام في النّصف من شعبانَ يُغفَرُ لَهُ ذُنُوبُهُ و لن يُكتَبَ عليه سيِّئَةٌ فی سنَتِهِ حَتّیٰ يَحولَ عليهِ الحولُ فإن زارَ في السّنَةِ المُقبِلَةِ غَفَرَ اللهُ لَهُ ذُنُوبَهُ

Imām Muḥammad al-Bāqir (A):

The sins of one who visits Imām Ḥusayn (A) on the 15th of Shaʿbān will be forgiven, and no sins will be recorded for him during the remainder of that year, and if he visits Imām Ḥusayn (A) again the following 15th Shaʿbān, Allāh will forgive all his sins.

Kāmil az-Ziyārah, P. 596

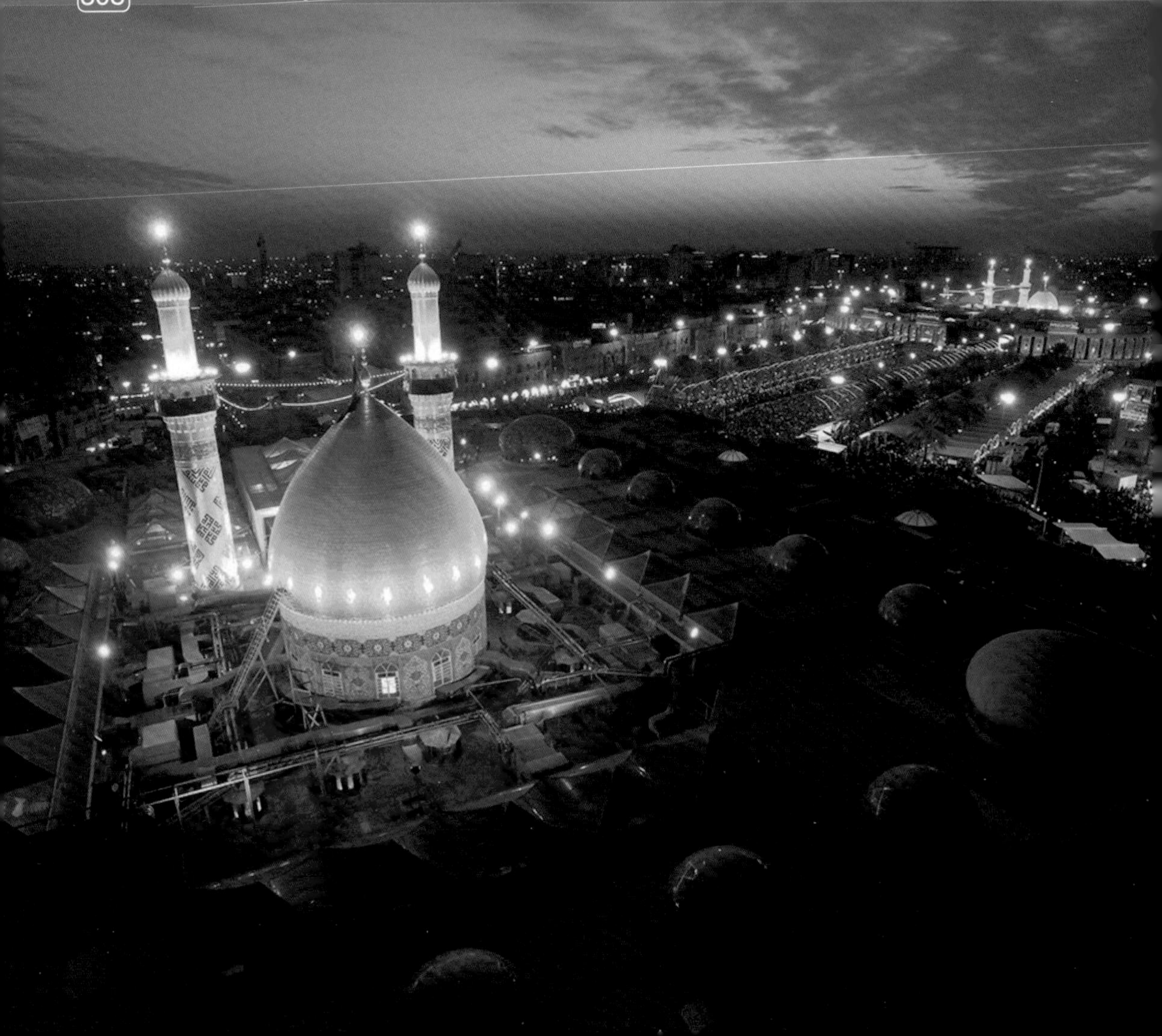

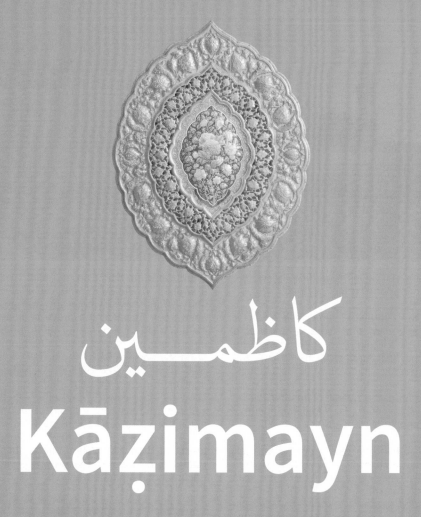

كاظمين

Kāẓimayn

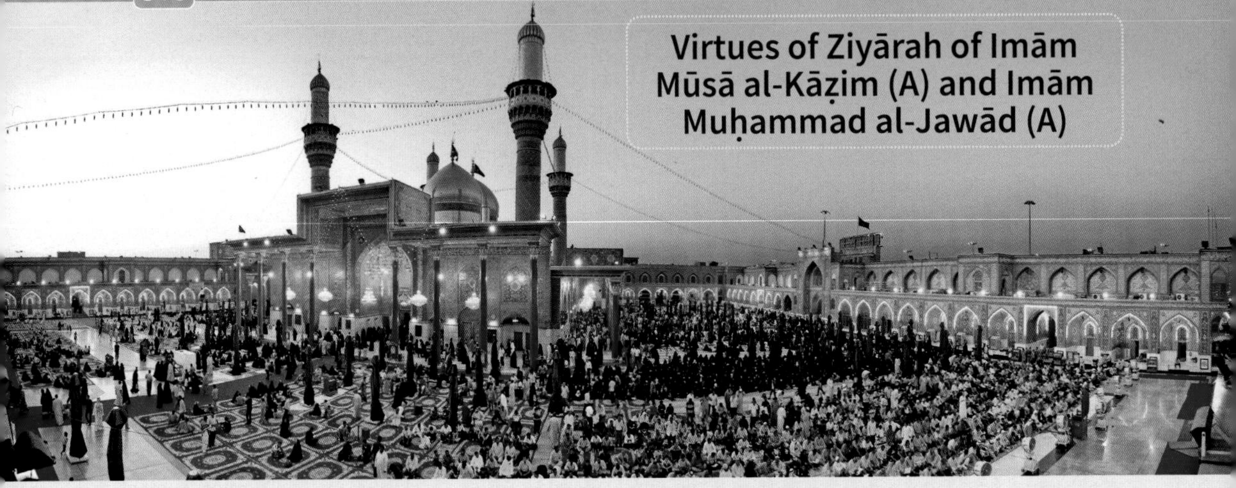

Virtues of Ziyārah of Imām Mūsā al-Kāẓim (A) and Imām Muḥammad al-Jawād (A)

There are many narrations regarding the virtues and bounties of performing their ziyārah:

- Performing the ziyārah of Imām Mūsā ibn Jaʿfar (A) is like performing the ziyārah of the Noble Prophet (S), and visiting him is like visiting the Noble Prophet (S), Amīr al-Mu'minīn (A), and Imām Ḥusayn (A).[1]

- Whoever performs the ziyārah of Imām Mūsā ibn Jaʿfar (A) [with maʿrifah (deep understanding) is among the people of Heaven.[2]

- Ibn Shahr Āshūb narrates from Khaṭīb al-Baghdādī, the author of *Tārīkh Baghdād*, from ʿAlī ibn Khilāl: Every problem that I faced was resolved and made easy by the Almighty through seeking refuge in the holy shrine of Mūsā ibn Jaʿfar (peace be upon him) and seeking his intercession.[3]

- Khaṭīb al-Baghdādī also narrates: I witnessed a woman in Baghdād who was running in a hurry. When asked where she was going, she answered, "Towards the grave of Imām Mūsā ibn Jaʿfar (A) to pray for my son to be released from prison." A man standing nearby made fun of her by saying, "Mūsā ibn Jaʿfar (A), himself, died in prison!" She replied, "O Allāh! By the right of the one who was martyred in prison, show us Your power! Soon after, her son was set free, and instead, the son of the man who made fun was taken into custody."[4]

- Imām ar-Riḍa (A): Allāh saved the city of Baghdād by placing the graves of Imām al-Kāẓim and Imām al-Jawād in it.

1. Wasā'il ash-Shīʿa, Vol.14, P. 545, 547
2. Ibid, P. 545
3. Ibn Shahr Āshūb, Manāqib Āl Abī Ṭālib, Vol. 4, P. 305
4. Ibid

الإمام موسى بن جعفر
الإمام محمد الجواد
Jawād means to give to one who does or doesn't deserve;
grant me a big heart, and in your way the chance to serve!

Biography of Imām al-Kāẓim (A) and Imām al-Jawād (A)

	Imām Mūsā al-Kāẓim (A): The 7th Imām	Imām Muḥammad al-Jawād (A): The 9th Imām
Name:	Mūsā	Muḥammad
Kunyah:	Abul Ḥasan the 1st[1], Abū Ibrāhīm	Abū Ja'far the 2nd
Title:	Al 'Abd Aṣ-Ṣaliḥ (the pious servant), Al-Kāẓim (the one who swallows his anger). Bāb al-Ḥawā'ij (the door to wishes), Ṣābir (the patient), and Amīn (the trustworthy)	Taqī (pious), Jawād (generous), Zakī (purified)
Parents:	Imām aṣ-Ṣādiq (A) & Ḥaḍrat Ḥumaydah (Ḥamīdah)	Imām ar-Riḍā (A) & Ḥaḍrat Khayzarān, Sabīka
Birthday:	Sunday, 7th Ṣafar, 128 AH	Friday, 10th Rajab, 195 AH
Birthplace:	Village of 'Abwā (between Makkah and Madīnah)	Madīnah
Ring Inscription:	اَلْمُلْكُ لِلّٰهِ وَحْدَه The Kingdom belongs exclusively to Allāh, the One	نِعْمَ الْقَادِرُ اللّٰه Allāh is the best of the powerful/capable ones
Number of Children:	37 children	4 children
Duration of Imāmah:	35 years	18 years
Date of Martyrdom:	25th Rajab, 183 AH	Last day of Dhūl Qa'dah, 202 AH
Place of Martyrdom:	Hārūn's prison, Baghdād	Baghdād
Cause of Martyrdom:	Poisoned by Hārūn ar-Rashīd	Poisoned by Mu'taṣim al-'Abbāsī
Lifespan:	55 years	25 years
Holy Shrine:	Kāẓimayn	Kāẓimayn
Eras of his Life:	■ Before Imāmah (128-148 AH) ■ During Imāmah (148-183 AH): 10 years during Manṣūr, 10 years during Mahdī al-'Abbāsī. 1 year during Hādi al-'Abbāsī & 15 years during Hārūn al-'Abbāsī. ■ Most of his Imāmah was spent in prison	■ Before Imāmah (183-190 AH) ■ During Imāmah (190-207 AH): under two evil khalīfahs, Ma'mūn and Mu'taṣim (7th & 8th Abbasid Caliphs) ■ He was the youngest Imām

[1] His most famous Kunyah was Abūl-Ḥasan. Although Amīr al-Mu'minīn and Imām Zayn al-'Ābidīn were also Abūl-Ḥasan, the books refer to the 7th Imām as the first Abul Ḥasan, Imām ar-Riḍā (A) as the second Abūl-Ḥasan, and Imām al-Hādī (A) as the third Abūl-Ḥasan (Muḥammad 'Alī Hāshim Khurāsānī, Muntakhab at-Tawārīkh, P. 516)

History of Kāẓimayn

- **145 AH:** This area used to be a garden called Shuniziyah next to Baghdād. Al-Manṣūr selected this garden to be the Graveyard of the Quraysh.
- **179 AH:** Upon the order of Hārūn ar-Rashīd, Imām Mūsā al-Kāẓim (A) was transported from Madīnah and imprisoned in Baghdād.
- **183 AH:** Sindī ibn Shāhik poisoned and martyred Imām Mūsā al-Kāẓim (A) upon the order of Hārūn ar-Rashīd.
- **183 AH:** The holy body of Imām al-Kāẓim (A) was buried in a land he had purchased earlier.
- **220 AH:** Imām al-Jawād (A) was poisoned and martyred upon the order of al-Muʾtaṣim and was buried alongside his grandfather. A structure was built over their holy and blessed graves, and that area was named Kāẓimiyyah.
- **336 AH:** Upon the order of Muʿizz ad-Dawlah (Buyid Dynasty), two new gravestones were built, along with two wooden ḍariḥs.
- **369 AH:** ʿAḍud ad-Dawlah extended the shrine and built a wall around the city, distinguishing Kāẓimayn.
- **441 AH:** A conflict between the Shīʿah and Sunnīs in Karkh, the western part of Baghdād, caused a fire that damaged the holy shrine.

- **490 AH:** The walls of the shrine were tiled by Majd al-Mulk. He also built a great masjid with two beautiful minarets on the northern side of the shrine.
- **569 AH:** Flooding of the Tigris River caused some damages to the holy courtyard, as well as the shrine.
- **575 AH:** Al-Nāṣir li-Dīn Allāh, with the help of his Shīʿah vizier, constructed rooms around the shrine and setup the Dār aḍ-Ḍiyāfah (guesthouse).
- **608 AH:** The ʿAbbāsid khalīfah converted the rooms around the shrine into an Islāmic seminary.
- **656 AH:** The Mongol ruler Hūlāgū Khān attacked Baghdād, damaging Kāẓimayn as well.
- **658 AH:** ʿAṭā Malik al-Juwaynī, the minister of Hūlāgū Khān, paid for the damages caused to Kāẓimayn and began rebuilding it.
- **776 AH:** Flooding of the Tigris River caused damage to the shrine. Sulṭān ʿUways Jalāyirī repaired these damages.
- **926 AH:** Shāh Ismāʿīl Ṣafawī constructed a magnificent building, a masjid, and two mosaic domes on the northern side of the shrine.
- **1045 AH:** Shāh Ṣafawī built four minarets on the corners of the courtyard, which still exist today.
- **1211 AH:** Āghā Muḥammad Khān Qājār gilded the two domes and covered the ground and courtyard of the shrine in marble.
- **1229 AH:** Fatḥ-ʿAlī Shāh Qājār adorned the interior of the shrine with intricate mirror work and gilded the minarets.
- **1255 AH:** Muʿtamid ad-Dawlah gilded the porches around the shrine.
- **1282 AH:** Shaykh al-ʻIrāqayn, the representative of Nāsīr ad-Din Shāh Qājār, adorned the porches with mirror work and gilded them; he also adorned the courtyard with mosaic tiles. Farhād Mīrzā, son of ʿAbbās Mīrzā, played an instrumental role in rebuilding the shrine and was buried inside the shrine.

On the southeast side of the shrine, there is a building with two small domes known as the "Children of Kāẓim."

Fawā'id al-Rijāliyah, Vol.1, P. 428

Map of the Ḥaram of Kāẓimayn

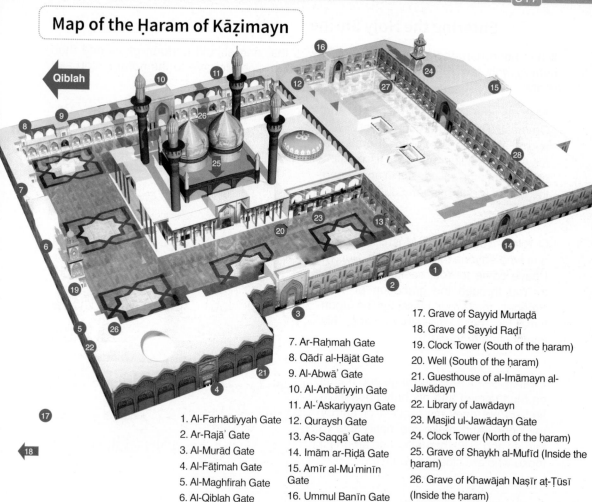

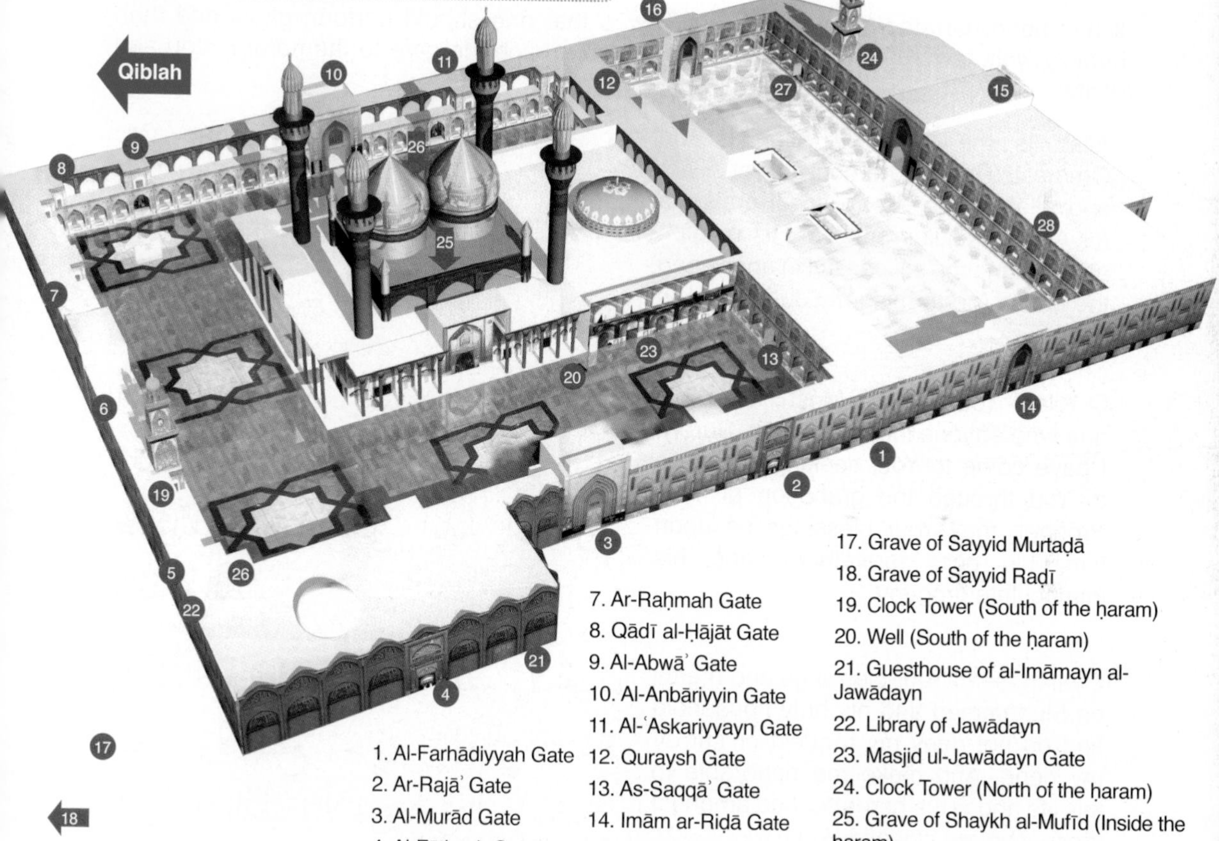

1. Al-Farhādiyyah Gate
2. Ar-Rajā' Gate
3. Al-Murād Gate
4. Al-Fāṭimah Gate
5. Al-Maghfirah Gate
6. Al-Qiblah Gate
7. Ar-Raḥmah Gate
8. Qāḍī al-Ḥājāt Gate
9. Al-Abwā' Gate
10. Al-Anbāriyyin Gate
11. Al-ʿAskariyyayn Gate
12. Quraysh Gate
13. As-Saqqā' Gate
14. Imām ar-Riḍā Gate
15. Amīr al-Muʿminīn Gate
16. Ummul Banīn Gate
17. Grave of Sayyid Murtaḍā
18. Grave of Sayyid Raḍī
19. Clock Tower (South of the ḥaram)
20. Well (South of the ḥaram)
21. Guesthouse of al-Imāmayn al-Jawādayn
22. Library of Jawādayn
23. Masjid ul-Jawādayn Gate
24. Clock Tower (North of the ḥaram)
25. Grave of Shaykh al-Mufīd (Inside the ḥaram)
26. Grave of Khawājah Naṣīr aṭ-Ṭūsī (Inside the ḥaram)
27. Al-Imām al-Ḥasan Gate
28. Al-Imām al-Ḥusayn Gate

Entering the Holy Shrine

It has been narrated from Sayyid ibn Ṭāwūs that one should perform ghusl and then humbly walk towards the holy shrine. When you reach the gate to the ḥaram, stop and recite:

Allāh is the Greatest! Allāh is the Greatest! There is no god except Allāh, and Allāh is the Greatest. All praise is for Allāh for guiding me to His religion and making me successful in answering the call to (performing my duties in) His path.	اَللّٰهُ اَكْبَرُ اَللّٰهُ اَكْبَرُ لَا اِلٰهَ اِلَّا اللّٰهُ وَاللّٰهُ اَكْبَرُ اَلْحَمْدُ لِلّٰهِ عَلَىٰ هِدَايَتِهِ لِدِيْنِهِ وَالتَّوْفِيْقِ لِمَا دَعَا اِلَيْهِ مِنْ سَبِيْلِهِ
O Allāh! You are the Most Honorable one who anyone intends to visit. Surely, I have come to You, seeking nearness to You through the grandson of Your Prophet, may Your blessings be upon him, his pure forefathers, and his immaculate progeny.	اَللّٰهُمَّ اِنَّكَ اَكْرَمُ مَقْصُوْدٍ، وَاَكْرَمُ مَأْتِيٍّ وَقَدْ اَتَيْتُكَ مُتَقَرِّباً اِلَيْكَ بِابْنِ بِنْتِ نَبِيِّكَ صَلَوَاتُكَ عَلَيْهِ وَعَلَىٰ آبَائِهِ الطَّاهِرِيْنَ وَاَبْنَآئِهِ الطَّيِّبِيْنَ
O Allāh, send Your blessings and mercy on Muḥammad and his holy household and do not deny my request or cut off my hope. And make me honorable in this life and in the hereafter and amongst those who are close to You.	اَللّٰهُمَّ صَلِّ عَلَىٰ مُحَمَّدٍ وَآلِ مُحَمَّدٍ وَلَا تُخَيِّبْ سَعْيِيْ وَلَاتَقْطَعْ رَجَائِيْ وَاجْعَلْنِيْ عِنْدَكَ وَجِيْهاً فِيْ الدُّنْيَا وَالْآخِرَةِ وَمِنَ الْمُقَرَّبِيْنَ.

When entering, enter with your right foot and recite:

بِسْمِ اللهِ وَبِاللهِ وَفِيْ سَبِيْلِ اللهِ وَعَلَىٰ
مِلَّةِ رَسُوْلِ اللهِ صَلَّى اللهُ عَلَيْهِ وَآلِهِ

With the name of Allāh (I begin), in Allāh (I trust), in the path of Allāh (I tread), and upon the creed of Rasūl Allāh (I proceed), may Allāh bless him and his household.

اَللَّهُمَّ اغْفِرْ لِيْ وَلِوَالِدَيَّ وَلِجَمِيْعِ
الْمُؤْمِنِيْنَ وَالْمُؤْمِنَاتِ

O Allāh, please forgive me, my parents and all the believing men and women.

When you reach the door to the room with the dariḥ, stop and ask permission to enter:

May I enter, O Messenger of Allāh? May I enter, O Prophet of Allāh? May I enter, O Muḥammad, son of ʿʿAbdullah?	أَأَدْخُلُ يَا رَسُوْلَ اللهِ أَأَدْخُلُ يَا نَبِيَّ اللهِ أَأَدْخُلُ يَا مُحَمَّدَ بْنَ عَبْدِاللهِ
May I enter, O Commander of the Faithful?	أَأَدْخُلُ يَااَمِيْرَالْمُؤْمِنِيْنَ
May I enter, O Abā Muḥammad, al-Ḥasan?	أَأَدْخُلُ يَا اَبَا مُحَمَّدٍ الْحَسَنَ
May I enter, O Abā ʿAbd Allāh, al-Ḥusayn?	أَأَدْخُلُ يَا اَبَا عَبْدِ اللهِ الْحُسَيْنَ
May I enter, O Abā Muḥammad, ʿAlī, son of Ḥusayn?	أَأَدْخُلُ يَا اَبَا مُحَمَّدٍ عَلِيَّ بْنَ الْحُسَيْنِ
May I enter, O Abā Jaʿfar, Muḥammad, son of ʿAlī?	أَأَدْخُلُ يَا اَبَا جَعْفَرٍ مُحَمَّدَ بْنَ عَلِيٍّ
May I enter, O Abā ʿAbd Allāh, Jaʿfar, son of Muḥammad?	أَأَدْخُلُ يَا اَبَاعَبْدِاللهِ جَعْفَرَ بْنَ مُحَمَّدٍ
May I enter, O my master, O Abā al-Ḥasan, Mūsā, son of Jaʿfar?	أَأَدْخُلُ يَا مَوْلَايَ يَا اَبَاالْحَسَنِ مُوْسَى بْنَ جَعْفَرَ
May I enter, O my master, O Abā Jaʿfar?	أَأَدْخُلُ يَا مَوْلَايَ يَا اَبَا جَعْفَرٍ
May I enter, O my master, Muḥammad, son of ʿAlī?	أَأَدْخُلُ يَا مَوْلَايَ مُحَمَّدَ بْنَ عَلِيٍّ

Ziyārah of Imām Mūsā al-Kāẓim (A)

Then, enter, say Allāhu Akbar 4 times, face the grave with your back to the qiblah and recite:

Peace be upon you, O guardian of Allāh and son of His guardian. Peace be upon you, O proof of Allāh and son of His proof.

اَلسَّلَامُ عَلَيْكَ يَا وَلِيَّ اللهِ وَابْنَ وَلِيِّهِ
اَلسَّلَامُ عَلَيْكَ يَا حُجَّةَ اللهِ وَابْنَ حُجَّتِهِ

Peace be upon you, O Allāh's chosen one and son of His chosen one. Peace be upon you, O Allāh's trustee and son of His trustee.

اَلسَّلَامُ عَلَيْكَ يَا صَفِيَّ اللهِ وَابْنَ صَفِيِّهِ
اَلسَّلَامُ عَلَيْكَ يَا اَمِيْنَ اللهِ وَابْنَ اَمِيْنِهِ

Peace be upon you, O Allāh's light in the darkness of the earth. Peace be upon you, O leader of true guidance. Peace be upon you, O the banner of religion and piety.

اَلسَّلَامُ عَلَيْكَ يَا نُوْرَ اللهِ فِيْ ظُلُمَاتِ الْاَرْضِ
اَلسَّلَامُ عَلَيْكَ يَا اِمَامَ الْهُدٰى
اَلسَّلَامُ عَلَيْكَ يَا عَلَمَ الدِّيْنِ وَالتُّقٰى

Peace be upon you, O the treasure of the Prophets' knowledge. Peace be upon you, O treasure of the Messengers' knowledge.

اَلسَّلَامُ عَلَيْكَ يَا خَازِنَ عِلْمِ النَّبِيِّيْنَ
اَلسَّلَامُ عَلَيْكَ يَا خَازِنَ عِلْمِ الْمُرْسَلِيْنَ

Peace be upon you, O deputy of the preceding successors (of the Prophets). Peace be upon you, O source of the clear revelation.

اَلسَّلَامُ عَلَيْكَ يَا نَآئِبَ الْاَوْصِيَآءِ السَّابِقِيْنَ
اَلسَّلَامُ عَلَيْكَ يَا مَعْدِنَ الْوَحْيِ الْمُبِيْنِ

Peace be upon you, O master of the certain knowledge. Peace be upon you, O treasure of the knowledge of the Messengers.	اَلسَّلَامُ عَلَيْكَ يَاصَاحِبَ الْعِلْمِ الْيَقِيْنِ اَلسَّلَامُ عَلَيْكَ يَا عَيْبَةَ عِلْمِ الْمُرْسَلِيْنَ
Peace be upon you, O righteous leader. Peace be upon you, O ascetic leader.	اَلسَّلَامُ عَلَيْكَ اَيُّهَا الْاِمَامُ الصَّالِحُ اَلسَّلَامُ عَلَيْكَ اَيُّهَا الْاِمَامُ الزَّاهِدُ
Peace be upon you, O worshipping leader. Peace be upon you, O guiding and nurturing leader and chief.	اَلسَّلَامُ عَلَيْكَ اَيُّهَا الْاِمَامُ الْعَابِدُ اَلسَّلَامُ عَلَيْكَ اَيُّهَا الْاِمَامُ السَّيِّدُ الرَّشِيْدُ
Peace be upon you, O slain martyr. Peace be upon you, O son of Allāh's Messenger and his successor.	اَلسَّلَامُ عَلَيْكَ اَيُّهَا الْمَقْتُوْلُ الشَّهِيْدُ اَلسَّلَامُ عَلَيْكَ يَابْنَ رَسُوْلِ اللهِ وَابْنَ وَصِيِّهِ
Peace be upon you, O my master, Mūsā, son of Jaʿfar. May Allāh's mercy and blessings be upon you.	اَلسَّلَامُ عَلَيْكَ يَا مَوْلَايَ مُوْسَى بْنَ جَعْفَرٍ وَرَحْمَةُ اللهِ وَبَرَكَاتُهُ
I bear witness that you faithfully conveyed that which Allāh ordered You to convey and that you safeguarded that which He entrusted with you.	اَشْهَدُ اَنَّكَ قَدْ بَلَّغْتَ عَنِ اللهِ مَا حَمَّلَكَ وَحَفِظْتَ مَا اسْتَوْدَعَكَ

And you made lawful all that which Allāh has deemed lawful and made unlawful that which Allāh has deemed unlawful.	وَحَلَّلْتَ حَلاَلَ اللهِ وَحَرَّمْتَ حَرَامَ اللهِ
And you established the commands of Allāh, recited the Book of Allāh, and endured harm for the sake of Allāh.	وَاَقَمْتَ اَحْكَامَ اللهِ، وَتَلَوْتَ كِتَابَ اللهِ وَصَبَرْتَ عَلَى الْاَذٰى فِيْ جَنْبِ اللهِ،
And you strove in the way of Allāh as it ought to be strove, until certainty (death) came to you.	وَجَاهَدْتَ فِيْ اللهِ حَقَّ جِهَادِهِ حَتّٰى أَتَاكَ الْيَقِيْنُ
I also bear witness that you passed away upon the same principles on which your immaculate fathers and pure forefathers, the successors, guides, leaders, and rightly guided ones, passed away.	وَاَشْهَدُ اَنَّكَ مَضَيْتَ عَلٰى مَا مَضٰى عَلَيْهِ آبَاؤُكَ الطَّاهِرُوْنَ وَاَجْدَادُكَ الطَّيِّبُوْنَ الْاَوْصِيَاءُ الْهَادُوْنَ الْاَئِمَّةُ الْمَهْدِيُّوْنَ،
You never preferred blindness over true guidance and never slanted from the truth to falsehood. I also bear witness that you acted sincerely for Allāh, His Messenger, and the Commander of the Faithful.	لَمْ تُؤْثِرْ عَمًى عَلٰى هُدًى وَلَمْ تَمِلْ مِنْ حَقٍّ اِلٰى بَاطِلٍ، وَاَشْهَدُ اَنَّكَ نَصَحْتَ لِلّٰهِ وَلِرَسُوْلِهِ وَلِاَمِيْرِ الْمُؤْمِنِيْنَ

وَاَنَّكَ اَدَّيْتَ الْاَمَانَةَ، وَاجْتَنَبْتَ الْخِيَانَةَ، وَاَقَمْتَ الصَّلَاةَ، وَآتَيْتَ الزَّكَاةَ، وَاَمَرْتَ بِالْمَعْرُوْفِ، وَنَهَيْتَ عَنِ الْمُنْكَرِ	You fulfilled the trust given to you, avoided betrayal, established the prayers, paid alms, enjoined good, forbade evil,
وَعَبَدْتَ اللهَ مُخْلِصاً مُجْتَهِداً مُحْتَسِباً حَتّٰى أَتَاكَ الْيَقِيْنُ	and served Allāh sincerely and painstakingly, expecting His reward until certainty (death) came to you.
فَجَزَاكَ اللهُ عَنِ الْاِسْلَامِ وَاَهْلِهِ اَفْضَلَ الْجَزَآءِ وَاَشْرَفَ الْجَزَاءِ	So, may Allāh reward you on behalf of Islām and its people with the best and most honorable reward.
اَتَيْتُكَ يَابْنَ رَسُوْلِ اللهِ زَآئِراً، عَارِفاً بِحَقِّكَ، مُقِرّاً بِفَضْلِكَ، مُحْتَمِلاً لِعِلْمِكَ، مُحْتَجِباً بِذِمَّتِكَ	I have come to visit you, O son of Rasūl Allāh, aware of your right, professing your virtues, knowing your knowledge, shielding myself with the greatness of your essence,
عَآئِذاً بِقَبْرِكَ، لَائِذاً بِضَرِيْحِكَ، مُسْتَشْفِعاً بِكَ اِلَى اللهِ، مُوَالِياً لِاَوْلِيَآئِكَ، مُعَادِياً لِاَعْدَآئِكَ	seeking protection with your grave, resorting to your tomb, seeking your intercession with Allāh, declaring loyalty to your loyalists, declaring animosity towards your enemies,

having insight of your status and true guidance you are upon, knowing the misguidance of your openents, and knowing the blind path they are upon.	مُسْتَبْصِراً بِشَأْنِكَ وَبِالْهُدَى الَّذِيْ اَنْتَ عَلَيْهِ، عَالِماً بِضَلَالَةِ مَنْ خَالَفَكَ وَبِالْعَمَى الَّذِيْ هُمْ عَلَيْهِ
May my father, mother, myself, my family members, my property, and my sons be sacrificed for you, O son of Rasūl Allāh.	بِاَبِيْ اَنْتَ وَاُمِّيْ وَنَفْسِيْ وَاَهْلِيْ وَمَالِيْ وَوَلَدِيْ يَا بْنَ رَسُوْلِ اللهِ
I have come to you seeking nearness to Allāh, the Exalted, by visiting you and seeking your intercession for me with Him; so, intercede for me with your Lord so that He may forgive my sins,	اَتَيْتُكَ مُتَقَرِّباً بِزِيَارَتِكَ اِلَى اللهِ تَعَالٰى، وَمُسْتَشْفِعاً بِكَ اِلَيْهِ فَاشْفَعْ لِيْ عِنْدَ رَبِّكَ لِيَغْفِرَ لِيْ ذُنُوْبِيْ
pardon my offenses, overlook my errors, erase my wrongdoings, grant me entrance to Heaven,	وَيَعْفُوَ عَنْ جُرْمِيْ، وَيَتَجَاوَزَ عَنْ سَيِّئَاتِيْ، وَيَمْحُوَ عَنِّيْ خَطِيْئَاتِيْ وَيُدْخِلَنِي الْجَنَّةَ
favor me with that which is befitting of Him, and forgive me, my forefathers, my brothers, my sisters,	وَيَتَفَضَّلَ عَلَيَّ بِمَا هُوَ اَهْلُهُ، وَيَغْفِرَ لِيْ وَلِآبَائِيْ وَلِاِخْوَانِيْ وَاَخَوَاتِيْ
and all the believing men and women in the east and west of the earth, out of His grace, magnanimity, and munificence.	وَلِجَمِيْعِ الْمُؤْمِنِيْنَ وَالْمُؤْمِنَاتِ فِيْ مَشَارِقِ الْاَرْضِ وَمَغَارِبِهَا بِفَضْلِهِ وَجُوْدِهِ وَمَنِّهِ

Then, kiss the ḍarīḥ, place both sides of your face on it, and ask for your needs. Then, come back near the holy head and say:

Peace be upon you, O my master, Mūsā, son of Jaʿfar. May Allāh's mercy and blessings be upon you.	اَلسَّلَامُ عَلَيْكَ يَا مَوْلَايَ يَا مُوْسَى بْنَ جَعْفَرٍ وَرَحْمَةُ اللهِ وَبَرَكَاتُهُ
I bear witness that you are surely the guiding leader and the guardian who nurtures (us) to true guidance.	اَشْهَدُ اَنَّكَ الْاِمَامُ الْهَادِيْ وَالْوَلِيُّ الْمُرْشِدُ
You are surely the core of the Revelation, the master of true interpretation, the bearer of the Torah and the Bible, and the knowledgeable, just, and truthful one who puts his knowledge into practice.	وَاَنَّكَ مَعْدِنُ التَّنْزِيْلِ وَصَاحِبُ التَّأْوِيْلِ وَحَامِلُ التَّوْرَاةِ وَالْاِنْجِيْلِ وَالْعَالِمُ الْعَادِلُ وَالصَّادِقُ الْعَامِلُ
O my master, I disocciate from your enemies in the presence of Allāh, and I seek nearness to Allāh through my loyalty towards you.	يَا مَوْلَايَ اَنَا اَبْرَأُ اِلَى اللهِ مِنْ اَعْدَائِكَ وَاَتَقَرَّبُ اِلَى اللهِ بِمُوَالَاتِكَ
So, may Allāh bless you, your fathers, your forefathers, your descendants, your followers, and your lovers. May Allāh's mercy and blessings be upon them.	فَصَلَّى اللهُ عَلَيْكَ وَعَلٰى آبَائِكَ وَاَجْدَادِكَ وَاَبْنَآئِكَ وَشِيْعَتِكَ وَمُحِبِّيْكَ وَرَحْمَةُ اللهِ وَبَرَكَاتُهُ

Offer a two rakaʿāt prayer of ziyārah; after Sūrat al-Fātiḥā, recite Sūrat Yāsīn, ar-Raḥmān, or any other sūrah of the Qurʾān that is easy for you. Then, ask for your wishes.

Ṣalawāt of Imām Mūsā al-Kāẓim (A)

Sayyid ibn Ṭāwūs narrates the following Ṣalawāt of Imām Mūsā bin Jaʿfar (A), which divulges the virtues and tragedies of the Imām (A):

O Allāh, send blessings upon Muḥammad and his household and send blessings upon Mūsā, son of Jaʿfar, the successor of the righteous ones,	اَللّٰهُمَّ صَلِّ عَلٰى مُحَمَّدٍ وَاَهْلِ بَيْتِهِ، وَصَلِّ عَلٰى مُوْسَى بْنِ جَعْفَرٍ وَصِيِّ الْاَبْرَارِ
the leader of the excellent ones, the treasure of illumination, and the inheritor of tranquility, dignity, wisdom, and traditions.	وَاِمَامِ الْاَخْيَارِ، وَعَيْبَةِ الْاَنْوَارِ، وَوَارِثِ السَّكِيْنَةِ وَالْوَقَارِ وَالْحِكَمِ وَالْآثَارِ
He used to stay awake during the night until early dawn, continuously imploring (Allāh) for forgiveness.	الَّذِيْ كَانَ يُحْيِي اللَّيْلَ بِالسَّهَرِ اِلَى السَّحَرِ بِمُوَاصَلَةِ الْاِسْتِغْفَارِ
He was inseparably attached to lengthy prostrations, heavy tears, long confidential talks, and unending implorations.	حَلِيْفِ السَّجْدَةِ الطَّوِيْلَةِ، وَالدُّمُوْعِ الْغَزِيْرَةِ، وَالْمُنَاجَاةِ الْكَثِيْرَةِ وَالضَّرَاعَاتِ الْمُتَّصِلَةِ
He was the center of understanding, justice, goodness, virtue, munificence, and generosity.	وَمَقَرِّ النُّهٰي وَالْعَدْلِ وَالْخَيْرِ وَالْفَضْلِ وَالنَّدٰى وَالْبَذْلِ

He was also accustomed to trials and patience, and he was oppressed wrongfully, buried unjustly, and tortured in the pits of jails and darkness of cells.	وَمَأْلَفِ الْبَلْوٰى وَالصَّبْرِ، وَالْمُضْطَهَدِ بِالظُّلْمِ، وَالْمَقْبُوْرِ بِالْجَوْرِ، وَالْمُعَذَّبِ فِيْ قَعْرِ السُّجُوْنِ وَظُلَمِ الْمَطَامِيْرِ
He is the one whose leg was bruised by the rings of chains and whose funeral was heckled with humiliating and belittling calls.	ذِي السَّاقِ الْمَرْضُوْضِ بِحَلَقِ الْقُيُوْدِ، وَالْجِنَازَةِ الْمُنَادٰى عَلَيْهَا بِذُلِّ الْاِسْتِخْفَافِ
He is the one who joined his grandfather (the Prophet), the chosen one, his father (Imām ʿAlī), the content one, and his mother (Sayyidah Fāṭimah), the leader of the women, with usurped inheritance, robbed loyalty, overpowered state, unavenged blood, and having drunk poison.	وَالْوَارِدِ عَلٰى جَدِّهِ الْمُصْطَفٰى وَاَبِيْهِ الْمُرْتَضٰى وَاُمِّهِ سَيِّدَةِ النِّسَاءِ بِإِرْثٍ مَغْصُوْبٍ وَوَلَاءٍ مَسْلُوْبٍ وَاَمْرٍ مَغْلُوْبٍ وَدَمٍ مَطْلُوْبٍ وَسَمٍّ مَشْرُوْبٍ
O Allāh, just as he patiently endured difficult ordeals, swallowed his grief and tragedies,	اَللّٰهُمَّ وَكَمَا صَبَرَ عَلٰى غَلِيْظِ الْمِحَنِ وَتَجَرَّعَ غُصَصَ الْكُرَبِ
submitted to Your pleasure, obeyed You sincerely, adopted (internal) humility towards You,	وَاسْتَسْلَمَ لِرِضَاكَ وَاَخْلَصَ الطَّاعَةَ لَكَ، وَمَحَضَ الْخُشُوْعَ

and adopted (internal) humility towards You, stood against innovation (bidʿat) and its bearers,	وَاسْتَشْعَرَ الْخُضُوْعَ وَعَادَى الْبِدْعَةَ وَاَهْلَهَا
and was not influenced by those who taunted him, in regards to following Your orders and refraining from Your prohibitions;	وَلَمْ يَلْحَقْهُ فِيْ شَيْءٍ مِنْ اَوَامِرِكَ وَنَوَاهِيْكَ لَوْمَةُ لَائِمٍ
thus, bless him with ever-increasing, lofty, and purified blessings that will allow all Your creations to receive his intercession.	صَلِّ عَلَيْهِ صَلَاةً نَامِيَةً مُنِيْفَةً زَاكِيَةً تُوْجِبُ لَهُ بِهَا شَفَاعَةَ اُمَمٍ مِنْ خَلْقِكَ، وَقُرُوْنٍ مِنْ بَرَايَاكَ
And convey to him our greetings and peace, and grant us from Your special blessings, favors, bounties, forgiveness, and pleasure on account of our loyalty to him.	وَبَلِّغْهُ عَنَّا تَحِيَّةً وَسَلَاماً، وَآتِنَا مِنْ لَدُنْكَ فِيْ مُوَالَاتِهِ فَضْلاً وَ اِحْسَاناً وَمَغْفِرَةً وَرِضْوَاناً
Surely, You are the Owner of prevalent favors and supreme exoneration. By Your Mercy, O the Most Merciful!	اِنَّكَ ذُوْالْفَضْلِ الْعَمِيْمِ، وَالتَّجَاوُزِ الْعَظِيْمِ، بِرَحْمَتِكَ يَا اَرْحَمَ الرَّاحِمِيْنَ

Ziyārah of Imām Muḥammad al-Jawād (A)

Then, turn towards the grave of Imām Muḥammad bin ʿAlī al-Jawād, which is next to the grave of his grandfather, and recite the following:

Peace be upon you, O guardian of Allah. Peace be upon you, O decisive proof of Allah.	اَلسَّلَامُ عَلَيْكَ يَا وَلِيَّ اللهِ اَلسَّلَامُ عَلَيْكَ يَا حُجَّةَ اللهِ
Peace be upon you, O light of Allah in the darkness of the earth.	اَلسَّلَامُ عَلَيْكَ يَا نُوْرَاللهِ فِيْ ظُلُمَاتِ الْاَرْضِ
Peace be upon you, O son of Rasūl Allāh.	اَلسَّلَامُ عَلَيْكَ يَا بْنَ رَسُوْلِ اللهِ
Peace be upon you and your forefathers. Peace be upon you and your offspring. Peace be upon you and your intimate friends.	اَلسَّلَامُ عَلَيْكَ وَعَلٰى آبَائِكَ اَلسَّلَامُ عَلَيْكَ وَعَلٰى اَبْنَائِكَ اَلسَّلَامُ عَلَيْكَ وَعَلٰى اَوْلِيَائِكَ
I bear witness that you established the prayer, paid alms, enjoined good, forbade evil, and recited the Qurʿān in its correct manner.	اَشْهَدُ اَنَّكَ قَدْ اَقَمْتَ الصَّلَاةَ، وَآتَيْتَ الزَّكَاةَ، وَاَمَرْتَ بِالْمَعْرُوْفِ، وَنَهَيْتَ عَنِ الْمُنْكَرِ، وَتَلَوْتَ الْكِتَابَ حَقَّ تِلَاوَتِهِ
And that you strove in the way of Allah as one ought to and patiently endured harm for the sake of Allāh until certainty (death) came to you.	وَجَاهَدْتَ فِيْ اللهِ حَقَّ جِهَادِهِ، وَصَبَرْتَ عَلَى الْاَذٰى فِيْ جَنْبِهِ حَتّٰى أَتَاكَ الْيَقِيْنُ،

Then, kiss the ḍarīḥ and place both sides of your face on it. Next, offer a two rakaʿāt prayer of ziyārah. Then, perform sajdah and recite:

اِرْحَمْ مَنْ اَسَاءَ وَاقْتَرَفَ وَاسْتَكَانَ وَاعْتَرَفَ

Have mercy on (s)he who has done wrong and committed sins, and confesses.

Then, place your right cheek on the turbah and recite:

اِنْ كُنْتُ بِئْسَ الْعَبْدُ فَاَنْتَ نِعْمَ الرَّبُ

If I am the worst servant, then You are the best Lord and Nurturer.

Then, place your left cheek on the turbah and recite:

عَظُمَ الذَّنْبُ مِنْ عَبْدِكَ فَلْيَحْسُنِ الْعَفْوُ مِنْ عِنْدِكَ يَا كَرِيْمُ

The greatest sin is from Your servant, and the best of pardon is from You, O the Most Generous!

Then, perform sajdah and recite شُكْرًا لِلّٰه "shukran lillāh" (Thank You Allah) 100 times.

Common Ziyārah of Imām al-Kāzim (A) and Imām al-Jawād (A)

The two great scholars Sheikh al-Mufīd and Muḥammad bin Mashhadī have said that the moment you reach the pure ḍarīḥ, stand there and recite the following:

اَلسَّلَامُ عَلَيْكُمَا يَا وَلِيَّيِ اللهِ اَلسَّلَامُ عَلَيْكُمَا يَا حُجَّتَيِ اللهِ اَلسَّلَامُ عَلَيْكُمَا يَا نُورَيِ اللهِ فِيْ ظُلُمَاتِ الْاَرْضِ

Peace be upon you O representatives of Allāh! Peace be upon you O proofs of Allāh! Peace be upon you O the lights of Allāh in the darkness of the earth.

اَشْهَدُ اَنَّكُمَا قَدْ بَلَّغْتُمَا عَنِ اللهِ مَا حَمَّلَكُمَا وَحَفِظْتُمَا مَا اسْتُوْدِعْتُمَا وَحَلَّلْتُمَا حَلَالَ اللهِ وَحَرَّمْتُمَا حَرَامَ اللهِ

I bear witness that you both faithfully conveyed that which Allāh ordered you to convey, and that you safeguarded that which He entrusted with you. I bear witness that you prescribed that which Allāh has made lawful and prohibited that which Allāh has made unlawful,

وَاَقَمْتُمَا حُدُوْدَ اللهِ وَتَلَوْتُمَا كِتَابَ اللهِ وَصَبَرْتُمَا عَلَى الْاَذٰى فِيْ جَنْبِ اللهِ مُحْتَسِبَيْنِ حَتّٰى اَتَاكُمَا الْيَقِيْنُ

and that you established the boundaries set by Allāh, recited the book of Allāh, and endured harm for the sake of Allāh patiently while directing affairs in the light of the divine rules until death came to you.

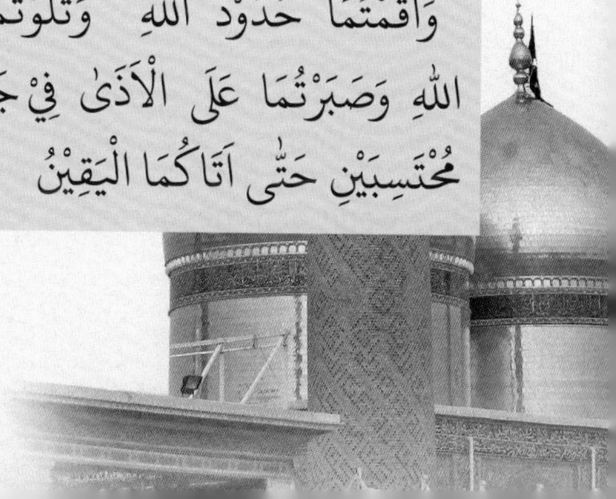

اَبْرَءُ اِلَى اللهِ مِنْ اَعْدآئِكُمَا وَاَتَقَرَّبُ
اِلَى اللهِ زَائِراً عَارِفاً بِحَقِّكُمَا مُوَالِياً
لِاَوْلِيآئِكُمَا مُعَادِياً لِاَعْدآئِكُمَا

I turn to Allāh by disassociating with your enemies, and I seek nearness to Allāh through your guardianship. I have come to visit you, fully aware of your rights, attached to your friends and averse to your enemies,

مُسْتَبْصِراً بِالْهُدَى الَّذِيْ اَنْتُمَا عَلَيْهِ
عَارِفاً بِضَلَالَةِ مَنْ خَالَفَكُمَا فَاشْفَعَا لِيْ
عِنْدَ رَبِّكُمَا فَاِنَّ لَكُمَا عِنْدَ اللهِ جَاهاً
عَظِيْماً وَمَقَاماً مَحْمُوْداً

having insight of the guidance that you are upon, and being aware of the misguidance of your opponents, so, intercede for me with your Lord, because, surely, you have a supreme standing and praiseworthy status with Allāh.

اَلسَّلَامُ عَلَيْكُمَا يَاحُجَّتَى اللهِ فِيْ اَرْضِهِ
وَسَمآئِهِ عَبْدُكُمَا وَوَلِيُّكُمَا زَائِرُكُمَا
مُتَقَرِّباً اِلَى اللهِ بِزِيَارَتِكُمَا

Peace be on both of you, O the decisive proofs of Allāh on His earth and in His heavens. Your servant and friend has come to visit you, in order to seek Allāh's nearness through your ziyārah.

اَللَّهُمَّ اجْعَلْ لِيْ لِسَانَ صِدْقٍ فِيْ اَوْلِيآئِكَ
الْمُصْطَفَيْنَ وَحَبِّبْ اِلَيَّ مَشَاهِدَهُمْ
وَاجْعَلْنِيْ مَعَهُمْ فِيْ الدُّنْيَا وَالْاٰخِرَةِ يَا اَرْحَمَ
الرَّاحِمِيْنَ

O Allāh, make me speak the truth about Your chosen friends, love and honor their shrines, and place me with them in this world and the Hereafter, O the Most Merciful!

Then, recite a two rakaʿāt prayer of ziyārah next to each Imām and ask Allāh for your ḥājāt.

Farewell Ziyārah of Imām Mūsā al-Kaẓim (A)

Peace be upon you, O my master, O Abā al-Ḥasan, and the mercy and blessings of Allah.	اَلسَّلَامُ عَلَيْكَ يَا مَوْلَايَ يَا اَبَاالْحَسَنِ وَرَحْمَةُ اللهِ وَبَرَكَاتُهُ
I entrust you in Allāh's care and send my salutations upon you. I have believed in Allāh, the Messenger, and that which he has brought and guided us to.	اَسْتَوْدِعُكَ اللهَ وَاَقْرَأُ عَلَيْكَ السَّلَامَ آمَنَّا بِاللهِ وَبِالرَّسُوْلِ وَبِمَا جِئْتَ بِهِ وَدَلَلْتَ عَلَيْهِ
O Allah, write our names amongst the martyrs.	اَللّٰهُمَّ اكْتُبْنَا مَعَ الشَّاهِدِيْنَ

Farewell Ziyārah of Imām al-Jawād (A)

Peace be upon you, O my master, O son of Rasūl Allāh, and the mercy and blessings of Allah.	اَلسَّلَامُ عَلَيْكَ يَا مَوْلَايَ يَاابْنَ رَسُوْلِ اللهِ وَرَحْمَةُ اللهِ وَبَرَكَاتُهُ
I entrust you in Allāh's care and send my salutations upon you. I have believed in Allāh, the Messenger, and that which he has brought and guided us to.	اَسْتَوْدِعُكَ اللهَ وَاَقْرَأُ عَلَيْكَ السَّلَامَ آمَنَّا بِاللهِ وَبِالرَّسُوْلِ وَبِمَا جِئْتَ بِهِ وَدَلَلْتَ عَلَيْهِ
O Allah, write our names amongst the martyrs.	اَللّٰهُمَّ اكْتُبْنَا مَعَ الشَّاهِدِيْنَ

Pray to Allāh for acceptance of your ziyārah and for this not to be the last one. Ask Allāh to grant you tawfīq to come more often; then, kiss the ḍarīḥ and place both sides of your face on it.

Stars of the Ḥaram

Important Figures Buried in the Shrine of Kāẓimayn

Khawājah Naṣīr al-Dīn Ṭūsī

Nasīr al-Dīn al-Ṭūsī was born on the 11th of Jamādi al-Awwal, 597 AH in Ṭūs and passed away on ʿĪd al-Ghadīr (18th Dhūl Hijjah), 672 AH in Baghdād. He is buried in the hall that faces the head of the holy Imām (A), in the women's side.

Nasīr al-Dīn al-Ṭūsī was forced to be a part of the Iranian government, but he used this opportunity to help others. He did not assume the position for power, but rather, he was there to serve others and prevent oppression. He was also an architect and helped build many structures. He also took advantage of this position to help further Islām. His contributions and service to the people is unparalleled, which is why he is known as Nasīr ad-Dīn aṭ-Ṭūsī, the "Helper of Religion." Imām Khumaynī has also praised him and mentioned his great qualities, and in Iran, there is a special day dedicated to his memory.

Shaykh al-Mufīd

Shaykh al-Mufīd was born in ʿUkbarā, a small town north of Baghdād, on 11th Dhūl Qaʿdah, 336 AH. He passed away on 3rd Ramaḍān, 413 AH. Sayyid Murtaḍā led his Ṣalāt al-Mayyit and buried him in the holy shrine. His grave is in the hall that faces the feet of the holy Imām (A), in the men's side. Shaykh al-Mufīd is the only person to have received letters from Imām az-Zamān (AJ) during the Greater Occultation. Some believe that he received 30 letters from the Imām (AJ) over the course of 30 years. Amongst his famous students are Shaykh aṭ-Ṭūsī, Sayyid Raḍī, and Sayyid Murtaḍā.

Ibn Qūliwayh Qumī

Abūl-Qāsim Jaʿfar ibn Muḥammad, was a teacher of Shaykh al-Mufīd and the author of *Kāmil az-Ziyārāt*. He passed away in 369 AH and is buried in the holy shrine in the hall that faces the feet of the holy Imām (A), alongside Shaykh al-Mufīd.

The Vivid Dream of Shaykh al-Mufīd

One day, Shaykh al-Mufīd was sitting with his students and delivering a lecture, when they suddenly saw him arise to greet a guest. They turned around and saw a woman standing at the door with her two sons.

After greeting the Shaykh, she said, "O Shaykh! Please teach these two sons of mine (Sayyid Murtaḍā and Sayyid Raḍī) fiqh."

The Shaykh's eyes were filled with tears and he replied, "The dream I had last night has come true! I dreamt that I was teaching in this masjid when Sayyidah Fāṭimah (A) entered our class along with her two dear sons, Imām al-Ḥasan (A) and Imām al-Ḥusayn (A). The entire masjid was illuminated. She told me, 'I have brought my sons to learn fiqh from you.' When I woke up, I was in awe of their remarkable presence, and was preoccupied by that dream until now."

Sayyid Murtaḍā & Sayyid Raḍī

Sayyid Murtaḍā, known as ʿAlam al-Hudā, was born in 355 AH in a shīʿah neighborhood of Baghdād, and his brother, Sayyid Raḍī, was born in 359 AH. They are paternal descendants of Imām Mūsā al-Kāẓim (A) by five generations and maternal descendants of Imām Zayn al-ʿĀbidīn (A) by six generations.

Their father, Sayyid Ḥusayn, was a community leader and led Ḥajj caravans. Their mother Fātimah was a pious scholar who requested Shaykh al-Mufīd to write the book Aḥkām an-Nisā' (Practical laws for Women).

Sayyid Raḍī is best known for gathering and compiling the sermons, letters, and sayings of Amīr al-Mu'minīn (A) into the famous book *Nahj al-Balāghah*. He passed away at the age of 47 in Muḥarram, 406 AH. He was buried inside his own home.

Sayyid Murtaḍā bore the title Niqāb aṭ-Ṭālibiyyīn, which means the "Confidante of the Seekers," because he would always help others, yet still guard their secrets. He was also considered the jurisprudential leader, theologian, and Marjaʿ of the shīʿah after his teacher, Shaykh al-Mufīd, passed away. One of his famous students was Shaykh aṭ-Ṭūsī, the author of *Tahdhīb* and *Istibṣār* (two of the four most reliable shīʿah books).

Sayyid Murtaḍā passed away in 436 AH. He was buried in the Kharkh region of Baghdād.

Sayyid Murtaḍa

Gravesite of Sayyid Raḍī and Sayyid Murtaḍa, southeast of the ḥaram

Sayyid Raḍī

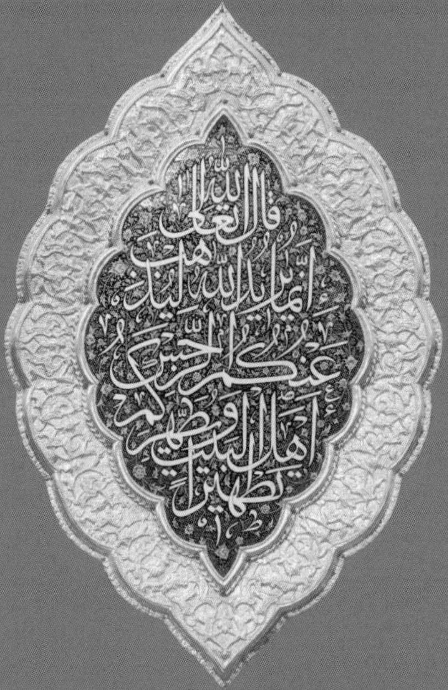

سامرا

Sāmarrā

Sāmarrā

Dear Zā'ir,

You have now entered the city of Sāmarrā. As you walk through this city, be aware that this the same land where our beloved 10th, 11th, and 12th Imāms (A) lived and were under house arrest. This is the place where our living Imām (A) was born and last seen before he entered into ghaybah (occultation). Make sure to especially pray for his quick reappearance, and for your families and communities to be included amongst his close companions and supporters.

The city of Sāmarrā is unique in that both Shī'ah and Sunnī populations peacefully coexist in this locale. This is beacuse they have found firm unity through their love for the Imāms (A) who reside in this land.

In this ḥaram, you will find one big darīḥ that has four holy graves within it:

- Imām 'Alī al-Hādī (A)
- Imām Ḥasan al-'Askarī (A)
- Ḥaḍrat Ḥakīmah Khātūn (The sister of the 10th Imām)
- Ḥaḍrat Narjis Khātūn (The mother of the 12th Imām)

Ṣalāh of Imām al-Hādī (A)

Offer a two rakaʿāt prayer in the following method:

- 1st Rakaʿah: Sūrat al-Fātiḥah and Sūrat Yāsīn
- 2nd Rakaʿah: Sūrat al-Fātiḥah and Sūrat ar-Raḥmān

Ṣalāh of Imām al-ʿAskarī (A)

Offer two sets of two rakaʿāt in the following method:

- 1st set: Sūrat al-Fātiḥah and Sūrat al-Zalzalah 15 times
- 2nd set: Sūrat al-Fātiḥah and Sūrat al-Ikhlāṣ 15 times

Biḥār ul-Anwār, Vol. 88, P. 189

Virtues of Performing Ziyārah of ʿAskarīyayn (A)

Without a doubt, the rewards and virtues of performing the ziyārah of the 10th and 11th Imāms (A) is equivalent to that of the other Imāms (A).

Imām as-Ṣādiq (A):
The one who performs ziyārah of any of the Imāms (A) is like one who has visited and performed ziyārah of the Noble Prophet (S).

Imām as-Ṣādiq (A):
Whoever performs ziyārah of an Imām (A), whom it is mandatory to follow, and offers a four rakaʿāt prayer in his ḥaram will be given the reward of performing Ḥajj and ʿUmrah.

ʿAllāmah Majlisī has reported 15 aḥādīth in regards to the rewards for rebuilding the graves of the Prophets and the Imāms. Some of these aḥadīth are below:

1. Imām Ḥasan al-ʿAskarī (A): My grave in “Sorra man ra ʾ” is a source of safety (from divine punishment) for both groups.

The two groups are the Shīʿah and Sunnī groups who were living there at the time, implicating that the Imām's (A) holy grave has such magnificent blessings that it has covered the entire region and is a general mercy for all.

2. Sheikh Ṭusī narrates in *Amālī* that someone asked Imām al-Hādī (A): O my master! Teach me a duʿāʾ through which I may gain closeness to Allāh, the Exalted. The Imām (A) replied, "I will teach you a duʿāʾ that I recite many times and call upon Allāh with. I have asked Allāh not to disappoint anybody who recites this duʿāʾ at my shrine:

O my means when I lack means. O my hope and trust! O my shelter and support!	يَا عُدَّتِيْ عِنْدَ الْعُدَدِ وَيَارَجَائِيْ وَ الْمُعْتَمَدَ وَ يَاكَهْفِيْ وَالسَّنَدَ
O the One! O the Only! O (He who is described in) "Say: He is Allāh, the One."	يَاوَاحِدُ يَا أَحَدُ وَ يَا قُلْ هُوَ اللهُ أَحَدٌ
I ask you, O Allāh, by the right of those whom you have created and have not made anyone like them	أَسْأَلُكَ اللَّهُمَّ بِحَقِّ مَنْ خَلَقْتَ مِنْ خَلْقِكَ وَلَمْ تَجْعَلْ فِيْ خَلْقِكَ مِثْلَهُمْ أَحَداً
to send blessings upon all of them and grant me...[ask for your wishes]	صَلِّ عَلَىٰ جَمَاعَتِهِمْ وَ افْعَلْ بِيْ...

3. Its been narrated in ʿUddat al-Dāʿī that one person had a difficult problem during the time of Imām al-Hādī (A). So, he asked Imām (A) to intercede on his behalf to the khalīfah. Before long, his problem was resolved, so he came to Imām (A) and asked, "Did you intercede for me at his palace?" The Imām (A) replied, "Allāh has trained us in a way that we only seek His help during difficult hardships and do not ask anybody else for help. I was afraid that if I took your request to the khalīfah, the Almighty would remove His Mercy from us, so I asked Him to grant blessings to those who recite this duʿāʾ at my shrine and accept their call." The Imām (A) then recited the above duʿāʾ.

	Imām al-Hādī (A): the 10th Imām	Imām al-ʿAskarī (A): the 11th Imām
Name:	ʿAlī	Ḥasan
Kunya:	Abū al-Ḥasan ath-Thālith	Abū Muḥammad
Title:	Hādī, Naqī	al-ʿAskarī, Ibn ar-Ridhā, as-Sirrāj
Parents:	Imām al-Jawād & Ḥaḍrat Samānah	Imām al-Hādī & Ḥaḍrat Sawsan
Birthday:	15th Dhul Ḥijjah, 212 AH	8th or 10th Rabīʿ ath-Thānī, 232 AH
Birth Place:	Sorayya, a village near Madīnah	Madīnah
Ring Inscription:	اَللهُ رَبِّيْ وَ هُوَ عِصْمَتِيْ مِنْ خَلْقِهِ Allāh is my Nurturer and Guardian from his creation	اِنَّ اللهَ شَهِيْدٌ Certainly Allāh is the witness
Number of Children:	5	1
Duration of Imāmah:	33 years	6 years
Date of Martyrdom:	Monday, 3rd Rajab, 254 AH	Friday, 8th Rabīʿ ul-Awwal, 260 AH
Place of Martyrdom:	Sāmarrā	Sāmarrā
Cause of Martyrdom:	Poisoned by Muʿtamid or Muʿtazz	Poisoned by Muʿtamid ʿAbbāsid
Lifespan:	42 years	28 years
Holy Shrine:	Sāmarrā	Sāmarrā
Eras of his life:	■ Before Imāmah: 212-220 AH ■ Imāmah prior to Mutawakkil: 220-232 AH ■ Imāmah during Mutawakkil: 232-254 AH (the most severe time for the Imām (A))	■ Before Imāmah: 232-254 AH ■ Imāmah: 254-260 AH (The Imām (A) was always under watch or in prison. He lived during the time of Muhtadī and Muʿtamid.)

History of Sāmarrā

- Sāmarrā is located on the east bank of the Tigris River in the Ṣalāḥuddīn Province, 78 miles north of Baghdād.
- Due to the good weather, the Sasanian Kings had erected some buildings here.
- Sāmarrā used to be the border city between the Persian and Roman empires. The Romans had control over it; therefore, its people were Christians.
- After the revelation of Islām, the city was conquered from the Romans through various battles, and was destroyed, leaving its people scattered.
- By the end of the 2nd century, there was only one temple left standing in this city.
- This city was famous even before the Muslims took over.
- In the year 221 AH, Muʿtaṣim, the 8th ʿAbbāsid khalīfah, rebuilt the city and appointed it as his capital. He named it "Sorra man rāʾ," which means "Whoever sees it will become happy."
- This name was engraved on the ʿAbbāsid coins during that time.
- From the death of Muʿtaṣim until 279 AH, seven ʿAbbāsid khalīfahs also selected Sāmarrā as their capital and constructed many buildings around it.
- Sāmarrā was extended during the time of al-Mutawakkil, and a new city named Mutiwakkiliya was established next to it.
- Once the capital of the khalīfahate was moved back to Baghdād, Sāmarrā's development slowed down.

Aerial view of Sāmarrā

The Holy Shrine (20th Century)

- Some of the magnificent buildings of Sāmarrā existed until the 4th century.
- During the 4th century, the city of Sāmarrā was slowly destructed, and nothing remained except for the Holy ʿAskarīyayn Shrine.
- Oppressors like Salāḥuddīn Ayyūbī and Saddam Hussein were born here and oppressed many of the Shīʿah here.

Ṣalāḥuddīn Province

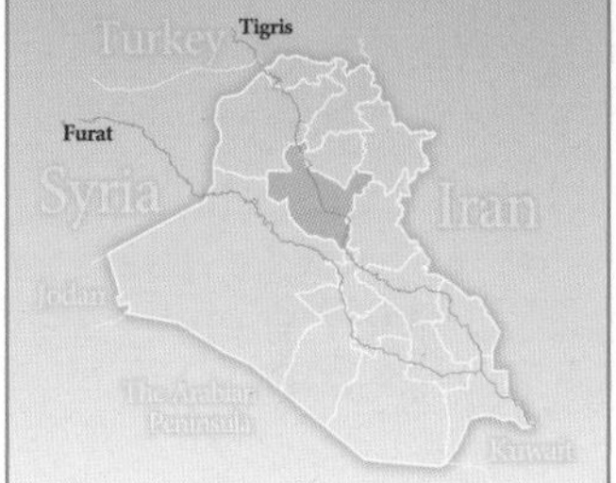

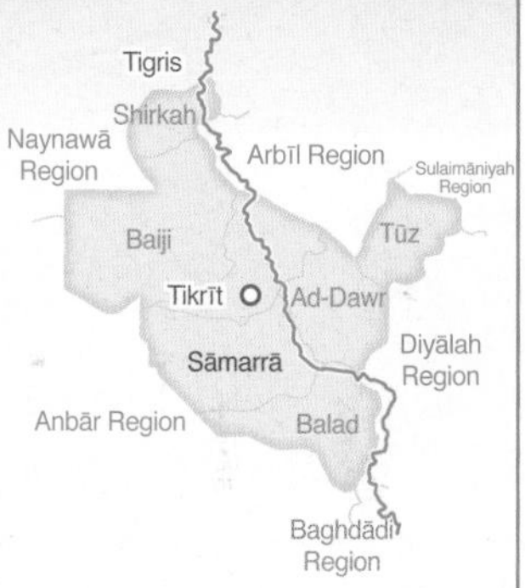

Aerial Map of the City of Sāmarrā

The Holy Shrine of Imām al-Hādī (A) & Imām Ḥasan al-Askarī (A)

Map of the Holy Shrine of Imām al-Hādī and Imām Ḥasan al-Askarī (A)

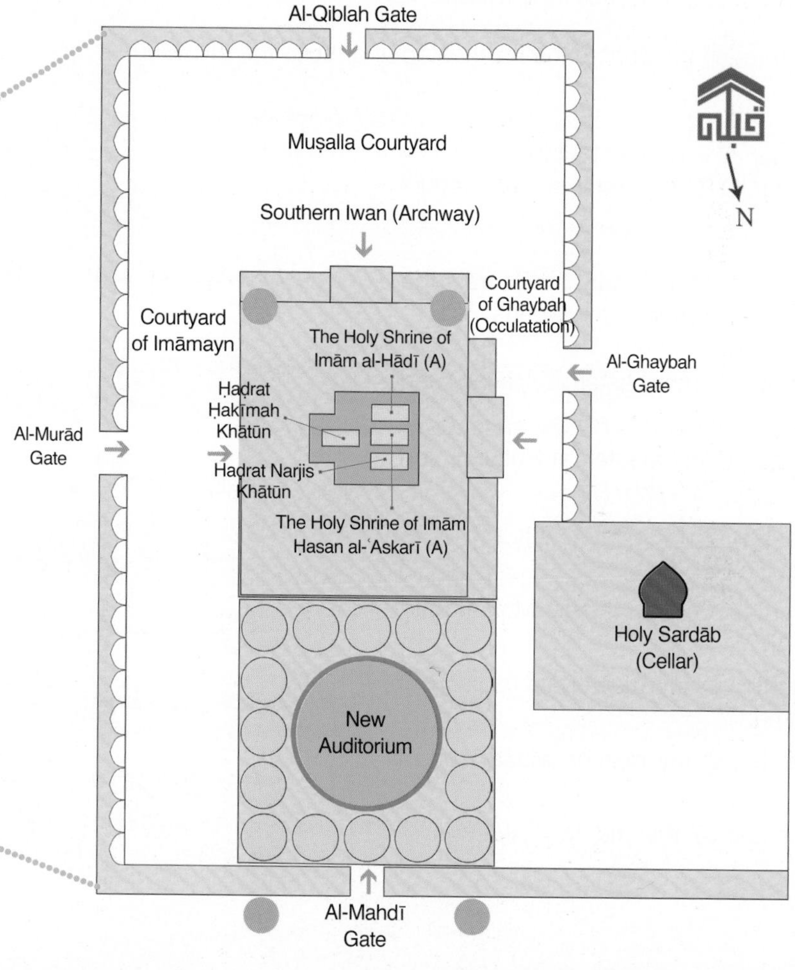

Idhn Dukhūl (Permission to Enter)

When you reach the door to the darīḥ, stop and recite the following:

May I enter, O Prophet of Allāh? May I enter, O Commander of the Faithful?	أَأَدْخُلُ يَا نَبِيَّ اللهِ أَأَدْخُلُ يَا اَمِيْرَالْمُؤْمِنِيْنَ
May I enter, O Fāṭimah az-Zahrāʾ, the leader of the women of the worlds?	أَأَدْخُلُ يَا فَاطِمَةُ الزَّهْرَاءُ سَيِّدَةُ نِسَاءِ الْعَالَمِيْنَ
May I enter, O my master, al-Ḥasan, son of ʿAlī?	أَأَدْخُلُ يَا مَوْلَايَ الْحَسَنَ بْنَ عَلِيٍّ
May I enter, O my master, al-Ḥusayn, son of ʿAlī?	أَأَدْخُلُ يَا مَوْلَايَ الْحُسَيْنَ بْنَ عَلِيٍّ
May I enter, O my master ʿAlī, son of al-Ḥusayn?	أَأَدْخُلُ يَا مَوْلَايَ عَلِيَّ بْنَ الْحُسَيْنِ،
May I enter, O my master, Muḥammad, son of ʿAlī?	أَأَدْخُلُ يَا مَوْلَايَ مُحَمَّدَ بْنَ عَلِيٍّ،
May I enter, O my master, Jaʿfar, son of Muḥammad?	أَأَدْخُلُ يَا مَوْلَايَ جَعْفَرَ بْنَ مُحَمَّدٍ،
May I enter, O my master, Mūsa, son of Jaʿfar?	أَأَدْخُلُ يَا مَوْلَايَ مُوسَي بْنَ جَعْفَرٍ،
May I enter, O my master, ʿAlī, son of Mūsa?	أَأَدْخُلُ يَا مَوْلَايَ عَلِيَّ بْنَ مُوسَىٰ،

May I enter, O my master, Muḥammad, son of ʿAlī?

أَأَدْخُلُ يَا مَوْلَايَ مُحَمَّدَ بْنَ عَلِيٍّ،

May I enter, O my master, Abul Ḥasan ʿAlī, son of Muḥammad?

أَأَدْخُلُ يَا مَوْلَايَ يَا أَبَا الْحَسَنِ عَلِيَّ بْنَ مُحَمَّدٍ

May I enter, O my master, Abā Muḥammad al-Ḥasan, the son of ʿAlī?

أَأَدْخُلُ يَا مَوْلَايَ يَا أَبَا مُحَمَّدٍ الْحَسَنَ بْنَ عَلِيٍّ،

May I enter, O angels of Allāh who are assigned to this holy shrine?

أَأَدْخُلُ يَا مَلَائِكَةَ اللهِ الْمُوَكَّلِيْنَ بِهَذَا الْحَرَمِ الشَّرِيْفِ

If your heart becomes soft and your eyes fill with tears, then this is a sign that you have been granted permission to enter.

Ziyārah of Imām al-Hādī (A)

Then, enter with your right foot. Stand facing the ḍarīḥ of Imām al-Hādī (A), with your back to the qiblah, and say "Allāhu Akbar" 100 times. Then, recite:

اَلسَّلَامُ عَلَيْكَ يَا اَبَاالْحَسَنِ عَلِيَّ بْنَ مُحَمَّدٍ الزَّكِيُّ الرَّاشِدُ النُّوْرُالثَّاقِبُ وَرَحْمَةُ اللهِ وَبَرَكَاتُهُ

Peace be upon you, O Abal-Ḥasan, ʿAlī, son of Muḥammad, the pure, guiding, and brightly shining light. May Allāh's mercy and blessings be upon you.

اَلسَّلَامُ عَلَيْكَ يَا صَفِيَّ اللهِ
اَلسَّلَامُ عَلَيْكَ يَا سِرَّ اللهِ

Peace be upon you, O chosen one of Allāh.
Peace be upon you, O confidante of Allāh.

اَلسَّلَامُ عَلَيْكَ يَا حَبْلَ اللهِ
اَلسَّلَامُ عَلَيْكَ يَا آلَ اللهِ

Peace be upon you, O rope of Allāh.
Peace be upon you, O household of Allāh.

اَلسَّلَامُ عَلَيْكَ يَا خِيَرَةَ اللهِ
اَلسَّلَامُ عَلَيْكَ يَاصِفْوَةَ اللهِ

Peace be upon you, O the elite of Allāh.
Peace be upon you, O chosen one of Allāh.

اَلسَّلَامُ عَلَيْكَ يَا اَمِيْنَ اللهِ
اَلسَّلَامُ عَلَيْكَ يَا حَقَّ اللهِ

Peace be upon you, O trustee of Allāh.
Peace be upon you, O truth of Allāh.

اَلسَّلَامُ عَلَيْكَ يَا حَبِيْبَ اللهِ
اَلسَّلَامُ عَلَيْكَ يَا نُوْرَ الْاَنْوَارِ

Peace be upon you, O beloved of Allāh.
Peace be upon you, O light of the lights.

Peace be upon you, O ornament of the righteous ones. Peace be upon you, O descendant of the upright ones.	اَلسَّلَامُ عَلَيْكَ يَا زَيْنَ الْاَبْرَارِ اَلسَّلَامُ عَلَيْكَ يَا سَلِيْلَ الْاَخْيَارِ
Peace be upon you, O essence of the purified ones. Peace be upon you, O proof of the Most Beneficent.	اَلسَّلَامُ عَلَيْكَ يَا عُنْصُرَ الْاَطْهَارِ اَلسَّلَامُ عَلَيْكَ يَا حُجَّةَ الرَّحْمَانِ
Peace be upon you, O pillar of faith. Peace be upon you, O master of the believers.	اَلسَّلَامُ عَلَيْكَ يَارُكْنَ الْإِيْمَانِ اَلسَّلَامُ عَلَيْكَ يَا مَوْلَي الْمُؤْمِنِيْنَ
Peace be upon you, O guardian of the righteous ones.	اَلسَّلَامُ عَلَيْكَ يَاوَلِيَّ الصَّالِحِيْنَ
Peace be upon you, O banner of guidance. Peace be upon you, O embodiment of piety.	اَلسَّلَامُ عَلَيْكَ يَا عَلَمَ الْهُدَىٰ اَلسَّلَامُ عَلَيْكَ يَا حَلِيْفَ التُّقَىٰ
Peace be upon you, O pillar of the religion.	اَلسَّلَامُ عَلَيْكَ يَا عَمُوْدَ الدِّيْنِ
Peace be upon you, O son of the seal of the Prophets.	اَلسَّلَامُ عَلَيْكَ يَا بْنَ خَاتَمِ النَّبِيِّيْنَ
Peace be upon you, O son of the chief of the Prophets' successors.	اَلسَّلَامُ عَلَيْكَ يَا بْنَ سَيِّدِ الْوَصِيِّيْنَ
Peace be upon you, O son of Fāṭimah az-Zahrāʾ, the leader of the women of the worlds.	اَلسَّلَامُ عَلَيْكَ يَا بْنَ فَاطِمَةَ الزَّهْرَاءِ سَيِّدَةِ نِسَاءِ الْعَالَمِيْنَ
Peace be upon you, O faithful trustee.	اَلسَّلَامُ عَلَيْكَ اَيُّهَا الْاَمِيْنُ الْوَفِيُّ

Peace be upon you, O banner of contentment.	اَلسَّلَامُ عَلَيْكَ اَيُّهَا الْعَلَمُ الرَّضِيُّ
Peace be upon you, O ascetic and pious one.	اَلسَّلَامُ عَلَيْكَ اَيُّهَا الزَّاهِدُ التَّقِيُّ
Peace be upon you, O decisive proof (of Allāh) over all creations.	اَلسَّلَامُ عَلَيْكَ اَيُّهَا الْحُجَّةُ عَلَىٰ الْخَلْقِ اَجْمَعِيْنَ
Peace be upon you, O reciter of the Qurʿān.	اَلسَّلَامُ عَلَيْكَ اَيُّهَا التَّالِيْ لِلْقُرْآنِ
Peace be upon you, O the distinguisher between the lawful and the unlawful.	اَلسَّلَامُ عَلَيْكَ اَيُّهَا الْمُبَيِّنُ لِلْحَلَالِ مِنَ الْحَرَامِ
Peace be upon you, O sincere guardian.	اَلسَّلَامُ عَلَيْكَ اَيُّهَا الْوَلِيُّ النَّاصِحُ
Peace be upon you, O evident path of truth.	اَلسَّلَامُ عَلَيْكَ اَيُّهَا الطَّرِيْقُ الْوَاضِحُ
Peace be upon you, O bright star.	اَلسَّلَامُ عَلَيْكَ اَيُّهَا النَّجْمُ اللَّائِحُ
I bear witness, O my master, O Abal Ḥasan, that you are verily the decisive proof of Allāh over His creations,	اَشْهَدُ يَا مَوْلَايَ يَا اَبَا الْحَسَنِ اَنَّكَ حُجَّةُ اللهِ عَلَىٰ خَلْقِهِ
His representative amongst His creations, His trustee in His lands, and His witness over His servants.	وَخَلِيْفَتُهُ فِيْ بَرِيَّتِهِ وَاَمِيْنُهُ فِيْ بِلَادِهِ وَشَاهِدُهُ عَلَىٰ عِبَادِهِ

وَاَشْهَدُ اَنَّكَ كَلِمَةُ التَّقْوىٰ

I also bear witness that you are surely the word of piety,

وَبَابُ الْهُدىٰ، وَالْعُرْوَةُ الْوُثْقىٰ

the door to true guidance, the firmest grip

وَالْحُجَّةُ عَلىٰ مَنْ فَوْقَ الْاَرْضِ وَمَنْ تَحْتَ الثَّرىٰ

and the proof over those who are on the earth and those who are beneath the layers of the soil.

وَاَشْهَدُ اَنَّكَ الْمُطَهَّرُ مِنَ الذُّنُوْبِ الْمُبَرَّأُ مِنَ الْعُيُوْبِ

I bear witness that you are purified from sins, cleansed from defects,

وَالْمُخْتَصُّ بِكَرَامَةِ اللهِ وَالْمَحْبُوُّ بِحُجَّةِ اللهِ

bestowed with the honor of Allāh, endowed with the proof of Allāh,

وَالْمَوْهُوْبُ لَهُ كَلِمَةُ اللهِ وَالرُّكْنُ الَّذِيْ يَلْجَأُ اِلَيْهِ الْعِبَادُ وَتُحْيَيْ بِهِ الْبِلَادُ

granted the word of Allāh, and the strong pillar to whom the servants (of Allāh) resort and by whom the lands are revived.

وَاَشْهَدُ يَامَوْلَايَ أَنِّيْ بِكَ وَبِآبَائِكَ وَاَبْنَائِكَ مُوْقِنٌ مُقِرٌّ

I bear witness, O my master, that I have faith in and submit to you, your forefathers, and your sons.

وَلَكُمْ تَابِعٌ فِيْ ذَاتِ نَفْسِيْ وَشَرَايِعِ دِيْنِيْ وَخَاتِمَةِ عَمَلِيْ وَمُنْقَلَبِيْ وَمَثْوَايَ

I follow all of you in my personal affairs, my religious performance, the completion of my actions, and in my return and final place.

I am loyal to your loyalists and an enemy of your enemies.	وَاَنِّيْ وَلِيٌّ لِمَنْ وَالَاكُمْ وَعَدُوٌّ لِمَنْ عَادَاكُمْ
I believe in all of the invisible and the visible, and the first and the last of you. May my father and mother be sacrificed for you.	مُؤْمِنٌ بِسِرِّكُمْ وَعَلَانِيَتِكُمْ وَاَوَّلِكُمْ وَآخِرِكُمْ بِاَبِيْ اَنْتَ وَاُمِّيْ
May Allāh's peace, mercy, and blessings be upon you.	وَالسَّلَامُ عَلَيْكَ وَرَحْمَةُ اللهِ وَبَرَكَاتُهُ

Then kiss the ḍarīḥ and place the right side of your face on it and recite:

O Allāh, send blessings upon Muḥammad and the household of Muḥammad	اَللّٰهُمَّ صَلِّ عَلَىٰ مُحَمَّدٍ وَآلِ مُحَمَّدٍ
and send blessings upon Your loyal proof, pure guardian,	وَصَلِّ عَلَىٰ حُجَّتِكَ الْوَفِيِّ وَوَلِيِّكَ الزَّكِيِّ
contented trustee, chosen guide,	وَاَمِيْنِكَ الْمُرْتَضَىٰ، وَصَفِيِّكَ الْهَادِيْ
straight path, the supreme avenue,	وَصِرَاطِكَ الْمُسْتَقِيْمِ وَالْجَادَّةِ الْعُظْمَىٰ
the moderate course, the light of the faithful believers' hearts,	وَالطَّرِيْقَةِ الْوُسْطَىٰ نُوْرِ قُلُوْبِ الْمُؤْمِنِيْنَ
the guardian of the God-conscious ones, and the companion of the sincere,	وَوَلِيِّ الْمُتَّقِيْنَ، وَصَاحِبِ الْمُخْلَصِيْنَ

اَللّٰهُمَّ صَلِّ عَلٰى سَيِّدِنَا مُحَمَّدٍ وَاَهْلِ بَيْتِهِ

O Allāh, send blessings upon our Master Muḥammad and his household

وَصَلِّ عَلٰى عَلِيِّ بْنِ مُحَمَّدٍ الرَّاشِدِ
الْمَعْصُوْمِ مِنَ الزَّلَلِ وَالطَّاهِرِ مِنَ الْخَلَلِ

and send blessings upon ʿAlī, son of Muḥammad, the guiding, nurturing, infallible guide, who is pure from defects.

وَالْمُنْقَطِعِ اِلَيْكَ بِالْاَمَلِ الْمَبْلُوِّ بِالْفِتَنِ
وَالْمُخْتَبَرِ بِالْمِحَنِ

He cut off hope from anyone except You, was afflicted with temptations, was tried with tribulations,

وَالْمُمْتَحَنِ بِحُسْنِ الْبَلْوٰى
وَصَبْرِ الشَّكْوٰى

was tested with beneficial trials and through patience against complaining.

مُرْشِدِ عِبَادِكَ وَبَرَكَةِ بِلَادِكَ وَمَحَلِّ
رَحْمَتِكَ

(He is) the spiritual guide of Your servants, the blessing for Your lands, the store of Your mercy,

وَمُسْتَوْدَعِ حِكْمَتِكَ وَالْقَآئِدِ اِلٰى جَنَّتِكَ
الْعَالِمِ فِيْ بَرِيَّتِكَ وَالْهَادِيْ فِيْ خَلِيْقَتِكَ

the storehouse of Your wisdom, the guide to Your paradise, the most knowledgeable amongst Your creations, and the true guide of Your creatures,

الَّذِيْ ارْتَضَيْتَهُ وَانْتَجَبْتَهُ وَاخْتَرْتَهُ لِمَقَامِ
رَسُوْلِكَ فِيْ اُمَّتِهِ وَاَلْزَمْتَهُ حِفْظَ شَرِيْعَتِهِ

whom You pleased, preferred, selected to take the place of Your Messenger, and entrusted with the protection of his laws.

فَاسْتَقَلَّ بِاَعْبَآءِ الْوَصِيَّةِ نَاهِضاً بِهَا وَمُضْطَلِعاً بِحَمْلِهَا	So, he fulfilled the heavy task, bore it perfectly, and undertook the responsibility of bearing it.
لَمْ يَعْثُرْ فِيْ مُشْكِلٍ وَلَا هَفَا فِيْ مُعْضِلٍ بَلْ كَشَفَ الْغُمَّةَ وَسَدَّ الْفُرْجَةَ وَاَدَّى الْمُفْتَرَضَ	He neither slipped in any difficulty, nor did he fail to solve any complexity. Rather, he relieved all distress, clarified any confusion, and fulfilled his responsibilities.
اَللَّهُمَّ فَكَمَا اَقْرَرْتَ نَاظِرَ نَبِيِّكَ بِهِ فَرَقِّهِ دَرَجَتَهُ	O Allāh, just as You made him a source of delight for Your Prophet, also raise his rank,
وَاَجْزِلْ لَدَيْكَ مَثُوْبَتَهُ وَصَلِّ عَلَيْهِ وَبَلِّغْهُ مِنَّا تَحِيَّةً وَسَلَاماً	give him the most fitting reward that suits him, bless him, convey our greetings and peace to him,
وَآتِنَا مِنْ لَدُنْكَ فِيْ مُوَالَاتِهِ فَضْلًا وَاِحْسَاناً وَمَغْفِرَةً وَرِضْوَاناً اِنَّكَ ذُو الْفَضْلِ الْعَظِيْمِ	and give us, on account of our love for him, from Your special bounties, favors, goodness, forgiveness, and pleasure. Surely, You are the Lord of supreme grace.

Then, offer a two rakaʿāt prayer of ziyārah. After the salām, recite the following duʿāʾ:

اَللّهُمَّ يا ذَا الْقُدْرَةِ الْجامِعَةِ وَالرَّحْمَةِ الْواسِعَةِ	O Allah! O Lord of omnipotent power and encompassing mercy!
وَالْمِنَنِ الْمُتَتابِعَةِ وَالْآلاءِ الْمُتَواتِرَةِ وَالْاَيادِي الْجَلِيْلَةِ وَالْمَواهِبِ الْجَزِيْلَةِ	O Lord of successive favors! O Lord of uninterrupted bounties! O Lord of magnificent bestowals! O Lord of abundant gifts!
صَلِّ عَلىٰ مُحَمَّدٍ وَآلِ مُحَمَّدٍ الصّادِقِيْنَ	Send blessings upon Muḥammad and the household of Muḥammad, the truthful ones,
وَاَعْطِنِيْ سُؤْلِيْ وَاجْمَعْ شَمْلِيْ وَلُمَّ شَعْثِيْ وَزَكِّ عَمَلِيْ	and grant me that which I ask from You, re-unify me (with my family), unite me (with my family), purify my deeds,
وَلا تُزِغْ قَلْبِيْ بَعْدَ اِذْ هَدَيْتَنِيْ وَلا تُزِلَّ قَدَمِيْ	do not cause my heart to stray after You have guided me, do not cause not my footstep to slip,
وَلا تَكِلْنِيْ اِلىٰ نَفْسِيْ طَرْفَةَ عَيْنٍ اَبَداً	do not leave me to myself even for even the blink of an eye,
وَلا تُخَيِّبْ طَمَعِيْ وَلا تُبْدِ عَوْرَتِيْ	do not disappoint my hopes, do not expose my secrets,
وَلا تَهْتِكْ سِتْرِيْ، وَلا تُوحِشْنِيْ وَلا تُؤْيِسْنِيْ	do not uncover my covering, do not cause me to feel lonely, do not cause me to despair,

وَكُنْ بِيْ رَؤُوْفاً رَحِيْماً	be affectionate and merciful to me,
وَاهْدِنِيْ وَزَكِّنِيْ وَطَهِّرْنِيْ وَصَفِّنِيْ وَاصْطَفِنِيْ وَخَلِّصْنِيْ وَاسْتَخْلِصْنِيْ وَاصْنَعْنِيْ وَاصْطَنِعْنِيْ	guide me (to the right path), sanctify me, purify me, cleanse me, select me, dedicate me to You, purify me, make and devote me to You alone,
وَقَرِّبْنِيْ اِلَيْكَ وَلَا تُبَاعِدْنِيْ مِنْكَ وَالْطُفْ بِيْ وَلَا تَجْفُنِيْ	draw me near You, do not take me far away from You, be gentle to me, do not turn away from me,
وَاَكْرِمْنِيْ وَلَا تُهِنِّيْ وَمَآ اَسْاَلُكَ فَلَا تَحْرِمْنِيْ	honor me, do not humiliate me, do not deprive me of that which I ask from You,
وَمَا لَا اَسْاَلُكَ فَاجْمَعْهُ لِيْ بِرَحْمَتِكَ يَا اَرْحَمَ الرَّاحِمِيْنَ	and give me that which I have not asked from You. (Please do all that) in the name of Your mercy, O the Most Merciful!
وَاَسْاَلُكَ بِحُرْمَةِ وَجْهِكَ الْكَرِيْمِ	I ask You by the sanctity of Your Honorable Face,
وَبِحُرْمَةِ نَبِيِّكَ مُحَمَّدٍ صَلَوَاتُكَ عَلَيْهِ وَآلِهِ	the sanctity of Your Prophet Muhammad, may Your blessings be upon him and his household,
وَبِحُرْمَةِ اَهْلِ بَيْتِ رَسُوْلِكَ اَمِيْرِ الْمُؤْمِنِيْنَ عَلِيٍ وَالْحَسَنِ وَالْحُسَيْنِ	and the sanctity of Your Messenger's household: ʿAlī, the Commander of the faithful, al-Ḥasan, al-Ḥusayn,

وَعَلِيٍّ وَمُحَمَّدٍ وَجَعْفَرٍ وَمُوسَىٰ وَعَلِيٍّ
وَمُحَمَّدٍ وَعَلِيٍّ وَالْحَسَنِ وَالْخَلَفِ الْبَاقِيْ
صَلَوَاتُكَ وَبَرَكَاتُكَ عَلَيْهِمِ

ʿAlī, Muḥammad, Jaʿfar, Mūsā, ʿAlī, Muḥammad, ʿAlī, Ḥasan, and the remaining successor (al-Mahdī). May your blessing be upon them.

اَنْ تُصَلِّيَ عَلَيْهِمْ اَجْمَعِيْنَ وَتُعَجِّلَ فَرَجَ
قَائِمِهِمْ بِاَمْرِكَ

(I ask You in their names) to send blessings upon all of them, hasten the relief of their rising Imām by Your command,

وَتَنْصُرَهُ وَتَنْتَصِرَ بِهِ لِدِيْنِكَ وَتَجْعَلَنِيْ فِيْ
جُمْلَةِ النَّاجِيْنَ بِهِ وَالْمُخْلِصِيْنَ فِيْ طَاعَتِهِ

support him, make him the means of victory of Your religion, and include me with those who shall be saved through him, and those who are sincerely obedient to him.

وَاَسْاَلُكَ بِحَقِّهِمْ لَمَّا اسْتَجَبْتَ لِيْ دَعْوَتِيْ
وَقَضَيْتَ لِيْ حَاجَتِيْ وَاَعْطَيْتَنِيْ سُؤْلِي

I also beseech You by their right to answer to my prayer, grant me my needs, bestow my requests,

وَكَفَيْتَنِيْ مَا اَهَمَّنِيْ مِنْ اَمْرِ دُنْيَايَ
وَآخِرَتِيْ يَا اَرْحَمَ الرَّاحِمِيْنَ

and suffice me against the [worrisome] affairs of this world and the hereafter. O the Most Merciful!

يَا نُوْرُ يَا بُرْهَانُ يَا مُنِيْرُ يَامُبَيِّنُ، يَا رَبِّ
اكْفِنِيْ شَرَّ الشُّرُوْرِ وَآفَاتِ الدُّهُوْرِ

O Light! O Evident! O Granter of Light! O Clarifier! O my Lord, save me from all evils and from the trials of life.

وَاَسْاَلُكَ النَّجَاةَ يَوْمَ يُنْفَخُ فِيْ الصُّوْرِ

I also ask You for salvation on the day when the trumpet is blown.

Then, ask Allāh for all your wishes and recite the following du'ā' abundantly:

O my means when I lack means! O my hope and my trust! O my shelter and my support!	يَا عُدَّتِيْ عِنْدَ الْعُدَدِ، وَيَا رَجَائِيْ وَالْمُعْتَمَدَ، وَيَا كَهْفِيْ وَالسَّنَدَ
O the One! O the Only! O (He who is described in) "Say: He is Allāh, the One."	يَا وَاحِدُ يَا اَحَدُ وَيَا قُلْ هُوَاللهُ اَحَدٌ
I ask You, O Allāh, by the right of those whom you have created and have not made anyone like them, to send blessings upon them all, and grant me...[ask for your wishes]	اَسْاَلُكَ اللَّهُمَّ بِحَقِّ مَنْ خَلَقْتَ مِنْ خَلْقِكَ وَلَمْ تَجْعَلْ فِيْ خَلْقِكَ مِثْلَهُمْ اَحَداً صَلِّ عَلَىٰ جَمَاعَتِهِمْ، وَافْعَلْ بِيْ ...

It is narrated that Imām has said: "I have requested to Allāh that who ever recites this du'ā' in my ḥaram will not return with empty hands."

Ziyārah of Imām Ḥasan al-ʿAskarī (A)

ʿAllāmah Majlisī in *Biḥār ul-Anwār* and Sayyid bin Ṭāwūs in *Miṣbāḥ az Zāʾir* both narrate that when you decide to perform the ziyārah of Imām Ḥasan al-ʿAskarī (A), first recite the ziyārah of Imām al-Hādī (A). Then, stand facing the holy ḍarīḥ of Imām al-ʿAskarī (A) and recite:

اَلسَّلَامُ عَلَيْكَ يَا مَوْلَايَ يَا اَبَا مُحَمَّدٍ الْحَسَنَ بْنَ عَلِيٍّ الْهَادِيَ الْمُهْتَدِيَ وَرَحْمَةُ اللهِ وَبَرَكَاتُهُ

Peace be upon you, O my Master Abā Muḥammad, al-Ḥasan, son of ʿAlī, the guide and well-guided. May Allāh's mercy and blessings be upon you.

اَلسَّلَامُ عَلَيْكَ يَا وَلِيَّ اللهِ وَابْنَ اَوْلِيَآئِهِ اَلسَّلَامُ عَلَيْكَ يَا حُجَّةَ اللهِ وَابْنَ حُجَجِهِ

Peace be upon you, O guardian of Allāh and the son of his guardians. Peace be upon you, O decisive proof of Allāh and son of His proofs.

Peace be upon you, O chosen one of Allāh and son of His chosen ones. Peace be upon you, O Allāh's representative, son of His representatives, and father of His representative.

اَلسَّلَامُ عَلَيْكَ يَاصَفِيَّ اللهِ وَابْنَ اَصْفِيَآئِهِ اَلسَّلَامُ عَلَيْكَ يَا خَلِيْفَةَ اللهِ وَابْنَ خُلَفَائِهِ وَاَبَا خَلِيْفَتِهِ

Peace be upon you, O son of the Seal of the Prophets. Peace be upon you, O son of the chief of the Prophets' successors.

اَلسَّلَامُ عَلَيْكَ يَا بْنَ خَاتَمِ النَّبِيِّيْنَ اَلسَّلَامُ عَلَيْكَ يَا بْنَ سَيِّدِ الْوَصِيِّيْنَ

Peace be upon you, O son of the Commander of the Faithful. Peace be upon you, O son of the leader of the women of the worlds.

اَلسَّلَامُ عَلَيْكَ يَا بْنَ اَمِيْرِ الْمُؤْمِنِيْنَ اَلسَّلَامُ عَلَيْكَ يَا بْنَ سَيِّدَةِ نِسَاءِ الْعَالَمِيْنَ

Peace be upon you, O son of the guiding leaders. Peace be upon you, O son of the guided and nurturing successors (of the Prophets.)

اَلسَّلَامُ عَلَيْكَ يَا ابْنَ الْاَئِمَّةِ الْهَادِيْنَ اَلسَّلَامُ عَلَيْكَ يَا بْنَ الْاَوْصِيَاءِ الرَّاشِدِيْنَ

Peace be upon you, O shelter of the pious. Peace be upon you, O leader of the successful ones.

اَلسَّلَامُ عَلَيْكَ يَا عِصْمَةَ الْمُتَّقِيْنَ، اَلسَّلَامُ عَلَيْكَ يَا اِمَامَ الْفَائِزِيْنَ

Peace be upon you, O pillar of the believers. Peace be upon you, O relief of the aggrieved ones.

اَلسَّلَامُ عَلَيْكَ يَا رُكْنَ الْمُؤْمِنِيْنَ اَلسَّلَامُ عَلَيْكَ يَا فَرَجَ الْمَلْهُوْفِيْنَ

اَلسَّلَامُ عَلَيْكَ يَا وَارِثَ الْاَنْبِيَاءِ الْمُنْتَجَبِيْنَ اَلسَّلَامُ عَلَيْكَ يَا خَازِنَ عِلْمِ وَصِيِّ رَسُوْلِ اللهِ	Peace be upon you, O inheritor of the the chosen Prophets. Peace be upon you, O treasure of the knowledge of Rasūl Allāh's successor.
اَلسَّلَامُ عَلَيْكَ اَيُّهَا الدَّاعِيْ بِحُكْمِ اللهِ اَلسَّلَامُ عَلَيْكَ اَيُّهَا النَّاطِقُ بِكِتَابِ اللهِ	Peace be upon you, O caller to the judgment of Allāh. Peace be upon you, O he who speaks with the Book of Allāh.
اَلسَّلَامُ عَلَيْكَ يَاحُجَّةَ الْحُجَجِ اَلسَّلَامُ عَلَيْكَ يَا هَادِيَ الْاُمَمِ	Peace be upon you, O proof of all the proofs. Peace be upon you, O guide of the nations.
اَلسَّلَامُ عَلَيْكَ يَا وَلِيَّ النِّعَمِ اَلسَّلَامُ عَلَيْكَ يَاعَيْبَةَ الْعِلْمِ	Peace be upon you, O guardian of blessings. Peace be upon you, O store of knowledge.
اَلسَّلَامُ عَلَيْكَ يَا سَفِيْنَةَ الْحِلْمِ اَلسَّلَامُ عَلَيْكَ يَا اَبَا الْاِمَامِ الْمُنْتَظَرِ	Peace be upon you, O ark of forbearance. Peace be upon you, O father of the Awaited Imām,
الظَّاهِرَةِ لِلْعَاقِلِ حُجَّتُهُ وَالثَّابِتَةِ فِي الْيَقِيْنِ مَعْرِفَتُهُ	whose proof is evident for rational people, whose recognition is undeniable,
الْمُحْتَجَبِ عَنْ اَعْيُنِ الظَّالِمِيْنَ وَالْمُغَيَّبِ عَنْ دَوْلَةِ الْفَاسِقِيْنَ	who is concealed from the oppressors' eyes and hidden from the governments of the transgressors.

وَالْمُعِيْدِ رَبُّنَا بِهِ الْاِسْلَامَ جَدِيْداً بَعْدَ الْاِنْطِمَاسِ وَالْقُرْآنَ غَضَّاً بَعْدَ الْاِنْدِرَاسِ

(He is the one) through whom our Lord shall restore Islām after it will be buried and He shall recover the Qurʿān after it will be neglected.

اَشْهَدُ يَامَوْلَايَ اَنَّكَ اَقَمْتَ الصَّلَاةَ وَآتَيْتَ الزَّكَاةَ وَاَمَرْتَ بِالْمَعْرُوْفِ وَنَهَيْتَ عَنِ الْمُنْكَرِ

I bear witness, O my master, that you established the prayers, gave alms, enjoined good, forbade evil

وَدَعَوْتَ اِلَىٰ سَبِيْلِ رَبِّكَ بِالْحِكْمَةِ وَالْمَوْعِظَةِ الْحَسَنَةِ وَعَبَدْتَ اللهَ مُخْلِصاً حَتَّىٰ اَتَاكَ الْيَقِيْنُ

called to the way of your Lord with wisdom and good admonitions, and that you worshipped Allāh sincerely until certainty (death) came upon you.

اَسْأَلُ اللهَ بِالشَّأْنِ الَّذِيْ لَكُمْ عِنْدَهُ اَنْ يَتَقَبَّلَ زِيَارَتِيْ لَكُمْ،

I ask Allāh by the standing that you have with Him that He accepts my visit to you,

وَيَشْكُرَ سَعْيِيْ اِلَيْكُمْ، وَيَسْتَجِيْبَ دُعَائِيْ بِكُمْ،

accepts my efforts with gratitude, responds to my prayers through you,

وَيَجْعَلَنِيْ مِنْ اَنْصَارِ الْحَقِّ وَاَتْبَاعِهِ وَاَشْيَاعِهِ وَمَوَالِيْهِ وَمُحِبِّيْهِ،

and include me with the supporters of the truth, its followers, its adherents, its devotees, and its lovers.

وَالسَّلَامُ عَلَيْكَ وَرَحْمَةُ اللهِ وَبَرَكَاتُهُ.

May Allāh's peace, mercy, and blessings be upon you.

Then, kiss the ḍarīḥ, place the right and left sides of your face on it, and recite the following duʿāʾ:

O Allāh, send blessings upon our master Muḥammad and his Ahl al-Bayt.	اَللَّهُمَّ صَلِّ عَلَىٰ سَيِّدِنَا مُحَمَّدٍ وَاَهْلِ بَيْتِهِ
and send blessings upon al-Ḥasan, son of ʿAlī, who guides to Your religion and invites to Your path.	وَصَلِّ عَلَىٰ الْحَسَنِ بْنِ عَلِيٍّ الْهَادِيْ اِلَىٰ دِيْنِكَ وَالدَّاعِيْ اِلَىٰ سَبِيْلِكَ
He is the banner of true guidance, the lantern of true piety, the core of rationale,	عَلَمِ الْهُدَىٰ وَمَنَارِ التُّقَىٰ وَمَعْدِنِ الْحِجَىٰ
the source of reason, the raining cloud (of goodness) over mankind,	وَمَاْوَى النُّهَىٰ وَغَيْثِ الْوَرَىٰ
the cloud of wisdom, the ocean of admonition,	وَسَحَابِ الْحِكْمَةِ وَبَحْرِ الْمَوْعِظَةِ
the inheritor of the Imāms (A), the infallible and well-mannered witness over the community,	وَوَارِثِ الأَئِمَّةِ وَالشَّهِيْدِ عَلَىٰ الْأُمَّةِ الْمَعْصُوْمِ الْمُهَذَّبِ
the virtuous, the close one (to Allah), the purified against impurity,	وَالْفَاضِلِ الْمُقَرَّبِ وَالْمُطَهَّرِ مِنَ الرِّجْسِ
the one who inherited knowledge of the book and You inspired with clear judgment.	الَّذِيْ وَرَّثْتَهُ عِلْمَ الْكِتَابِ وَاَلْهَمْتَهُ فَصْلَ الْخِطَابِ

You appointed him as the banner for those who follow Your direction. You have made his obedience attached to Your obedience,	وَنَصَبْتَهُ عَلَماً لِاَهْلِ قِبْلَتِكَ وَقَرَنْتَ طَاعَتَهُ بِطَاعَتِكَ
and You have imposed love for him upon all Your creatures.	وَفَرَضْتَ مَوَدَّتَهُ عَلَىٰ جَمِيْعِ خَلِيْقَتِكَ
O Allāh, as he always turned to You with excellent sincerity in Your Oneness,	اَللَّهُمَّ فَكَمَا اَنَابَ بِحُسْنِ الْاِخْلَاصِ فِيْ تَوْحِيْدِكَ
defeated those who attempted to materialize You, and defended those who faithfully believed in you;	وَاَرْدَىٰ مَنْ خَاضَ فِيْ تَشْبِيْهِكَ وَحَامَىٰ عَنْ اَهْلِ الْاِيْمَانِ بِكَ
so, O my Lord, pour down on him Your blessings so that he joins the rank of those who are (inwardly) humble towards You and surmounts in paradise to the rank of his grandfather, the Seal of the Prophets.	فَصَلِّ يَا رَبِّ عَلَيْهِ صَلَاةً يَلْحَقُ بِهَا مَحَلَّ الْخَاشِعِيْنَ وَيَعْلُوْ فِي الْجَنَّةِ بِدَرَجَةِ جَدِّهِ خَاتَمِ النَّبِيِّيْنَ
And convey to him greetings and peace from us,	وَبَلِّغْهُ مِنَّا تَحِيَّةً وَسَلَاماً
grant us from Your special favor, on account of our loyalty to him, grave, goodness, forgiveness, and pleasure.	وَآتِنَا مِنْ لَدُنْكَ فِيْ مُوَالَاتِهِ فَضْلاً وَاِحْسَاناً وَمَغْفِرَةً وَرِضْوَاناً
Surely, You are the Lord of supreme favors and large gifts.	اِنَّكَ ذُوْ فَضْلٍ عَظِيْمٍ وَمَنٍّ جَسِيْمٍ

Then offer two rakaʿāt prayers of ziyārah. After the salām, recite the following duʿāʾ:

يَا دَائِمُ يَا دَيْمُوْمُ يَا حَيُّ يَا قَيُّوْمُ يَا كَاشِفَ الْكَرْبِ وَالْهَمِّ	O All-eternal Lord! O Everlasting! O Ever-living! O Self-subsisting! O Dispeller of hardships and grief!
وَيَا فَارِجَ الْغَمِّ وَيَابَاعِثَ الرُّسُلِ وَيَا صَادِقَ الْوَعْدِ	O Reliever of sadness! O Appointer of Messengers! O Truthful to His promises!
وَيَا حَيُّ لَا اِلَهَ اِلَّا اَنْتَ اَتَوَسَّلُ اِلَيْكَ بِحَبِيْبِكَ مُحَمَّدٍ وَوَصِيِّهِ عَلِيٍّ ابْنِ عَمِّهِ،	O Ever-living! There is no god except You. I intercede to You through Your beloved one, Muḥammad, and his successor, cousin, and son in-law, ʿAlī,
وَصِهْرِهِ عَلَى ابْنَتِهِ اللَّذَيْنِ خَتَمْتَ بِهِمَا الشَّرَايِعَ وَفَتَحْتَ بِهِمَا التَّأْوِيْلَ وَالطَّلَايِعَ	through both of whom you have completed your laws and opened the door to interpretation and analysis.
فَصَلِّ عَلَيْهِمَا صَلَاةً يَشْهَدُ بِهَا الْاَوَّلُوْنَ وَالْآخِرُوْنَ وَيَنْجُوْبِهَا الْاَوْلِيَاءُ وَالصَّالِحُوْنَ	So, send upon both of them blessings that are witnessed by the ancient and coming generations, and through which the intimate servants and the righteous ones are saved.

I also intercede to You through Fāṭimah az-Zahrā᾽, the mother of the rightfully guided Imāms, and the leader of the women of the worlds,	وَاَتوَسَّلُ اِلَيْكَ بِفَاطِمَةَ الزَّهْرَاءِ وَالِدَةِ الْاَئِمَّةِ الْمَهْدِيِّيْنَ وَسَيِّدَةِ نِسَاءِ الْعَالَمِيْنَ
who shall be allowed to intercede for the Shīʿah of her pure descendants. So, send upon her blessings that are as endless as time.	الْمُشَفَّعَةِ فِيْ شِيْعَةِ اَوْلَادِهَا الطَّيِّبِيْنَ فَصَلِّ عَلَيْهَا صَلَاةً دَائِمَةً اَبَدَ الْآبِدِيْنَ وَدَهْرَ الدَّاهِرِيْنَ
I also intercede to You through al-Ḥasan, the pleased, the immaculate, and the pure, and through al-Ḥusayn, the oppressed, the pleased, the pious, and God-conscious; (they both are) the masters of the youth of paradise,	وَاَتَوَسَّلُ اِلَيْكَ بِالْحَسَنِ الرَّضِيِّ الطَّاهِرِ الزَّكِيِّ وَالْحُسَيْنِ الْمَظْلُوْمِ الْمَرْضِيِّ الْبَرِّ التَّقِيِّ سَيِّدَيْ شَبَابِ اَهْلِ الْجَنَّةِ
the two virtuous, immaculate, God-conscious, pure, immaculate, martyred, oppressed, and murdered Imāms.	الْاِمَامَيْنِ الْخَيِّرَيْنِ الطَّيِّبَيْنِ التَّقِيَّيْنِ النَّقِيَّيْنِ الطَّاهِرَيْنِ الشَّهِيْدَيْنِ الْمَظْلُوْمَيْنِ الْمَقْتُوْلَيْنِ
So, send blessings upon them whenever the sun rises and sets, blessings that are consecutive and successive.	فَصَلِّ عَلَيْهِمَا مَا طَلَعَتْ شَمْسٌ وَمَا غَرَبَتْ صَلَاةً مُتَوَالِيَةً مُتَتَالِيَةً

وَاَتَوَسَّلُ اِلَيْكَ بِعَلِيِّ بْنِ الْحُسَيْنِ سَيِّدِالْعَابِدِيْنَ الْمَحْجُوْبِ مِنْ خَوْفِ الظَّالِمِيْنَ

I also intercede to You through ʿAlī, son of al-Ḥusayn, the chief of the worshippers and the one who was not afraid of the oppressors.

وَبِمُحَمَّدِبْنِ عَلِيٍّ الْبَاقِرِ الطَّاهِرِ النُّوْرِ الزَّاهِرِ

and through Muḥammad, son of ʿAlī, the splitter of knowledge, the pure, the bright light.

الْاِمَامَيْنِ السَّيِّدَيْنِ مِفْتَاحَيِ الْبَرَكَاتِ وَمِصْبَاحَيِ الظُّلُمَاتِ فَصَلِّ عَلَيْهِمَا مَا سَرَىٰ لَيْلٌ وَمَا اَضَاءَ نَهَارٌ صَلَاةً تَغْدُوْ وَتَرُوْحُ

(They both are) two Imāms and masters, the keys to blessings, and the lanterns in darkness. So, send blessings upon them whenever night falls and daylight breaks, blessings that are endless.

وَاَتَوَسَّلُ اِلَيْكَ بِجَعْفَرِ بْنِ مُحَمَّدٍ الصَّادِقِ عَنِ اللهِ وَالنَّاطِقِ فِيْ عِلْمِ اللهِ

I also intercede to You through Jaʿfar,son of Muḥammad, the truthful in what he conveys from Allāh and the spokesman of Allāh's knowledge

وَبِمُوْسَىٰ بْنِ جَعْفَرٍ الْعَبْدِ الصَّالِحِ فِيْ نَفْسِهِ وَالْوَصِيِّ النَّاصِحِ

and through Mūsā, son of Jaʿfar, the self-righteous servant (of Allāh) and the sincere successor (of the Prophet);

(they both are) the guiding and well-guided Imāms who are adequate and sufficient (guides). So, send upon them blessings whenever an angel glorifies you and whenever a planet moves,	الْاِمَامَيْنِ الْهَادِيَيْنِ الْمَهْدِيَّيْنِ الْوَافِيَيْنِ الْكَافِيَيْنِ فَصَلِّ عَلَيْهِمَا مَا سَبَّحَ لَكَ مَلَكٌ وَتَحَرَّكَ لَكَ فَلَكٌ
blessings that are increasing and neverending. I also intercede to You through ʿAlī, son of Mūsā, the content one.	صَلَاةً تُنْمىٰ وَتَزِيْدُ وَلَا تَفْنىٰ وَلَا تَبِيْدُ وَاَتَوَسَّلُ اِلَيْكَ بِعَلِيِّ بْنِ مُوْسَي الرِّضَا
and through Muḥammad, son of ʿAlī, the well-pleased, the two purified and divinely appointed Imāms.	وَبِمُحَمَّدِ بْنِ عَلِيٍّ الْمُرْتَضىٰ الْاِمَامَيْنِ الْمُطَهَّرَيْنِ الْمُنْتَجَبَيْنِ
So, send upon them blessings whenever morning glows, such blessings that promote them to the rank of Your extreme pleasure in the highest level of Your paradise.	فَصَلِ عَلَيْهِمَا مَا اَضَاءَ صُبْحٌ وَدَامَ صَلَاةً تُرَقِّيْهِمَا اِلَىٰ رِضْوَانِكَ فِيْ الْعِلِّيِّيْنَ مِنْ جِنَانِكَ
I intercede to You through ʿAlī, son of Muḥammad, the rightly guidde, and in the name of al-Ḥasan, the son of ʿAlī, the guide,	وَاَتَوَسَّلُ اِلَيْكَ بِعَلِيِّ بْنِ مُحَمَّدٍ الرَّاشِدِ وَالْحَسَنِ بْنِ عَلِيٍّ الْهَادِيْ
the two Imāms who supervised the affairs of your servants, were tested by unbearable ordeals, and acted patiently against the hypocritical enemies' grudges.	الْقَائِمَيْنِ بِاَمْرِ عِبَادِكَ الْمُخْتَبَرَيْنِ بِالْمِحَنِ الْهَائِلَةِ وَالصَّابِرَيْنِ فِي الْاِحَنِ الْمَائِلَةِ

فَصَلِّ عَلَيْهِمَا كِفَاءَ اَجْرِ الصَّابِرِيْنَ وَاِزَاءَ ثَوَابِ الْفَائِزِيْنَ

So, send upon them blessings that are equivalent to the reward of the patient ones and the prize of the successful ones,

صَلَاةً تُمَهِّدُ لَهُمَا الرِّفْعَةَ، وَاَتَوَسَّلُ اِلَيْكَ يَا رَبِّ بِاِمَامِنَا وَمُحَقِّقِ زَمَانِنَا

such blessings that pave for them the way to exaltation. I also intercede to You, O my Lord, through our Imām, the fullfiller (of the prophecy) of our time,

الْيَوْمِ الْمَوْعُوْدِ وَالشَّاهِدِ الْمَشْهُوْدِ وَالنُّوْرِ الْاَزْهَرِ وَالضِّيَاءِ الْاَنْوَرِ

the promised day (when he will bring peace and justice), the witnessed observer, the luminous light, the bright illumination,

الْمَنْصُوْرِ بِالرُّعْبِ وَالْمُظَفَّرِ بِالسَّعَادَةِ

who will guide (people to success) through reverential fear and glad tidings.

فَصَلِّ عَلَيْهِ عَدَدَ الثَّمَرِ وَاَوْرَاقِ الشَّجَرِ وَاَجْزَاءِ الْمَدَرِ وَعَدَدَ الشَّعْرِ وَالْوَبَرِ

So, send upon him blessings that are as numerous as the amount of fruits, the leaves of trees, the stones and pebbles, the hairs of people and animals,

وَعَدَدَ مَا اَحَاطَ بِهِ عِلْمُكَ وَاَحْصَاهُ كِتَابُكَ صَلَاةً يَغْبِطُهُ بِهَا الْاَوَّلُوْنَ وَالْاٰخِرُوْنَ

such numerous blessings that are only in Your knowledge and enumerated in Your book, such blessings due to which all the ancient and coming generations wish to have.

اَللّٰهُمَّ وَاحْشُرْنَا فِيْ زُمْرَتِهِ وَاحْفَظْنَا عَلٰى طَاعَتِهِ وَاحْرُسْنَا بِدَوْلَتِهِ

O Allāh, include us in his group, maintain our obedience to him, guard us through his government,

وَاَتْحِفْنَا بِوِلَايَتِهِ وَانْصُرْنَا عَلٰى اَعْدَائِنَا بِعِزَّتِهِ

delight us through his guardianship, give us victory over our enemies through his power,

and include us, O my Lord, amongst those who constantly repent to You. O the Most Merciful!	وَاجْعَلْنَا يَارَبِّ مِنَ التَّوَّابِيْنَ يَا اَرْحَمَ الرَّاحِمِيْنَ
O Allāh, Iblīs, the accrsed rebel, asked You to grant him respite so that he could mislead Your creatures, and You granted him so.	اَللّٰهُمَّ وَاِنَّ اِبْلِيْسَ الْمُتَمَرِّدَ اللَّعِيْنَ قَدِ اسْتَنْظَرَكَ لِاِغْوَاءِ خَلْقِكَ فَاَنْظَرْتَهُ
He asked You to postpone his punishment so that he would misguide Your servants, and You granted it to him. This is because You had already known about him. He thus coneverted many of them to follow him.	وَاسْتَمْهَلَكَ لِاِضْلَالِ عَبِيْدِكَ فَاَمْهَلْتَهُ بِسَابِقِ عِلْمِكَ فِيْهِ، وَقَدْ عَشَّشَ وَكَثُرَتْ جُنُوْدُهُ
So, his armies have been overcrowding, and his propagandists are widespread in all the corners of this earth. They have mislead Your servants, deformed Your religion,	وَازْدَحَمَتْ جُيُوْشُهُ وَانْتَشَرَتْ دُعَاتُهُ فِيْ اَقْطَارِ الْاَرْضِ فَاَضَلُّوْا عِبَادَكَ وَاَفْسَدُوْا دِيْنَكَ
displaced words from their rightful places, and divided Your servants into diverse groups and rebellious parties.	وَحَرَّفُوْا الْكَلِمَ عَنْ مَوَاضِعِهِ وَجَعَلُوْا عِبَادَكَ شِيَعاً مُتَفَرِّقِيْنَ وَاَحْزَاباً مُتَمَرِّدِيْنَ
You promised that You would demolish his platform and destroy his standing. So, defeat his sons and armies,	وَقَدْ وَعَدْتَ نَقْضَ بُنْيَانِهِ وَتَمْزِيْقَ شَأْنِهِ فَاَهْلِكْ اَوْلَادَهُ وَجُيُوْشَهُ

وَطَهِّرْ بِلَادَكَ مِنِ اخْتِرَاعَاتِهِ وَاخْتِلَافَاتِهِ وَارِحْ عِبَادَكَ مِنْ مَذَاهِبِهِ وَقِيَاسَاتِهِ

purify Your lands from his inventions and fabrications, relieve Your servants from his sects and prejudices,

وَاجْعَلْ دَائِرَةَ السَّوْءِ عَلَيْهِمْ وَابْسُطْ عَدْلَكَ وَاَظْهِرْ دِيْنَكَ

make the disaster of evil surround them, extend Your justice, make apparent Your religion,

وَقَوِّ اَوْلِيَآءَكَ وَ اَوْهِنْ اَعْدآءَكَ وَ اَوْرِثْ دِيَارَ اِبْلِيْسَ وَ دِيَارَ اَوْلِيَائِهِ اَوْلِيَاءَكَ وَخَلِّدْهُمْ فِيْ الْجَحِيْمِ وَاَذِقْهُمْ مِنْ الْعَذَابِ الْاَلِيْمِ

give strength to Your intimate servants, weaken Your enemies, make Your intimate servants inherit the lands of Iblīs and his followers, destine the followers of Iblīs to remain in the blazing fire forever, make them taste the painful torment,

وَاجْعَلْ لَعَائِنَكَ الْمُسْتَوْدَعَةَ فِيْ مَنَاحِسِ الْخِلْقَةِ وَمَشَاوِيْهِ الْفِطْرَةِ دَائِرَةً عَلَيْهِمْ

and place Your curses on those people who spend their time in corrupt places and have left the realm of the fiṭrah (divine nature),

وَمُوَكَّلَةً بِهِمْ وَجَارِيَةً فِيْهِمْ كُلَّ صَبَاحٍ وَمَسآءٍ وَغُدُوٍّ وَرَوَاحٍ

and as a result, they will have removed themselves from the mercy of Allāh, and remain there day and night.

رَبَّنَا آتِنَا فِيْ الدُّنْيَا حَسَنَةً وَفِي الْآخِرَةِ حَسَنَةً وَقِنَا بِرَحْمَتِكَ عَذَابَ النَّارِ يَا اَرْحَمَ الرَّاحِمِيْنَ

O Our Lord, grant us goodness in this world and goodness in the hereafter, and save us, out of Your mercy, from the punishment of the fire. O the Most Merciful!

Common Ziyārah of Imām al-Hādī (A) and Imām al-ʿAskarī (A)

When you decide to perform the ziyārah of Imām al-Hādī (A) and Imām al-ʿAskarī (A), stand by the holy ḍarīḥ and recite:

Peace be upon you both, O the guardians of Allāh! Peace be upon you both, O the proofs of Allāh!	اَلسَّلَامُ عَلَيْكُمَا يَا وَلِيَّيِ اللهِ اَلسَّلَامُ عَلَيْكُمَا يَا حُجَّتَيِ اللهِ
Peace be upon you both, O the lights of Allāh in the darkness of the earth!	اَلسَّلَامُ عَلَيْكُمَا يَا نُوْرَيِ اللهِ فِيْ ظُلُمَاتِ الْاَرْضِ
Peace be upon you both, whose will was the will of Allāh.	اَلسَّلَامُ عَلَيْكُمَا يَا مَنْ بَدَا لِلّٰهِ فِيْ شَأْنِكُمَا
I have come to visit you, aware of your rights,	اَتَيْتُكُمَا زَائِراً وَعَارِفاً بِحَقِّكُمَا
displaying hostility towards your enemies, showing loyalty to those who are loyal to you, believing in whatever you believed in,	مُعَادِيًا لِأَعْدَآئِكُمَا مُوَالِيًا لِأَوْلِيَآئِكُمَا مُؤْمِناً بِمَا آمَنْتُمَا بِهِ
disbelieving in whatever you disbelieved, verifying that which you deemed true, and invalidating that which you deemed wrong.	كَافِراً بِمَا كَفَرْتُمَا بِهِ، مُحَقِّقاً لِمَا حَقَّقْتُمَا مُبْطِلاً لِمَا اَبْطَلْتُمَا

I ask Allāh, my Lord and your Lord,	أَسْأَلُ اللهَ رَبِّيْ وَرَبَّكُمَا
to make the reward of my visit to you be given in the form of sending blessings upon Muḥammad and his Household (as that increases my reward)	أَنْ يَجْعَلَ حَظِّيْ مِنْ زِيَارَتِكُمَا الصَّلَاةَ عَلَىٰ مُحَمَّدٍ وَآلِهِ
and that He may grant me the favor of accompanying you both in the gardens of Paradise with your righteous fathers,	وَأَنْ يَرْزُقَنِيْ مُرَافَقَتَكُمَا فِي الْجِنَانِ مَعَ آبَائِكُمَا الصَّالِحِيْنَ
And I ask Him to save me from the hellfire, to grant me your intercession and your company, and that He may allow me to get to know you better,	وَأَسْأَلُهُ أَنْ يُعْتِقَ رَقَبَتِيْ مِنَ النَّارِ وَيَرْزُقَنِيْ شَفَاعَتَكُمَا وَمُصَاحَبَتَكُمَا وَيُعَرِّفَ بَيْنِيْ وَبَيْنَكُمَا
to never remove the love for you and your righteous fathers from my heart,	وَلَا يَسْلُبَنِيْ حُبَّكُمَا وَحُبَّ آبَائِكُمَا الصَّالِحِيْنَ
not to make this my last visit to you,	وَأَنْ لَّا يَجْعَلَهُ آخِرَ الْعَهْدِ مِنْ زِيَارَتِكُمَا
and to include me with you all in paradise, out of His Mercy.	وَيَحْشُرَنِيْ مَعَكُمَا فِي الْجَنَّةِ بِرَحْمَتِهِ
O Allāh, grant me love for them, and make me die while I am upon their creed.	اَللَّهُمَّ ارْزُقْنِيْ حُبَّهُمَا وَتَوَفَّنِيْ عَلَىٰ مِلَّتِهِمَا

O Allāh, curse and punish those who usurped the right of the family of Muḥammad.	اَللَّهُمَّ الْعَنْ ظَالِمِيْ آلَ مُحَمَّدٍ حَقَّهُمْ وَانْتَقِمْ مِنْهُمْ
O Allāh, curse their enemies from the past and coming generations, increase their punishment,	اَللَّهُمَّ الْعَنِ الْاَوَّلِيْنَ مِنْهُمْ وَالْآخِرِيْنَ وَضَاعِفْ عَلَيْهِمُ الْعَذَابَ
send them and their adherents, lovers, and followers to the deepest pit of the hellfire. Surely, You have power over all things.	وَاَبْلِغْ بِهِمْ وَبِاَشْيَاعِهِمْ وَمُحِبِّيْهِمْ وَمُتَّبِعِيْهِمْ اَسْفَلَ دَرْكٍ مِنَ الْجَحِيْمِ اِنَّكَ عَلَىٰ كُلِّ شَيْءٍ قَدِيْرٌ
O Allāh, hasten the relief (reappearance) of Your guardian and the son of Your guardian, and cause our relief to accompany his relief. O the Most Merciful!	اَللَّهُمَّ عَجِّلْ فَرَجَ وَلِيِّكَ وَابْنِ وَلِيِّكَ وَاجْعَلْ فَرَجَنَا مَعَ فَرَجِهِمْ يَا اَرْحَمَ الرَّاحِمِيْنَ.

Ziyārah of Ḥaḍrat Narjis Khātūn (A)

Ḥaḍrat Narjis Khātūn, the wife of Imām al-ʿAskarī (A) and mother of Imām al-Mahdī (AJ) is buried behind Imām Ḥasan al-ʿAskarī (A). Turn towards her grave and recite:

Peace be on the Messenger of Allāh, may the blessings of Allāh be upon him and his truthful, trustworthy family.	اَلسَّلَامُ عَلَىٰ رَسُوْلِ اللهِ صَلَّى اللهُ عَلَيْهِ وَآلِهِ الصَّادِقِ الْاَمِيْنِ
Peace be on our Master, the Commander of the Faithful. Peace be on the pure Imāms and auspicious proofs.	اَلسَّلَامُ عَلَىٰ مَوْلَانَا اَمِيْرِ الْمُؤْمِنِيْنَ اَلسَّلَامُ عَلَىٰ الْاَئِمَّةِ الطَّاهِرِيْنَ الْحُجَجِ الْمَيَامِيْنِ
Peace on the mother of the Imām, who was entrusted with the secrets of All-Knowing Master and bore the best of creations.	اَلسَّلَامُ عَلَىٰ وَالِدَةِ الْاِمَامِ وَالْمُوْدَعَةِ اَسْرَارَ الْمَلِكِ الْعَلَّامِ وَالْحَامِلَةِ لِاَشْرَفِ الْاَنَامِ
Peace be upon you, O the truthful, the contented.	اَلسَّلَامُ عَلَيْكِ اَيَّتُهَا الصِّدِّيْقَةُ الْمَرْضِيَّةُ
Peace be upon you, O the one who is similar to the mother of Mūsā (A) and the daughter of the disciple of ʿĪsā (A). Peace be upon you, O the pious, the pure.	اَلسَّلَامُ عَلَيْكِ يَا شَبِيْهَةَ اُمِّ مُوْسَىٰ وَابْنَةَ حَوَارِيِّ عِيْسَىٰ اَلسَّلَامُ عَلَيْكِ اَيَّتُهَا التَّقِيَّةُ النَّقِيَّةُ

اَلسَّلَامُ عَلَيْكِ اَيَّتُهَا الرَّضِيَّةُ الْمَرْضِيَّةُ،

Peace be upon you, O the pleased, the content.

اَلسَّلَامُ عَلَيْكِ اَيَّتُهَا الْمَنْعُوْتَةُ
فِي الْاِنْجِيْلِ الْمَخْطُوْبَةُ مِنْ رُوْحِ اللّٰهِ
الْاَمِيْنِ

Peace be upon you, whose praise has been mentioned in the Bible, the one whose proposal came from the trustworthy spirit of Allāh,

وَمَنْ رَغِبَ فِيْ وُصْلَتِهَا مُحَمَّدٌ سَيِّدُ
الْمُرْسَلِيْنَ، وَالْمُسْتَوْدَعَةُ اَسْرَارَ رَبِّ
الْعَالَمِيْنَ

the one whose marriage union was pleasing to Muḥammad, the leader of the Messengers, the one who was entrusted with the secrets of the Lord of the worlds.

اَلسَّلَامُ عَلَيْكِ وَعَلٰى آبَائِكِ الْحَوَارِيِّيْنَ
اَلسَّلَامُ عَلَيْكِ وَعَلٰى بَعْلِكِ وَوَلَدِكِ

Peace be upon you and upon your forefathers, the followers of ʿĪsā (A). Peace be upon you and upon your husband and son.

اَلسَّلَامُ عَلَيْكِ وَعَلٰى رُوْحِكِ وَبَدَنِكِ
الطَّاهِرِ اَشْهَدُ اَنَّكِ اَحْسَنْتِ الْكَفَالَةَ
وَاَدَّيْتِ الْاَمَانَةَ وَصَبَرْتِ فِيْ ذَاتِ اللّٰهِ

Peace be upon you and on your pure soul and body. I bear witness that you were the best guardian and nurtured that which was entrusted to you (Imām al-Mahdī), strove in the path of Allāh's pleasure,

وَحَفِظْتِ سِرَّ اللّٰهِ وَحَمَلْتِ وَلِيَّ اللّٰهِ
وَبَالَغْتِ فِيْ حِفْظِ حُجَّةِ اللّٰهِ وَرَغِبْتِ فِيْ
وُصْلَةِ اَبْنَاءِ رَسُوْلِ اللّٰهِ

endured patience in the way of Allāh, protected the secret of Allāh, bore the guardian of Allāh, and endeavoured In maintaining relation with the sons of the Messenger of Allāh (S).

عَارِفَةً بِحَقِّهِمْ، مُؤْمِنَةً بِصِدْقِهِمْ، مُعْتَرِفَةً بِمَنْزِلَتِهِمْ، مُسْتَبْصِرَةً بِاَمْرِهِمْ، مُشْفِقَةً عَلَيْهِمْ، مُؤْثِرَةً هَوَاهُمْ	You recognized their rights, believed in their truthfulness, attested to their position, had insight and sympathy for their affairs, were compassionate to them, and gave preference to their wishes.
وَاَشْهَدُ اَنَّكِ مَضَيْتِ عَلٰى بَصِيْرَةٍ مِنْ اَمْرِكِ، مُقْتَدِيَةً بِالصَّالِحِيْنَ	I also bear witness that you passed away while you had foresight in religion, were following the righteous ones,
رَاضِيَةً مَرْضِيَّةً تَقِيَّةً نَقِيَّةً زَكِيَّةً فَرَضِيَ اللهُ عَنْكِ وَاَرْضَاكِ	and were pleased, contented, pious, pure, chaste. So, may Allāh be satisfied with you and keep you satisfied,
وَجَعَلَ الْجَنَّةَ مَنْزِلَكِ وَمَأْوَاكِ فَلَقَدْ اَوْلَاكِ مِنَ الْخَيْرَاتِ مَا اَوْلَاكِ	and may He make paradise your place and abode. And certainly you are deserving of all goodness.
وَاَعْطَاكِ مِنَ الشَّرَفِ مَا بِهِ اَغْنَاكِ فَهَنَّاكِ اللهُ بِمَا مَنَحَكِ مِنَ الْكَرَامَةِ وَأَمْرَاكِ	And because of your nobility, He has given you the means to be self-sufficient. May Allāh make the honor He gave you abundantly joyous.

Then, raise your head towards the sky and recite:

اَللّٰهُمَّ اِيَّاكَ اعْتَمَدْتُ وَلِرِضَاكَ طَلَبْتُ وَبِاَوْلِيَائِكَ اِلَيْكَ تَوَسَّلْتُ	O Allāh, I rely only upon You, seek only Your satisfaction, and seek intercession only through Your intimate servants,

Your forgiveness and forbearance do I trust, and in You do I seek protection and in the grave of the mother of Your representative, do I take refuge	وَعَلَىٰ غُفْرَانِكَ وَحِلْمِكَ اتَّكَلْتُ وَبِكَ اعْتَصَمْتُ وَبِقَبْرِ اُمِّ وَلِيِّكَ لُذْتُ
So, bless Muḥammad and the household of Muḥammad, let me benefit from visiting her, keep me steadfast in my love for her,	فَصَلِّ عَلَىٰ مُحَمَّدٍ وَآلِ مُحَمَّدٍ وَانْفَعْنِيْ بِزِيَارَتِهَا وَثَبِّتْنِيْ عَلَىٰ مَحَبَّتِهَا
do not deprive me of her and her son's intercession, grant me her companionship,	وَلَا تَحْرِمْنِيْ شَفَاعَتَهَا وَشَفَاعَةَ وَلَدِهَا وَارْزُقْنِيْ مُرَافَقَتَهَا
and gather me with her and her son, just as You have bestowed upon me the opportunity of visiting her and her son.	وَاحْشُرْنِيْ مَعَهَا وَمَعَ وَلَدِهَا كَمَا وَفَّقْتَنِيْ لِزِيَارَةِ وَلَدِهَا وَزِيَارَتِهَا
O Allāh, I turn to You through the pure Imāms, and intercede to You through the auspicious proofs from the progeny of Ṭā Ha and Yā Sīn (the Noble Prophet)	اَللّٰهُمَّ اِنِّيْ اَتَوَجَّهُ اِلَيْكَ بِالْاَئِمَّةِ الطَّاهِرِيْنَ وَاَتَوَسَّلُ اِلَيْكَ بِالْحُجَجِ الْمَيَامِيْنِ مِنْ آلِ طٰهٰ وَيٰسٓ
that You bless Muḥammad and the household of Muḥammad, the pure ones,	اَنْ تُصَلِّيَ عَلَىٰ مُحَمَّدٍ وَآلِ مُحَمَّدٍ الطَّيِّبِيْنَ
include me amongst the content, successful, joyous, and cheerful ones	وَاَنْ تَجْعَلَنِيْ مِنَ الْمُطْمَئِنِّيْنَ الْفَائِزِيْنَ الْفَرِحِيْنَ الْمُسْتَبْشِرِيْنَ

اَلَّذِيْنَ لَاخَوْفٌ عَلَيْهِمْ وَلَاهُمْ يَحْزَنُوْنَ وَاجْعَلْنِيْ مِمَّنْ قَبِلْتَ سَعْيَهُ وَيَسَّرْتَ اَمْرَهُ وَكَشَفْتَ ضُرَّهُ وَآمَنْتَ خَوْفَهُ	those who have no fear and do not grieve, and include me amongst those whose efforts You accept, affairs You make easy, difficulties You solve, and fear You convert into security.
اَللّٰهُمَّ بِحَقِّ مُحَمَّدٍ وَآلِ مُحَمَّد صَلِّ عَلٰى مُحَمَّدٍ وَآلِ مُحَمَّدٍ وَلَا تَجْعَلْهُ آخِرَ الْعَهْدِ مِنْ زِيَارَتِيْ اِيَاهَا	O Allāh, by the right of Muḥammad and the household of Muḥammad, send blessings upon Muḥammad and his household, do not make this my last visitation to her,
وَارْزُقْنِيْ الْعَوْدَ اِلَيْهَا اَبداً مَا اَبْقَيْتَنِيْ، وَاِذَا تَوَفَّيْتَنِيْ فَاحْشُرْنِيْ فِيْ زُمْرَتِهَا	grant me the good fortune of returning to visit her again and again for as long as I live.
وَاَدْخِلْنِيْ فِيْ شَفَاعَةِ وَلَدِهَا وَشَفَاعَتِهَا وَاغْفِرْ لِيْ وَلِوَالِدَيَّ وَلِلْمُؤْمِنِيْنَ وَالْمُؤْمِنَاتِ	And include me amongst those who receive the intercession of her and her son, and forgive me, my parents, and all the believing men and the women.
وَآتِنَا فِي الدُّنْيَا حَسَنَةً وَفِيْ الْآخِرَةِ حَسَنَةً وَقِنَا بِرَحْمَتِكَ عَذَابَ النَّارِ	Grant us goodness in this world and the hereafter and protect us from the punishment of Hell, by your mercy.
وَالسَّلَامُ عَلَيْكُمْ يَا سَادَاتِيْ وَرَحْمَةُ اللّٰهِ وَبَرَكَاتُهُ	May the peace, mercy, and blessings of Allāh be upon you, O my leaders!

Ḥaḍrat Ḥakīmā Khātūn (A)

Ḥaḍrat Ḥakīmā Khātūn is the daughter of Imām al-Jawād (A), sister of Imām al-Hādī (A), and aunt of Imām Ḥasan al-ʿAskarī (A). Her holy grave is located beneath the foot of Imām al-Hādī (A) and Imām al-ʿAskarīi (A) in Sāmarrā. This noble lady witnessed the Imāmate of four Imāms. In addition, Imām al-Hādī (A) appointed her to be the teacher of Ḥaḍrat Narjis Khātūn, the mother of Imām az-Zamān (AJ), so she could learn about Islām even after the martyrdom of Imām Ḥasan al-ʿAskarī (A) she maintained the position of representation by Imām Zamān (AJ). She also witness the birth of Imām az-Zamān (AJ).

ʿAllāmah Majlisī says, "I wonder why there is no specific ziyārah for this noble and pious lady, despite her being among true companions of the Imāms (A), being present at the birth of Imām Zamān (AJ), and constantly being around Imām al ʿAskarī (A) and being his intermediary after his martyrdom. By the same reasoning, Marhūm Muḥaddith Qummī mentions in Mafātīḥ al-Jinān that it is proper to recite her ziyārah using the phrases that are used for her aunt, Sayyidah Maʿṣūmah, the daughter of Imām Mūsa bin Jaʿfar (A).

Ziyārah of Ḥaḍrat Ḥakīmā Khātūn (A)

Peace be upon Ādam, the chosen one of Allāh. Peace be upon Nūḥ, the Prophet of Allāh. Peace be upon Ibrāhīm, the intimate friend of Allāh.

اَلسَّلَامُ عَلٰى آدَمَ صَفْوَةِ اللهِ
اَلسَّلَامُ عَلٰى نُوْحٍ نَبِيِّ اللهِ
اَلسَّلَامُ عَلٰى اِبْرَاهِيْمَ خَلِيْلِ اللهِ

Peace be upon Mūsā, the one spoken to by Allāh. Peace be upon ʿĪsā, the spirit of Allāh. Peace be upon you, O Messenger of Allāh.

اَلسَّلَامُ عَلٰى مُوْسٰى كَلِيْمِ اللهِ
اَلسَّلَامُ عَلٰى عِيْسٰى رُوْحِ اللهِ
اَلسَّلَامُ عَلَيْكَ يَارَسُوْلَ اللهِ

Peace be upon you, O best creation of Allāh. Peace be upon you, O chosen one of Allāh.

اَلسَّلَامُ عَلَيْكَ يَا خَيْرَ خَلْقِ اللهِ
اَلسَّلَامُ عَلَيْكَ يَا صَفِيَّ اللهِ

Peace be upon you, O Muḥammad, son of ʿAbdullāh, the Seal of the Prophets.

اَلسَّلَامُ عَلَيْكَ يَا مُحَمَّدَ بْنَ عَبْدِ اللهِ
خَاتَمِ النَّبِيِّيْنَ

Peace be upon you, O Commander of the Faithful, ʿAlī, son of Abī Ṭālib, the successor of the Messenger of Allāh.

اَلسَّلَامُ عَلَيْكَ يَا اَمِيْرَ الْمُؤْمِنِيْنَ عَلِيَّ بْنَ
أَبِيْ طَالِبٍ وَصِيَّ رَسُوْلِ اللهِ

Peace be upon you, O Fāṭimah, the leader of the women of the worlds. Peace be upon you both, O the leaders of mercy and leaders of the youth of paradise.

اَلسَّلَامُ عَلَيْكِ يَافَاطِمَةُ سَيِّدَةُ نِسَاءِ
الْعَالَمِيْنَ، اَلسَّلَامُ عَلَيْكُمَا يَا سِبْطَيِ
الرَّحْمَةِ وَسَيِّدَيْ شَبَابِ اَهْلِ الْجَنَّةِ

Peace be upon you, O ʿAlī, son of Ḥusayn, chief of the worshippers and the delight of the people's eyes.	اَلسَّلَامُ عَلَيْكَ يَا عَلِيَّ بْنَ الْحُسَيْنِ سَيِّدَ الْعَابِدِيْنَ وَقُرَّةَ عَيْنِ النَّاظِرِيْنَ
Peace be upon you, O Muḥammad, son of ʿAlī, the splitter of knowledge after the Prophet.	اَلسَّلَامُ عَلَيْكَ يَا مُحَمَّدَ بْنَ عَلِيٍّ بَاقِرَ الْعِلْمِ بَعْدَ النَّبِيِّ
Peace be upon you, O Jaʿfar, son of Muḥammad, the truthful one, the good, the trustworthy.	اَلسَّلَامُ عَلَيْكَ يَا جَعْفَرَ بْنَ مُحَمَّدٍ الصَّادِقَ الْبَارَّ الْاَمِيْنَ
Peace be upon you, O Mūsā, son of Jaʿfar, the pure and purified. Peace be upon you, O ʿAlī, son of Mūsā, the contented and well-pleased.	اَلسَّلَامُ عَلَيْكَ يَا مُوْسَي بْنَ جَعْفَرٍ الطَّاهِرَ الْطُّهْرَ اَلسَّلَامُ عَلَيْكَ يَا عَلِيَّ بْنَ مُوْسَي الرِّضَا الْمُرْتَضَىٰ
Peace be upon you, O Muḥammad, son of ʿAlī, the pious. Peace be upon you, O ʿAlī, son of Muḥammad, the pure and sincere trustee.	اَلسَّلَامُ عَلَيْكَ يَا مُحَمَّدَ بْنَ عَلِيٍّ التَّقِيَّ اَلسَّلَامُ عَلَيْكَ يَا عَلِيَّ بْنَ مُحَمَّدٍ النَّقِيَّ النَّاصِحَ الْاَمِيْنَ
Peace be upon you, O Ḥasan, son of ʿAlī. Peace be upon you, O the successor after him (Imām al-Mahdī).	اَلسَّلَامُ عَلَيْكَ يَا حَسَنَ بْنَ عَلِيٍّ اَلسَّلَامُ عَلَىٰ الْوَصِيِّ مِنْ بَعْدِهِ

O Allah, send blessings upon Your light, Your lantern, my guardian and Your guardian, my successor and Your successor, and Your proof over Your creation.	اَللّٰهُمَّ صَلِّ عَلٰى نُوْرِكَ وَسِرَاجِكَ وَوَلِيِّ وَلِيِّكَ وَوَصِيِّ وَصِيِّكَ وَحُجَّتِكَ عَلٰى خَلْقِكَ
Peace be upon you, O daughter of the Messenger of Allāh. Peace be upon you, O daughter of Fāṭimah and Khadījah.	اَلسَّلَامُ عَلَيْكِ يَا بِنْتَ رَسُوْلِ اللّٰهِ اَلسَّلَامُ عَلَيْكِ يَا بِنْتَ فَاطِمَةَ وَخَدِيْجَةَ،
Peace be upon you, O daughter of the Commander of the Faithful. Peace be upon you, O daughter of al-Ḥasan and al-Ḥusayn.	اَلسَّلَامُ عَلَيْكِ يَا بِنْتَ اَمِيْرِالْمُؤْمِنِيْنَ، اَلسَّلَامُ عَلَيْكِ يَابِنْتَ الْحَسَنِ وَالْحُسَيْنِ
Peace be upon you, O daughter of the guardian of Allāh. Peace be upon you, O sister of the guardian of Allāh. Peace be upon you, O aunt of the guardian of Allāh.	اَلسَّلَامُ عَلَيْكِ يَا بِنْتَ وَلِيِّ اللّٰهِ اَلسَّلَامُ عَلَيْكِ يَا اُخْتَ وَلِيِّ اللّٰهِ اَلسَّلَامُ عَلَيْكِ يَا عَمَّةَ وَلِيِّ اللّٰهِ
Peace be upon you, O daughter of Muḥammad, son of ʿAlī, the pious. And May Allāh's mercy and blessings be upon him	اَلسَّلَامُ عَلَيْكِ يَا بِنْتَ مُحَمَّدِ بْنِ عَلِيٍّ التَّقِيِّ وَرَحْمَةُ اللّٰهِ وَبَرَكَاتُهُ
Peace be upon you, the one to whom Allāh will introduce us in heaven, gather us in your group, and bring us to the Prophet's (S) pond (Kawthar).	اَلسَّلَامُ عَلَيْكِ عَرَّفَ اللّٰهُ بَيْنَنَا وَبَيْنَكُمْ فِي الْجَنَّةِ وَحَشَرَنَا فِيْ زُمْرَتِكُمْ وَاَوْرَدَنَا حَوْضَ نَبِيِّكُمْ

And quench our thirst with the refreshing water by the hand of your grandfather, ʿAlī, son of Abī Ṭālib, may Allāh's blessings be upon you. I ask Allāh to grant my happiness through your relief (the hastening of the Imām),	وَسَقَانَا بِكَأْسِ جَدِّكُمْ مِنْ يَدِ عَلِيِّ بْنِ أَبِيْ طَالِبٍ صَلَوَاتُ اللهِ عَلَيْكُمْ اَسْأَلُ اللهَ اَنْ يُرِيَنَا فِيْكُمُ السُّرُوْرَ وَالْفَرَجَ
gather us and you in the group of your grandfather, Muḥammad, may Allāh's blessings be upon him and his household, and not remove your recognition from us. Certainly, He is the Most Powerful Guardian.	وَاَنْ يَجْمَعَنَا وَاِيَّاكُمْ فِيْ زُمْرَةِ جَدِّكُمْ مُحَمَّدٍ صَلَّى اللهُ عَلَيْهِ وَآلِهِ وَاَنْ لَا يَسْلُبَنَا مَعْرِفَتَكُمْ اِنَّهُ وَلِيٌّ قَدِيْرٌ
I seek nearness to Allāh, through my love for you, dissociation from your enemies,	اَتَقَرَّبُ اِلَى اللهِ بِحُبِّكُمْ وَالْبَرَاءَةِ مِنْ اَعْدَائِكُمْ
submission to Allāh, contentment with Him without denying or being arrogant,	وَالتَّسْلِيْمِ اِلَى اللهِ رَاضِيًا بِهِ غَيْرَ مُنْكِرٍ وَلَا مُسْتَكْبِرٍ
certainty of that which Muḥammad brought, and I am content with it. Through this, I seek your pleasure, O my Master!	وَعَلَى يَقِيْنِ مَا اَتَى بِهِ مُحَمَّدٌ، وَ بِهِ رَاضٍ نَطْلُبُ بِذٰلِكَ وَجْهَكَ يَا سَيِّدِيْ

اَللَّهُمَّ وَرِضَاكَ وَالدَّارَ الْآخِرَةَ، يَا
حَكِيْمَةُ اشْفَعِيْ لِيْ فِيْ الْجَنَّةِ فَاِنَّ لَكِ
عِنْدَ اللهِ شَأْناً مِنَ الشَّأْنِ

O Allāh, I seek your contentment and the abode of the hereafter. O Ḥakīma, intercede for me in heaven, for surely, you hold an honorable status with Allāh.

اَللَّهُمَّ اِنِّيْ اَسْاَلُكَ اَنْ تَخْتِمَ لِيْ بِالسَّعَادَةِ
فَلَا تَسْلُبْ مِنِّيْ مَا اَنَافِيْهِ

O Allah, certainly, I ask you for my end to be felicitous, so do not remove from me the state that I am in.

وَلَاحَوْلَ وَلَا قُوَّةَ اِلَّا بِاللهِ الْعَلِيِّ الْعَظِيْمِ

There is no might and power, except trhough Allāh, the Exalted, the Supreme.

اَللَّهُمَّ اسْتَجِبْ لَنَا وَتَقَبَّلْهُ
بِكَرَمِكَ وَعِزَّتِكَ وَبِرَحْمَتِكَ وَعَافِيَتِكَ

O Allāh, answer us and grant our requests, through Your generosity, dignity, mercy, and felicity.

وَصَلَّى اللهُ عَلَىٰ مُحَمَّدٍ وَآلِهِ اَجْمَعِيْنَ وَسَلَّمَ
تَسْلِيْماً يَا اَرْحَمَ الرَّاحِمِيْنَ

May Allāh's blessings and complete peace be upon Muḥammad and his household, O the Most Merciful!

Farewell Ziyārah of ʿAskarīyayn (A)

Peace be upon you both, O guardians of Allāh. I entrust you in Allāh's care and send my salutations upon you.	اَلسَّلَامُ عَلَيْكُمَا يَا وَلِيِّيَ اللهِ اَسْتَوْدِعُكُمَا اللهَ وَاَقْرَأُ عَلَيْكُمَا اَلسَّلَامُ
I have believed in Allāh, the Messenger, and that which he has brought and guided us to.	آمَنَّا بِاللهِ وَبِالرَّسُوْلِ وَبِمَا جِئْتُمَا بِهِ وَدَلَلْتُمَا عَلَيْهِ
O Allāh, write our names amongst the martyrs.	اَللَّهُمَّ اكْتُبْنَا مَعَ الشَّاهِدِيْنَ
O Allāh, please do not make this my last visit to them, and allow me to return to them.	اَللَّهُمَّ لَا تَجْعَلْهُ آخِرَ الْعَهْدِ مِنْ زِيَارَتِيْ اِيَاهُمَا وَارْزُقْنِيْ الْعَوْدَ اِلَيْهِمَا
And gather me with them, their immaculate forefathers, and the upright proof from their progeny. O the Most Merciful!	وَاحْشُرْنِيْ مَعَهُمَا وَمَعَ آبَائِهِمَا الطَّاهِرِيْنَ وَالْقَآئِمِ الْحُجَّةِ مِنْ ذُرِّيَّتِهِمَا يَا اَرْحَمَ الرَّاحِمِيْنَ

	Imām Muḥmmad al-Mahdī (AJ) (12th Imām)
Name:	Muḥammad
Kunya:	Abū Qāsim
Title:	Mahdī, Imām al-ʿAsr (Leader of the Time), Ṣaḥib az-Zamān (Master of the Time), Baqīyatullāh (Remainder of Allāh), Qāʾim (The Upright)
Parents:	Imām Ḥasan al ʿAskarī (A) & Ḥaḍrat Narjis Khātūn
Birthday:	Friday, 15th Shaʿbān, 255 AH
Birth Place:	Sāmarrā
Ring Inscription:	أنا حِجَّةِ الله وَ خاصَّتِه I am the proof of Allāh and His the elite one
Start of Imāmah:	260 AH
Start of Greater Occultation:	329 AH
Duration of Imāmah:	Allāh knows best
Lifespan:	1184 years
Stages of his life:	■ Childhood (up to 5 years old) ■ Minor Occultation (about 70 years) ■ Major Occultation (until today, about 1114 years) ■ Re-appearance (God willing, very soon)

Holy Sardāb (Cellar)

In ʿIrāq, it was common to build basements as shelters against the heat. These basements or cellars are called sardāb, and are essentially houses built underground that contain a cold water fountain to keep the home cool in the summer.

Imām al-Hādī's (A) house in Sāmarrā was home to three of the Imāms (A). They spent many years living and worshipping the Almighty in there. Hence, it is very significant for the Shīʿāh and lovers of the Imāms (A).

The sardāb is located on the northwest side of the holy shrine and has recently undergone major construction. The sardāb is only considered sacred due to the previous presence of the Infallibles (A) in it, but it is not considered to be the place of occultation.

The term "Sardāb al-Ghaybah" (the Basement of Occultation) is made up by those who have biased opinions about Shīʿāh beliefs. In some Sunnī sources, very harsh language and accusations have been reported against this regard.

Many mistakenly think the place the 12th Imām went to occultation in this basement, but this is a baseless claim. If it were true at all, many people would have seen the Imām as he was heading towards the basement, but there are no such reports. This indicates that his occultation had started since the day of his blessed birthday and was maintained by his blessed parents, Imām al-ʿAskarī and Narjis Khātūn (A).

Best Time to Perform the Ziyārah of Imām az-Zamān (AJ)

Sulaymān ibn ʿĪsā narrates from his father:

I asked Imām as-Ṣādiq (A), "When I am incapable of visiting you physically, then how can I offer my ziyārah?"

The Imām (A) replied, "O ʿĪsā! If you are unable to come to us, perform a ghusl or wuḍū on Friday and stand under the sky and offer a two rakaʿāt prayer. Then, focus your attention towards me. Whoever visits me during my lifetime is like one who has visited me after my lifetime, and whoever performs my ziyārah after my lifetime is like one who has visited me during my lifetime!"

Based on this ḥadīth, it is clear that one can perform ziyārah of the living Imām at any time and in any place. While we should perform ziyārah of our Imām (AJ) everyday, we should at least offer our greetings on Friday, as this day holds special significance.

Nāṣir Makārim Shērāzī, Mafātīḥ Nawīn, Pg 243,

Ziyārah of Imām az-Zamān (AJ)

O Allāh, certainly, I am standing at one of the many doors of the house of your Prophet, may Your blessings be upon him and his household.

اَللّٰهُمَّ اِنِّيْ وَقَفْتُ عَلٰى بَابٍ مِنْ اَبْوَابِ بُيُوْتِ نَبِيِّكَ صَلَوَاتُكَ عَلَيْهِ وَ آلِهِ

Certainly, it is impermissible for people to enter except with his permission.

وَقَدْ مَنَعْتَ النَّاسَ اَنْ يَدْخُلُوْا إِلَّا بِإِذْنِهِ

For You have said, "O you who believe! Do not enter the houses of the Prophet, except when you have been given permission."

فَقُلْتَ يَا اَيُّهَا الَّذِيْنَ آمَنُوْا لَا تَدْخُلُوْا بُيُوْتَ النَّبِيِّ إِلَّا اَنْ يُؤْذَنَ لَكُمْ

O Allāh, certainly I believe in the sanctity of the owner of this noble place in his absence the same way that I have believed in it in his presence.

اَللّٰهُمَّ اِنِّيْ اَعْتَقِدُ حُرْمَةَ صَاحِبِ هٰذَا الْمَشْهَدِ الشَّرِيْفِ فِيْ غَيْبَتِهِ كَمَا اَعْتَقِدُهَا فِيْ حَضْرَتِهِ

I know that Your messenger and representatives, peace be upon them, are always alive and are being sustained with You.

وَاَعْلَمُ اَنَّ رَسُوْلَكَ وَخُلَفَاءَكَ عَلَيْهِمُ السَّلَامُ اَحْيَاءٌ عِنْدَكَ يُرْزَقُوْنَ

The see where I am standing and hear my words, and they reply to my greetings. And certainly, You have concealed their words from my ears,

يَرَوْنَ مَقَامِيْ، وَيَسْمَعُوْنَ كَلَامِيْ، وَيَرُدُّوْنَ سَلَامِيْ، وَاَنَّكَ حَجَبْتَ عَنْ سَمْعِيْ كَلَامَهُمْ

وَفَتَحْتَ بَابَ فَهْمِي بِلَذِيْذِ مُنَاجَاتِهِمْ،
وَإِنِّي اَسْتَأْذِنُكَ يَا رَبِّ اَوَّلاً وَاَسْتَأْذِنُ
رَسُوْلَكَ صَلَّى اللهُ عَلَيْهِ وَآلِهِ ثَانِياً

and have opened the door of my understanding with pleasurable confidential talks. I first ask for permission to enter from You, O my Lord, and secondly from Your Messenger, may Your blessings be upon him and his household.

وَاَسْتَأْذِنُ خَلِيْفَتَكَ الْإِمَامَ الْمَفْرُوْضَ
عَلَيَّ طَاعَتُهُ حُجَّةَ بْنَ الْحَسَنِ الْمَهْدِيْ
عَجَّلَ اللهُ تَعَالَىٰ فَرَجَهُ الشَّرِيْفُ

Thirdly, I ask permission from Your representative, the Imām whose obedience is obligatory upon me, the Proof, son of Ḥasan, al-Mahdī, may Allāh hasten his reappearance,

وَالْمَلَائِكَةَ الْمُوَكَّلِيْنَ بِهٰذِهِ الْبُقْعَةِ
الْمُبَارَكَةِ ثَالِثاً

and the angels who have been appointed to this blessed grave.

أَأَدْخُلُ يَا رَسُوْلَ اللهِ
أَأَدْخُلُ يَاحُجَّةَ اللهِ
أَأَدْخُلُ يَا مَلَائِكَةَ اللهِ الْمُقَرَّبِيْنَ
الْمُقِيْمِيْنَ فِيْ هٰذَا الْمَشْهَدِ

May I enter, O Messenger of Allāh?
May I enter, O Proof of Allāh?
May I enter, O close angels of Allāh, who have been appointed to this holy place?

فَأْذَنْ لِيْ يَا مَوْلَايَ فِيْ الدُّخُوْلِ اَفْضَلَ مَا
اَذِنْتَ لِاَحَدٍ مِنْ اَوْلِيَائِكَ فَإِنْ لَمْ اَكُنْ
اَهْلاً لِذٰلِكَ فَاَنْتَ اَهْلٌ لِذٰلِكَ

So grant me permission, O my Master, to enter in the best way that you have ever allowed any of your intimate servants to enter. So, if I am unworthy of this blessing, You are worthy of giving it to me.

Then, say:

With the name of Allāh (I begin), in Allāh (I trust), in the path of Allāh, and upon the creed of Rasūl Allāh (I proceed), may Allāh bless him and his Household.	بِسْمِ اللهِ وَبِاللهِ وَفِيْ سَبِيْلِ اللهِ وَعَلىٰ مِلَّةِ رَسُوْلِ اللهِ صَلَّى اللهُ عَلَيْهِ وَآلِهِ
O Allāh, forgive me, have mercy upon me, and accept my repentance and return. Certainly, You are the Most Clement (accepting of repentance), the Most Merciful!	اَللَّهُمَّ اغْفِرْ لِيْ وَارْحَمْنِيْ وَتُبْ عَلَيَّ اِنَّكَ اَنْتَ التَّوَّابُ الرَّحِيْمُ

Ziyārat Āle Yāsīn

Shaykh Tūsī narrates in *Sharīf Iḥtijāj* that Imām al-Mahdī (AJ) said, "Whenever you desire to reach Allāh through us and wish to turn your attention towards us, then recite this ziyārah."

Peace be upon the family of Yāsīn. Peace be upon you, O caller of Allāh and the manifestation of His signs.	سَلَامٌ عَلىٰ آلِ يٰسٓ اَلسَّلَامُ عَلَيْكَ يَا دَاعِيَ اللهِ وَ رَبَّانِيَ آيَاتِهِ
Peace be upon you, O the door of Allāh and the devout one of His religion. Peace be upon you, O the representative of Allāh and the supporter of His truth.	اَلسَّلَامُ عَلَيْكَ يَا بَابَ اللهِ وَدَيَّانَ دِيْنِهِ، اَلسَّلَامُ عَلَيْكَ يَا خَلِيْفَةَ اللهِ وَ نَاصِرَ حَقِّهِ

اَلسَّلَامُ عَلَيْكَ يَا حُجَّةَ اللهِ وَ دَلِيْلَ
إِرَادَتِهِ اَلسَّلَامُ عَلَيْكَ يَا تَالِيَ كِتَابِ
اللهِ وَ تَرْجُمَانَهُ

Peace be upon you, O the proof of Allāh and the guide towards His will. Peace be upon you, O the reciter and interpreter of Allāh's book.

اَلسَّلَامُ عَلَيْكَ فِيْ آنَاءِ لَيْلِكَ وَاَطْرَافِ
نَهَارِكَ اَلسَّلَامُ عَلَيْكَ يَا بَقِيَّةَ اللهِ
فِيْ اَرْضِهِ

Peace be upon you in your night and in your day. Peace be upon you, O the remnant of Allāh on His earth.

اَلسَّلَامُ عَلَيْكَ يَا مِيْثَاقَ اللهِ الَّذِيْ
اَخَذَهُ وَوَكَّدَهُ اَلسَّلَامُ عَلَيْكَ يَا وَعْدَ
اللهِ الَّذِيْ ضَمِنَهُ

Peace be upon you, O the covenant of Allāh, which He took and strengthened. Peace be upon you, O the promise of Allāh which He has guaranteed.

اَلسَّلَامُ عَلَيْكَ اَيُّهَا الْعَلَمُ الْمَنْصُوْبُ
وَالْعِلْمُ الْمَصْبُوْبُ وَالْغَوْثُ وَالرَّحْمَةُ
الْوَاسِعَةُ، وَعْداً غَيْرَمَكْذُوْبٍ

Peace by upon you, O the one who raises the flag, the one who is filled with knowledge, the one who answers the calls for help, and the vast mercy, and the promise that will not be broken.

اَلسَّلَامُ عَلَيْكَ حِيْنَ تَقُوْمُ، اَلسَّلَامُ
عَلَيْكَ حِيْنَ تَقْعُدُ، اَلسَّلَامُ عَلَيْكَ
حِيْنَ تَقْرَأُ وَتُبَيِّنُ ،

Peace be upon you while you are standing. Peace be upon you while you are sitting. Peace be upon you while you are reading and explaining.

اَلسَّلَامُ عَلَيْكَ حِيْنَ تُصَلِّيْ وَتَقْنُتُ
اَلسَّلَامُ عَلَيْكَ حِيْنَ تَرْكَعُ وَتَسْجُدُ

Peace be upon you when you are praying and supplicating. Peace be upon you when you are bowing (in rukuʿ) and prostrating.

اَلسَّلَامُ عَلَيْكَ حِيْنَ تُهَلِّلُ وَتُكَبِّرُ
اَلسَّلَامُ عَلَيْكَ حِيْنَ تَحْمَدُ وَتَسْتَغْفِرُ

Peace be upon you when you attest to the oneness and greatness of Allāh. Peace be upon you when you praise Allāh and seeking forgiveness.

اَلسَّلَامُ عَلَيْكَ حِيْنَ تُصْبِحُ وَتُمْسَىٰ
اَلسَّلَامُ عَلَيْكَ فِيْ اللَّيْلِ اِذَا يَغْشَىٰ
وَالنَّهَارِ اِذَا تَجَلَّىٰ

Peace be upon you in the morning and the evening. Peace be upon you in the night when it covers and the day when it emerges.

اَلسَّلَامُ عَلَيْكَ اَيُّهَا الْاِمَامُ الْمَأْمُوْنِ
اَلسَّلَامُ عَلَيْكَ اَيُّهَا الْمُقَدَّمُ الْمَأْمُوْلُ

Peace be upon you, O the trusted leader. Peace be upon you, O he who will carry out my hopes.

اَلسَّلَامُ عَلَيْكَ بِجَوَامِعِ السَّلَامْ، اُشْهِدُكَ
يَا مَوْلَايَ اَنِّيْ اَشْهَدُ اَنْ لَا اِلَهَ اِلَّا اللهُ
وَحْدَهُ لَا شَرِيْكَ لَهُ

Peace be upon you by the collections of the salutations. I call you as a witness, O my Master, that I testify that there is no god except Allāh, He is alone, without any partner,

وَاَنَّ مُحَمَّداً عَبْدُهُ وَرَسُوْلُهُ لَا حَبِيْبَ اِلَّا
هُوَ وَاَهْلُهُ،

and that Muḥammad is His servant and Messenger; there is no beloved except him and his progeny.

وَاُشْهِدُكَ يَا مَوْلَايَ اَنَّ عَلِيّاً
اَمِيْرَالْمُؤْمِنِيْنَ حُجَّتُهُ وَالْحَسَنَ حُجَّتُهُ
وَالْحُسَيْنَ حُجَّتُهُ

And I call you as a witness, O my Master, that ʿAlī, the Commander of the Faithful, is His proof. And Ḥasan is His proof. And Ḥusayn is His proof.

وَعَلِيَّ بْنَ الْحُسَيْنِ حُجَّتُهُ وَمُحَمَّدَ بْنَ
عَلِيٍّ حُجَّتُهُ، وَجَعْفَرَ بْنَ مُحَمَّدٍ حُجَّتُهُ

And ʿAlī, son of Ḥusayn, is His proof. And Muhammad, son of ʿAlī, is His proof. And Ja'far, son of Muḥammad, is His proof.

وَمُوْسَىٰ بْنَ جَعْفَرٍ حُجَّتُهُ، وَعَلِيَّ بْنَ
مُوْسَىٰ حُجَّتُهُ، وَمُحَمَّدَ بْنَ عَلِيٍّ حُجَّتُهُ

And Mūsā, son of Jaʿfar, is His proof. And ʿAlī, son of Mūsā, is His proof. And Muhammad, son of ʿAlī, is His proof.

وَعَلِيَّ بْنَ مُحَمَّدٍ حُجَّتُهُ، وَالْحَسَنَ بْنَ عَلِيٍّ
حُجَّتُهُ، وَاَشْهَدُ اَنَّكَ حُجَّةُ اللهِ

And ʿAlī, son of Muḥammad, is His proof. And Ḥasan, son of ʿAlī, is His proof. And I testify that surely, you are the proof of Allāh.

اَنْتُمُ الْاَوَّلُ وَالْآخِرُ وَاَنَّ رَجْعَتَكُمْ حَقٌّ
لَارَيْبَ فِيْهَا يَوْمَ لَايَنْفَعُ نَفْساً اِيْمَانُهَا
لَمْ تَكُنْ آمَنَتْ مِنْ قَبْلُ اَوْ كَسَبَتْ فِيْ
اِيْمَانِهَا خَيْراً

All of you are the first and the last. And surely your return is true; there is no doubt in it. The day when believing will not benefit oneself if he previously did not believe or acquire goodness through his belief.

وَاَنَّ الْمَوْتَ حَقٌّ، وَاَنَّ نَاكِراً وَنَكِيْراً
حَقٌّ، وَاَشْهَدُ اَنَّ النَّشْرَ حَقٌّ، وَالْبَعْثَ
حَقٌّ، وَاَنَّ الصِّرَاطَ حَقٌّ،

And indeed death is a truth. And indeed Nākir and Nakīr are truths. And I testify that indeed the scattering (on the Day of Judgment) is a truth. And the resurrection is a truth. And indeed the bridge (over hell) is a truth.

And the watching place is a truth. And the scale (of deeds) is a truth. And the gathering is a truth. And the accounting (of deeds) is a truth.

وَالْمِرْصَادَ حَقٌّ، وَالْمِيْزَانَ حَقٌّ، وَالْحَشْرَ حَقٌّ، وَالْحِسَابَ حَقٌّ

And heaven and hell are truths. And the promise (of reward) and threat (of punishment) are truths. O my Master, one who opposes you is wretched, and one who obeys you is felicitous.

وَالْجَنَّةَ وَالنَّارَحَقٌّ، وَالْوَعْدَ وَالْوَعِيْدَ بِهِمَا حَقٌّ، يَا مَوْلَايَ شَقِيَ مَنْ خَالَفَكُمْ وَسَعِدَ مَنْ اَطَاعَكُمْ،

Then testify to whatever I have testified. Surely, I am your ally and denounce your enemy. So, the truth is whatever you are satisfied with.

فَاشْهَدْ عَلَىٰ مَا اَشْهَدْتُكَ عَلَيْهِ، وَاَنَا وَلِيٌّ لَكَ بَرِيْءٌ مِنْ عَدُوِّكَ، فَالْحَقُّ مَا رَضِيْتُمُوْهُ،

And falsehood is whatever you are displeased with. And the goodness is whatever you ordered.

وَالْبَاطِلُ مَا اَسْخَطْتُمُوْهُ، وَالْمَعْرُوْفُ مَا اَمَرْتُمْ بِهِ،

And the evil is whatever you have prohibited. So, I am a believer in Allāh alone — He has no partner, and in His Messenger, and in the Commander of the Faithful, and in you, O my Master, the first of you and the last of you.

وَالْمُنْكَرُ مَا نَهَيْتُمْ عَنْهُ، فَنَفْسِيْ مُؤْمِنَةٌ بِاللهِ وَحْدَهُ لَاشَرِيْكَ لَهُ وَبِرَسُوْلِهِ وَ بِاَمِيْرِالْمُؤْمِنِيْنَ وَبِكُمْ يَا مَوْلَايَ اَوَّلِكُمْ وَآخِرِكُمْ،

And my help is intended for you. And my love is purely for you. Amen! Amen! (Accept! Accept!)

وَنُصْرَتِيْ مُعَدَّةٌ لَكُمْ وَمَوَدَّتِيْ خَالِصَةٌ لَكُمْ آمِيْنَ آمِيْنَ

After this, you may recite the special duʿāʾ that can be found in Mafātīh al-Jinān.

Biography of Sayyid Muḥammad

Name:	Sayyid Muḥammad
Kuniyah:	Abu Jaʿfar, Abū ʿAlī, Abū Aḥmad
Title:	Sabuʿ al-Dujayl, Buʿaj
Parents:	Imām ʿAlī al-Hādī (A) & Ḥṣaḍrat Salīl
Birthday:	228 AH
Place of Birth:	Suraya, around Medina
Date of Death:	22nd Jamadi ath-Thani, 252 AH
Place of Death:	Balad (between Baghdad and Sāmarrā)
Age:	24 years
Caliphs of his time:	Wathiq, Mutawakkil, Muntasir, Musta'in and Mu'tazz

Sayyid Muḥammad ibn ʿAlī

Sayyid Muḥammad was a very noble man; because of his virtuous traits, many Shīʿāh thought that he would inherit the imāmate from Imām al-Hādī (A).

A group of Banī Hāshim, such as Ḥasan ibn Ḥasan Aftas, narrate, "On the day of Sayyid Muḥammad's death, I went to Imām al-Hādī (A). They had made food and were hosting people as they would come in and express their condolences to Imām al-Hādī (A). Close to 150 descendants of Abī Ṭālīb, the Banī Hāshim, and the Quraysh were present. All of a sudden, Imām Ḥasan al-ʿAskarī (A) entered the house grieving the death of his brother and stood next to his father. We did not recognize the young Imām. After some time, Imām al-Hādī (A) turned to Imām al-ʿAskarī and said:

يَابُنَىَّ أَحدِثُّ للهِ شُكْراً فَقَدْ أَحَدَثَ فِيْكِ أَمْراً

O my son! Thank Allāh, as He has blessed you with a bounty.

Imām Ḥasan al-ʿAskarī (A) cried and said:

اَلْحَمْدُ لِلهِ رَبِّ الْعَالَمِيْنَ، إِيّاهُ نَشْكُرُ نِعَمَهُ عَلَيْنَا وَ إِنَّا لِلهِ وَ إَنَّا إِلَيْهِ رَاجِعُوْنَ

All praise is for Allāh, Lord of the worlds! We thank him for blessing us, and surely we are from Allāh, and surely we are returning to Him.

I asked, "Who is this?"

Someone replied, "Ḥasan (A), the son of Imām ʿAlī an-Naqi (A)."

He seemed about 20 years old. We realized that after Imām al-Hādī (A), he will be the Imām.

Sayyid Muḥammad is renowned for his glory and generosity. Many people perform his ziyārah and ask Allāh for their requests through his intercession. Those living close to his shrine have a special reverence for him and narrate many stories from him, such as:

- If anybody takes a false oath on this noble Sayyid, he or she will die within one or two days; therefore, people in this area resolve their conflicts with each other by taking an oath upon his name.
- Whoever takes something from his shrine and wants to leave, his vehicle will not move until he or she returns the stolen good to the shrine.
- Those families who cannot bear children ask Allāh through him, and most of them have been able ot have a child after doing so. In the past, some cradles were placed inside of the shrine upon which people would tie a piece of cloth until their request was fulfilled.

Abū Jaʿfar Muḥammad ibn al-Imām ʿAlī al-Hādī (A) is known as Sayyid Muḥammad and is also known among the natives as Sabu' al-Dujayl (the lion of Dujayl). He was the eldest son of Imām al-Hādī (A).

Sayyid Muḥammad's shrine is located in the city of Balad, about 50 kilometers south of Samarra. Balad is part of the Ṣalāḥuddīn Province and is also known as al-Balad as-Sayyid Muḥammad. This shrine is respected greatly by the Shi'as, especially in ʿIrāq.

He intended to perform Hajj in the year 252 AH, but when he entered the city of Balad, he fell sick and passed away. This happened two years prior to the martyrdom of Imām al-Hādī (A). His brother, Imām Ḥasan al-ʿAskarīi (A) mourned for him profusely.

Many karamat (supernatural wonders) have been attributed to Sayyid Muḥammad. In al-Najm al-Thāqib, Mirza Ḥasan Nūrī writes:

Sayyid Muḥammad has many Karamat and is very well-known even among the Sunnis. The people of ʿIrāq, even the nomads living in the desert, are fearful to take an oath in his name. If they are accused of stealing, they would rather return the money than take an oath on Sayyid Muḥammad's name because they have witnessed the punishment.

Ziyārah of Sons of the Imām

Peace be upon you, O pure, immaculate leader, guardian, caller, and representative.	اَلسَّلَامُ عَلَيْكَ اَيُّهَا السَّيِّدُ الزَّكِيُّ الطَّاهِرُ الْوَلِيُّ وَالدَّاعِيْ الْحَفِيُّ
I bear witness that you spoke truthfully and honestly, and called towards my Master and your Master, both openly and secretly.	اَشْهَدُ اَنَّكَ قُلْتَ حَقّاً وَنَطَقْتَ حَقّاً وَصِدْقاً وَدَعَوْتَ اِلَىٰ مَوْلَايَ وَمَوْلَاكَ عَلَانِيَةً وَسِرّاً
The one who follows you is successful. The one who verifies you is saved. The one who rejects and opposes you is a loser.	فَازَ مُتَّبِعُكَ وَنَجَا مُصَدِّقُكَ وَخَابَ وَخَسِرَ مُكَذِّبُكَ وَالْمُتَخَلِّفُ عَنْكَ
Bear witness to my testimony so that I may be amongst those who are successful by recognizing you, verifying you, and following you.	اِشْهَدْ لِيْ بِهٰذِهِ الشَّهَادَةِ لِاَكُوْنَ مِنَ الْفَائِزِيْنَ بِمَعْرِفَتِكَ وَطَاعَتِكَ وَتَصْدِيْقِكَ وَاتِّبَاعِكَ
Peace be upon you, O my leader, and the son of my leader, You are the door of Allāh through which He gives and accepts.	وَالسَّلَامُ عَلَيْكَ يَا سَيِّدِيْ وَابْنَ سَيِّدِيْ اَنْتَ بَابُ اللهِ الْمُؤْتَىٰ مِنْهُ وَالْمَأْخُوْذُ عَنْهُ
I have come to visit you, entrusting you with my needs,	اَتَيْتُكَ زَائِراً وَحَاجَاتِيْ لَكَ مُسْتَوْدِعاً،

entrusting with you my faith, the performance of my deeds, and all my hopes until the end of my life.	وَهَا اَنَا ذَا اَسْتَوْدِعُكَ دِيْنِيْ وَ اَمَانَتِيْ وَخَوَاتِيْمَ عَمَلِيْ وَجَوَامِعَ اَمَلِيْ اِلَىٰ مُنْتَهٰى اَجَلِي
So, may Allāh's peace, mercy, and blessings be upon you.	وَالسَّلَامُ عَلَيْكَ وَرَحْمَةُ اللهِ وَبَرَكَاتُهُ

Gravesite of Sayyid Muḥammad

Another Ziyārah of Sons of the Imām

Stand before the grave and recite the following ziyārah

Peace be upon your grandfather, al-Muṣṭafā (the chosen one). Peace be upon your father, al-Murtaḍa, ar-Riḍa (the pleased and pleasing to Allāh).	اَلسَّلَامُ عَلَىٰ جَدِّكَ الْمُصْطَفَىٰ اَلسَّلَامُ عَلَىٰ اَبِيْكَ الْمُرْتَضَىٰ الرِّضَا
Peace be upon our leader, al-Ḥasan and al-Ḥusayn.	اَلسَّلَامُ عَلَىٰ السَّيِّدَيْنِ الْحَسَنِ وَالْحُسَيْنِ
Peace be upon Khadījah, the mother of the leader of the women of the worlds.	اَلسَّلَامُ عَلَىٰ خَدِيْجَةَ اُمِّ سَيِّدَةِ نِسَاءِ الْعَالَمِيْنَ
Peace be upon Fāṭimah, the mother of the pure Imāms.	اَلسَّلَامُ عَلَىٰ فَاطِمَةَ اُمِّ الْاَئِمَّةِ الطَّاهِرِيْنَ
Peace be upon the ones who are sources of pride, seas of knowledge,	اَلسَّلَامُ عَلَىٰ النُّفُوْسِ الْفَاخِرَةِ بُحُوْرِ الْعُلُوْمِ الزَّاخِرَةِ
intercessors in the hereafter, my guardians near whom the bones decompose, the leaders of creation, and the rightful leaders.	شُفَعَائِيْ فِي الْآخِرَةِ وَاَوْلِيَائِيْ عِنْدَ عَوْدِ الرُّوْحِ اِلَى الْعِظَامِ النَّاخِرَةِ اَئِمَّةِ الْخَلْقِ وَوُلَاةِ الْحَقِّ
Peace be upon you, O noble, pure, and honorable being.	اَلسَّلَامُ عَلَيْكَ اَيُّهَا الشَّخْصُ الشَّرِيْفُ الطَّاهِرُ الْكَرِيْمُ

I bear witness that there is no god except Allāh, Muḥammad is His servant and chosen one, and ʿAlī is His guardian and chosen one.

اَشْهَدُ اَنْ لَا اِلٰهَ اِلَّا اللّٰهُ وَاَنَّ مُحَمَّداً عَبْدُهُ وَمُصْطَفَاهُ وَاَنَّ عَلِيّاً وَلِيُّهُ وَمُجْتَبَاهُ

And (I bear witness) that the Imāms from his lineage are the true leaders until the Day of Judgment.

وَاَنَّ الْاِمَامَةَ فِيْ وُلْدِهِ اِلَىٰ يَوْمِ الدِّيْنِ

We know this for certain, are their confidantes, and will do our best to support them.

نَعْلَمُ ذٰلِكَ عِلْمَ الْيَقِيْنِ وَنَحْنُ لِذٰلِكَ مُعْتَقِدُوْنَ وَفِيْ نَصْرِهِمْ مُجْتَهِدُوْنَ

Gravesite of Zayd bin ʿAlī

Gravesite of Abū ʿAlī Ḥamzah Sharqī

Gravesite of Ibrahīm Aḥmar al ʿAynayn

Gravesite of ʿĪsā bin Zayd

Gravesite of ʿUmar Ashraf

Gravesites of the ʿAskarīyayn (A) household

It is said that the graves of some Sādāt (Prophet's descendants) are located in Sāmarrā:

Sawsan (Mother of Imām Ḥasan al ʿAskari (A))

Sawsan is the grandmother of Imām az-Zamān (AJ), and has therefore been referred to as the "Jaddah" as well. This noble and pious lady is also sometimes known as Hādīth, Hādīthe, Salīl, and Reyhānah. In some texts, she has been called the wakīl or representative of Imām al-Mahdī (AJ), because when the Shīʿās had asked Hakīmah Khātūn whom they should refer their questions to, she had appointed Ḥaḍrat Sawsan. She passed away in 262 AH and was buried in her house.

Ḥaḍrat Narjis Khātūn (Mother of Imām Zamān (AJ))

Narjis Khātūn was the mother of Imām az-Zamān (AJ). This noble lady was the daughter of Yashūʿā, son of the Roman Caesar, and was brought to Sāmarrā as a slave. Imām al-Hādī (A) purchased her and married her to his son Imām Ḥasan al-ʿAskarī (A). Her Roman name is Malika, and through her mother, her lineage traces back to Shamūn, the successor of Prophet ʿĪsā (A). After embracing Islām, she changed her name to Narjis. She passed away in 260 AH and and was buried in her house in Sāmarrā, next to Imām al-ʿAskarī (A).

Sayyid Ḥusayn ibn ʿAlī (Brother of Imām Ḥasan al ʿAskarī (A))

Muḥaddith Qumī writes in Mafatiḥ al-Janān:
I have not found any bio about this great Sayyid; however, it can be concluded from some narrations that our Leader compared Imām Ḥasan al-ʿAskarī (A) and his brother, Ḥusayn ibn ʿAlī (A), to the two holy sons of the Holy Prophet (S): Imām Ḥasan (A) and Imām Ḥusayn (A). It has also been mentioned in the Hādīth of Abu al-Ṭayyib that Imām az-Zamān's (AJ) voice was like the voice of his uncle Ḥusayn.

Sayyid Ḥusayn believed in the Imāmate of his brother Imām Ḥasan ʿAskarī (A) and was among his followers. He was known as one of the most devoted and ascetic people of his time. He was buried beneath the foot section of Imām al-Hādī and Imām ʿAskarī (A).

Sayyid Jaʿfar (Brother of Imām Ḥasan al ʿAskarī (A))

Abu ʿAbdillah Jaʿfar is another son of Imām al-Hādī (A). They say Jaʿfar was not a pious person and was given the title al-Kaḍāb, which means the liar. Imām al-Hādī (A) says about his son Jaʿfar, "Stay away from my son Ja'far; his relationship to me is like the relationship of Kanʿan to Prophet Nūḥ (A)."

Imām Ḥasan al-ʿAskarī (A) said, "The example of Jaʿfar and I is like Kabil and Habil, the two sons of Prophet Adam (A). If it were possible, Ja'far would have killed me, but Allāh did not allow him to do so."

After the martyrdom of Imām al-Hādī (A), Ja'far claimed the Imāmate. He went to the current Caliph of the time and told him, "I will send you 2,000 Ashrafi if your order the Imāmate to be transferred from my brother to me."

The Caliph replied, "If the position of Imāmate was in our hands, we would have taken it and guarded it for ourselves. If the Shīʿās see miracles and generosity from you as they saw from your father and brother, they will choose you as their Imām, and you would not need our help."

After the martyrdom of Imām Ḥasan al-ʿAskarī (A), Jaʿfar once again claimed the Imāmate, but Allāh knows all.

It has been narrated in Bihār ul-Anwār from Tafsri Ayyashi from Mufazil ibn Amr that Imām as-Ṣadiq (A) was asked about the following ayah:

وَإِنْ مِنْ أَهْلِ الْكِتَابِ إِلاَّ لَيُؤْمِنَنَّ بِهِ قَبْلَ مَوْتِهِ

And there is no one from the People of the Book except that he will surely believe in him before his death. (4:159)

The Imām (A) replied:

نزلت فينا خاصّه انه ليس رجل من ولد فاطمه يموت و لا يخرج عن الدنيا حتّى يقر لامامه بإمامته كما أقر ولد يعقوب ليوسف قالُوا تَا للهِ لَقَدْ آثَرَكَ اللهُ عَلَيْنا

"This ayah has been revealed for us. Indeed, no son of Lady Faṭimah (A) will leave this world without acknowledging the Imām of his time, just like the sons of Ya'qūb confessed the prophecy of Yūsuf and said, "They said, 'By Allāh, Allāh has certainly preferred you over us, and we have indeed been erring."

Ḥaḍrat Samānah (Mother of Imām al-Hādī (A))

Ḥaḍrat Samānah is the mother of Imām al-Hādī (A) and is known as "Um al-Faḍl (mother of Grace)l" and "Sayyidah." She was among the righteous, wise, and ascetic women of her time who would fast most of the days and pray through the nights. She passed away in Imām al-Hādī's (A) house and was buried there alongside her son.

Abu Hashim Ja'farī

Dawūd ibn Qāsim, son of Ishāq ibn 'Abdullah ibn Ja'far ibn Abi Ṭālib, known as Abu Hāshim, is a descendent of Ja'far at-Tayyār. The lineage of this noble man from his mother can be traced back to Muḥammad ibn Abī Bakr. He was a companion of Imām ar-Ridha (A), Imām al-Jawad (A), Imām al-Hādī (A), and Imām al-'Askarī (A). His grave is also inside of the holy shrine.

Jamīl ibn Darrāj Kūfī

Jamīl ibn Darrāj is among the trustworthy narrators (ath-thiqā) who has narrated ahādīth through Zurārāh from Imām aṣ-Ṣādiq (A) and Imām Mūsā al-Kaẓim (A).

His tomb is in Dajil, in the Tarimiya village on the right side of Baghdad's main road, about 12 km away from Baghdad and close to the Tigris River.

Ibrāhīm ibn Mālik al-Ashtar

Abū Nuʾman Ibāhīm, the brave son of Mālik al-Ashtar, was the commander of Mukhtār's army. He was raised by his father, and despite his young age, he participated in the Battle of Ṣiffīn alongside his father and Amīr ul-Muʾminīn (A). Ibrāhīm rose against the khalīfah of his time, ʿAbdul Malik Marwān, and took over Baṣrah, Kūfah, and other parts of ʿIrāq.

He was able to defeat the khalīfah's army and kill their commanders, such as ʿUbaydullāh ibn Zīyād, Shimr ibn Dhiʾl-Jawshan, Hurmalah, and Khūlī.

After Mukhtār was martyred, Ibrāhīm remained as the leader of Mosul, Jazīrah, Azerbaijan, and Armenia until ʿAbdul Malik attacked ʿIrāq in 72 AH. When his commander ran away, the ʿIrāqi army was defeated, and Ibrāhīm was surrounded. Despite his great resistance, they were able to martyr Ibrāhīm and send his head to ʿAbdul Mālik, who then burnt his body.

Ibrāhīm was martyred on the 13th of Jamādī ul-Awwal in Dayr al-Jathaliq, which is south of Dujail, and was buried there as well. This grave is known as Shaykh Ibrāhīm today.

Allāmah Majlisī: Ibrāhīm did not have any doubt in his faith. He did not go astray in his belief and never lost his certainty. He participated in avenging the blood of Imām Ḥusayn (A). He was a loyalist of the Prophet (S) and Ahl al-Bayt (A), and their flagbearer.

Conclusion

Dear Zāʿir,

You have reached the conclusion of your spiritual journey and attained the lofty status of a zāʿir. According to aḥadīth, for 40 days after completing your ziyārāt, angels do tawāf around you. For 40 days, you are the qiblah for the angels, and thus, you become the qiblah of guidance. Take advantage of this opportunity by demonstrating love and obedience to the Ahl al-Bayt (A) through your words and actions.

It is important to remember that the ḥarams of the Ahl al-Bayt (A) are symbols. Their true place is in the hearts of the believers. Performing ziyāarah is a chance for us to rekindle our love and obedience towards our beloved Maʿṣūmīn. Coming to their graves and performing their ziyārah was a means for us to rejuvenate our love and connection with them, but as we return home, they are just as close to us, as long as we maintain our proximity towards them and continue to build that connection. Seize that spiritual connection you are feeling right now and strive towards maintaining this feeling after you return home. Resolve to bring about a change within yourself that will help you maintain the spiritual fervor that comes with a successful ziyārah trip. Above all, ask Allāh, through the intercession of the Ahl al-Bayt (A), to help you remain steadfast on the path of the Ahl al-Bayt (A) and strive in His way.